INSTITUTIONS UNBOUND

Institutions—like education, family, medicine, culture, and law—are powerful social structures shaping how we live together. As members of society we daily express our adherence to norms and values of institutions as we consciously and unconsciously reject and challenge them. Our everyday experiences with institutions not only shape our connections with one another, they can reinforce our binding to the status quo as we struggle to produce social change. Institutions can help us do human rights. Institutions that bridge nation-states can offer resources, including norms, to advance human rights. These institutions can serve as touchstones to changing minds and confronting human rights violations. Institutions can also prevent us from doing human rights. We create institutions, but institutions can be difficult to change. Institutions can weaken, if not outright prevent, human rights establishment and implementation. To release human rights from their institutional bindings, sociologists must solve riddles of how institutions work and determine social life. This book is a step forward in identifying means by which we can loosen human rights from institutional constraints.

David L. Brunsma is Professor of Sociology at Virginia Tech and co-editor of *The Leading Rogue State*.

Keri E. Iyall Smith is Associate Professor of Sociology at Suffolk University and author of *States of Indigenous Movements*.

Brian K. Gran is Associate Professor of Sociology and Law at Case Western Reserve University whose publications have appeared in *The International Journal of Children's Rights* and in *Child Welfare*. Gran edits the journal *Societies Without Borders*.

INSTITUTIONS UNBOUND
SOCIAL WORLDS AND HUMAN RIGHTS

Edited by

David L. Brunsma,
Keri E. Iyall Smith, and
Brian K. Gran

NEW YORK AND LONDON

First published 2016
by Routledge
711 Third Avenue, New York, NY 10017

and by Routledge
2 Park Square, Milton Park, Abingdon, Oxon, OX14 4RN

Routledge is an imprint of the Taylor & Francis Group, an informa business

© 2016 Taylor & Francis

The right of the editors to be identified as the authors of the editorial material,
and of the authors for their individual chapters, has been asserted in accordance
with sections 77 and 78 of the Copyright, Designs and Patents Act 1988.

All rights reserved. No part of this book may be reprinted or reproduced or
utilised in any form or by any electronic, mechanical, or other means, now
known or hereafter invented, including photocopying and recording, or in any
information storage or retrieval system, without permission in writing from the
publishers.

Trademark notice: Product or corporate names may be trademarks or registered
trademarks, and are used only for identification and explanation without intent
to infringe.

Library of Congress Cataloging in Publication Data
A catalog record for this book has been requested

ISBN: 978-1-138-65548-5 (hbk)
ISBN: 978-1-138-65551-5 (pbk)
ISBN: 978-1-315-62244-6 (ebk)

Typeset in Goudy Oldstyle Std
by Swales & Willis Ltd, Exeter, Devon, UK

CONTENTS

Introduction		1
1	Medical Sociology *Susan W. Hinze and Heidi L. Taylor*	9
2	Crime, Law, and Deviance *Joachim J. Savelsberg*	20
3	Education *Nathalia E. Jaramillo, Peter McLaren, and Jean J. Ryoo*	31
4	Family *Angela J. Hattery and Earl Smith*	41
5	Organizations, Occupations, and Work *J. Kenneth Benson*	52
6	Political Sociology *Thomas Janoski*	69
7	Culture *Mark D. Jacobs and Lester R. Kurtz*	80
8	Science, Knowledge, and Technology *Jennifer L. Croissant*	90
9	Sociology of Law *Christopher N. J. Roberts*	97
10	Religion *David V. Brewington*	107
11	Economic Sociology *Clarence Y. H. Lo*	118

Discussion Questions	*128*
List of Acronyms	*132*
Bibliography	*134*
About the Editors	*213*

INTRODUCTION

David L. Brunsma, Keri E. Iyall Smith, and Brian K. Gran

INSTITUTIONS: SOCIALLY CONSTRUCTED SOCIAL BINDINGS

Institutions are fundamental social constructions. While people build institutions, institutions definitely reflect their time and place. The design and functioning of institutions are organized around patterns of power and resources. Institutions often fulfill organizational purposes, but frequently organizations seem to obstruct rather than support their stated goals. They produce intended and unintended consequences. Institutions connect people. Sometimes these connections promote inequality, violence, and regressive policies and practices. Sometimes these connections foster strong and enduring social ties that are progressive, peaceful, and encourage justice and dignity.

The concept (and reality) of institutional life can be both quite abstract and at the same time is always very real. Yet, because of this dual reality, institutions are often difficult to think and talk about, let alone know how to identify, study, understand, and change. As such, we discuss the complexities of institutions before embarking on grappling with the chapters in this book. The eleven chapters in this book carve paths of sociological understanding of specific institutions and how they may look and operate differently *if the ideas of human rights are taken seriously by society and/or sociologists.* Yet, human rights are not yet fully taken seriously either.

If this were a traditional sociology textbook for, say, an Introduction to Sociology course, you might read that a social institution is "a set of roles and behaviors centered on the performance of important social tasks." This arguably vague definition is meant to encourage you to think about, for instance, education as a social institution (which it is) where there are roles (e.g., teachers, students) and associated expected behaviors (e.g., "to lecture, to teach," "to listen, to learn") which, as a social structure, come together to "educate." This is all true, but education as a social institution facilitates other social tasks as well, such as socialization (see Ballantine and Spade 2011). From the perspective of an individual in that human community (or perhaps from the "voice" and

2   David L. Brunsma, Keri E. Iyall Smith, and Brian K. Gran

"perspective," if you will, of that community itself) one might think about an institution by filling in the following blank: "in this society/community, there is a *way* to do _____."

Thus, take "citizenship as an institution" as an example. In many societies, such as the United States, there is a *way* to do citizenship. While formally a person who wants to become a U.S. citizen is not obligated to forego her ethnic identity, she must fulfill residency requirements, pay fees, and sit for exams that are designed to ensure that this individual is informed of U.S. history, laws, and rights and duties. Indeed, a person who becomes a U.S. citizen may be more familiar with her rights and duties than many "native-born" citizens. In contrast, when a person becomes a French citizen, there are distinct ways to do citizenship. A prominent difference is that a person who wants to become a French citizen is expected to become French. The institution of citizenship differs because it is fully grounded in social and cultural worlds. Dalton Conley recently defined institutions in a more critical and dynamic way for introductory students: "Social institutions are networks of structures in society that work to socialize the groups of people within them" (Conley 2011). As such, institutions are not just out there, unchanging, they are purposefully structured the way they are structured and change over time within a structure of power relations too. We are the people within institutions—socialized by others and socializing others.

Take family as another exemplar institution. In a society like the United States there is a *way* to do family. When one mentions the word "family" one is invoking a cultural script as well as a social structure—certain bodies come to mind, certain expectations, certain relationships, certain beginnings and outcomes. This is, perhaps, why certain family structures experience a struggle for recognition and equality—families founded by same-sex couples, with only one head of household, with extended relations, or families made of cohabitating couples (see Chapter Five in this volume). As the institution "family" changes, it does not reflect the socialization that we experienced. Institutions are fluid and constantly being made and remade by the people within them.

We draw our understanding of social institutions from all of the above notions but also from a highly acclaimed piece of theoretical sociology by one of our leading scholars, Patricia Yancey Martin. Martin's 2004 "Gender as Social Institution" article offers one of the most dynamic definitions of an institution, and how institutions operate, through the multifaceted lens of gender. To paraphrase this inspirational piece of sociological theory, institutions are profoundly social entities that endure across time and space with distinct social practices. These practices constrain as well as facilitate behavior. The practices are features of social positions with which we attribute expected norms and behaviors. As part of social groups, people construct, support, and change institutions.

Typically, institutions are vitally important to members of social groups. Expectations arising from institutions are relied upon without thinking and typically become connected to identities of individuals and the social groups of which they are members. While people adapt to institutions, they can remake

INTRODUCTION 3

them, as well as dismantle them. Social institutions have attendant legitimating ideologies, organized and permeated by power, and, at the same time, are inconsistent, contradictory and rife with conflict—institutions continuously change and occasionally fall apart. Now, that should clear things up. No? Let's walk through this discussion bit by bit by elaborating on Martin's conceptual apparatus (2004, 1,256–1,259).

First, to conceive of institutions as "profoundly social . . . [as] characteristics of groups" is to understand that they are features of the collective body of society, that they are features of our relationships, and are built by you and the people you interact with extensively. Through this social interaction, you develop practices that tether you to that collectively created institution. These practices are meaningful to you and to the others in your social networks. Over time this institutional creation is transferred through socialization processes; often this institution reproduces itself from generation to generation.

As social facts, institutions can be studied as such. That is, we can study institutions as facts that people make together. Thus, the most powerful institutions (e.g., family, religion) "endure/persist across extensive time and geographical space," allowing sociologists to study them historically and comparatively. Changes in the particular institution, over time and space, can be tracked. Studying institutional change can help us understand who we now are, who we have been, as well as the potential that we can become.

Martin maintains that "institutions entail distinct social practices that recur, recycle, or are repeated (over time) by group members." How do social practices of institutions recur, recycle, and repeat? Consider your experience in the institution of higher education at this very moment. Think about all of the social practices (your conversations, your schedules, your studying, your exams, your interaction with peers, with professors, with folks from the town, your note-taking, etc.) and how these continuously happen, daily. What's more, other peers (whom you may not even know, or who may not even attend your college/university) are walking the same institutional grooves. Taken together these collective practices fundamentally make and remake the institution of higher education. As a result, our everyday choices and behaviors often go unquestioned, accepted as "natural" realities—"That's just how it works here"—when really these institutional practices are created, fostered, and sometimes challenged by everyone, every day.

These institutions, the institutional structures of which we are a part, both "constrain and facilitate behavior/actions by societal/group members." Institutional structures provide opportunities to some people, and deny opportunities to others. Why? Institutions have collective preferences built into their fabric. As such, some actions are prevented, some alternatives are prescribed, some ideas are squelched, and some choices are empowered. Consider institutions that hinder scientists and philosophers from discovery. In some parts of the world, governments persecute scholars and researchers who are merely trying to advance science. This problem is not new: think of scientists who argued that the world was round when the government-sanctioned view was that the

4　*David L. Brunsma, Keri E. Iyall Smith, and Brian K. Gran*

world was flat. Despite demonstrating through systematic observations that the world is round, the reigning institutions of the time—primarily the Church and institutionalized forms of religion—offered no meaningful place at the societal table for such notions. As a result, scientists calling for evidence and exploration were imprisoned and exiled. In the meantime, as a society, we have yet to acknowledge African explorations to the "new world" happening centuries before Columbus (Van Sertima 1976).

Institutions "have social position and relations that are characterized by particular expectations, rules/norms, and procedures," according to Martin. Institutions help to map social relationships and their meanings for us. The institution of the family has dramatically changed over time and even now significantly differs across societies, yet rules govern expected behaviors of children, parents, and other family members. Those who claim the title of "parent" have certain cultural norms governing their behaviors as seen by others within the shared institutional framework. A person who is designated a "bad parent" is accused of violating institutional requirements of family.

One could say that institutions are made, supported, and changed by people—this is certainly true. The academic version adds some important meat to those bones, though, by saying that institutions are "constituted and reconstituted by embodied agents." While saying virtually the same thing, the latter adds the important recognition that we are *embodied*—that the skin we are in, the shape of our bodies, the experience of being in a body is crucially important to understanding institutions and how they work. We are part of a collective body, yes, but we are also a collection of bodies that are in institutional relations to each other in meaningful and profoundly important ways.

So important, in fact, that institutions are "internalized as identities and selves and they are displayed as personalities." Note the deep implication of this contour! Our interactions with institutions as well as our interactions in those institutions become a part of who we think we are. These interactions shape our knowledge of self and actions from that knowledge of self. While perhaps seeming abstract, we analyze this important fact of social constructions of difference in this textbook. *Because* a person has a self-understanding, for instance, *as* a Christian, and because the institution of religion structures that experience, then this institutional experience becomes invisible, unmarked, and unquestioned—therein lies part of the incredible power of institutions.

Institutions are seen widely as "the way things are," despite the fact that there actually are many ways to reach social objectives. For Martin, institutions "have a legitimating ideology," a set of stories, narratives, and meanings that argue that the arrangements and practices within, say, elementary education (as an institution) are right and, because they are "right," they should remain as they are—unchanged. Sociologists of education have been keen to understand why approaches to elementary education persist despite failing many young people. Often, the institutional structure of, say, elementary education and the relationships, norms, and expectations it sustains are ideologically legitimated because the elite in the social system benefit from such an institutional structure. Sociologists of education have been keen to understand why approaches to elementary education persist despite failing many young people.

While you may now be thinking that institutions are all-powerful and highly determinative of our lives, institutions are, indeed, very messy and "inconsistent, contradictory, and rife with conflict." Social groups are constantly pushing against boundaries of institutions. As such, institutions "continuously change." Over time and over space, individuals and their collectivities slowly, sometimes quickly, work to redefine their identities and their institutional practices. Change in one institution, say government, can affect changes in other institutions, say family. Occupy Wall Street represents a significant contemporary social movement pressing against the institutional grooves of government and the economy. President Obama's campaign slogan in 2008, "Change we can believe in," recognizes the roles of citizens in the institution of government. It also acknowledges that evolution is essential for institutions.

Institutions are "organized with and permeated by power." Organizing forces of institutions so fundamentally shape our social relations that power is a central fulcrum of social life. Later in this book we will discuss ways in which institutions affect your sense of who you think you are, how these institutions are created, maintained, and changed with the social constructions of race, gender, class, and sexuality as collectively understood. Families are powerful institutions—perhaps one of the most powerful. Our lives are nestled within a matrix of economic and occupational structures that also shape our health (another institution). The structure of education as well as the realities of crime, law, and deviance help to shape our opportunities and constraints in life. Institutions are indeed powerful—and often, very often, shaped by elites within each institution—an embodied element of power.

Finally, Martin (2004) highlights that "[i]nstitutions and individuals mutually constitute each other; they are not separable into micro and macro phenomena." As you now know, institutions are powerful structures. You are constantly creating institutions and they are constantly creating you. As individuals and groups respond to institutional structures, these same institutions respond to them, creating a continuous feedback loop. Thus, institutions are dynamic, always changing, never static, and we are always a part of them and they a part of us. Furthermore, it is human created institutions that mean we are not limited to Darwinian notions of "survival of the fittest." With institutions, we can create space for ourselves and others, regardless of "fitness" to survive. This not only renders us uniquely human, it also enables us to honor and render us human through the institution of human rights.

Social institutions and practices construct groups and foster differences, including political, religious, and legal institutions. Political institutions and practices rely on categories, such as citizen and non-citizen. One right that many citizens have is the ability to use voting to hold governments accountable. Such a construction means non-citizens cannot hold government accountable through voting. Instead, if non-citizens are to hold a government accountable, they must use other means. When it comes to voting and other rights, when governments do not enforce citizenship rights, citizens and non-citizens will turn to human rights to seek justice and access socially acceptable living standards, among other rights. In addition, religious institutions often distinguish between adherents and non-adherents. The basis of professions is a difference between the professional and non-professional, a distinction typically sanctioned by governments. Government uses its power to maintain national secrets and what are not secrets, what is a military actor and a contractor, and what is child abuse and what is parental discipline. "Law" cannot only be used to distinguish between the haves and the have nots, it can help the haves come out ahead. Law can help members of social groups who have historically been in institutionally weak positions. Indeed, rights can indicate membership in a society and that members of a social group are entitled to fair treatment and consideration. Laws can and have been used to challenge and weaken economic discrimination arising from employment practices, such as lawsuits brought to end pay inequities and hazardous work practices.

Social Institutions and Human Rights

Representing an exciting moment for sociology to further energize and develop a sociology of human rights (or, more to the point, sociologies of human rights), *Institutions Unbound: Social Worlds and Human Rights* brings together leading and emergent scholars who seriously engage in revolutionary questions, resituate their substantive concerns within new terrains, and begin mapping the intellectual and practical contours of a human rights-sociology. Each chapter responds to two primary questions: (1) How does a human rights perspective change the questions that sociologists ask, the theoretical perspectives that sociologists utilize, the methods that sociologists use, and the implications of sociological inquiry? And (2) How can the sociological enterprise (its epistemologies, theories, methodologies, results) inform and push forward human rights theory, discourse, and implementation towards a better world for all humanity?

When we began this project the American Sociological Association sponsored forty-five sections that supports its members' interests in substantive, theoretical, methodological, and applied areas (there are now fifty-two, with Human Rights being added just after we started this project, followed by sections on Altruism, Morality and Social Solidarity; Body and Embodiment; Global and Transnational Sociology; Inequality, Poverty and Mobility; The Sociology of Development; and Consumers and Consumption). We approached progressive, critical scholars in the hope they would contribute work to this project that would accomplish several goals. The first objective was to present a brief summary of the state of the area of sociological inquiry and a reckoning of the central concerns and questions that motivate the area. The second objective was to give readers a summary of the key findings in the area as well as the most prominent methods its practitioners use. The third objective is to provide readers with a critical discussion of what the human rights paradigm can learn from the work in their area as well as to describe how the human rights paradigm might resituate the area and its constituent questions, methods, theories, and findings, and, in turn, reorient readers toward a new set of questions, particularly how human rights redefines the research situation and what new questions can and should be asked. Finally, given this, we encouraged the authors to think broadly and critically about doing the work of human rights sociology, a look forward—new questions, new possibilities for both the area/field and human rights realizations.

We asked these authors to pay particular attention to major institutions in society including medicine, crime/deviance, education, family, work/occupations, politics, culture, science/technology, law, religion, and the economy. We asked them to take seriously the ideas of human rights for a new, energetic sociology of [insert institution here]. The results, as you will see, are astounding.

HUMAN RIGHTS INSTITUTIONS: SOCIALLY CONSTRUCTED, SOCIALLY UNBOUND

In recognizing the existence and role of institutions in the lives of individuals and groups in society, it is possible to observe how institutions transform over time and identify how their functions change and why some institutions fail. Opening our eyes to the roles of institutions in our daily lives allows us to understand what we see not only did not just happen "naturally," but that institutions will not always exist—for instance, you may have once thought that there would always be poor people. Yet poverty is not inherent in the human condition, nor is it inherent in society. Institutions in societies can, in fact, end poverty; even institutions in capitalist societies can end poverty.

Within institutions, norms govern our behavior. We engage in this behavior not only as social beings, but as social beings with bodies. Not only do we embody institutions, our very personalities are products of institutions with which we grow up, are educated, form relationships, and work, among other aspects of doing things together. Institutions frame how we understand who we are, how we live within society and express our personality, our bodies, and our affiliations as individuals and as groups. Institutions are both enduring over time and always being both reaffirmed and reshaped by both individuals and groups in our society. Every day when you get dressed you affirm your identity and affiliation with groups. Did you wear a backpack today? Are you wearing a baseball cap? Is there a cross on a chain around your neck? Do you wear a claddagh ring? Which way does the heart face? Do you have piercings or tattoos? These are just a few of the ways that we express our own relationships to institutions. They are also symbols that we use to understand how other individuals in society are or are not expressing their relationships to institutions.

As embodied members of society with personality, on a daily basis we express our adherence to the norms and values of institutions. Everyday we consciously and unconsciously reject other institutions. We recognize the people we interact with based upon the institutions that we see in their bodies, personalities, and the norms and values they adopt and adhere to. Through these behaviors we not only express our adherence to institutions but we create and recreate institutions in society. We also create and recreate ourselves within institutions—personality, body, and social being.

The presence and absence of institutions in human social life is represented not only in sociology but also in popular media as exemplified by television shows such as *The Walking Dead, Orange Is the New Black, Manhattan,* and most reality shows (which are unreal because they frequently exaggerate institutions or remove people from their institutional roots).

As we write this chapter, institutions that seemed fixed and static have in fact shifted, meaning that by the end of the summer of 2015 same-sex marriage exists throughout the United States. Marriage vows no longer inherently produce a man and a wife. After a year of turning a critical eye to policing and the deaths of non-white people at the hands of police, cities around the country are re-examining the methods of policing, who police are, and the relationships of police agencies with the communities they are supposed to serve and protect. At the same time, people living in the United States are again examining what it means to be embodied as a non-white person. These examinations may mean a change in the institutions of crime, law, and deviance. These shifts in the institutions of marriage and "criminal justice" are changing what it means to be able to experience dignity, self-determination and life itself.

Changing institutions with a human rights lens expands the dignity and self-determination of all of us as embodied individuals with personality. Changing institutions also means creating social structures and institutions that *unbound* our personalities, our bodies, and even our social groups. We become more human as we express our human right to dignity and self-determination. Institutions unbound allow us—as individuals and members of society—to be more fully and freely human, more fully and freely members of societies. As we are more free to be you and me, we are also more free to create institutions which will only expand our unboundedness and unleash unknown potential of individuals in society and society itself.

CHAPTER ONE

MEDICAL SOCIOLOGY

Susan W. Hinze and Heidi L. Taylor

Medical sociology emerged as a distinct subfield in the early to mid-twentieth century as sociologists brought their research skills to medical settings, studying doctor-patient relationships, the expansion of medicine as a profession, and the organization of medical systems, health care, and health policy (Bird, Conrad, and Fremont 2000; Bloom 2000). While the establishment of a formal American Sociological Association (ASA) section in 1959 is relatively recent, the intellectual roots of the specialty date back to the 1840s in classical works such as Friedrich Engels's writings on the health of factory workers and German pathologist Rudolph Virchow's work on the social origins of illness (Waitzkin 1981). Indeed, the struggle for economic and political rights for the working classes in the mid-nineteenth and early twentieth centuries was intertwined with concerns about the health status and rights of workers and citizens.

Fast-forward to the present, and medical sociology in the early twenty-first century is one of the largest subfields in the ASA, continuing to expand and diversify at a rapid speed as scholars explore societal consequences of the swift growth of the institution of medicine, the organizational fluidity of the health-care system, and the rapidly changing health conditions of global citizens. The internationalization of sociology is evident in publications by medical sociologists around the world in the past two decades, although the use of a human rights perspective within medical sociology is infrequent (see Dumas and Turner 2007 and Turner 2006 for exceptions).

While medical sociologists have rarely used the language of human rights in framing their scholarship, work within medical sociology contributes to a human rights framework in three important ways: (1) by providing evidence of and explanations for the unequal distribution of health within and between countries; (2) by presenting comparative research on access to health care and the evolution of health policies; and (3) by highlighting the dangers of the expansion of (Western) biomedicalization and the concomitant rise in corporate power—processes that may threaten the right to health, health care, and self-determination at local, national, and global levels.

Barriers to the Right to Health

Article 25 of the Universal Declaration of Human Rights (UN General Assembly, 1948) specifies, "Everyone has the right to a standard of living adequate for the health and well-being of himself and his family, including . . . medical care . . . and the right to security in the event of . . . sickness [and/or] disability." Implicit in the human rights framework is an understanding that the protection and promotion of human rights is essential to the protection and promotion of health (Mann 1996). Others have eloquently called for the protection and promotion of health as fundamental to protecting and promoting human rights (Farmer 2010). Clearly, human rights and the right to health are reciprocal and mutually constitutive. In short, the right to health is a basic human right, a sentiment captured by the language used in the Constitution of the World Health Organization (1948) specifying the enjoyment of the highest attainable standard of health as a fundamental right of every human being. Furthermore, the constitution champions equal development of the promotion of health and control of disease and the extension of the benefits of medical, psychological, and related knowledge to all.

How close are we—as a global community—to meeting the standards laid out by the Universal Declaration of Human Rights and the World Health Organization? Medical sociologists have helped to answer this question by documenting the disproportionate burden of illness, disability, and early mortality for certain individuals, groups, countries, and regions. Furthermore, medical sociologists explore the social conditions that produce health inequalities or violate the "right-to-health" principle. Virchow asked scholars to collect medical statistics in order to "weigh life for life, and see where the dead lie thicker, among the workers or among the privileged" (1848, 182). In general, decades of empirical research reveal the short answer to be "among the workers," or among individuals, groups, countries, and regions where social power is low (Marmot 2004; Robert and House 2000; Wilkinson 1992, 1996). The enduring survival gap between those in the upper versus the lower social echelons persists across times and place, even as causes of mortality shift from infectious disease to chronic illness due to rising standards of living, nutrition, and sanitation (Olshansky and Ault 1986; Omran 1971).

A major contribution by medical sociologists to our understanding of health inequalities is the focus on macro-level social structural conditions, rather than genetic, biological, and psychological conditions, that contribute to poor health. Social scientists employing a wide range of methodologies have used within-country, between-country, and individual-level data analysis to understand how macro-level forces (e.g., political economy, social-class relations, racism) and micro-level forces (e.g., individual risk factors, social support, patient-provider relationships) together contribute to health inequalities.

For the better part of two centuries, persistent health inequalities have closely mirrored social hierarchies, and sociologists (along with epidemiologists, health-service researchers, public health scholars, and others) have tracked how and why poor health accumulates in poor communities. One well-established empirical regularity in population health is the strong association between per capita income and life expectancy. Life expectancy rises rapidly with increasing GNP per capita, but the relationship holds only up to a certain level, after which there are diminishing returns (Wilkinson 1992, 1996). Income distribution within the country is also of critical importance; countries with the smallest income differentials have the highest average life expectancies.

From a human rights perspective, then, the right to health is more easily accomplished when citizens have a basic level of economic stability and live in countries or regions with less economic inequality. Farmer (2003) reminds us that macro-level forces, including global class relations, can do "violence" to individuals and communities by depriving them of the conditions necessary for good health. Analyses of health and medicine that incorporate critical views of class relations are important contributions by sociologists. For example, Navarro asks, how do "class structure, class exploitation, and class struggle appear, reproduce, and affect the health and quality of life of our populations?" (2004, 92–93).

Also important are studies using individual-level data, such as occupational indicators, income, and education, to reveal how poor social and economic circumstances affect health throughout the life course (House et al. 1994; Mirowsky, Ross, and Reynolds 2000; Robert and House 2000). In their watershed piece, Link and Phelan (1995) propose a theory of fundamental causes to explain persistent inequalities in overall health and mortality across time, despite the changing nature of diseases and risk factors.

Sociological research on individual-level health inequalities supports policies that address fundamental or root causes of poor health. Providing high-quality educational opportunities for all would go a long way toward improving health, as would protections against poverty and economic instability. Improving health also requires protecting workers and providing the right to autonomy on the job (Marmot 2004).

Other social factors that place people at risk for poor health outcomes include race/ethnicity, gender, and sexuality. Early sociologist W. E. B. DuBois (1899) implicated racial inequality as a social factor in the high levels of poor health for blacks. Unfortunately, DuBois's insights were overlooked because, for many decades, racial differences in health were generally viewed as biological (due to genetic differences) or as behavioral (due to lifestyle choices). However, we now have a wealth of evidence to show how one's life circumstances—especially in confronting classism, racism, and sexism—are increasingly viewed as leading sources of illness and death in the United States (Krieger et al. 1993; Krieger 2000). While recognizing race as a social construction and not a biological reality, most contemporary medical sociologists still use race and ethnicity as variables in research (for criticisms, see LaVeist 2002) primarily because, while imperfect, they highlight the disproportionate burden of disease, disability, and death borne by African Americans, Hispanic Americans, Native Americans, and some Asian Americans. In their overview of racial and ethnic inequalities in health, Williams and Sternthal (2010) illustrate how social exposures combine with biology to affect the social distribution of disease. They emphasize the disproportionate impact of socioeconomic status on certain racial/ethnic groups at the individual level (e.g., lower incomes, less education, less wealth, higher unemployment, increased occupational hazards) and community level (e.g., racial segregation, economic hardship, concentrated disadvantage, environmental toxins, poor-quality housing, criminal victimization). As well, they implicate racism—expressed through institutional and individual-level discrimination, stigma, racial prejudice, and stereotypes—as detrimental to the health of certain racial/ethnic minority groups.

Medical sociologists have been at the forefront in their examination of how gender "gets under the skin" with dramatic consequences for the health of women and men. In short, women get sicker, but men die quicker: in almost every nation, women live longer than men but have higher morbidity rates and a diminished quality of life in later years (Lorber and Moore 2002; Rieker, Bird, and Lang 2010). Much of this difference can be captured by social factors such as higher rates of alcoholism, substance abuse, and death by homicide and accident in part to due to expectations surrounding the male gender role or, as contemporary gender scholars phrase it, the risks of "doing gender" in line with hegemonic masculinity. In nations facing extreme poverty, both women and men die at relatively early ages, with women being particularly at risk because they often have fewer resources, such as education, food, and medical care (Rieker, Bird, and Lang 2010). Women in poor countries and poor women in better-off countries are at higher risk for complications from childbearing.

On a global level, members of the LGBT community experience higher rates of physical violence, suicide, depression, substance abuse, and other indicators of psychological distress than do heterosexuals (Herek and Berrill 1992; Krieger and Sidney 1997). Also, transwomen and transmen are especially at risk of homicide.

Since health disparities reflect social relations between people and not inherent qualities possessed by them, scholars caution against the use of certain variables, such as race/ethnicity or gender, as "explanatory." Smaje writes, "People do not experience the world through a set of partial coefficients, but as embodied social actors" (2000, 116). As sociologists have long asserted, these social factors are intertwined and intersect in important ways. For example, differences in health status by race/ethnicity often disappear when we adjust for social class; yet at each socioeconomic level, blacks have worse health status than whites (Williams and Sternthal 2010). Scholars employing a feminist, intersectionality perspective remind us to pay attention to how the mutually constitutive dimensions of race/ethnicity, gender, sexual orientation, and social class influence health (e.g., Hinze, Lin, and Andersson 2011; Richardson and Brown 2011).

Removing barriers to good health for members of marginalized groups necessitates bringing attention to racism and sexism as features of institutions. For example, policies and practices adopted by governments and corporations contribute to racial segregation and environmental racism (Bullard 1993; LaVeist 2002; Takechi, Walton, and Leung 2010), including toxic dumps and increased risk of pollution in certain areas (Brown 2000; Brown and Mikkelsen 1990).

MEDICAL SOCIOLOGY   13

Medicine as an institution is not exempt. Historically, health-care providers in the Western world have held prejudices and biases that have resulted in poorer care for members of certain groups, including racial/ethnic minorities, women, members of the LGBT community, and people of lower socioeconomic status (Hinze et al. 2009; Sarver et al. 2003; McKinlay 1996).

In summary, health inequalities are not inevitable but are inherent in social systems where distributions of power are vastly unequal. As the next section makes clear, health services are not evenly distributed either among social groups within societies or between nations (Quadagno 2005; Wright and Perry 2010). After providing an overview of critical scholarship by medical sociologists on how nations finance and deliver health care, we consider how the spread of biomedical approaches to health is a risky proposition and a potential threat to human rights.

National Approaches to Health Care as a Human Right

The constitutions of 67 percent of UN member nations make provisions guaranteeing the right to universal health care, reflecting broad ideological support for the Universal Declaration of Human Rights. Unfortunately, no association has been found between a nation's constitutional pledge and its financial investment in health-care resources (Kinney and Clark 2004). Without concrete government action, affirming the right to health care is an empty promise if access is limited, quality is poor, and cost is prohibitive. The constitution of Haiti, for example, decrees, "The state has the absolute obligation to guarantee the right to life and health." This assurance is impossible in a country plagued by government corruption and economic and political instability (Farmer 2011).

In the struggle to ensure population health, nations must balance three inherently competing goals: equity, cost containment, and quality. Which of these goals becomes central to shaping a country's system, and how, is influenced by each nation's ideological, social, political, and economic realities (Gran 2008; Mechanic 1997; Wright and Perry 2010). Medical sociologists have developed useful comparative frameworks for examining national health-care systems and advancing research into the linkages between health outcomes and health-delivery systems of different countries (Kikuzawa, Olafsdottir, and Pescosolido 2008; Matcha 2003; Mechanic and McAlpin 2010; Stevens 2001). While not grounded in rights-based discourse, this comparative work is increasingly turning from examination of structural components to exploring principles and ideals underlying health-care systems. Challenging assumptions about the value neutrality of medical policy and practice lays bare culturally specific notions about distributive justice and human rights.

The growing comparative focus in medical sociology is also useful for understanding points of convergence and divergence between national approaches to health-care delivery and the multiplicity of factors shaping a country's system (Stevens 2001). In a landmark twenty-one-nation study, Kikuzawa, Olafsdottir, and Pescosolido (2008) found that residents of "Insurance Model" nations such as the United States, with a small state role in the provision of health care, are much less likely than people in National Health Service countries to agree that government should be responsible for health care. Yet a majority of people in countries such as the United States retain a belief in the fundamental right to health and health care (Jenkins and Hsu 2008). Medical sociologists can provide empirical data and theoretical underpinnings to illuminate the disjuncture between the moral convictions of individuals and health-care policies that do not uphold these values.

Along with international comparisons of health-care systems, it is essential to examine the rights of those individuals who remain on the sidelines of health-care policy. Though citizenship guarantees health-care services in most industrialized nations, indigenous and immigrant populations are often denied equal access to care (Turner 1993). Medical sociologists have chronicled health-policy barriers to access for indigenous populations, including the Roma in Europe (Sienkiewicz 2010), Aboriginals in Canada and Australia (Benoit, Carroll, and Chaudhry 2003), and Native Americans in the United States (Garroutte 2001, 2003), among others.

Of particular concern, from a health and human rights perspective, is the absence of provisions for illegal immigrant populations in almost all areas of policy. Even in the European Union, with a newly ratified health and human rights treaty, only Spain guarantees care for illegal immigrants (Romero-Ortuno 2004). Immigrants, both legal and illegal, face ineligibility and may forgo health services due to fears of arrest or deportation. Individual-level barriers include lack of knowledge of available services, language barriers, and cultural insensitivity of providers (Shuval 2001). Meeting the health needs of immigrant populations requires not only extending the right to health care to noncitizens and working to improve access for this population but providing a broader bundle of services, including translation, housing, education, and occupational opportunities. Immigrant health is particularly a problem for nations with large numbers of refugees (e.g., Kenya), rapidly growing immigrant populations (e.g., Spain), and nations such as the United States with millions of undocumented immigrants.

As the only industrialized nation that does not guarantee health-care access to all its citizens, the United States is uniquely situated in the debate over the right to health care. With health-care spending standing at nearly 18 percent of the GDP, the US system relies on a patchwork of public and private services that, despite being the most expensive system in the world, leaves 50 million people, or 17 percent of the US population, without health care. Fully one-third of young adults are uninsured, and at all ages insurance status is highly associated with race/ethnicity, with 14 percent of whites, 22 percent of blacks, and 34 percent of Latinos lacking health insurance (Streeter et al. 2011) The uninsured face higher levels of morbidity and mortality, delayed treatment, and inferior medical care; they have poorer medical outcomes and are more likely to be denied care (Chirayath 2007; Quesnel-Vallee 2004). While the 2010 Obama health-care legislation increases access to care, it does little to address health-care quality or cost, and many foresee a potential shift toward explicit rationing due to insufficient resources and health-care personnel to care for millions of newly insured.

Nations with universal health-care systems prioritize the goal of access, treating health care as a collective good and containing costs through implicit rationing based on medical need. However, the value placed on individual responsibility in the United States renders health care a commodity, not a right, and services are rationed on the basis of income instead of medical need (Jost 2003). Though the highest burden of disease lies with the poor, it is the wealthier and healthier Americans who "earn" the privilege of accessing the medical care required to maintain their physical and mental well-being. While policy-makers in the United States decry the rationing used in universal health-care systems, medical sociologists have been on the forefront of demonstrating ways in which explicit rationing occurs at multiple levels in the US system (Mechanic 1997; Stevens 2001). Medical sociologists (among others) point to the failure of competition in the medical marketplace to control costs and argue that health care cannot be considered a commodity because ill patients are not rational actors who can "shop around" for medical care as they can with other goods and services (Matcha 2003; Mechanic 1997). Navarro (2004) reminds us that wherever the corporate class is very strong and the working class is very weak, you find weak welfare states in which social services, including health care, are paltry. Without dismantling the market-driven commodification of health care, the US health-care system will stand at odds with the values of distributive justice and human rights.

The promotion of health care as a human right cannot be achieved through national health-care policy alone. Recent studies in Canada and the United Kingdom remind us that universal health-care systems do not ameliorate health disparities (Wright and Perry 2010). Access to health care must be coupled with political and financial investments in other "life-affirming opportunities" that protect disadvantaged populations from daily acts of structural violence (Matcha 2003, 184; Farmer 2003). Research in medical sociology confirms that the poor have difficulties seeking medical care if they do not have transportation, cannot leave work, or do not have child care. Physical and mental well-being suffer if housing is substandard, food is unsafe, crime goes unchecked, air quality is poor, working conditions are dangerous, and employment is scarce. Governing bodies at local, national, and global levels must recognize their role in the protection and promo-tion of health and take proactive steps to uphold the human rights of their peoples.

EXPANSION OF (WESTERN) BIOMEDICALIZATION

As the above sections make clear, medical sociologists have been at the forefront of research on inequalities in health and health care, providing contextual explanations that emphasize ideological barriers as well as social, political, and economic structures. In this section, we explore how a primary focus on biomedical solutions has potential to violate the "first, do no harm" axiom taught to health-care providers early in their medical educations. In short, medical sociologists have cautioned that the ascendancy, dominance, and expansion of biomedical approaches to health and illness, along with increasing commodification of medical care, carry significant risks to local, national, and global health, in part because they eclipse contextual explanations but also because they raise the specter of biomedical colonialism. Whether they frame it as medicalization (Conrad 2007), biomedicalization (Clark et al. 2003), geneticization (Lippman 1991; Shostak and Freese 2010), or pharmaceuticalization (Abraham 2010), medical sociologists and other scholars of trends in medicine warn of the dangers inherent in promoting Western biomedical models worldwide. A few examples bring to light the dilemmas and highlight potential threats to human rights.

First, sociologist Troy Duster's (2003, 2005) scholarship on the problematic social consequences of genetic research is a case in point. Genetic research is supported by extensive public-sector investment, yet reinforces the individualization of health and illness and reifies racial categories. The advent of "personalized medicine" (reserved primarily for the well-off) is based upon individual genetic profiles and locates health problems inside the body rather than with the social forces, social arrangements, and government policies that contribute to poor health. Additionally, racialized medicine promotes biomedical fixes for different races without attention to the role of structural forces that create racial and ethnic health disparities. (See also Conrad [2000] and Shostak and Freese [2010] for sociological critiques of the rise of the genetic paradigm, or genetic medicalization.)

Second, while sociologists are at the forefront (along with epidemiologists and public health scholars) of data collection on health disparities, it has become increasingly clear that data collection can impede the provision of health services. According to Adams (2010), global health efforts rooted in bench science can shift resources from the delivery of vaccines and treatment to laboratory research—often for pharmaceutical development—with clinical trial subjects and blood samples. Adams asserts that "turning the world of international health into a laboratory space for research" can interrupt the practices of physician activists and caregivers and divert scarce resources away from the provision of care to people and toward "good statistics" that accompany evidence-based medicine (2010, 54). If the only way for the poor to obtain health care is to enroll in clinical trials, then the objectives of public health are displaced.

Third, the promotion of Western biomedical models globally introduces a phenomenon Gaines (2011) terms "the biomedical entourage." In short, global health programs grounded in the Western biomedical model can impose costly and impersonal curative medicine resulting in a form of biocultural colonialism. A biomedical entourage comprised of pharmaceutical companies and medical technologies (both with enormous influence over medical research and practice), along with a universal bioethical approach that neglects local context (and is gender biased), accompanies many global health programs without attention to local biology, healing alternatives from the local culture, and even local medicines and medical practice.

Finally, while scholars and activists worldwide recognize the value of medical advances and technologies for improving health, Conrad (2007) reminds us of the "dark side" of medicalization. As more human conditions and problems come to be identified and treated as medical conditions, medicine and accompanying industries (e.g., insurance and pharmaceutical companies) become institutions of surveillance and control, laying claim to birth, death, and everything in between. At a general level, greater exposure to medical treatment opens the door to higher rates of medical abuses and iatrogenesis. For example, approximately two hundred thousand people die each year due to preventable medical errors (Harmon 2009). As well, history books are rife with examples of medical abuses, such as the infamous Tuskegee study, thalidomide deaths, and complications from the Dalkon Shield. In addition, and as touched upon above, certain health conditions, like depression or obesity, become decontexualized with a focus on diagnosis and biomedical treatment trumping collective social action necessary to change social conditions that contribute to increases in physical and mental illnesses. Karp's (1996) work on the experience of depression raises important questions about a postmodern world that may contribute to emotional exhaustion and alienation. As well, several scholars have exposed the role upstream social conditions (e.g., tobacco and fast-food industries) play in contributing to health problems downstream (McKinlay 1974). Yet, the biomedical model—and even public health and epidemiology—can very narrowly focus on individual risk behaviors and medical interventions. Medical sociologists keep health and human rights issues on the table by pushing questions of political economy and the market-based commodification of medicine to the forefront of academic attention.

Indeed, the spread of biomedicalization in its current form also invites exploitation by corporations, including pharmaceutical and technology companies, which may place medical treatments outside the realm of possibility for the poor, further exacerbating existing health inequalities. As Farmer and Smith note, "The better the therapy, the more injustice meted out to those not treated" (1999, 267). Market-based approaches to health care, combined with shrinking state investment in public solutions, will only deepen structural inequality, widening the health gaps between those with and those without resources. Roberts asserts, "The social immorality of biotechnological advances not only will ensure that their benefits are distributed unequally to the most privileged citizens, but will reinforce inequitable social structures and neoliberal political trends that impede social change" (2010, 69).

CONCLUSION

Anthropologist and physician Paul Farmer (2010) and the late public health scholar Jonathan Mann (1996) have argued that taking a "health angle" will help promote human rights globally. Medical sociologists contribute by providing vital theory and data on the causes and consequences of early mortality, excessive morbidity, and disability. In this chapter, we've argued that some bodies are more at risk than others and that structural forces and institutions have collective power to protect vulnerable bodies or do great damage to them. Turner argues for grounding sociological analyses of human rights in the concept of human frailty, generating "collective sympathy for the plight of others" and leading to the creation of moral communities in support of human rights (1993, 489). Since human frailty is a universal condition, bringing the plight of the vulnerable to light can increase collective support for a human rights paradigm.

Furthermore, a focus on health brings much to the struggle for human rights because public health, medicine, and social scientists occupy privileged spaces from which to promote a broader human rights agenda (Farmer 2010). One enduring conundrum is how scholars from Economic North countries often argue for "positive" civil rights (e.g., economic, social, and cultural) across the globe when their own countries fail to uphold the right to food, shelter, and medical care as human rights. Critical sociologists draw attention to the ideological and cultural resistance to the notion that the right to health care is a legitimate, basic human right (see, e.g., An-Na'im 2001). Findings from research in this tradition sharpen our understanding of the political processes at work in many Economic North countries and foster a greater understanding of cultural and geographic differences around the question of who deserves basic human rights. Sociologists can highlight the tensions between public support for civil and political rights worldwide on the one hand and public inability to support economic and social rights on the other. Bringing the tensions to light helps scholars, policy-makers, and activists craft agendas for the promotion of economic and social rights locally, nationally, and globally.

In the early years of the subdiscipline, medical sociologists embraced the academic tradition of moral neutrality in order to earn legitimacy within the scientific world of medicine. Currently, sociologists versed in the study of tangible social phenomena struggle with the conceptual vagueness of the language of human rights, which is "distinctly slippery, polysemic, and promiscuous" (Somers and Roberts 2008, 412). Yet, in the past fifty years, public sociology, feminist theory, and critical race theory have emancipated sociology from claims of moral neutrality, paving the way for a burgeoning sociology of human rights. According to Blau, while the role of sociologists has long been limited to observation and analysis of social inequalities, "human rights provide sociologists with the authority to assert that homelessness is *wrong*, racism is *wrong*, poverty is *wrong* (and, yes, even capitalism is wrong, if you are so inclined)" (2006, 1). Increasingly, medical sociologists are adopting rights-based frameworks in their study of health inequalities and rejecting a rigid form of positivism (and even its later shift to cultural relativism), which led them to eschew normative judgments and universal values (Frezzo 2008; Turner 1993).

As social actors, medical sociologists inhabit multiple roles through which to make a case for health as a human right. We can advance awareness of human rights efforts through research drawing on local knowledge and "capturing realities on the ground" (Moncada and Blau 2006, 120). Medical sociologists need to guard against becoming handmaidens of the biomedical paradigm and must ensure that rights-based work remains guided by sociological perspectives. Blau and Smith argue that though they are rarely leaders in activism and policy, sociologists "become their advocates when they conceptualize the forms and the processes [and disseminate] their findings and interpretations in publications" (2006, xiv). For medical sociologists to embrace their role in advocating for health as a human right, a commitment must extend from their positions as authors, editors, and members of professional organizations and the broader academic community.

We also have the option of weaving advocacy for the basic right to health into our academic home: the classroom. Paolo Freire (2000) would remind us that our pedagogy cultivates humanitarian values and social action when we forge community with our students—future leaders who will harness new forms of social engagement to advocate for the protection and promotion of health as a fundamental human right.

Medical sociology is uniquely positioned to lay bare the ways in which myriad inequities around the world strip individuals, particularly the disenfranchised, of their basic right to health and well-being. By making the case for a right to health, to health care, and to autonomy from medical sovereignty, medical sociologists can help lay a solid foundation for the human rights paradigm.

CHAPTER TWO

CRIME, LAW, AND DEVIANCE

Joachim J. Savelsberg

The relationship between the sociology of crime, law, and deviance and the study of human rights—those basic political, civil, and social rights that are granted to all human beings irrespective of their citizenship—is crucial but problematic. It is crucial because violations of human rights (and humanitarian law) constitute not just deviant but also law-breaking and at times criminal behaviors. They include war crimes, crimes against humanity, and genocide that have cost manifold more human lives and caused more suffering than all street crimes combined in the twentieth century alone. The relatively recent definition of these behaviors as crimes poses challenges to criminology and to the practice and sociology of law.

The relationship between crime, law, and deviance and human rights issues is also problematic. Scholars who address human rights and their criminal violations, especially political scientists, historians, lawyers, and philosophers, tend to know little about the wealth of sociological insights into issues of crime and law. Simultaneously, only a few sociologists of crime, law, and deviance have investigated human rights violations and legal responses to them (early: Turk 1982; Chambliss 1989; Barak 1991; more recently: e.g., Brannigan and Hardwick 2003; Ermann and Lundman 2002; Friedrichs 2009; Hagan 2003; Hagan and Greer 2002; Hagan and Levi 2005; Hagan, Rymond-Richmond, and Parker 2005; Hagan, Schoenfeld, and Palloni 2006; Hagan and Rymond-Richmond 2008, 2009; Maier-Katkin, Mears, and Bernard 2011; Mullins, Kauzlarich, and Rothe 2004; Savelsberg 2010; Savelsberg and King 2011; Woolford 2006). Yet, these themes should find a central place in the sociology of crime, law, and deviance, while these sociological specialties should simultaneously export their insights to other disciplines.

ATROCITIES: A MAINSTAY OF HUMAN HISTORY

Atrocities, today defined as humanitarian and human rights crimes, are a mainstay of human history. Myths and history tell us about mass killings during antiquity, hundreds of thousands slaughtered at the command of rulers and

CRIME, LAW, AND DEVIANCE   21

conquerors such as Genghis Khan and his successors, sultans of the Ottoman Empire, or rulers of the Aztecs (Rummel 1994). Europeans contributed to this history. In 1099, after the conquest of Jerusalem, Christian Crusaders butchered forty to seventy thousand of the city's Jewish and Muslim inhabitants. Eyewitnesses depict unimaginable cruelties and bloodshed (William, Archbishop of Tyre 1943). During the plagues of the fourteenth century, European Christians used their Jewish neighbors as scapegoats, and tens of thousands were killed. The Spanish Crown murdered some eighteen thousand Protestants in the Low Countries between 1567 and 1573, and the French royal court initiated the massacre of tens of thousands of Protestant Huguenots during the infamous St. Bartholomew night of 1572. The Revolutionary Councils of the French Revolution ordered the execution of some twenty thousand members of the nobility, political opponents, and alleged traitors. The Catholic Church had tens of thousands of heretics killed by fire, miserable prison conditions, and torture between 1480 and 1809, and Protestant witch hunts cost the lives of thousands of women (Jensen 2007).

Colonial rule also involved massive atrocities that victimized millions, including the early twentieth-century genocide against the Herero in today's Namibia by German colonial forces (Steinmetz 2007). Further, between the sixteenth and nineteenth centuries, up to 2 million African slaves were killed by the deplorable conditions of their voyage across the Atlantic Ocean. Millions more perished during transports to the Middle East and the Orient. The total death toll is estimated at somewhere between 17 and 65 million (Rummel 1994, 48).

Those responsible for atrocities throughout most of human history were not prosecuted and condemned but typically celebrated as heroes. "Victims," those on whom "heroes" imposed great sacrifices, were discounted, perceived as evil or "polluted" (*victima* in Latin means those set aside to be sacrificed) (Giesen 2004).

The long history of state-committed or -sponsored mass killings continued, as we know, into current times. The twentieth century outdid many of its predecessors in light of the technological advances and organizational potentials of modern states, especially totalitarian ones (Bauman 1989; Cooney 1997; Horowitz 2002). Rummel (1994) estimates the number of people killed by governments from the beginning of the twentieth century until 1987 at close to 170 million, not counting tens of millions who died as a consequence of regular warfare. Here, the percentage of civilian casualties of war increased from fourteen in World War I to sixty-seven in World War II and up to ninety in the century's final decades (Hagan and Rymond-Richmond 2009, 63f.). These horrifying numbers do not even account for the millions of women raped, houses and cities looted, and lands and livelihoods destroyed. The degree of victimization is of a magnitude that easily dwarfs that caused by regular street crime.

Reactions to atrocities have changed, however. While denial is still common (Cohen 2001), perpetrations often cause moral outrage, and the search for preventive measures and remedies and the punishment of offenders has begun. Several international conventions and UN initiatives speak to such innovation.

22   JOACHIM J. SAVELSBERG

Consider also diverse ad hoc courts and the new International Criminal Court (ICC), truth commissions (Hayner 2001), apologies (Bilder 2006), amnesties (Mallinder 2008), and other mechanisms of transitional justice (Teitel 2000).

EXPLANATIONS OF HUMANITARIAN AND HUMAN RIGHTS CRIMES

Crimes against humanitarian and human rights law always involve collective, often organizational action, but they can never be committed without individual action. In this respect they resemble white-collar crime, and terminology from that literature can be applied to human rights crimes too: *organizational crimes*, supported by often legitimate organizations whose goals they are meant to advance; *organized crimes*, committed by organizations set up for the purpose of engaging in law-breaking behavior; and *occupational crime*, "committed by individuals in the course of their occupation for their personal gain and without organizational support" (Coleman 2006, 11). Individual actors involved in such crime include frontline, low-level perpetrators who execute the dirty work (Hughes 1963), as well as leaders whose hands remain untainted by the blood they ultimately bear responsibility for shedding. These crimes demand complex explanatory approaches that go beyond much of what criminology has developed to address juvenile delinquency and street crimes (Chambliss 1989).

Innovative work on human rights crime thus seeks to link distinct levels of analysis and types of actors. Consider a simultaneous application of Randall Collins's micro-sociological, situation-focused approach to violence and Diane Vaughan's organizational model to the explanation of massacres (Savelsberg 2010, 75–85). Discussing the My Lai massacre against hundreds of civilians, committed by an American military company in the course of the Vietnam War, Collins focuses on situations that are "shaped by an emotional field of tension and fear" (2008, 18), turned into emotional energy that drives violent action. Resulting "forward panics" are particularly frequent in the context of guerrilla warfare, especially when troops are brought into a landing zone by helicopter in the middle of enemy territory (as in My Lai). Here "frenzied attacks of forward panic" become likely.

Importantly, military leadership frequently placed American soldiers in such situations during the Vietnam War (see also the 1972 documentary film *Winter Soldier*). Thus, actions by members of Company C cannot be understood without considering organizational context. Diane Vaughan (1999, 2002) stresses that members of organizations are likely to resort to the violation of laws, rules, and regulations in order to meet organizational goals, especially where divisions by hierarchy and specialization create "structural secrecy," where risk of detection is minimized. Organizational processes such as the "normalization of deviance" (i.e., acceptance of deviant behavior as normal) provide normative support for illegality, as has previously been documented in white-collar crime literature. Further organizational conditions (all identified for My Lai) include ambiguous orders and pleas for more aggressiveness perceived as authorization

CRIME, LAW, AND DEVIANCE   23

to engage in "sanctioned massacres" (Kelman and Hamilton 2002, 210); organized rituals that drive emotions to a high pitch (e.g., a funeral of a fallen comrade when orders for the attack were given); and organizational culture ("permissive attitude toward the treatment and safeguarding of non-combatants . . . almost total disregard for the lives and property of the civilian population" [Goldstein, Marshall, and Schwartz 1976, 314]).

A sufficiently complex approach needs to incorporate, in addition to micro-dynamics and organizational conditions, the larger environment of organizations, where environmental uncertainty and "liability of newness" (Vaughn 2002, 275) further advance routine nonconformity (e.g., in My Lai, brief military training, neglected knowledge about local culture, and "the handling and treatment of civilians or refugees" [Goldstein, Marshall, and Schwartz 1976, 81]). The organizational environment also included definitions of the enemy as "commies," fighters for "ultimate evil" in the Cold War, and racist attitudes, reflected in the derogatory term "gooks" (Kelman and Hamilton 2002, 215).

In short, a complex approach that merges the study of situational, organizational, and environmental conditions is needed to explain grave human rights violations. Individual agency also matters. Some soldiers refused to participate in the My Lai case as elsewhere (for Police Battalion 101 during the Holocaust, see Browning 1998).

The sociology of crime has also finally begun to address genocide, the "crime of crimes," introducing innovative and complex methodological and theoretical tools (e.g., Hagan 2003; Hagan and Rymond-Richmond 2008, 2009; Savelsberg 2010). John Hagan and collaborators, after work on genocidal action in the Balkan wars and the building of the International Criminal Tribunal for the Former Yugoslavia (ICTY) (Hagan 2003), engaged the genocide in the Darfur region of Sudan (Hagan and Rymond-Richmond 2008, 2009). They utilized the Atrocities Documentation Survey, a rich victimization survey of some eleven hundred Darfurians in the refugee camps in neighboring Chad.

Horrifying narratives of victimization are backed up by statistical analysis: most victimization occurred where the land was most fertile, and total and sexual victimization were highest where attacks were most often accompanied by racial slurs. Expressions of racial hatred thus appear to ignite collective fury that encourages killing and raping. In a "joint criminal enterprise," individual liability exists in the context of collective action. Genocide is documented as the criteria of its legal definition are backed up with empirical evidence: members of a group are being killed, serious bodily and mental harm is being inflicted, conditions of life calculated to bring about their physical destruction are imposed, and empirical evidence of intent to destroy, in whole or in part, a racial or ethnic group is produced. The tools of crime, law, and deviance scholarship are thus used to document genocide.

Tools from crime, law, and deviance scholarship are also suited to explain genocide. Hagan and Rymond-Richmond (2009) put to productive use Ross Matsueda's (2006) complex criminological theory that links together Sutherland's expansion of social-psychological ideas about differential association toward differential organization, associated network ideas, and Goffmanian framing analysis. Collective-action frames (Benford and Snow 2000) are especially effective if they define the root of the problem and its solution collectively ("we are all in this together"), the antagonists as "us" versus "them" (e.g., "Jews versus Arians"; "blacks versus Arabs"), and a problem or injustice caused by "them" that can be challenged by "us." Closed and dense social networks with such collective-action frames are most likely to produce collective efficacy, "the willingness . . . [of groups] to intervene for the common good [evil from the perspective of the other side]" (Sampson and Raudenbusch 1999, 919). "Social efficacy" of actors who are central to local networks, but who also are linked to the outside world, enables creation of "consensus over group . . . objectives and procedures, and translate[s] these procedures into action" (Matsueda 2006, 24). Capable of recognizing interests of their local group and of outside institutions and able to switch between local and universal codes, such actors play crucial roles in manipulating local groups on behalf of collective goals, including a state's genocidal project. Hagan and Rymond-Richmond link central elements of the Matsueda model with Coleman's (1990) famous micro/macro scheme and creatively apply this amalgam to explain the genocide in Darfur.

Linking theoretical arguments by Collins and Vaughan, applying them to massacres (Savelsberg 2010, 75–85), and merging models by Matsueda and Coleman to explain genocide (Hagan and Rymond-Richmond 2009, 117–121, 162–169) takes into account micro and macro factors and organizational and individual actors at different levels of hierarchy, thus engaging traditional tools from the sociology of crime in the explanation of the gravest of offenses. Other traditional criminological approaches await application to human rights crimes, including Messner and Rosenfeld's (2007) ideas about the imbalance of societal sectors, ideas on criminal learning and culture as enduring versus adaptive (Anderson 1994), especially if enriched by a wealth of differentiated ideas on the emergence of anti-Semitism (Friedländer 2007), and ideas about anomie and strain (Merton 1938) and their interaction with social instability (for suggestions, see Savelsberg 2010, 49–66; Maier-Katkin, Mears, and Bernard 2011, 239–247).

Legal Regulation: Norms and Court Intervention

Responses to atrocities have changed dramatically in recent history. They limit the notion of national sovereignty, according to which domestic rulers can act toward their populations at will. Resulting from the 1648 Peace Treaty of Westphalia that ended the Thirty Years' War, sovereignty was meant to reduce foreign interventions and international warfare, but it opened up room for massive domestic abuses. The nineteenth century saw the establishment of humanitarian law (Geneva and Hague conventions), seeking to protect non-combatants against mistreatment in times of international warfare while still respecting national sovereignty. Yet, the Nazis' domestic terror and their later expansion into occupied and allied lands brought into plain sight the need for international regulation not only in the pursuit of war but also when states engage in outrageous victimization during times of peace. The foundation was laid, in immediate reaction to the Nazi terror, by the 1948 Universal Declaration of Human Rights (UDHR), guaranteeing civil, political, social, and economic rights. Also in 1948 the Convention on the Prevention and Punishment of the Crime of Genocide was approved by representatives of fifty nations. It finally entered into force on January 12, 1951. Genocide now constituted a crime, and perpetrators were to be punished, be they "constitutionally responsible rulers, public officials or private individuals" (Article 4). Other human rights conventions address the protection of women (1979), children (1990), and indigenous peoples (1991). The Convention against Torture and Other Cruel, Inhumane and Degrading Treatment or Punishment (1987), like the genocide convention, applies standards of criminal liability. Finally, the Rome Statute of the ICC established the first independent and permanent international criminal court to try "persons accused of the most serious crimes of international concern" (ICC 2011). It entered into force on July 1, 2002, and had been joined by 105 nations by October 2008, not including the United States. With jurisdiction over genocidal atrocities, crimes against humanity, and war crimes, it backs up a multitude of domestic and foreign courts (for critical debate on the criminalization of human rights offenses, see Blau and Moncada 2007a; Hagan and Levi 2007; Cerulo 2007).

Why did the twentieth century, despite its many competitors in the execution of excessive cruelties, become the first to get serious about developing control responses (Minow 1998, 2002)? Satisfactory explanations should simultaneously draw on human rights literature, the sociology of law, and other branches of sociology. They need to speak to the universalization of human rights (global norms trump state sovereignty), individualization of responses (individuals, not just nations, can be held liable), and criminalization of offenses.

Universalization was advanced by the globalization of economies and new technologies that enhanced the flow of ideas, capital, goods, and workers across national boundaries. New international governmental organizations, such as the United Nations, were supplemented by international nongovernmental organizations that now represent a form of civil society at the global level (Keck and Sikkink 1998). Comparable to national civil societies, they contribute to the creation of global cognitive and normative scripts, which, once produced, direct actions of national governments (Meyer et al. 1997). Policies passed in compliance with international human rights norms spread and become effective at the local level (e.g., Boyle 2002; Boyle and Corl 2010 on female genital cutting; for more cautionary conclusions, see Cole 2005).

Individual criminal accountability in international human rights law is advanced by structural and cultural forces: the changing balance of power (growing inter-dependence of nations), the emergence of global civil society, and the occasional backing of criminal justice intervention by powerful countries or international government organizations. The rapid establishment of

26 JOACHIM J. SAVELSBERG

criminal liability after the 1980s was advanced by the end of the Cold War, during which the two superpowers blocked any move toward international criminal justice (Turk 1982). The selection of leaders from relatively weak countries for criminal prosecution partially mirrors massive power differentials in the international community.

Cultural forces also promote criminalization of offenses. Émile Durkheim wrote—as Erving Goffman would later do—about the most sacred good in modern society, expressed in the "cult of the individual" (Smith 2008, 18). This new dignity of individuals combines with the sensitization of modern humans to physical violence resulting from the civilizing process with its massive decrease in interpersonal violence in everyday life (Elias 1978; Johnson and Monkkonen 1996). A cultural approach simultaneously recognizes punishment not as (just) a rational application of disciplinary knowledge but as a didactic exercise (Garland 1990; Smith 2008). Rituals of court trials signify, in line with Durkheimian ideas, the sacred—human dignity in modern society—versus the evil.

But what about the timing of the criminalization of human rights violations, specifically in the post–World War II era? In light of the new sensibilities to which Durkheim and Elias speak, the Holocaust evoked responses that created a universal cultural trauma: through symbolic extension of the Shoah and psychological identification with the victims, members of a world audience became traumatized by an experience that they themselves had not shared (Alexander et al. 2004, 251). The legal proceeding of the International Military Tribunal, subsequent Nuremberg trials (Heberer and Matthäus 2008), and punishment of leading Nazi perpetrators were performative or demonstrative in Durkheim's terms. They provided images, symbols, totems, myths, and stories and thus contributed to the formation of a collective memory of evil. Once established as universal evil, the Holocaust served as "analogical bridging" to reinterpret and dramatize later events in light of this earlier trauma (Alexander 2004, 245–249). Cultural trauma thus further advanced global consensus regarding the dignity of individuals.

In short, as a result of structural and cultural changes, human rights law became universalized, and individual criminal liability was introduced for perpetrators of state-organized crimes. The application of such law by courts poses the next challenge to which the sociology of law responds.

Recent work in the sociology of law has addressed the conditions of domestic, foreign, and international human rights courts (e.g., Hagan 2003 applying Bourdieu's field theory to the ICTY). Yet, central debates on consequences of human rights trials tend to bypass the sociology of law—much to their detriment. While conservative lawyers and political scientists (e.g., Goldsmith and Krasner 2003; Snyder and Vinjamuri 2003/2004) express skepticism about the application of international or domestic criminal law, liberals are optimistic regarding the effects of human rights trials (e.g., Sikkink 2011; Payne 2009). The former base their often effective arguments on case studies. The latter, however, have stronger ammunition in the form of systematic data sets with large numbers of transitional justice situations. Sikkink's analyses, for example, indicate that countries with truth commissions and trials substantially improved human rights records; countries with criminal trials alone still showed significant improvement. Yet, these analyses do not resolve the issue of causality. Could third factors, such as past states of democracy and liberal law, explain both the holding of trials in transitional situations and the later improvement of human rights?

Also, what might explain the effectiveness of trials, should the association indeed represent a causal relation? Classical and new arguments from the sociology of crime, law, and deviance provide a look into the black box between intervention and outcomes. A long line of research on deterrence, consistent with rational-choice ideas, suggests that the certainty of punishment deters more than its severity (Matsueda, Kreager, and Huizinga 2006). In the case of human rights crimes, the certainty of punishment moves away from zero, suggesting a deterrent effect (Sikkink and Kim 2009).

Newer cultural arguments focus on the memory-building functions of trials that may thoroughly delegitimize previous regimes and their atrocities (Osiel 1997; Savelsberg and King 2007, 2011). This new line of work on collective memory (Halbwachs 1992) and cultural trauma (Alexander et al. 2004) is inspired by classic Durkheimian ideas. It is in line with arguments by historic actors such as President Franklin D. Roosevelt and Justice Robert H. Jackson, who assigned a history-writing function to the international military tribunal (Landsman 2005, 6). A cautionary note is warranted though. Trials follow a particular institutional logic, targeting individuals, not the social processes and cultural patterns sociologists might focus on; focusing on actions covered by legal classifications (producers of inflammatory rhetoric may not be criminally liable); focusing on defendants (voices of victims are heard only when they serve the court; on the ICTY, see Stover 2005); and considering defendants guilty or not guilty, a gross simplification by psychological standards.

Historical case studies indicate that trials do shape memory—albeit in line with the institutional logic of law (Bass 2000; Giesen 2004; Landsman 2005; Heberer and Matthäus 2008). Further, trials that unfold under conditions of regime continuity typically focus on low-level perpetrators and may be less successful. Most American history textbooks, for example, do not mention the My Lai massacre. Those that do tend to present the crime in line with the trial outcome, focusing on the deeds of 2nd Lt. William Calley, while silencing the role played by higher ranks and the attempted cover-up of the massacre (Savelsberg and King 2011). Such processing of past atrocities may have advanced uncritical attitudes toward the institution of the military (Smith 2009) and contributed to a willingness by American military in current conflicts to offend against norms of humanitarian law (Mental Health Advisory Team IV 2006).

In short, through deterrence and collective-memory functions, criminal trials may—under specific conditions—help transitions to democracy and peace and prevent the repetition of past evil. Optimism, however, must be tempered by insights into the selectivity and inaccuracy of trial-based memories, by the

28   JOACHIM J. SAVELSBERG

focus on "small fish" in the absence of regime transitions, and by transition problems that trials may cause in some contexts. Much more work on the conditions and effects of national, foreign, and international courts is needed.

MUTUAL GAINS IN METHODS AND THEORY: SOCIOLOGY OF CRIME, LAW, AND DEVIANCE AND HUMAN RIGHTS SCHOLARSHIP

This chapter indicates that the study of human rights and grave offenses such as genocide, mostly executed by historians, lawyers, and political scientists, can gain conceptually, theoretically, and methodologically from the sociology of crime, law, and deviance—and vice versa. Many human rights offenses constitute crimes, but the fields that most prominently study human rights have barely sought inspiration from the sociology of crime, law, and deviance, which has engaged issues of crime and its control for more than a century. This particularly striking example of the problems of disciplinary segmentation should be remedied. There are many potential gains. On the conceptual front, genocide scholars discuss totalitarianism, war and social instability, and racist and anti-Semitic ideologies. Crime, law, and deviance scholars tend to use broader concepts such as learning and culture, strain and anomie, social control and social disorganization. The application of each, historically specific and broader theoretical concepts, comes with costs and benefits, and drawing on both should yield substantial gain.

Genocide scholars' frequent concern with single cases yields profound insights. It contrasts with crime, law, and deviance scholars' typical interest in general patterns. Linking insights from both perspectives and advancing historical-comparative studies is highly promising (e.g., Weitz 2003 on genocide).

Historians are primarily concerned with past cases, while crime, law, and deviance scholars tend to focus on current-day phenomena. Yet, there is a history of the present (or very recent past), and historical criminology has become an important branch of this field.

While crime, law, and deviance scholars often proceed deductively, testing general theories with empirical data, genocide scholars commonly proceed inductively, weaving together a rich tapestry of empirical findings to arrive at explanations. In practice elements of induction and deduction enrich each other in the work of both historians and sociologist-criminologists. Mutual recognition is warranted.

Human rights scholars and sociologists of crime, law, and deviance tend to work with different types of data (e.g., archives versus surveys). Merging insights from different data sources can only enrich our understanding of social phenomena generally and of grave human rights violations specifically. One example for the use of crime, law, and deviance data that are new to human rights scholarship is large-scale victimization surveys and accompanying sophisticated statistical analysis, as in the work on Darfur by Hagan and Rymond-Richmond (2008, 2009). Also the use of nonparticipant observation and in-depth interviews can enrich human rights scholarship (e.g., Hagan 2003). Other methods include systematic content analysis to capture the memory and framing of grave human rights violations (e.g., Savelsberg and King 2011), historic comparative analysis, and—already common in human rights scholarship—archival research (e.g., Chambliss 1989).

Crime, law, and deviance scholars typically focus on individuals and their offenses (or aggregations to rates), much in line with criminal law's notion of individual criminal liability. Leviathan, the state as the creator and enforcer of law, is typically excluded as the potential culprit. In both respects, genocide scholars show much more independence from a state-centered perspective (e.g., on the role of physicians and lawyers in the service of the state, see Stolleis 2007; on collaborating governments, Fein 1979).

Human rights scholars speculate on the effect of criminal justice intervention on abuses. Crime, law, and deviance scholarship's deterrence research (Matsueda, Kreager, and Huizinga 2006) and new work on the collective-memory function of criminal trials (Osiel 1997; Savelsberg and King 2011) can provide guidance.

Sociologists of crime, law, and deviance have engaged in at-times-sterile debates on cultural versus structural conditions of crime. Historical genocide scholarship holds profound lessons on ways in which both are intertwined (e.g., Friedländer 2007).

Finally, and not covered in this chapter, responses to street crime, excessive incarceration, and the death penalty may at least potentially constitute human rights offenses. Much common crime, law, and deviance sociology should thus be examined through the human rights prism. Today, many Native Americans and African Americans live in miserable conditions, partly due to a legacy of discriminatory practices (Sampson and Wilson 1995). The federal and state governments have used massive force against members of these groups (Hagan and Peterson 1995; see also Hagan and Rymond-Richmond's 2009 link between Darfur and the position of minorities in the United States). The "war on drugs" has been a major contributor to the vast overrepresentation of blacks in America's prisons, and federal authorities anticipated this consequence from the outset (Tonry 1995). Felon disenfranchisement laws have been motivated by aggressive attitudes against African Americans and have further weakened their political representation (Manza and Uggen 2006). The practice of capital punishment has also been driven by resentments against minorities, and it continues to disproportionally affect blacks (Peffley and Hurwitz 2007; Jacobs et al. 2007).

CONCLUSION

To address major humanitarian law and human rights violations, crime, law, and deviance scholarship must develop more complex approaches. Previous work on white-collar and organizational crime particularly might lead the way. Crime, law, and deviance scholarship must also abandon its state centeredness, recognizing the state as a potential perpetrator, and adjust its conceptual and theoretical tools accordingly. Simultaneously, the response side of crime, law, and deviance scholarship must contribute to our understanding of the newly founded institutions of human rights law and international criminal justice. Debates in international relations reveal profound uncertainties about the likely outcomes of interventions. This is not surprising, as much human rights scholarship has only recently recognized criminal behavior and criminal-justice institutions as subjects of study and, indeed, as international institutions of criminal justice are historically new. Work on this front is only beginning, and cooperation between traditional human rights scholarship and the sociology of crime, law, and deviance is crucial.

CHAPTER THREE

EDUCATION

Nathalia E. Jaramillo, Peter McLaren, and Jean J. Ryoo

The importance of education as a human right has become widely accepted, in theory, with the 1948 publication of the Universal Declaration of Human Rights and the subsequent 1990 UNESCO World Declaration on Education for All. Both these documents, partial artifacts of a post–World War II climate, referenced existing educational disparities among states as well as an ideological shift toward addressing the "root" causes of social turmoil and strife. These documents also advanced a predominantly modernist paradigm for education in the wake of massive industrialization and uneven economic and social development/exploitation between the world's periphery states and the capitalist core (Ishay 2008). The growing connections among education, state building, capitalist development, and liberal-progressive models of democratic governance gave credence to universal tropes associated with education as a human right within these global frameworks in terms of education providing means necessary for citizens' meaningful participation in society. This is not to suggest, however, that either of these treaties provided an elaborate or even sufficient definition of education per se. In fact, neither did. While Education for All identified literacy, numeracy, and basic problem-solving skills as fundamental to social progress and human welfare, many questions remained unanswered about how to justify education as a human right and how to define education altogether, given cultural, historical, and material differences (Spring 2000).

We could say, however, that a general consensus supports the notion that education is necessary and central to development of a state and its people. Education is considered, in the simplest sense, an institution and social practice that can aid in "self-reliance," as well as personal and social improvement, and contribute to a "safer, healthier and more prosperous sound world" (UNESCO 1990). Within the sociology of education, these preliminary understandings have resulted in various analyses and theoretical contributions to education as a human right. Interrogating relations between social and educational actors at both individual and societal levels, the sociology of education has, for the most part, focused on questions of access, inclusion, and exclusion and how they are addressed in both industrial and so-called developing nations. In more contemporary terms, the sociology of education has also examined roles of race/ethnicity, gender, sexuality, class, and disability in relation to differentiated distribution of educational services and practices (Sadovnik 2007; Weis 2008). It has given primary concern to the individual situated in a wider sphere of social relations and antagonisms that limit equal access to education. Further, questions about the relationship among schooling, states, and development of an active and participatory citizenry have been of concern from the sociology of education's inception.

Social inquiries into education as a human right have looked very different south of the equator, however, with questions of colonialism, coloniality and sanctity of culture, freedom of expression (religious, linguistic, or otherwise), and spatial sovereignty central to understanding and analyzing the relationship between education and society. Documented by friars and missionaries during brutal colonization efforts, indigenous testimonies and narratives have yielded profound historical archives from which to examine teaching's role and learning as a strategy for "conquering" mind, body, and spirit. We are confronted with the continuing legacy of what Nelson Maldonado-Torres (2007) refers to as "coloniality of being"—the idea that effects of colonialism do more than subjugate subaltern knowledges and practices through imposition of sovereign discourses; they also constitute a way of being that is embodied or enfleshed (McLaren 1999). Here the emphasis is on how lived oppression becomes naturalized as a way of life.

While we share the belief that education is a human right, our intent is not to reify the modernist tropes of progressive education as they have been articulated within the literature. Rather, we propose a decolonial and materialist shift in addressing social and pedagogical dimensions of knowledge production mutually evident in our conceptions of self, state, and rights/justice.

KEY FINDINGS IN THE SOCIOLOGY OF EDUCATION

Sociological research into education has traditionally been broken down into three general categories: functionalism, conflict theory, and symbolic interactionism. Following Durkheim (1956, 1962, 1977), functionalists focus on ways schools establish and maintain social order. Many believe that schools serve the interests of society's dominant groups/citizens by teaching children mainstream moral values, inculcating attributes of civic and national patriotism, manufacturing consent to that society's dominant political and social order, ensuring that students acquire academic skills necessary to understand majority-shared forms of knowledge, and facilitating a smooth ideological transition into the capitalist workplace. Modern functionalists often focus on the role of education in fostering a belief in meritocracy—an ideological disposition that assumes all people have more or less equal opportunities and that individual hard work and determination (not social or economic status) produce educational results—and thus suggest that students who fail to succeed in school or society are not meant to be its leaders (Davis and Moore 1945; Parsons 1959). Conflict theorists, on the other hand, illuminate how education imposes dominant groups' ideas on nondominant populations through subordination and manipulation in school spaces where administrators/teachers, teachers/students, teachers/parents, and so on engage in constant power struggles. Conflict theorists reveal how schools sort students based on social status instead of abilities, such that schools' organizations reflect organization of power relations in society at large (Bowles and Gintis 1976). Finally, sociologists in education who work from a symbolic interactionism perspective consider how peoples' engagement with education or learning is constantly in dialogue with socially constructed processes of making meaning of schooling experiences or practices (Rist 1970, 1973, 1977). Sociologists of education have offered analyses of schooling that complicate these three theoretical frameworks, pushing us to reconsider the relationship between society and educational institutions. For example, Basil Bernstein's (1970, 1977, 1990, 1996) "code theory" illuminates how differences in communication systems reflect differences in class, power relations, and social division of labor and how, due to ways schools value certain communication systems and language-use patterns over others, only specific groups are slated to succeed in such schools.

The conflict-theory school has strongly influenced work in social justice education and human rights, including early work within sociology of knowledge (Durkheim, Mannheim, Weber) and later work by Michel Foucault, the Frankfurt School, and Michael D. F. Young, as well as Joe Feagin and Hernan Vera's (2008) liberation sociology, Michael Burawoy's (2004, 2006) development of a public sociology, and phenomenological sociology. Sociologists of education working within this "critical school" recognize that larger society's asymmetrical relations of power and privilege are largely reproduced in school settings in which class exploitation and other social differences continue to obstruct access to equitable educational opportunities for student populations outside the dominant social order. However, such a view often fails to consider social and political agency of nondominant individuals and groups. Thus, several scholars have made an effort to highlight that schools can be sites of resistance that disrupt and challenge schools' dominant social arrangements (Freire 2000; Giroux 1983a, 1983b; Illich 1971; McLaren and Jaramillo 2007). For example, Freire (2000) notes how education is a potentially liberating space where oppressed and oppressor, student and teacher alike, can challenge educational and societal power hierarchies, examine personal roles in society, and create new visions of participation in our communities that are humanizing for all. In this sense, Freire recognized that education is a political act.

Antonio Gramsci's (1982) work—especially development of the theory of hegemony and function of organic intellectuals—has also been foundational to development of a critical sociology of education. For Gramsci, hegemony signified moral and intellectual leadership and management used to produce consent to specific interests of the ruling class or historic bloc. Here, Gramsci teaches that social integration at the level of culture and ideology required practice of moral and intellectual leadership in producing a unified will of the masses. Political power always involves coercion and consent, or a balance between political (coercive) forces and social (normative) functions. Gramsci distinguishes between a war of position (ideological battle for the "will" of the people) and a war of maneuver (a direct and violent frontal assault on the state) as two possible strategies for social transformation.

Freire's ideas, like those of Gramsci, have proved to be profoundly influential in the field of progressive education, providing the ideational spine for many of critical pedagogy's theoretical trajectories (Giroux 1983a, 1983b; McLaren 1989) and for those of revolutionary critical pedagogy (Allman 2001; McLaren 2005; McLaren and Jaramillo 2007) that recognize the potential for students and teachers to accomplish social-justice agendas.

As an emancipatory philosophy committed to empowering nondominant students, critical pedagogy urges educational researchers, theorists, and practitioners to (1) recognize traditional schooling's political nature (Giroux 1997; McLaren 1989; Shor 1992), (2) understand how educational reform must engage communities' experiences and belief systems (Duncan-Andrade and Morrell 2008; Valenzuela 1999), (3) replace banking education and rote memorization practices with classroom and teaching practices that support critical-thinking skills (Freire 2000), (4) challenge the teacher-student hierarchy by employing a dialogic approach to pedagogy (Freire 2000; McLaren 1989, 2005), (5) encourage student agency by providing students with support and knowledge necessary to understand and change the world in positive ways (Morrell 2008; Freire 2000; Freire and Macedo 1987), and (6) support a dialectical perspective that embraces critical praxis—uniting theory and practice—as a tool for envisioning and fomenting social change through engaged inquiry, reflection, dialogue, and collective action (Freire 2000; Giroux 1997; McLaren 1989).

Going further, revolutionary critical pedagogy proves useful for both sociology of education and human rights by reframing how we think about knowledge production and the purpose of learning through an anticapitalist framework and decolonialization of human subjectivity and struggle. Recognizing its own intellectual, historical roots in a white, male, Western, heterosexual, academic world, revolutionary critical pedagogy acknowledges the importance of self-critique and reflexivity in knowledge production and analysis of schooling.

This move to both historicize and draw attention to material social relations that yield knowledge production provides a fecund ground for extending more orthodox interpretations of Marxist theory in education. Sandy Grande (2004) has given due consideration to both omissions and affordances of revolutionary critical pedagogy from an indigenous standpoint. Grande's (2004) examination of teleological and linear tendencies of predominantly Western social theory occasions consideration of "deep structures of colonialist consciousness" that defines progress as change, separates faith and reason in overly positivistic, empirical ways of knowing, marks divine conceptualizations of reality as "primitive superstition,"

Education 35

values individualism over community, and considers humans the only creatures capable of rational thought (69–70).

Catherine Walsh (2010) has extended such work in terms of "interculturality," a concept she characterizes as an analysis and reflection of the foundational principles of knowledge production that include both marginal and dominant ways of knowing. For Walsh, interculturality provokes "social, political, ethical, and epistemic considerations regarding society, State, life, and even ourselves" (2010, para. 16). An intercultural framework's intent is to avoid merely thinking about subaltern subjects and, rather, to enter into dialogue and thinking with such subjects and to learn from their "distinct knowledges, beings, logics, cosmovision, and forms of living" (Walsh 2010, para. 16). Such thinking and dialogue has as its aim transformation of social structures and institutions that continue to inflict colonialist ways of knowing and being upon aggrieved populations. Here, sociology of education becomes concerned with questions of identity, in the sense of the identity politics associated not with the postmodern turn in social theory but with what Walter Mignolo (2010) describes as "identity in politics," or historicity of identities. Questions raised by scholars and activists working within an intercultural framework concern the right of peoples to express their identities, knowledges, and ways of being in the context of existing social institutions and formations. Inquiries into "rights" and "access" to education have less to do with gaining entry into the assemblage of educational services and credentials offered by states/public agencies and more to do with transforming existing monolithic forms of thought into more inclusive and pluriversal understandings of the social organization of learning. The concept of social difference in this instance is seen as a way to open "new intercultural perspectives of living 'with,' of co-living or co-existence" (Walsh 2010, para. 16).

Key Methods in the Sociology of Education

Research methods used to explore how society affects schooling and how schooling, in turn, affects society include quantitative and qualitative approaches. While efforts have been made to be purely objective when conducting educational research in sociology, a critique of such scientific positivism has been embraced by many sociologists of education who recognize that complete objectivity—even in quantitative methods—is simply impossible. Drawing from Kant's (1993 [1788]) work that explored how pure objectivity and knowledge of "truth" are unattainable for humans submerged in a world where popular dogma masquerades as "truth," Marx and Engels (1976 [1846]) in *The German Ideology* develop a critical theory of consciousness that has proven useful for researchers in sociology of education. Contesting that human consciousness is separate from material world experiences, as well as that all consciousness is simply a sensory projection of that material world, Marx and Engels (1976 [1846]) describe a dialectical relationship between consciousness and material practice, human objectivity and subjectivity, such that only praxis between human thought and sensuous activity—attainable through researcher reflexivity—can reveal deeper understanding and consciousness. In response, critical researchers in sociology of education have sought to be more rigorous in their methods by using a "self-conscious criticism" that Kincheloe and McLaren describe as an awareness of "the ideological imperatives and epistemological presuppositions that inform their research as well as their own subjective, intersubjective, and normative reference claims" (1994, 140).

Recent work has explored more participatory, action-oriented research and decolonial research practices in an effort to describe educational experiences from the perspectives of actors involved rather than from the researcher's perspective. In such research methods, researchers, educators, and students collaborate to analyze classroom practice and social relations that inform their daily lives. The act of research becomes more pedagogical in the sense that guided inquiry is intended to provide students with tools necessary to generate their own conclusions about social reality and the potential transformative activity within their surroundings (see Duncan-Andrade and Morrell 2008). Questions about the subject-neutrality of research are considered, given the premises from which many educators-activists conduct their inquiries. Orlando Fals-Borda (1988), the founding "father" of participatory action research, clearly refuted the objective neutrality often associated with positivist research practice. Fals-Borda, a native Colombian, recognized early on the political and politicized elements of social research. For Fals-Borda (1988), participatory research methods needed to bring together action-reflection and theory-practice, in participation with others. Research needed to be "endogenous" so as to foster mutual confidence in shared goals of social transformation and people's power in the research process. Further, Fals-Borda encouraged educators-scholars-activists to connect the development of "local" knowledge and practices with the wider goals of democratic social change as part of the stated objectives or goals of a research project. The research process itself needed to be determined by the social-political-economic necessities of the very people who were both the subjects and objects of research.

Indigenous and decolonizing scholars have been at the forefront of articulating educational research practices that support community development. Importantly, research in this vein has sought not only to critique and dispel colonizing forces of imperialist research practices but to advance in its stead a humanizing and grounded research praxis that benefits communities. While recognizing the heterogeneous, multifaceted characteristic of native peoples, Linda Smith is among the most prominent researchers/educators to reshape qualitative methods by what she terms "Kaupapa Maori research" (2005, 125). The "genealogy of indigenous approaches to research" utilized by Smith takes into consideration relationships and connections between "indigenous aspirations, political activism, scholarship and other social justice movements and scholarly work" (2007, 87). Research is guided by the ethic of self-determination and development in an effort to undo the historical legacy of research practices that extract information/observations from the "native" rather than contributing to the community. As Smith reflects on the role of power in the research process, a particular Maori research methodology emerges that "sets out to make a positive difference for Maori that incorporates a model of social change or transformation, that privileges Maori knowledge and ways of being" (2007, 90). Though this is but one example, we can see how methodologically indigenous and decolonizing scholars within the sociology of education have extended the field to incorporate notions of power and self-determination as constitutive of the research process. Such efforts are different from those of the earliest progenitors of the field, who examined the school-society relationship from the macro structures of nation building, religious orthodoxy, and an evolving capitalist society. We could say that in the latter case, the subjective dimensions of social inquiry take precedence (at the level of "identity in politics"), given the immediacy of needs that present themselves in communities that have experienced grave degrees of isolation and exploitation.

THE SOCIOLOGY OF EDUCATION IN RELATION TO HUMAN RIGHTS

Research findings in sociology of education reveal that the current human rights paradigm regarding peoples' rights to education, as defined by Article 26 of the Universal Declaration of Human Rights, fails to acknowledge how schooling is affected by class exploitation, racism, sexism, colonization, and neoliberal globalization.

The human rights paradigm acknowledges that all parents have a right to choose what kind of education their children receive and that all people have a right to an education that is free, equally accessible, and merit based toward the development of a personality that respects human rights, freedom, tolerance, and peace.

Yet, applying the sociology of education to this human rights paradigm, one might begin to ask, While everyone has a right to education, to what kind of education do people have a right? Who determines the core subject matter that should make up that education and how such subjects are taught? Should literacy learning involve engaging critical-thinking skills necessary to read and write in multiple media forms so that one is able to read into deeper or hidden meanings found in advertising, film, television, radio, and so on? In many countries, education may be free, but are all schools equally accessible to all students? The sociology of education's exploration of US public education paints a picture of glaring inequality for nonwhite students (Velez et al. 2008; Yosso et al. 2009). How can we address differences in access to quality education based on overriding relations of class exploitation in capitalist society? How can we address differences in access to quality education based on other factors, such as race, gender, sexuality, or religion? How does such difference affect the ways that students learn about tolerance, human rights, and understanding across nations, races, or religions? Indeed, the human rights paradigm may uphold the importance of tolerance; yet education in all nations across the globe is fraught with intolerable inequalities based on race, gender, sexuality, religion, language, and more.

38   Nathalia E. Jaramillo, Peter McLaren, and Jean J. Ryoo

Needed is a globalized curriculum grounded in human rights education. No one has provoked more international debate on a globalized curriculum grounded in the human right to education than Joel Spring. The universal right to education should, in Spring's view, be underpinned by the struggle for happiness and longevity and accompanied by progressive human rights and environmental traditions. Spring has developed a prototype for a global school that combines eco-pedagogy to protect the biosphere and human rights to support the well-being of students, staff, teachers, and the immediate community. In Spring's own words, "The goal is to promote the longevity and happiness of school administrators, teachers, and students, while preparing students to assume the responsibility to ensure their own long life and happiness and that of others" (2007, 135).

In addition, Spring has been instrumental in drawing the link between colonialism/postcolonialism and the universal right to education. For Spring, it is necessary to justify the universal right to education according to people's culture and their location in an overriding global economy. The justification for the universal right to an education, according to Spring, includes the need for all people to know how the global culture and economy created by colonialism and postcolonialism affect their lives and what benefits or harm might result; the necessity of achieving other human rights that guarantee equal economic and social opportunities in the global economy; protection against economic and social exploitation; freedom of expression and thought; and the right to an education that does not serve nationalistic or particular political ends by indoctrination, and so on (2000, 75).

Resituating the Human Rights Paradigm through the Sociology of Education

To resituate the human rights paradigm using sociology of education as a crucial theoretical and methodological lens, we must acknowledge a deeper purpose in schooling beyond preparing students merely to be workers in our global, capitalist, military-industrial system. We must engage in sociology of education that is intercultural at the root—in both theory and practice—and that opens up new spaces for interrogating the relationship between education and various social formations. The focus here is on developing an approach that allows for individuals to express themselves freely, to exercise their rights to maintain and produce multiple knowledges, and to develop their capacities to participate fully in the social world. Of course, there is the danger of falling prey to a reductive solipsism that does not lend itself to building solidarity or community across groups or to developing a universal understanding of what it means to advance a human rights paradigm in education. We argue, however, that it is possible to generate a universal conception of human rights in sociology of education that attends to various geopolitical conditions of peoples across the globe and simultaneously addresses the overriding logic of capitalist exploitation that hinders overall human development. In this sense, our review of sociology of education has yielded two primary considerations for situating the field in a human rights paradigm: (1) an examination of the "objective" structures and internal relations of class exploitation characteristic of capitalist society, and (2) a due deliberation on "subjective" dimensions of what Mignolo (2010) terms "identity in politics" in relationship to the historical legacy of coloniality and imperialism through the apparatus of schooling. On these points we elaborate further.

Theoretically and methodologically, this paradigm must acknowledge the multiple ways in which people define "rights." Human rights must move beyond liberal-progressive notions of equity and access and into the deeper spheres of addressing human development. Taking into consideration macro-level structures and relations that shape our global social order, we find it necessary to reflect upon Marx's thinking on human development. Marx envisioned a society that emphasized full development of human beings as a result of protagonistic activity in revolutionary praxis—the simultaneous changing of circumstances and human activity, or self-change. This key link in Marx is the concept of human development and practice. In other words, as Marx makes clear, there are always two products resulting from our activity, change in circumstances and change in people themselves. Socialist human beings produce themselves only through their own activity (Lebowitz 2010). So the question becomes, How do we transcend the conflicts today that lead to overidentification and disidentification? According to Marx, transcendence means not only abolishing dehumanizing conditions under capitalism but going beyond the given to create conditions of possibility for individuals to shape their own destiny, read anew the past, and demythify and generate meaning from multiple contexts people inhabit. It is a process, one in which we have in mind the betterment of our social condition, of which education forms a central part.

Sociology of education within a human rights paradigm can and should address social structures and social relations that negate us as human beings. This includes aspects of classroom life: authoritarianism but not authority, apathy and a heightened sense of individualism, fear of speaking about difficult topics, resistance to moving outside disciplinary boundaries, and questioning the interrelationship of ideas and practices. If we could depict our own unity, what would we create? And furthermore, how would we define human development in the context of class antagonisms and social contradictions at the epistemological and ontological levels? The answer for us comes down to praxis. Sociology of education grounded in a critical praxis has potential to become both a reading practice, where we read the word in the context of the world, and a practical activity, where we write ourselves as subjective forces into the text of history. Praxis is directed at understanding the word and the world dialectically as an effect of contradictions. An engaged and grounded sociology of education is a way of challenging the popular imaginary (which has no "outside" to the text) that normalizes the core cultural foundations of capitalism and normative force of the state. A critical sociology of education is a reading of and acting upon the social totality by turning abstract "things" into a material force, by helping abstract thought lead to praxis, to revolutionary praxis, to bringing about a social universe concerned with human development as opposed to human exploitation.

This brings us to the distinction between abstract and concrete utopian praxis. A concrete utopianism is grounded in creative potential of human beings living in the messy web of capitalist social relations to overcome and transform conditions of unfreedom. Knowledge production as a liberatory act must include an *actio in proximis*, meaning that the epistemology in question must have a practical effect in the world. This echoes Walter Benjamin's argument that if we merely contemplate the world, we will only arrive at a knowledge of evil (see McNally 2001). Knowledge of the good is knowledge of a practice designed to change reality; it derives from action, from contemplation. We judge the truth of our actions in their effects on the lives of the oppressed. But an epistemology of everyday praxis is not enough, because such acts or forms of praxis need a larger rudder and heavier ballast, something to give the emancipatory act direction. That is, it must also be implicated in an *actio in distans*, or the utopian aspect of knowledge production, which, in our case, is part of our struggle to diminish exploitation and suffering and promote justice. An *actio in proximis* is very much like a form of emancipatory praxis, whereas the *actio in distans* is the larger movement within these forms of praxis toward a utopia built upon the principles of equality and participatory democracy. It is precisely the double valence, or mixture of the two acts, that prevents the utopia from becoming abstract and metaphysical and prevents everyday acts of emancipatory praxis from becoming free floating and directionless, detached from the larger project of global emancipation. It directs praxis toward a concrete utopia, grounded in everyday struggle.

Looking Forward

Sociology of education is ripe with possibilities for developing a transformative research praxis. The questions we have posed in this chapter are intended to incite debate and consideration of those issues that we deem relatively absent in a human rights paradigm in education. These have to do with attending to the complexity of defining "rights" within the multilayered and multidimensional social system in which we live that largely ascribes meaning to education as a mechanism for inculcating in generations of youth the norms of a preexisting social order. Our fundamental premise is simple. The global capitalist social order in which we live denies people the right to pursue a meaningful and humane life. To undo education's historical legacy as a means of social control and assimilation into a preexisting mode of work, citizenship, and general livelihood, sociology of education must address capitalist society's fundamental contradictions. This approach, which some may claim is universalizing in its approach and economically reductionist in its philosophy, needs to be considered in light of popular struggles currently waged on behalf of the disenfranchised. It is on this point that work on decoloniality and an engagement with the geopolitics of knowledge becomes fundamental to expanding the field into a pluriversal and intercultural undertaking.

~

CHAPTER FOUR

FAMILY

Angela J. Hattery and Earl Smith

As we enter the second decade of the twenty-first century, sociologists of the family consider changes in family form and ask, Is the family dying, or is it merely changing in response to social conditions? In a 2010 poll of American millennials—aged eighteen to twenty-nine—the PEW Research Center reports that marriage is no longer a top priority. In fact, though half of millennials indicate that they prioritize being a good parent, less than a third prioritize having a successful marriage (see Figure 4.1).

Simultaneously, but with very little awareness of the other, scholars of human rights—a relatively new paradigm—are raising questions about the fundamental rights of individuals and groups everywhere. In this chapter, we use the human rights paradigm to frame questions and a discussion about the contemporary American family. We argue that the family is not only an appropriate area for study but also in desperate need of attention by human rights scholars. Second, we argue that reframing many of the discussions around the central tenets of human rights would significantly advance family sociology. Third, the bulk of the chapter is devoted to a discussion of specific issues facing the contemporary family and the insights that a human rights approach brings to bear on the study of these issues.

KEY QUESTIONS FACING FAMILY SCHOLARS

In addition to the debate around the changing nature of the American family, a second key question seeks to investigate the health of the American family in the twenty-first century; the focus is on the degree to which families are able to provide for the basic needs of their members and how any shortfall is being filled. Third is the question of choice: Do all Americans have an equal right to found families, marrying and engaging in childbearing as they see fit? These questions bring us around to the role that the human rights paradigm can play

42   Angela J. Hattery and Earl Smith

Figure 4.1 Percentage of millennials saying that ___ is one of the most important things in their lives

Being a good parent	52
Having a successful marriage	30
Helping others in need	21
Owning a home	20
Living a very religious life	15
Having a high-paying career	15
Having lots of free time	9
Becoming famous	1

Note: Based in adults ages 18–29

in researching and interrogating US families in the twenty-first century. We begin by reviewing some of the major changes in the American family over the last hundred years.

An Overview of the Evolving American Family

As a result of many social forces, including changes in the economy, urbanization, lower fertility rates, access to birth control, the civil rights movement, the "feminist revolution," and others, the shape of the American family is changing (Collins 1994; Coontz 1992, 1997). For example, the percentage of families that are "nuclear" dropped across the second half of the twentieth century from a high of 45 percent in 1960 to fewer than 25 percent in 2010 (Cherlin 2008). The most recent analysis by the Marriage Project (2010) reveals that these changes in marriage and the nuclear family form are largely shaped by race and social class. In short, the more highly educated and those with more financial stability are more likely to marry, less likely to divorce, and more likely to live in nuclear family households. A peculiar aspect of marriage decline and cohabitation increase in heterosexual relationships in the United States is that more Americans are turning to social media for relationships, love, and marriage.

Women's labor force participation changed dramatically across the twentieth century, such that the *Leave It to Beaver* family form, which hit its peak in the 1950s, is not only more or less a myth but certainly no longer exists today (Coontz 1992, 1997). According to a Bureau of Labor Statistics report in 2007, not only were 70 percent of married women employed, but 60 percent of mothers with preschoolers were as well (Cohany and Sok 2007).

Marriage also changed. Overall, marriage has declined. In 1960, 70 percent of Americans were married; today, that number has dropped to approximately 50 percent, with tremendous differences by race and social class (Marriage Project 2010). And those who do marry do so later—the average age of first marriage for women has risen to twenty-five (from twenty in 1960), and for men it has risen to twenty-seven (from twenty-two in 1960) (Marriage Project 2010).

Because there are structural advantages to marriage—for example, health benefits, inheritance-law preferences, and taxes—and because the middle and upper classes and whites have significantly higher rates of marriage, the advantages of being married and the disadvantages of not being married—in addition to those benefits and disadvantages already associated with differences related to class location—accrue disproportionately by social class and race.

Divorce remains common. The divorce rate more than doubled between 1970 and 1980, with financial stress being the greatest risk factor influencing one's chances of becoming divorced. The impact of social class on the likelihood of divorce stems from many factors, including arguments about money, differences regarding financial management, which can be more difficult to resolve in families with fewer resources, and the potential gains of staying married, which are highly tied to the perception that divorce results in a decline in social class for women (Stevenson and Wolfers 2007). Perhaps most importantly, unemployment and underemployment of men is a key risk factor for divorce, according to Stevenson and Wolfers (2007, 49), because of the perception that the male is not meeting expectations associated with masculinity and breadwinning (Kimmel 2005). Divorce rates peaked in 1980 and have since declined slightly and leveled off. In 1960 only 2 percent of the population was divorced, and in 2010 nearly 10 percent was; the overall divorce rate is 40 to 50 percent for new marriages, but because many divorced people get remarried, the percentage of Americans who are divorced at any given time remains approximately 10 percent. As Bumpass and Sweet (1989) predicted twenty years ago, by 2000 half of all children in the United States spent at least some of their childhood in single-parent households. As with most changes in the American family, divorce is also shaped significantly by social class in ways that compound class disadvantages, especially for children (Marriage Project 2010).

In contrast to declining rates of marriage, the rate of cohabitation has exploded. Today nearly 10 percent of all families involve a cohabitating couple, some of whom are raising their own children or are raising children as part of a blended family. One question that many scholars raise, including ourselves, is what role cohabitation does or does not play in supplanting marriage. The cohabitation rate increased fifteen times between 1960 and 2010. Today 25 percent of people between the ages of twenty-five and thirty-nine are cohabiting; an additional 25 percent reportedly cohabited in the past, and 60 percent of all marriages are preceded by cohabitation (Marriage Project 2010). In addition to the question of cohabitation supplanting marriage, it is also important to consider the question of resources, especially for children, and the degree to which children are shaped by the living arrangements of parents. For example, do children living in

44 ANGELA J. HATTERY AND EARL SMITH

a household with cohabiting parents suffer in any measurable ways relative to those living in households in which parents are married? This is a complex question to answer and may be most easily understood by considering who chooses to marry and who does not. The Marriage Project (2010) data show that cohabitation rates are strongly shaped by race and social class. That is, cohabitation is on the rise, but not for every race/ethnic group. African Americans remain one ethnic group that generally chooses cohabitation over marriage. And, increasingly, middle-class Americans are cohabiting and never marrying.

The fertility behaviors of American families have changed over the last century. Fertility, by and large, has been steadily declining since 1900 (Coontz 1997; Hattery 2001). This may be one of the most significant trends in American families over the last hundred years. That said, fertility rates vary tremendously by race and social class; African American and Hispanic families have significantly higher fertility rates than whites (National Data Book). Because African Americans are disproportionately likely to be poor, and due to changes in the welfare laws that create significant burdens for women who continue to have children while receiving welfare, these differences in fertility likely contribute significantly to a racialized gap in standard of living for women and their children. We address this issue at length later in the chapter.

Perhaps one of the biggest changes in family life is the dramatic increase in nonmarital childbearing; in 2007, 40 percent of all babies were born to single mothers, more than double the rate in 1980. And, as is the case with most of the statistics associated with the family, this phenomenon is particularly racialized: 75 percent of African American babies are born to single mothers. Thus, the new norm of childbearing in the African American community is for marriage and childbearing to be decoupled (Burton 1990; Hattery and Smith 2007; Burton et al. 2010).

Finally, perhaps the key touch-button issue facing Americans in the early twenty-first century is the issue of gay marriage. As any casual news consumer is well aware, gay marriage is a highly contentious issue on which Americans have polarized views. Battles over gay marriage are currently fought in US voting booths, courts, and churches. That said, same-sex marriages are up. Period. Though gay marriage is still only legal in a handful of states and, at the time of this writing, is being fought over in the California court system, clearly the number of gay marriages has exponentially increased relative to just a decade ago. The issue of gay marriage is perhaps the one area of family scholarship in which a human rights paradigm has been applied; thus it is critical for us to review this argument. However, our focus in this chapter builds on the ways in which gay marriage as a human rights issue can shape our discussions of other issues facing the contemporary family.

In sum, the reader can see that the American family has been changing for at least the last hundred years, and there is no evidence to suggest that it will stop evolving. Though this perspective is highly contentious among sociologists who study the family, we stand firmly in our belief that when taking a longer, historical perspective, it is clear that there is no evidence to suggest that the family is disappearing in importance in American life; rather, it is evolving in response to a variety of institutional, legal, economic, and cultural pressures. Operating from this assumption, in this chapter we focus on the American family as a site for interrogation by the human rights paradigm. We focus our discussion on two key issues: (1) the right to create a family—to marry, have children, adopt, and so on—and (2) the right to have one's basic needs—for housing, food, access to education, and personal safety—met inside the family. We argue that on both accounts, the US government is not supporting the basic rights or meeting the basic needs of the family. We conclude by suggesting some changes to US policies regarding families that would result in both the basic rights and the basic needs of families being met (or restored) in ways that return the family, rather then the government, to the position of being the building block of society.

How Are Families Studied by Sociologists?

The primary methods that have been used to investigate families, attitudes toward families, and trends in everything from rates of interracial marriage to labor-force participation are surveys, specifically the national-level surveys conducted by the US Census Bureau and its related "arms," including the Bureau of Labor Statistics and the Current Population Survey; interviews (Garey 1999; Hattery 2001; Hays 2003); and ethnography (Burton 1990). In particular we highlight the use of government surveys, including data collected by the decennial census and Bureau of Labor Statistics, as these allow sociologists to examine trends among the entire US population. Because these data have been collected for decades, we can examine trends and changes across time.

As noted above, central to a human rights analysis of the American family are two basic rights: (1) the right to form one's own family—to marry and to control fertility—and (2) the right to have one's basic needs met inside the family. And though traditional sociological methods help to address these questions in terms of trends and predictions, as we will argue when data are collected primarily via large-scale surveys, there are limits to the analysis that can be performed through the lens provided by the human rights paradigm. Thus, in order to address human rights concerns as they apply to the evolving US family, additional methods will have to be employed. Specifically, human rights scholars who wish to study family life would rely on many qualitative methods, including interviews, ethnographic research, and policy analysis in order to generate the types of data appropriate for analysis and theory building. We point to the work of Linda Burton (1990) as an example of how ethnographic research can be used to disrupt underdeveloped and widely held beliefs and theories about teen childbearing.

The Scope of Human Rights Concerns Regarding the US Family

We would argue that, largely, the core questions we are raising regarding the US family are national as well as global issues. The question of who controls

46   ANGELA J. HATTERY AND EARL SMITH

the right to form a family—who can marry and who controls childbearing—is indeed global in scope. For example, the majority of other countries in the developed and developing world have either recently confronted or are currently grappling with the same issues, including gay marriage and abortion rights. Similarly, though the United States has long been characterized as one of the richest nations in the world, the recession that impacted us here is also global; the impact in Europe, for example, is particularly devastating. Outside the developed world, where the recession itself may have less impact, the conditions themselves threaten the very survival of most individuals and families living there. Thus, the questions we pose are indeed of both national and global importance.

INSTITUTIONS AND LEADERS SHAPE THE US FAMILY

Based on our definitions of the human rights issues facing American families, the key structures that impact or prohibit access to rights are (1) the legal structure, (2) the political structure, (3) the institution of religion, (4) the criminal justice system, (5) the economy, and (6) the system of social welfare.

First and foremost, the social structures that govern our lives are heavily shaped by our laws. Quite simply, for example, if gay marriage is not legal, then the right to form a family is threatened by the legal system. More complexly, the laws that shape eligibility for welfare indirectly threaten the fundamental right of the poor (and not those with financial resources) to control their childbearing. Other examples of this include issues such as retirement and financing a college education. For example, low-income individuals and families who live with employment instability or employment without benefits will rely entirely on the Social Security system to fund their retirement, whereas those with professional or unionized employment will likely have private, employer-contributed retirement plans. Similarly, though there are some programs for low-income students to attend college, these are competitive and often underfunded. For example, the most widely used government-funded program, the Pell Grant, recently limited awards to $2,500 per year. In contrast, middle- and upper-income families may be able to take advantage of 529 programs, which permit anyone to contribute to a student's college savings and benefit from tax deductions for the contribution, and the earnings are tax-free. Thus, the law is critical in shaping the basic human rights of families with regard to family formation. Similarly, with regard to the right to meet the basic needs of one's family, laws that shape the economy as well as the receipt of welfare are critical. For example, the minimum wage is set by law. The fact that the minimum wage does not provide a living wage is a major contributor to families' inabilities to meet their basic needs, as illustrated by the debate at the end of 2010 about the extension of unemployment benefits for the long-term unemployed.

We cannot undersell the importance of the development of hegemonic ideologies in shaping the options for families. At the most basic level, hegemonic ideologies impact and shape individuals' beliefs such that, for example, they may or may not support gay marriage rights. As important as this is, the real power of hegemonic ideology is how it is generated by the "state" (Therborn 1980), which in turn shapes state policies—for example, the law! Thus, hegemonic ideologies are a powerful force in shaping marriage rights and welfare. And, as Therborn (1980) notes, hegemonic ideologies are always constructed to uphold the interests of the state rather than individual citizens, and thus it is not uncommon for hegemonic ideologies and therefore policies to lag behind public opinion. Gay marriage rights and Don't Ask, Don't Tell are two contemporary examples of this.

The power elite—leaders of the government and corporate America (Zweigenhaft and Domhoff 2006)—influence all the major US institutions, including the military, the legal system, the criminal justice system, the economy and financial system, the system of education, the institution of religion, and the creation of ideology. Thus, the power elite either directly or indirectly influence the American family. Directly the elite influence the family by making laws that impact family rights—for example, the right to marry—and indirectly they influence the family, for example, through an economic system and set of laws and policies that prevent the minimum wage from being a living wage. The working poor barely live above the poverty line and find it difficult, if not impossible, to meet the basic needs—for shelter, food, and clothing—of the family.

Relevant Empirical Findings

We focus our discussion around two key issues: the right to form a family and the right to meet the basic needs of the family.

The Right to Form a Family

The right to form a family and to determine who will be a part of that family is not a guaranteed human right in the United States. Here we explore two different aspects of this issue: the right to marry and the right to bear children. Beginning with the right to marry, the United States—both the citizenry and the polity—is embroiled in a heated debate surrounding the rights of gays and lesbians to marry. This debate has been raging for the last decade and centers on several key issues. First and foremost are the beliefs of individuals regarding the fundamental right to marry. Currently, a third of Americans believe that gay marriage should be legal, and nearly half (41 percent) believe that civil unions— legal arrangements that provide the same legal benefits as marriage—should be legal (PEW Research Center for the People and the Press 2010). In contrast, the support for gay marriage among the power elite is far smaller, at least publicly. For example, more than a decade ago, in 1996, then–President Bill Clinton signed the Defense of Marriage Act (DOMA), which was intended to create a federal prohibition on gay marriage that would override the rights of individual states to grant marriages to gay and lesbian citizens. While the percentage of

Americans favoring some sort of legal relationship for gays and lesbians continues to grow, both President George W. Bush and President Barack Obama affirmed the key tenets of DOMA.

At the heart, the fight for gay marriage rights is about the right of all Americans to form families. Additionally, of course, legal marriage carries many benefits, including the right to inherit property or visit one's partner in the emergency room or intensive care unit, as well as countless other rights and financial benefits that are part of various laws. Thus, the fight for gay marriage is about more than the right to form a family; it is also about the right to care for one's family and take advantage of the same benefits that married heterosexuals enjoy.

Rarely talked about is another aspect of family formation: the right to have and raise children. With regard to gay and lesbian couples and single parents, this issue centers primarily on adoption. A number of states currently allow gays and lesbians to adopt, but most have some policies that make it difficult, and several prohibit adoption by gays and lesbians, including Florida, Mississippi, Nebraska, Oklahoma, Utah, and Virginia. Additionally, we know anecdotally that in our home community of Winston-Salem, North Carolina, physicians at North Carolina Baptist Hospital refused to perform an in vitro fertilization procedure on a colleague of ours who happens to be a lesbian. Thus, the gap between policies and actual practices may be a gulf.

Even more invisible are the ways in which the welfare system seeks to control the family formation and reproductive rights of low-income Americans. At the height of the most recent welfare reform that culminated in the 1996 Personal Responsibility and Work Opportunity Act, various "experiments" were explored. "Bridefare" was a program that paid higher welfare benefits to single mothers who married the fathers of their children. On the surface this may sound like a palatable idea, but when one digs deeper, one realizes that it is no more than an attempt at social engineering for the poor.

Though "bridefare" did not last long, one element of social engineering of poor families has become a central piece of our current welfare system. Hays (2003) explicates a policy designed explicitly to limit the fertility of women on welfare; a stipulation in the eligibility rules for Temporary Aid to Needy Families states that any child born to a woman currently receiving welfare benefits—termed a "CAP baby"—is permanently ineligible for benefits. Though again, on the surface, this might seem like a prudent idea designed to reduce childbearing among women who are receiving welfare, we identify at least two key problems with this policy. First, though designed to penalize the mother, the impact of this rule effectually penalizes the child. The child will not be covered by Medicaid, and due to her mother's ineligibility, the child will not benefit from additional cash assistance, food stamps, housing allowances, or child-care subsidies. This penalty continues into adulthood; as an adult, the child is ineligible for welfare assistance. Second, like "bridefare," this policy uses financial incentives to place restrictions on poor women's family formation, thereby restricting, even outright denying, the basic human right to bear children.

The Right to Provide for the Family's Basic Needs

Many structures make it difficult for a family to meet the basic needs of its members—namely, the economy, the labor market, and the welfare system. As the reader and authors are well aware, the recession that began in 2007 has wreaked havoc on American families, though as scholars of poverty and social inequality have argued, this has been a slow process that has been happening for years. Kristoff summarizes the data on the trend of growing income and wealth inequality in the United States by noting, "C.E.O.'s of the largest American companies earned an average of 42 times as much as the average worker in 1980, but 531 times as much in 2001. Perhaps the most astounding statistic is this: From 1980 to 2005, more than four-fifths of the total increase in American incomes went to the richest 1 percent" (Kristoff 2010).

Another way of examining this trend is to note that if the minimum wage had kept pace with CEO pay, today the minimum wage would be about $15 per hour and provide an annual income for full-time workers of $30,000—$10,000 above the poverty line for a family of four. Thus, since 1980, the average worker has been falling behind. As a result, not only is the middle class being virtually eliminated, but the average worker has lost his or her ability to provide the basic necessities for a family. In the 1960s and 1970s, families with a full-time minimum-wage worker were able to afford to buy a home and, with scrimping and saving, even send a child to college. Today, a family relying on a single minimum-wage worker will fall below the poverty line—full-time minimum-wage employment yields about $16,500 per year, and the poverty line for a family of three is around $20,000—and will be eligible for welfare. Thus, a worker's right to earn a living that can provide for a family has been eroded, and that same worker must now rely on the government in order to meet the family's basic needs. And welfare dependency "costs" in terms of rights. A simple example will illustrate: Imagine two families in the local grocery store. One family is paying for its purchases with cash (or check or debit card), and the other is paying for its purchases with food stamps. Now imagine that a youngster in both families would like a candy bar in the checkout line. The family paying with cash has the right to decide whether to indulge the youngster or not. In contrast, the family paying with food stamps has to forfeit this right; candy is not an eligible purchase for food stamps. Though this is a simple example, the point remains that families of today who work in minimum-wage jobs—which, we note, are an increasingly large sector of the economy—often not only face difficulties in providing for basic necessities but must forfeit some of their rights because of their welfare reliance. The shedding of relatively high-paying, often unionized manufacturing jobs has been exacerbated by the recession. Thus, as Kristoff (2010) argues, income and wealth inequalities are likely to continue to grow in the United States. Accompanying this trend will be the forfeiture of more individuals' basic human right to earn a living wage.

Applying a Human Rights Perspective to the Study of the Family

Rarely do family sociologists frame anything with regard to rights—for example, the right to marriage, the rights of children, or the basic right of families to control their own destinies. In this chapter, we have provided two examples of critical issues facing contemporary US families and how these issues might be reframed as human rights issues. Here we conclude the chapter with specific examples of the ways in which a human rights approach would transform the study of the family.

Family sociology would be transformed if it were to consider the human rights paradigm. For example, if intimate-partner violence were recast as a denial of rights to personal safety and security, then questions and solutions proposed would be very different (Hattery 2009). A welfare system that focused on the child, rather than the parent, would prioritize a child's right to stable, secure housing and nutritious food, regardless of parents' decisions about marriage, employment, drug use, and so on. If the right to marry were considered a "human right," then the debate over gay marriage and its impact would change. If the right to work included the right to earn a living wage, then not only would minimum-wage and employment laws change, but US income inequality would decrease, as would related threats to human rights, such as dependence on welfare and other social-welfare programs.

Processes of research would change. Quite obviously, how researchers frame their questions determines the data that are generated. So, for example, if family scholars interested in marriage simply ask respondents for their marital status and do not ask if they would like the right to marry, then data on the right to family formation will not be generated. Thus, applying a human rights perspective to the study of the contemporary family will change, in many significant ways, the types of questions that scholars ask and the kinds of data collected for analysis.

Applying Family Sociology to Human Rights Research

Just as family sociology is ripe for transformation through application of the human rights paradigm, the field of human rights can be transformed by family sociology. Quite simply, human rights research and theory rarely focus on the institution of the family; nor is the family generally conceptualized as a unit for analysis. In fact, as we have shown, the family is one of the most basic and fundamental institutions in which human rights play out. For example, human rights scholars study and pontificate about bride burning in India. Few rigorously examine intimate-partner violence in the United States, a phenomenon annually affecting millions of Americans and resulting in fifteen hundred murders. Similarly, human rights scholars conceptualize the US welfare system as a class (or race) issue but rarely examine the ways in which it restricts family life. Thus, we argue that scholars of the human rights paradigm are obligated to turn their attention to family sociology issues.

We agree with our colleagues Blau and Moncada that "every human being has moral rights to equality and has moral obligations not to violate or ignore the rights of others" (2005, 5). The right to equality and the protection of this right includes the family. Our chapter encourages family sociologists to see the ways in which the human rights paradigm would transform the field and, in turn, challenges human rights scholars to consider how their work could impact family sociology.

CHAPTER FIVE

ORGANIZATIONS, OCCUPATIONS, AND WORK

J. Kenneth Benson

A commitment to the advancement of human rights for all people underlies this chapter. In the following pages, I analyze the implications of this commitment for the study of organizations, occupations, and work. I am indebted to the call of Gideon Sjoberg, Ted Vaughan, and their coauthors who have argued for the development of a sociology of human rights and for the grounding of the discipline in a concern with human rights. Burawoy (2005, 2006) recognizes different kinds of sociologies—professional, critical, policy, and public—and argues for reflexive interactions between them. Professional studies then would provide knowledge of existing realities, and critical and public sociologies would criticize those realities and design ways to alter them. In this view, human rights concerns would be a part of critical and public sociologies that take account of the theories and findings of professional sociology but subject those findings to critical, reflexive examination and advocate alternative realities. Organic public sociologists directly participate in publics—for example, social movements—carrying on an extended dialogue between the discipline and the publics (Burawoy 2005, 7). I distinguish between forms of sociological work along the lines suggested by Burawoy and deal with their interactions. I argue that existing studies of organizations, occupations, and work offer many conceptual and theoretical insights relevant to the analysis and realization of human rights. At the same time I contend that a practical and theoretical concern with the realization of human rights requires a thorough rethinking of these fields. The social organization of human societies has profound implications for the realization of human freedom and development of human potentialities. Systems of domination built into organizations, occupations, and work contribute to powerlessness, social isolation, and meaninglessness in human life. Social systems consisting in large part of interdependent patterns of work, occupations, and organizations can destroy the possibility of realizing the potentiality for people to democratically produce their social worlds. Guarantees and protections of human rights provide openings for the collective activity, the social movements, through which new, more humane social worlds might be created. Studies of organizations, occupations, and work have been dominated by deterministic theories and methodologies that make existing systems appear inevitable and necessary (Gouldner 1955).

In recent decades, however, critiques and alternative theories and methodologies have gained a foothold. The dominant perspectives are now contested by a number of alternatives. The critical alternatives have gained a hearing and some influence within the professional discourse of sociology and related fields such as management and political science.

ORGANIZATIONS, OCCUPATIONS, AND WORK: THE STATE OF THE FIELD

FOUNDATIONAL PUZZLES

I focus here on a series of theoretical puzzles pursued in these fields that intersect in significant ways with human rights. I consider the implications of these puzzles for our understanding of human rights—that is, how these puzzles illuminate the tasks of developing and defending human rights. I also deal with the implications of a human rights–oriented praxis for the study of organizations, occupations, and work.

Although joined in the American Sociological Association's Section on Organizations, Occupations, and Work, these fields are somewhat distinct. It is common in the curricula of sociology departments to find separate courses for each field. However, here I identify some central theoretical puzzles that tie the fields together and argue that these central puzzles have profound implications for the realization of human rights.

A theoretical puzzle consists of a set of intersecting arguments about an aspect of social life. The arguments identify a centrally important complex of social phenomena and a set of possible, but potentially conflicting, explanations for those phenomena. Often the puzzles originate in the works of a classical theorist, such as Karl Marx, Émile Durkheim, or Max Weber (1968 [1920]), who defended opposing conceptions of the phenomena and conflicting explanations. These puzzles derive from the efforts of early theorists to understand the modernization of human societies, especially in the West.

The foundational puzzles include the following:

1. *The causes and consequences of bureaucracy:* Why do human societies undergoing modernization organize many spheres of activity into highly differentiated, hierarchical structures featuring elaborate systems of rules? What are the consequences of these organizational structures for the performance of the tasks of human societies and for the development of human societies? Are there any viable alternatives to bureaucracy for modernizing societies?

2. *The causes and consequences of technological change:* Why do human societies develop increasingly complex and sophisticated technologies, including especially increasingly complex machines and coordinated routines, that

54 J. KENNETH BENSON

reorganize work and the administrative control structures governing work? How do these technological changes and diverse technological forms affect the development of human societies? Are there alternative technologies and work organizations that are effective but less alienating for people?

3. *The causes and consequences of structural inequality:* Why do human societies develop organizational structures featuring varied forms of inequality between positions, organizations, and institutional sectors? How do these structured inequalities affect the development of human actors? Are alternative organizational forms featuring less inequality possible?

4. *The causes and consequences of such decentralized, participatory organizational systems:* "Professional control" (Freidson 2001), "responsible autonomy" (Friedman 1977), "workers' participation" (Poole 1975), and "self-management" (Markovíc 1974) offer some measure of relief from bureaucracy.

5. *The causes and consequences of alienation:* Marx (1964 [1844]) argued that alienation in the sense of powerlessness, meaninglessness, and self-estrangement is driven by the normal operation of the capitalist mode of production. Bureaucracy, industrial technology, and power inequalities are endemic features of capitalist societies that break down the possibilities of people to control their own lives and their communities. Civil societies are destroyed by the advance of these forces. Durkheim's (1964 [1893]) analysis of the division of labor draws out similar themes. The human-relations approach to industrial management (Mayo 1933; Roethlisberger and Dickson 1947) developed techniques for engaging industrial workers in their tasks and integrating them into their work groups.

OPPOSING EXPLANATORY PARADIGMS IN THE STUDY OF ORGANIZATIONS, OCCUPATIONS, AND WORK

Theoretical work in this area has produced a lively debate about the causes of variation in social organization. Distinct paradigms and research programs developed out of the theoretical puzzles. These are a part of what Burawoy (2005) calls "professional sociology." A rational model growing out of the work of Weber (1968 [1920]) and the practical problems of industrial management (Taylor 1967 [1910]) has been challenged by a number of alternatives. The rational model remains especially powerful in organizational and industrial sociology and had considerable impact on studies of work and occupations. Alternatives drew to a considerable extent on the work of Durkheim as channeled through structural-functional theories of Parsons (1951), Merton (1968), and others. Influential occupation/work scholars (Hughes 1971; Strauss 1978) often formulated their ideas in conflict with the rational and functional approaches.

The Rational Model

Some influential organization theorists developed deterministic arguments linking causes and effects through the tendency of the organization to make rational choices. Thus, for example, in order to be effective, complex technologies require a decentralized and somewhat flexible organizational structure (Perrow 1967), or large organizations require a hierarchical and differentiated structure (Blau and Schoenherr 1971). These kinds of arguments assume, explicitly or implicitly, a rational decision process producing efficient or effective organizations (Benson 1983). Organizations choose structures and practices that produce efficiency or effectiveness. The perspective is based on two major elements.

> *Boundary assumption:* The organization is a self-controlling entity with boundaries allowing it to select its own internal structural arrangements. In much of the literature, the boundaries of organizations are taken to be real and effective limits, containing the causal forces that shape the organization.
>
> *Selection assumption:* The organization selects its tasks, strategies, and structures in ways intended to produce success in reaching goals. Thus, observed organizational patterns—hierarchies, divisions of labor, technologies, reward systems, and other features—are explained by the rational pursuit of goals.

The boundary and selection assumptions are obviously based on a simplification of reality. Selections of strategies and structures are often imposed from outside the organization—for example, in legislation, contracts, or incorporating documents. But the model permits the formulation of predictions and explanations.

Transaction-cost theory (Williamson 1985), a version of the rational model, was developed by economists extending rational-choice theory to explain the social organization of firms and industries. They offer explanations for the development of bureaucratic organizations (firms and other hierarchies) rather than markets to govern economic activities. They argue that the cost of transactions in markets sometimes makes it more efficient to merge firms or extend the boundaries of firms rather than to connect to other firms through markets and contracts. In this way the presence of nonmarket arrangements can be given a rational explanation, and predictions can be generated.

Challenges to the Rational Model

Challenges to rational explanations are numerous. Here I briefly review some of the prominent alternatives. Dobbin (2005) provides a similar review of theoretical approaches.

Open-systems theory challenges the boundary and selection assumptions. The boundaries are seen as porous and vulnerable to intrusions by social forces beyond the control of the organization. Political, economic, and cultural conditions shape the options of the organization and its decision-makers. Internally, too, there are opposing tendencies, recalcitrant units, interest conflicts, and competing loyalties. The organization must also meet its needs to

56 J. Kenneth Benson

maintain itself as a system, and the fulfillment of needs sometimes requires the sacrifice or compromise of goals. Decision-makers monitor the external environment and respond to its pressures, threats, and opportunities. They also try to manage the internal sources of resistance, irrationality, and apathy. Balancing these various pressures, they try to ensure the survival, health, and success of the organization. Scott (1998) covers this view extensively in his encyclopedic textbook, in which even Marxist ideas find a place within the open-system framework.

Symbolic interaction studies of organizations and work developed alternatives to bureaucracy. Strauss (1978, 1993), Hall (1972), Hall and McGinty (2001), and others developed a negotiated-order model. They have seen this as an alternative to the bureaucracy model derived from the work of Max Weber and developed in mainstream studies of organizations. Strauss and his associates in various studies showed that hospitals do not follow a bureaucratic model of hierarchical authority, strict role differentiation, and extensive rule-following behavior. They observed many situations in hospitals and elsewhere where professionals controlled their own work through "negotiations" carried out in everyday work situations. Hierarchies and strict divisions of labor broke down in the face of work to be accomplished and problems to be solved.

There are also power theories where Heydebrand (1977), Clegg (1989), Perrow (2002), Roy (1997), and others developed explanations focused on opposing interests and differential power to pursue interests. They contend that various interests have a stake in the shaping of organizations, and organizational practices are controlled by those with more power to defend their interests. There are factional divisions within organizations, and they are often linked to external interest formations. So, interest divisions and related power structures determine the strategies and structures of organizations. In work and occupation studies too, power approaches are prominent. Freidson (1970) analyzed the US medical-care system as a case of "medical dominance."

Constructionist theories, like that of Czarniawska (1997), argue that organizational practices are repeated and become accepted, normalized rituals. So, people repeat them many times over without engaging in a rational decision to select them.

Institutionalists—old (Selznick 1947, Stinchcombe 1997) and new (Scott 2001)—contend that organizations are shaped by previously established practices that have become normative and entrenched in relationships to other organizations (Nee 2005). In a classic formulation, Selznick (1947) argued that the Tennessee Valley Authority (TVA), in an effort to survive in an established organizational environment, compromised its goal of reducing the social inequalities of the American South and developed mutually supportive relations with the previously existing power holders and entrenched organizations of the region. The TVA had to adjust to an environment consisting of other organizations and established authorities with entrenched power bases. Goals were developed and modified through the struggle to survive as an organization in such an environment. Selznick drew ideas and inspiration from Michels's

(1962 [1915]) study of a left-wing political party that became internally oligarchical in violation of its democratic ideology.

The "new institutionalists" propose normative and cultural explanations for organizational patterns. These arguments stress regulations, normative practices, and cognitive models as explanations for organizational structural formations (Scott 2001). Dobbin (1994), for example, has argued that during the nineteenth century, France, Britain, and the United States enacted different systems for organizing and regulating railroads, and the selected systems grew out of previously established organizing models in the societies. Here, too, there is an argument about repetition of previously established patterns of thinking. These repetitions come not only from practices required by law or rules but also from cognitive models, ideas carried in the minds of participants. The argument at this point is similar to theories of Bourdieu (1984) about cultural transmission and reproduction of established practices.

Institutionalism shows that there are variant forms of organizations, occupational systems, and work arrangements. Bureaucratization is affected by forces such as increasing scale (size) and technology, but these are not immutable forces beyond the control of human actors (agents) or independent of shaping by political, economic, and cultural contexts. These variant forms have differing implications for the realization of human rights. Different forms of capitalism have varying implications for the welfare of human beings and the realization of human rights (Sabel and Zeitlin 1997; Hall and Soskice 2001). The differences are not just a matter of culture but depend also on combinations of circumstances in the formative stages of institutions. Varying sets of interest combinations might have the upper hand in particular times and places, thus institutionalizing different forms of capitalism (Roy 1997, 263).

Marxist theories of industrial-capitalist societies (Burawoy 1983; Braverman 1974; Burawoy and Lukacs, 1992) identify the macro structures composed of multiple organizations, institutional sectors, and their organizing logics and contradictions. The recent literature on the labor process (Knights and Willmott 1990) was stimulated by the work of Braverman (1974). Working in the Marxist tradition, Braverman thought of the labor process as the seeking of capitalists to extract surplus value from the employment of labor power. He argued that capitalists seek more and more efficient ways to use labor and to link labor power efficiently to increasingly sophisticated machines. Increasing mechanization of production reduces the skills necessary in workers. Workers then are deskilled as the conception of work is separated from its execution. Braverman's argument predicts an inevitable deskilling of labor as capitalists seek profits through changes in technologies and divisions of labor. Some of the counterarguments (Clawson 1980) stress power, for example, contending that capitalists seek power and control over the labor process through rationalization of work and technologies. Bureaucratic organization and mechanization take skill and control away from workers and deliver control to managers and owners. Some (Burawoy 1979) see capitalists gaining greater control by creating ideologies, technologies, and incentive systems that harness workers to

58   J. KENNETH BENSON

capitalist objectives. Power and ideology arguments were mounted to challenge deterministic rationalism in both cases. Some analysts, Murphy (1990) shows, extended the deskilling hypothesis to the professions and argued that they are undergoing proletarianization.

THE KEY CONCERNS OF THE FIELD

The concerns underlying and expressed in the fields of organizations, occupations, and work are varied and contested. Here I review the major alternatives.

RATIONAL STRUCTURING

Organizations, occupations, and work are studied in order to find and implement the most rational ways of organizing. The ideas of the field are still shaped to a considerable degree by the practical problems of making organizations, occupations, and work more efficient, productive, and profitable. These are legitimate and important questions but should not, and do not, define the boundaries of acceptable discourse. Rational structuring is not only a concern of business and industrial production but also an issue in government, professional, religious, and other organizations. In some settings questions about efficiency can challenge patterns of domination—for example, the excessive bureaucratic centralization of the Soviet bureaucracies. But values, beyond efficiency and effectiveness in reaching goals, should be part of the discourse about organizations. The human rights paradigm should be a part of the ongoing debates about organizational forms. The commitment to rational structuring may be lodged in decision-making bodies external to the organization—for example, ownership groups such as shareholders or governing authorities—that intervene periodically to keep the organization on track to achieve its goals.

INTERPRETIVE CONCERNS

Some scholars are concerned with providing interpretations of people and events in organizations and work situations. They typically utilize subjective research methods, including both observational studies and analysis of texts produced or utilized in a setting. The intent is to render a sensitive account of events and actions that permits others to better understand the situation. Abolafia (2001) analyzed the social construction of markets by traders on the New York Stock Exchange. He shows both how trading is shaped by its institutional context and how traders construct their work.

MORAL CONCERNS

The classic theorists—Marx, Durkheim, Weber, Simmel, Tönnies, and others— were morally concerned with the state of contemporary societies, and their theories were tied into their moral concerns (Wardell and Turner 1986). The human rights paradigm offers an opportunity to reflect upon the moral issues embedded in studies of social organization and to develop a set of explicit moral concerns about social organization. Reflecting on descriptive findings of social scientists opens alternative possibilities for organizing human societies and for moral engagement with the alternatives. The human rights paradigm provides an explicit formulation of a set of moral concerns that can challenge the dominance of the praxis of rational structuring.

EXPLANATORY CONCERNS

Much of the work in these fields is driven by a search for causal explanations, with practical concerns with efficiency or effectiveness in the background. Which organizational structures are associated with particular functions or tasks? For example, are research-and-development units structured in a less hierarchical way than production units? Are decentralized firms quicker to make technological innovations or to enter new markets? Are professionals less alienated in less centralized, participatory organizations? In many of these inquiries, the researchers may say little or nothing about the search for the most rational or efficient ways of organizing. However, the rationality concern is so deeply institutionalized that such inquiries are implicitly tied into the praxis of rational structuring. Czarniawska (1997) uses a narrative method to give the reader an understanding of how people working in organizations follow routines that have grown up around the established tasks or functions. With repetition these become rituals that are disconnected from the goals and formal procedures of the bureaucracies. These accounts provide a unique understanding of the settings. Her accounts are similar to those from interactionist studies in the research tradition of Strauss (1993).

EMANCIPATORY CONCERNS

These fields include some scholars who focus explicitly on liberation or emancipation of people and institutions from centers of power and domination. They invoke values beyond the pursuit of "formal rationality" through making organizations effective and efficient in reaching goals. There are a number of important directions of emancipatory work (for example, Alvesson 2009; Alvesson and Willmott 1992, 2003; Adams and Balfour 1998). Some of these are emancipatory by undercutting the claims of rationality within the rational model. Dorothy Smith (1990, 1987, 1999) accomplishes this by revealing another social world hidden but coexisting within the bureaucracies.

FINDINGS

The study of organizations, occupations, and work has produced a large number of findings over the years. The findings are embedded in and grow out of

60   J. KENNETH BENSON

research programs. The "findings" are contentions supported by empirical evidence to some degree but also by the orienting arguments of research groups. The research programs represent a "contested terrain" (Edwards 1979).

Rationalization accompanies and grows with the modernization of societies. Thus, organizations, occupations, and work in modernizing societies are increasingly governed by norms of rationality extending across an array of institutions—industry, government, science, education. For example, see Thomas et al. (1987).

Bureaucracy increases in extent and complexity with the size of organizations (Blau and Schoenherr 1970). Specifically, organizations become more hierarchical and differentiated as they grow in size. This relationship is said to be a result of organizations seeking to reach goals efficiently as organizations grow. It is assumed that hierarchy and differentiation are effective means for coordinating work in large organizations. For critiques of this line of research, see Gouldner (1965) and Turner (1977). For an influential defense, see Donaldson (1987).

Administrative structures—hierarchy, differentiation, and rule systems—vary with the technologies, goals, and/or functions of organizations. It is assumed that the structures are selected for their fit. Etzioni (1961), Perrow (1967), and others developed this argument in the 1960s. The perspective remains as an important set of explanatory ideas that are invoked, sometimes in conjunction with other arguments.

Administrative structures vary with the strategic decisions of managers, owners, and administrators. These strategic decisions represent rational judgments made in specific circumstances such as market conditions or opportunities. This is a finding from managerialist studies, which generally see managers making rational decisions in the context of the circumstances and opportunities confronting their firms at particular times. These findings by scholars such as Chandler (1962, 1977) in his series of business histories open the way to another kind of argument and supporting set of findings. These involve the analysis of changing management ideologies and reasoning frameworks or logics, a direction that Child (1972) used to open managerial logics to analysis. Managers' strategic decisions are an independent source of variation, not just rational responses to circumstances and opportunities presented by the market or new technologies. If the managerial logics are not simply based on objectively rational responses to the challenges and opportunities faced by an organization, then many alternative outcomes are possible. Child's work connects to an older stream of thought associated with March and Simon (1958), which suggests careful studies of management decision-making, including the internal political processes in organizations through which powerful departments select managers with strategic views supportive of their interests (Cyert and March 1963).

Organizations with their associated work and occupational practices are shaped by their institutional, organizational, and political environments (Fligstein 2001). Organizations, occupations, and work are arranged in different ways, find different solutions to similar problems, and develop in accord with different institutional models and political systems. Politically negotiated regimes enforce models and control systems. These effects blunt or redirect the effects of rational choice, technology, and size. Organizational arrangements are swept along by forces beyond their boundaries and their control (March and Olson 1984).

Technologies are shaped by social and political processes in organizations and the larger social world. Thomas (1994) has shown how high-technology manufacturing companies develop and adopt new technologies through a complex political negotiation among interest groups based in the different departments of the organizations.

Organizational, occupational, and work structures and practices are shaped by the modes of production—for example, different forms of capitalist, social democratic, and socialist systems. The contradictions of the larger mode of production and its class conflicts shape the organization of work and power structures in organizations. Burawoy (1983) and others have developed this line of thought. Burawoy and Lukács (1992) in particular analyzed the similarities and differences in work organizations between capitalist and socialist industrial work. They found that factories in the United States and in socialist Hungary were incorporated into larger corporate or state administrative structures, but the Hungarian factories were subjected to scarcities that caused workers to be innovative and resourceful in order to do their work and earn their pay. In earlier comparative work, Burawoy (1983) argued that "factory regimes," the systems of discipline and control of factory workers, varied among capitalist countries. Thus, there is not just one capitalist mode of production but multiple forms of capitalism featuring divergent ways of organizing production and distribution (Hall and Soskice 2001; Sabel and Zeitlin 1997).

Multiorganizational systems are beset by contradictions and tensions that generate opposing interests and social movements within and beyond the systems (Offe 1984, 1985). These interests and movements produce instability and social change in the operation of the organizations and systems. Studies of the policy process by Hall and McGinty (1997) show that public policies, once made by legislation, are transformed through the pulling and hauling of the implementers; so they conclude that policy-making is the "transformation of intentions." Social movements form around the contradictions and tensions and reshape the directions of the organizations and systems (Davis et al. 2005).

Networks are increasingly powerful compared to hierarchical bureaucracies in contemporary societies (Castells 2000). Clegg (1990) argues that recent decades have seen a reversal of the long-term trend toward centralization of administrative

62 J. Kenneth Benson

structures and consolidation of power in bureaucratic organizations. Guillén (2001) finds that international business networks provide opportunities for innovation leading to diverse national models rather than convergence.

Many organizations persist despite failures to develop internally rational practices and meet objectives (Brunsson 1985; Meyer and Zucker 1989). This finding challenges the rational model.

Levels of alienation from work are affected by types of technologies of industries and varied ways of organizing workplaces. Assembly lines, bureaucratic hierarchies, responsible autonomy, and so on (Blauner 1964; Friedman 1977).

Research Methodologies

The methodologies of these fields are varied and, to a considerable extent, contested by the advocates and critics of particular approaches. Here I describe the contested methodological claims.

Fact/value separation versus fact/value contestation. The dominant methodological stance in these fields separates facts and values. Separation is defended by advocates of an exclusively scientific, empirically based discipline. Empirical observations are sought as a basis for building and testing theories. Statements of value or morality are separated from descriptive and predictive/explanatory theories, and this stance discounts the study of emergent possibilities and alternate models based on ideals. The scholar pursues empirical regularities and generalizations about causes and consequences based on rigorous empirical observations. If he or she has moral concerns about the phenomena observed, these might be set off in a footnote or an appendix or perhaps another kind of document altogether. In this methodology one must be careful not to allow values or moral concerns to contaminate the scientific observations and analyses. By contrast, Sjoberg and others argue that theories and methods (paradigms) in professional sociology have moral values and commitments inextricably built into them. The idea of a completely value-free sociology is illusory; thus it is necessary to illuminate those underlying moral values and commitments (Sjoberg, Gill, and Williams 2001).

Theorizing only the empirically observable versus challenging existing "realities" through "countersystem models." The positivist view is to deal only with concepts that can be observed and verified through empirical methods. This methodological stance makes it more difficult to see alternatives to the present realities and to analyze the possibilities for realization of human rights. Sjoberg, Gill, and Cain (2003) call these alternatives "countersystem models." The analyst might construct a model of how an organization based on human rights would be structured and compare that model to empirically observed organizations. Countersystem models then can be partly normative, based on human rights principles, and partly empirical, resting upon alternative realities held by participants. In an earlier formulation Gouldner (1965) suggested an "iron law of democracy" to counter the deterministic pessimism of Michels's "iron law of oligarchy" and Weber's "iron cage" of inevitable bureaucratization. Blau and Moncada (2005), in an argument compatible with countersystem analysis, develop an ideal type of a society built on human rights for all people.

Value neutrality versus reflexive engagement with social movements. The positivist methodology requires that research be carried out from a detached, distinterested stance. Touraine (1981, 1983), by contrast, advocates reflexive engagement with social movements. He argues that sociologists can assist activist groups in analyzing their objectives and strategies, interpreting their movements, and locating them within historical trajectories. The observer assists the group in self-study to reach a reflexive understanding of its position and objectives. In doing so, the sociologist must be immersed in the work of the group but still maintain distance to permit objective analysis. The sociologist must be reflexive about his or her engagement with the movement and with the analytical tools and theories of the discipline. This engagement by the sociologist can help to keep the group engaged with the larger society and developing its discourse (Touraine 1981, 167–222). Touraine (1983) engaged in such reflexive intervention with the Solidarity social movement in Poland. In this way the sociologist can look for emerging possibilities, alternative conceptions of reality, repressed ideas, and social movements within organizations and their extensions beyond their conventional boundaries. A human rights concern leads to a sensitivity to oppressed and hidden movements and fractures of the organizational order of things. Giving voice to these movements may open routes to transformations of the organizations. Davis et al. (2005) call attention to the intersections of organization studies and the study of social movements.

Separating versus contextualizing organizations, occupations, and work in larger social formations and analyzing how the transformations of the social formations move back and forth through the micro, meso, and macro levels of analysis. Burawoy (2006) argues that a professional sociology connected to public sociology must address the embedding of observed phenomena in larger institutional contexts. It must analyze the connections between local and international events. In recent decades the neoliberal political agenda has overwhelmed the protective barriers that restrained market forces in the past. The defenses afforded by labor unions, professional associations, tenure systems, retirement systems, and health-care systems have been gradually compromised and threatened. Market forces have been allowed freer movement of workplaces and reorganizations of firms to pursue market advantages (Streeck 1992). Shareholder value as a logic of action has been allowed to destroy firms and disrupt communities (Fligstein 2001). States have retreated from their powers to shape and defend the systems of economic organizations, networks, and industries. It is important to sustain forms of sociological analysis that examine and critique the larger forces shaping the fields

64   J. KENNETH BENSON

of economic action (Bourdieu 1998). It also important to develop the methodological resources for understanding forces emanating from the micro and meso levels of social formations. Hall and his associates have developed ways of conceptualizing and examining the back-and-forth, up-and-down movements of public policies. Policies emanating from one level are transformed during implementation at other levels (Hall and McGinty 1997).

Determinism versus possibilism. Studies of organizations, occupations, and work have been guided to a considerable extent by a search for deterministic variables that provide causal explanations and predictions. The proposed determinants include economic rationality in the prediction that the most efficient or effective social arrangements will prevail. Mancur Olson (1982) argued that nation-states and other political-economic units that had discarded their entrenched bargains, regulations, and restrictions on capital were most likely to experience rapid economic growth. Olson's view was characterized by Esping-Anderson as a thesis of "institutional sclerosis" (1994, 723). Douglas North argued that stability and order in regulatory regimes are essential to the growth and prosperity of business organizations. Weberian scholars have argued that rationalization of organizations and work is an inevitable tendency in modernizing societies, driven by the persistent search for more and more rational social arrangements. Some Marxists have predicted the inevitability of class conflict and reorganization of capitalist institutions toward production efficiency (Bottomore 1985). However, many scholars in these fields have argued for a kind of "possibilism" stressing multiple causes and contingent combinations of causes and uncertainty of outcomes. Weber himself took such a position (Kalberg 1994) as did Henri Lefebvre (1968), a French Marxist. Touraine (1981, 1983) develops a similar stance in his social-movement approach to social organization, as does Prechel (2000) in his work on corporate organizational structures, specifically, the development of firms with many subsidiaries. In the study of professions, historical comparative studies have challenged the adequacy of deterministic arguments such as Braverman's deskilling thesis (Murphy 1990).

LEARNING FROM STUDIES OF ORGANIZATIONS, OCCUPATIONS, AND WORK

The sociology of organizations, occupations, and work offers some lessons for the development of a human rights paradigm. Social organization has significant implications for the realization of human rights. Often human rights are denied or diminished by the social organization in these areas. The problems include the following: First, excessive domination denying actors the opportunity to control or participate meaningfully in the construction of their work settings, political systems, and communities. The result can be a pervasive alienation both in the structural sense and the social-psychological sense. In some cases it produces the complete collapse of the civil society through which people form communities and identities.

Second, the excessive and debilitating differentiation of work and other organizational settings denies people the opportunity to develop their capacities as human beings, narrowing the freedoms of people to pursue their own intellectual, cultural, and social development.

Third, inequalities and uneven development of social organization can narrow the range of opportunities available to minorities and to regional and sectoral divisions. Often the divisions of organizations, occupational categories, and work assignments correspond to spatial and ethnic differentiations of a society or international formation. The differentiations of the population are built into the structure of the organizations and occupational categories. Durkheim (1964 [1893]) referred to this pattern as the "forced division of labor," one of his "abnormal forms." Weber referred to "closure," and Marx wrote about "uneven development." Contemporary writers (Baron 1984) have analyzed the contribution of organizations to the construction and reproduction of social inequalities.

Fourth, multiorganizational networks, differentiated but coordinated systems, and competing fields (linked industries and governmental departments) exert control over huge sectors of social life. Policy-making and implementing organizations bring together the interests and powers of these multiorganizational systems. These multiorganizational systems are highly stratified with well-understood positions of dominance and subordination among the units. Policy-makers who would change or reform these systems struggle to find traction for movement and power resources to influence directions. Korpi (1983) analyzed such political processes in Sweden. Benson (1975, 1982) provided some early theoretical ideas on the topic. Many others have contributed to the development of the problem. Scott et al. (2000) drew upon several strands of theory to analyze the US healthcare system. Bourdieu (1984, 1998), DiMaggio and Powell (1983), Fligstein (2001), and others have utilized the "field" as a meso-level concept for dealing with these issues.

The forces and powers outlined above show the need for the declaration, implementation, and protection of human rights. These forces and powers greatly restrict the capacity of human beings to collectively, democratically, and cooperatively construct their social worlds and build alternative futures that realize more nearly the dignity and potentiality of the human condition. Yet dismantling the complex networks, organizations, and fields in favor of free and open markets is not a viable option. Bourdieu (1998), among many others, has stated effectively the dangers of that option. Instead we have to reconstruct the organizations, occupations, networks, and fields.

I suggest six steps in the reconstruction:

1. *Working reflexively as organic intellectuals in the social-movement organizations supporting human rights.* Touraine's (1981, 1983) model of engagement with social movements provides some guidelines. Sociologists and others studying human rights organizations may choose to be critical partisans

rather than objective, detached observers. In this way theory and praxis may be more perfectly and fruitfully connected.

2. *Broadening decision-making in organizations to include participants and recipients in more significant ways.* Critical organization theory challenges the powers of central authorities and centers of power. We must develop stakeholder theory to guide this effort.

3. *Challenging the rights of business corporations.* Corporations are treated in American law and practice as actors with legal rights and powers. Vaughan, Sjoberg, and Reynolds (1993) and Sjoberg, Gill, and Williams (2001) have made this point very strongly in several publications. The powers vested in corporations must be challenged, debated, limited, and revised through democratic processes. In social democratic societies such debates and limitations have been accomplished to some extent, for example, in codetermination laws.

4. *Designing multiorganizational systems extending and defending human rights regimes.* The system of property rights must be challenged and redesigned. Limits must be placed on the property rights of capitalist corporations, in effect reducing the power of corporations, for example, by limiting the right to reorganize the labor process in pursuit of profit.

5. *Designing new institutional arrangements to make possible a viable civil society, following up Burawoy's argument that both the market and the state must be countered by civil society.* What kinds of organizational structures would be supportive of civil society? Network and field studies can be utilized in the development of these objectives. Can you build a set of interdependent relationships between organizations that support a robust discourse in civil society?

6. *Recognizing the variety of organizational arrangements and taking a constructionist view of possibilities.* This would entail rejecting the assumption that "there is no alternative" (Clegg 1990). But possibilism does not mean that anything is possible. Markovíc (1974) argued there were only three possible futures for Yugoslavia: bureaucracy, capitalism, or self-management. Rather, possibilism entails analyzing the possibilities for effective action for human rights at a particular time and place. Some possibilities are open and others are closed at a given time. The set of boundaries and limits to negotiation at a given time is an aspect of social structure (Abbott 1988). Activists for human rights must analyze the situation, mobilize resources, and institutionalize their gains. Consider Korpi's (1983) argument about mobilizing power resources, husbanding them wisely, utilizing them effectively, building investments of resources into the system, and preparing for the next opening. Also, consider building movement organizations that are dialectical in the sense that diverse perspectives are included rather than excluded and the processes for democratically confronting differences is built. White (1974) calls this kind of system a "dialectical organization."

A Resituation of the Area/Field

Here we consider how the study of organizations, occupations, and work might be reshaped by its connection to the human rights paradigm. Previously I argued that the field should be guided by a praxis of liberating people from systems of domination (Benson 1977). A "public sociology for human rights" (Burawoy 2006) gives more specificity to that proposal. The discipline would be concerned with building organizations and reorganizing work and occupational structures to realize human rights, specifically the right to participate meaningfully in the design and control of work and the right to democratically, collectively, and cooperatively guide the development of societies.

A praxis of human rights would also shape the research agendas of these fields. Social-movement organizations and NGOs concerned with human rights can be studied and made more effective. Conventional organization theory and social-movement theory may be useful in this connection. It may be possible to study human rights organizations in ways that connect their goals and strategies more effectively—that is, to make strategic choices and develop administrative means that move the organizations more efficiently toward the realization of their goals. However, the range of studies must include critical, reflexive perspectives. The organizational means that are used to address human rights must themselves be operated in a way that upholds human rights. The internal methods of governing the social-movement organizations and relationships with constituents must be consistent with human rights principles. Exploitation, domination, subordination, and other methods resulting in alienation of participants must be resisted. Also the role of the scholar must be addressed. One way is to follow Touraine's (1981, 1983) model of reflexive engagement with the movement. Extending organizational liberation beyond the borders of any one nation and studying how to build global networks of democratic organizations would be important too.

Concentrations of power must be continuously challenged. Burawoy (2006) and others argue that this ongoing challenge requires a strong "civil society" consisting of social movements and movement organizations that can mobilize the population and develop power resources for limiting and revising the powers of centralized corporate and governmental bureaucracies. Scholars who criticized Soviet bureaucracies noted the destruction of mediating organizations and institutions. The Soviet bureaucracy drew all powers into itself and crushed organizations outside its control. Two Polish scholars (Kostecki and Mrela 1984) writing in the period of the Solidarity movement referred to these as "powdered" societies in the sense that all sources of possible challenge to bureaucratic power had been pulverized, leaving people as isolated particles subject to absolute control from above. They argued that these bureaucracies had produced a vacuum in the space that had been civil society. Solidarity was able to move into this space and create an effective challenge to the bureaucracy.

Developing stakeholder theory (Freeman 1984) is an approach to business management that runs counter to shareholder value as the dominant criterion for decisions. The general idea is that many different kinds of interests are affected by corporate actions. These include employees, the community, consumers, and so on. In this view, actions such as building a plant, closing a factory, or investing in a new technology would be made through consideration of and consultation with the various stakeholders. We might argue that human rights would call for the expansion and implementation of something similar to stakeholder rights. Also, it would be important that the rights of people not be infringed by corporate decisions in which these individuals have no voice or mechanism for being heard.

A robust civil society would include an extensive array of interorganizational networks. While some have championed networks as a more democratic step forward, networks do not necessarily end systems of domination (Sjoberg, Gill, and Williams 2001). We already have numerous studies that reveal power inequalities in networks (Laumann and Knoke 1987). Peter Bogason (2006), a social scientist in Denmark, is associated with a Centre on Democratic Network Governance and has written about such networks.

Developing nongovernmental network organizations can resolve many conflicts. Elinor Ostrom (1990) has studied and advocated the formation of networks that various interests form to settle differences and arrive at solutions to common problems. For example, farmers and other interests sometimes form associations to govern water rights. For her efforts in this direction she was awarded a Nobel Prize in economics a few years ago.

A Look Forward: New Questions and New Possibilities for Both the Area/Field and Human Rights Realizations

Alvin Gouldner (1965) confronted the pessimistic determinism of the classical theorists. We now face new sources of metaphysical pathos in current assessments of the future of democracy. The nation-state as a protector of human rights has diminished power vis-à-vis international corporations. In any case its policies are dominated by the unregulated powers of those corporations. The labor movement has lost much of its power to protect even workers' rights. International organizations facilitate the movements of capital and industrial jobs to low-wage countries where rights are not protected. The rational model, in new forms such as transaction-cost economics, still legitimates these developments. Studies of organizations, occupations, and work have never been more important.

The history of research and theory in these fields includes many challenges to the dominance of the rational model. But rationalization goes on and reaches new heights of achievement and degradation. It is to be hoped that the human rights movement will successfully challenge these trends. The events themselves generate increasingly glaring contradictions. By addressing those in the interest of human rights, we can contribute to the emancipatory possibilities of human action. Theories of the past and present provide openings for thought and action.

CHAPTER SIX

POLITICAL SOCIOLOGY

Thomas Janoski

Influenced by nineteenth-century Enlightenment universalism, the concept of human rights has deep roots in the politics of Europe and America (Delanty 2009). After World War II, human rights became pervasive as states derived much of their legitimacy from being embedded in the larger world of the United Nations, with its legitimating values in human rights declarations. As notions of citizenship, human rights, and individuality spread across state boundaries as well, more organizations, institutions, and social movements created a common human rights culture in the world, especially after the fall of communism. Yet, human rights still has many tensions, contradictions, and violations.

Political sociology has thoroughly addressed citizenship rights within countries, but it has been in slow opening up to global human rights. This survey of political sociology and human rights examines four areas concerning this relationship. First, it looks at key questions of morality and philosophies of law, then major theories of political sociology. Second, the most important findings in the field are examined in the area of revolutions, internal rights processes, world governments, and the most current human rights scenario. Third, the different methods in the field are reviewed. Fourth, the reorientation of political sociology toward human rights and future research is addressed.

KEY QUESTIONS AND THEORIES

HUMAN RIGHTS AS A SOCIOLOGICAL TOPIC

Theories of human rights often invoke morality and are at odds with value-free social science. Human rights theories tend to come out of a particular philosophy of law called natural law. Yet, at the same time, two other philosophies of law—legal positivism and legal realism—would not cede human rights to natural law alone. However, developing empirical proof of human rights as residing

70 THOMAS JANOSKI

in religion is generally not possible, nor is finding the sociological evidence for some natural condition of humanity embedded in all of us. Political sociology frequently has a stronger basis in legal positivism, which is typically tied to ideas of rationality and/or legal realism, which are approached in terms of interests, emotions, and traditions. Even though sociologists commonly assume that these rights are innate, sociology has difficulty with human rights as natural rights because human rights' truth claims are difficult to pin down. However, sociology need not verify the truth claims of natural human rights because, according to the W. I. Thomas theorem, a sociologist views a situation as real if people define it as such and consequences follow. Thus, political sociologists can make claims for the consequences of people following ethics or natural law.

One weakness of the human rights tradition is that it tends to avoid duties and obligations. Rights and obligations exist in a system; speaking about one without the other is problematic (Janoski 1998). Because of the human rights focus on massive deprivations of rights, obligations may not stand out as important, but they are needed to enforce rights. Thus, the political sociologist must have a clear-minded view of both rights and duties.

POLITICAL THEORIES OF HUMAN RIGHTS

Five theories of political sociology deal with human rights. First, convergence theories claim that states respond to common social forces, social movements, and international organizations to adopt similar cultural norms that reinforce human rights. This may often occur through a diffusion process, but with theories of globalization, this process itself becomes an isomorphic force that pressures states to adopt human rights conventions. An initial component of this pressure is identifying inconsistencies in application of internal state constitutions and laws that obligate a state to treat everyone as equally endowed with various rights. Although China has been a significant exception, a second component, international human rights requirements, is powerful. Unless those requirements are satisfied, access to markets is not assured, and states will face boycotts or other sanctions.

This type of convergence theory can have an implicit structural-functionalist undercurrent. For instance, some claim that states must have a strong bourgeoisie and a capitalist system to gain democratic rights (Lipset 1981; Huntington 1991) because democracies and rights only emerge from the capitalist system with economic growth. Thus, as resources catch up to needs, societies will increasingly fulfill those needs. Convergence theories can be subject to the weaknesses of functionalism in that the mechanisms for the global convergence of ideas and human rights sometimes remain vague. Given emphases on convergence, retrenchment of rights is often ignored.

Second, power-constellations theory takes an interest-driven approach to human rights (Huber and Stephens 2001). People whose rights are not protected eventually realize their interests and mobilize resources to influence the state to enact those rights. Whether citizenship or human rights are enacted within states depends upon power resources of various social movements and political parties. Originally focused on class, this theory requires vigilance concerning the power bases of various human rights groups in their abilities to create membership, organization, finances, and even military capacities to press their claims. A wealth of information exists on how social movements and political parties gain these power resources within states to pass new legislation, change constitutions, or press legal claims in courts. The power-constellations approach has generalized power-resources approaches to consider gender, racial and ethnic, and other groups that mobilize resources to press human rights claims. Often these groups must operate within an institutionally structured environment that constrains state formation, but these constraints are usually what they are trying to change. The social movements it examines may often invoke human rights, but the theory itself sees interests rather than natural rights as motivating political processes.

Third, world polity is a global system of creating value through authority with rules, frames, or models (Meyer 2010; Boli and Thomas 1997, 172). States and organizations in civil society enact global models that create "more structuration" than internal societal processes of states would produce (Meyer et al. 1997, 173). These global movements have widely shared principles of human rights. The United Nations and voluntary civil society associations have played salient roles in implementing this order and spreading its moral culture. Once enacted, world culture consists of states as rational actors that operate according to formal and often universalistic rules. World culture exerts isomorphic pressure on human rights with causal factors based on seeking good will or assuaging guilt. The institutionalization of these world-cultural models leads to structural similarity as states adopt similar constitutional, public-educational, and welfare systems. International voluntary associations promote, extend, and sometimes actually implement global cultural principles (Boli and Thomas 1997). Inside states, this global culture pressures organized interests to enact new policies. This results in a social "dynamism that is generated by the rampant inconsistencies and conflicts within world culture itself" (Meyer et al. 1997, 172). Different ways to resolve those tensions lead to a variety of world-cultural models. World polity-theory then leads to empirical analysis of various human rights policies using new institutional theories (Schofer and Meyer 2005).

Fourth, Marxist theory and human rights constitute a paradox in political sociology. Marx was dismissive of individual rights in general as a "bourgeois ruse" that would prevent the eventual liberation of workers. Marxist discussion has derided rights as individualistic solutions to social problems and maintained that group rights—specifically workers' or working-class rights—are solutions. On the other hand, Marxist activists and scholars have always been very concerned about human rights abuses and open to ethnic and women's rights. But to a large degree, human rights became a major weakness in communist societies once the capitalist system was eliminated.

As a version of Marxist theory, world-systems theory, with its focus on core and peripheral nation-states, has a twist on human rights. Starting

72 Thomas Janoski

with the Dutch in the United Provinces, the core power has an interest in toleration and human rights within the core. World-systems theory sees this relationship as being in the core's interests to develop new ideas and attract talent from the periphery in order to pursue political-economic dominance and empire (Wallerstein 1974; Hall 2002). However, human rights in the periphery continue to be trampled upon. World-systems theory does not propose a unique solution to promoting human rights, but it does lay open the contradiction that often exists between rights in the core and the periphery (Hardt and Negri 2009).

Fifth, cosmopolitanism theory has developed along with globalization in the 1990s and promotion of universalistic human rights (Delanty 2009; Beck 2007a). This theory focuses on supranational organizations as guarantors of justice (e.g., world courts, government, and media) and transnational or international nongovernmental organizations (INGOs) and social movements as dynamic factors that create and motivate these institutions (Held 2010; Archibugi 2008). Cosmopolitan theory is highly normative, claiming that the state no longer has sovereignty as INGOs assume power. While state decline is exaggerated, cosmopolitan theory makes recommendations about how to change global institutions and enhance human rights.

Key Findings in Political Sociology

The findings of political sociology on human rights consist of four historical contexts of revolutions, states, world governments, and the current and complex global human rights situation.

Human Rights Revolutions

The age of revolutions directly brought down repressive regimes and indirectly affected many other states, including encouraging steps toward democracy. Explanations of these political changes are theories of state centrism and rising expectations that lead to mobilization (Goodwin 2001). Two outcomes emerged from the ensuing revolutions. First, the American and eventually the French revolutions brought democracy directly to those countries and established foundational documents concerning human rights, the Declaration of Independence in 1776 and the Declaration of the Rights of Man in 1789 (Hunt 2007). Second, communist movements emerged out of the Industrial Revolution to create a second burst of revolutions that resulted in an emphasis on social rights. But these Soviet-led communist revolutions exhibited difficulty in adopting political rights after the first group of democratic countries attained their social and participation rights (Janoski 1998). As a result, communist revolutions led to (1) state-led deprivations of political and human rights that were not overcome, and (2) an East-West stalemate on rights enforcement in the United Nations during the Cold War. The difficulties of communist states

POLITICAL SOCIOLOGY   73

adopting human/citizenship rights remains important since mainland China, Cuba, and North Korea are still caught in this conundrum.

While the prevalence of revolutions and human rights was marked during this period, two nonrevolutionary movements should not be ignored. First, internal abolitionist movements from 1820 to 1870 led to states rejecting the slave trade and then banning slavery inside their borders (Hunt 2007). Second, the Crimean War led to a long-term international social movement to prevent inhumane treatment during wars. From 1859 to 2008, two major transnational institutions were created: the International Red Cross and the Geneva Conventions for the treatment of prisoners (Forsythe 2007; Bennett 2006). The women's rights movement started during this period but did not peak until the end of the twentieth century.

CREATING RIGHTS INSIDE STATES

Although constitutional conventions sometimes create human rights, they are generally enacted out of the proposals made by legislative political parties. These proposals are often propelled by developments in civil society, the media, and social movements. For the Organization for Economic Cooperation and Development (OECD) countries, modern-welfare-state research has shown how citizenship rights were developed through the efforts of left parties with the support of labor and civil rights movements (Huber and Stephens 2001). Cultural values shape developments in different countries. More liberal and left parties, along with some religious groups, promoted human rights in earlier periods. In the courts, judges have influenced internal human rights. Where democracy is weak, social movements may prove especially important, as with Solidarity in Poland or the Mothers of the Plaza de Mayo demonstrations in Argentina. In sum, every country has an internal explanation.

WORLD GOVERNMENTS

After the armistice of 1918, sentiment arose to end arms races, secret diplomacy, and nation-state ambitions. The Paris Peace Conference created the League of Nations in the final Treaty of Versailles. But from a political standpoint, the treaty was flawed by failure to pass the Japanese proposal on the equality of races and then doomed by the American refusal to ratify it.

World War II proved to be even more horrible, with mass genocide, prompting strong international pressure from the Allies to act decisively on guaranteeing peace. The leaders of the most powerful states worked with internal elites to establish the United Nations. The human rights movement with independent elites and INGOs stressed universal and global rights and a responsibility to support these rights in the world, independent of state boundaries. After the Security Council was established, representing the dominant states, and the General Assembly was created, representing all member states, the United Nations passed a series of human rights declarations that large numbers of states ratified (Cole 2005; Donnelly 2006; Wejnert 2005; Morsink 1999).

74   THOMAS JANOSKI

Research studies have tracked the rapid expansion of human rights treaties, intergovernmental organizations, INGOs, and popular and professional discourses advocating human rights (Pubantz 2005). Since 1970, the world human rights movement has expanded its earlier focus on individual legal protections to a more empowering focus on human rights education. INGOs and social movements have taken the place of states as primary forces. The United Nations expanded refugee protection through an international asylum regime led by the UN High Commission on Refugees (Morris 2010). By the 1980s, refugees and asylum seekers became an official category with their own statistics collected by the OECD and others. While there are still problems and sometimes backlashes, the focus on human rights with institutions helping refugees and other victims has risen to a new and encouraging level.

Part of the reason for creating the United Nations was to prevent genocide. This was capped in the post–World War II era with events such as the Nuremberg trials, which prosecuted and punished war criminals. Perhaps the greatest achievement in terms of human rights was the relatively peaceful end of the apartheid regime in South Africa, which was followed by the Truth and Reconciliation Commission hearings that created a mass mea culpa with no intention of prosecution. While some were dissatisfied with the lack of convictions, the subsequent calm and democracy that characterized the country compares favorably to the condemnation of all Bath Party leaders in Iraq, which led to their recruitment as terrorists.

The United Nations created the International Court of Justice in 1945 to resolve disputes between nation-states, but this has proven to be ineffective concerning human rights claims. The court requires that both states acquiesce to its decisions, and one country usually does not do so. However, the United Nations created the International Criminal Court in the 1990s, which has convicted individuals representing states or rogue groups. Nonetheless, preventing genocide remains a difficult issue.

THE CURRENT GLOBAL HUMAN RIGHTS SCENARIO

The usefulness of the United Nations in promoting human rights was limited by the deadlock of the Cold War. But the fall of communism led to a new approach to human rights throughout the world. Four processes and institutions are important in these developments: INGOs, the United Nations, new courts, and global agencies.

First and perhaps foremost in these developments have been the INGOs, such as Amnesty International and Human Rights Watch, that pressure and expose governments on human rights violations (Hafner-Burton and Montgomery 2008; Hopgood 2006; Shanks, Jacobson, and Kaplan 1996; Smith and Wiest 2005). Many of these organizations annually provide detailed information on how well governments are fulfilling human rights expectations. WikiLeaks falls into this category, but its impact is in revealing information and indirectly in judging human rights. Another type of INGO (e.g., the Red Cross or Green

Crescent, Oxfam, and Doctors Without Borders) has provided direct relief aid and services while proliferating and gaining direct access to various arms of the United Nations, including the Security Council. Many of these INGOs are religious organizations that raise considerable money but may conflict with other cultures. The impact of these efforts on human rights abuses is somewhat mixed (Lebovic and Voeten 2006). Hafner-Burton (2008, 713) shows that from 1975 to 2000 in 145 countries, "naming and shaming" by INGOs, the UN Commission on Human Rights, and the media had some positive impact on political rights but also increased political terror. Definitive solutions can be elusive. A critical indirect issue is how much these same policies influence the world polity to bring pressure on governments to improve human rights policies.

Second, the United Nations has continued to be active throughout this period, with increasing influence in creating international criminal courts and additional human rights declarations. However, the enforcement of these declared rights is a weakness of the UN rights regime, and this has not been aided by a number of corruption scandals at the United Nations.

Many international bureaucracies have filled this enforcement gap, and two cosmopolitan thinkers, Held (2010) and Archibugi (2008), make strong arguments that new types of political institutions need to be developed to improve UN action on human rights. Archibugi recommends the expansion of the UN Security Council to include a few more members on a rotating basis and limit the use of the veto power of permanent members. More powerful states would oppose adding to the Security Council, so Singer (2009) recommends proportional representation. Both authors recommend strengthening the General Assembly on human rights by (1) having the people of each country elect an additional representative to the assembly (the other would continue to be appointed by state leaders), and (2) creating an independent UN law-enforcement organization to keep the peace and enforce directives. Archibugi recommends expanding to all countries the International Court of Justice and International Criminal Court and establishing a World Parliamentary Assembly that would perform national citizenship audits, steer political action toward democracy, and evaluate the human rights regimes using smart sanctions (i.e., targeted toward specific and workable areas) for violators. And Held would create a world referendum process across country boundaries at regional and global levels to implement human rights policies. These recommendations are unlikely to pass anytime soon, but this plan for reform delineates clear reforms that would make the United Nations more responsive to human rights crises. A promising development since 2006 is the UN Human Rights Council, which conducts four-year periodic reviews of violations and makes its findings known to member states (OHCHR 2010).

Third, the United Nations established the International Criminal Tribunal for the Former Yugoslavia (ICTY). It has grown from an unfunded UN resolution to an institution with more than a $100 million budget and one thousand employees. Its success opens up international justice to serious consideration by offending states as it is the first effective international court since Nuremberg. The ICTY has crossed borders, overcoming political and organizational difficulties to create a

76 THOMAS JANOSKI

new and effective tribunal. Chief prosecutors Louise Arbour and Carla del Ponte worked with others to reverse its initial failures to arrest and convict significant figures and advance the tribunal's agenda. In particular, they used secret indictments and unexpected arrests to bring prominent war criminals, from soldiers to Slobodan Milošević, to justice. Using the investigations and criminal proceedings of the tribunal, Hagan and Levi (2005) show how the ICTY as an institution was founded and transformed by determined prosecutors into a new transnational legal field (Ginsburg 2009).

The establishment of the world criminal courts brought some triumphant cases and convictions, but subsequent events have been less successful (Hagan and Levi 2005; Hagan and Kutnjak 2006). The UN peacekeeping effort in Rwanda had too few troops and came too late, and the International Criminal Tribunal for Rwanda faced major obstacles. Many efforts in Somalia were fraught with the contradiction of peacekeeping creating more violence (Hagan and Kutnjak 2006; Power 2002). Later difficulties emerged with the prosecution of Sudanese leaders responsible for the tragedy in Darfur. While problems with these courts and peacekeeping efforts to prevent genocide have not been solved, these courts are an important new development.

In a "multicultural critique of international human rights," Stacy (2009) asks whether universal standards of human behavior can gain any real traction in a world of diverse religious, cultural, and national beliefs. Regional courts can help solve this problem. The European Court of Justice and, more recently (1998), the European Court of Human Rights provide an increasingly popular way to address human rights violations. In the Americas, the Organization of American States has the Inter-American Court of Human Rights, which plays an important but not decisive role in protecting those rights. The African Union has an African Court on Human and Peoples' Rights, which is a promising start. The countries of the Association of Southeast Asian Nations have a fledgling human rights system. But the Muslim countries in the Middle East and Africa lack a larger regional framework, which is important since their laws are generally decentralized but powerful within states. Currently, the European regional courts are the strongest institutions in this category, but many liken the Europeanization process to state building, and others contend that the various European courts concentrate too much on interstate jurisdictional disputes (rather than within-state problems). Nonetheless, these European courts are an example to be followed by other regions. Finally, two powerful states have been reluctant participants in these and wider types of courts—the United States and China—except when referring to other countries' violations (Blau et al. 2008; Quigley 2009; Amnesty International 2010).

Fourth, human rights can also be enforced or abridged in organizations such as the World Trade Organization (WTO), World Bank, and International Monetary Fund (Hafner-Burton 2009). These organizations have formulated rules and forums that displace parts of many state legal systems. Held (2010) wants these organizations to be more open, perhaps with the public election of representatives who would be more likely to uncover hidden practices.

Archibugi (2008) indicates that these organizations should endorse human rights, democracy, and nonviolence and exert pressure for these values inside authoritarian and transitional states.

This legal implementation can be achieved in at least four ways (Kingsbury, Krisch, and Stewart 2005). First, transnational networks may coordinate with various states under the umbrella of a global decision-making structure that has little or no coercive power (e.g., the Basel Committee on Banking Supervision that coordinates central bank policy). Second, distributed administration exists where the regulatory agencies of states act in concert with INGOs to create policies that are then returned to the regulatory agencies of all states (e.g., the WTO appellate body) (Alvarez-Jimenez 2009). Third, hybrid (intergovernmental-private) administration exists with INGOs that give feedback to a federation that produces policy that it transfers to a larger global government. In turn, this governmental agency directs standards for the INGO members. This reflects the most common interaction of INGOs and global governments through humanitarian services (e.g., the WTO, International Labour Organization, and UN institutions described in Reimann 2006). Fourth, private governments consisting of INGOs regulate limited areas (e.g., the Codex Alimentarius Commission that develops food-safety regulations or the Internet Corporation for Assigned Names and Numbers that manages part of the Internet).

There are two larger problems in enforcing global rights. First, NGOs are given a very strong role to play but may not be strong enough to enforce global citizenship rights and obligations. If organizational learning improves, these INGOs may enforce multidimensional citizenship. Second, states may withdraw from international organizations when they do not like decisions or possible prosecutions, and many states are still not willing to delegate these functions within their borders (Quigley 2009).

KEY METHODOLOGICAL ISSUES

There are many methodological approaches to the political sociology of human rights. Some of the most compelling are qualitative case studies of personal and group struggles. Other studies have been historical and legal and examine evidence and court documents. Welfare-state studies that involve citizenship rights, which strongly overlap with human rights, have used many different types of quantitative regression methods, often with pooled time and space techniques. The world-polity literature has examined large numbers of countries with event history methods, and the world-systems approach has used network analysis to look at economic organization and sometimes human rights (Meyer et al. 1997; Meyer 2010).

Recent cosmopolitan theorists have been extremely critical of using the state for human rights analysis because focusing on the state draws attention away from central actors in global human rights struggles (Beck and Sznaider 2006; Levy and Sznaider 2006). World-systems theorists frequently tout an "n of one"

78   THOMAS JANOSKI

as their unit of analysis (Hall 2002; Wallerstein 1974). They call for the use of social-network analysis of the world-system. However, the nodes of these networks (i.e., their units of analysis) are still states. Beck and Sznaider advocate "alternative units of research" and mention "transnational regimes of politics" and "transnational spaces and cultures of memory" (2006, 14–15). This suggests an institutional approach that might be a form of "policy domain" where a variety of state, corporate, and nonstate actors may reach various decisions.

One possible solution to this issue is to seek the smallest political unit possible and then to use various forms of hierarchical linear modeling or multilevel statistical analysis. For instance, one might take the county, parish, or census tract as a unit of analysis and then see how various influential regional, national, and supranational entities (including corporations) influence human rights. Or one could use states, provinces, or departments as the unit of analysis. This might be a way of operationalizing Beck and Sznaider's (2006) politics of "perspectives" or "scale" where they describe the integration of local, national, transnational, and global foci. This challenge is far from settled.

CRITIQUE OF POLITICAL SOCIOLOGY AND HUMAN RIGHTS

Sociology in general and political sociology in particular have been criticized for not taking on the moral cause of human rights more actively, whether in an explanatory or normative context (Sjoberg, Gill, and Williams 2001; Blau and Moncada 2005; Turner 1993). It is clear that cosmopolitan theory embracing human rights has been much more active in the United Kingdom and Germany than in the United States (e.g., two special issues of the *British Journal of Sociology* were voted to the topic in 2006 and 2010). Political sociology has touched but not embraced human rights, yet it can have a much stronger impact in this area. Action research combined with service learning within universities may present opportunities (Touraine 1981). Finally, Sociologists Without Borders is one of a number of possible extensions of the political-sociological charge, as are many other political party and social-movement activities (Moncado and Blau 2006).

REPOSITIONING POLITICAL SOCIOLOGY VIS-À-VIS HUMAN RIGHTS

Given the critique of political sociology, how can this field better position itself toward human rights without abandoning any claim to being a social science? Political sociology would appear to be caught between opposing theories. On the one hand, there is an optimistic cosmopolitan naïveté of a withered state being tamed by INGOs. On the other hand, the pessimistic view of world-systems theory sees multinational corporations and capitalism pushing societies and states into their global shadow. Neither is convincing. A more useful theory might recognize the importance of states, while making morally driven policy recommendations about improving international institutions and rights protections.

Further, a more general theory of globalization might well recognize the usefulness of reforming international institutions with INGOs and social movements.

Political sociology could benefit from a more global and process-oriented view of policy. One indicator of this change is that political sociologists (as opposed to political scientists) have not published much in international relations or organizations journals. The age of globalization would call for a redirection into international political sociology. Cosmopolitan solutions point to these innovative solutions, and political sociological research could be designed to improve the implementation of cosmopolitan recommendations and reforms of the exploitative aspects of the global economy.

LOOKING FORWARD TO THE POLITICAL SOCIOLOGY OF HUMAN RIGHTS

Political sociology will continue to examine power conflicts over inequality and human rights violations in both rich and poor countries. These studies will require new methods to fulfill the nonstate approach, but case-study comparisons and participant-observation studies will continue to be undertaken. This process will not be unilinear, but what is different at this point in history is the existence of transnational movements, global institutions, and bureaucracies that will continue to focus attention on human rights abuses. As such, the politics of fighting human rights abuses will no longer be built from within countries alone.

CHAPTER SEVEN

CULTURE

Mark D. Jacobs and Lester R. Kurtz

A major legacy of the Enlightenment, first formalized as a result of the American and French revolutions, wrought upon the experience of twentieth-century Holocaust and given worldwide legitimacy and force by the declarations, treaties, and institutions of the United Nations, the concept of human rights would seem to be one of the signature triumphs of the modern age. Yet systematic abuses of human rights persist. Indeed the very concept of human rights remains ambiguous. The sociology of culture—whose force derives more from the series of exegetical questions it asks than a body knowledge it has accumulated—can turn that ambiguity to productive use by posing a series of questions salient to human rights.

Are human rights defined *globally* or *locally*? Are they *universal*, a foundation of natural law, or *particularistic*, dependent on uniquely individual contexts? Are they *essential*, one of the very defining characteristics of what it means to be human, or *constructed*, negotiated through emergent processes of social interaction? Is their purpose *instrumental*, to increase societal effectiveness or efficiency, or *expressive*, to endow human experience with deeper meaning? How can social actors exercise *agency* to resist or transform a *structure* that appears to them all-powerful and impervious to change? And perhaps of greatest practical consequence, is the social order they help constitute *beneficial* or *exploitative* for the mass of the population?

Cultural analysis cuts through to the root issues of freedom and necessity, existence and identity. The sociology of culture is of special relevance to human rights because it has the capacity to denaturalize and reenvision categories of understanding them. If, as Gideon Sjoberg, Elizabeth Gill, and Norma Williams (2001) insist, human rights are best defined as "claims against organized power," the sociology of culture is especially useful in revealing and demystifying the ordinary workings of power embedded in habit or "common sense." As both neoliberal theorists of "soft power" and neo-Marxist proponents of the "dominant ideology thesis" argue, power functions most effectively when it does so seamlessly— without recourse to coercion—because subjects unreflectively regard as natural

CULTURE   81

ways of acting that serve its ends. A cultural lens helps foreground the social dynamics that marginalize and victimize groups according to class, race, gender, sexuality, or nationality to penetrate more fully the underlying complexity of social process. Analysis that focuses exclusively on the ways that culture aligns with power or material interests, however, falls into a trap of reductionism by ignoring the autonomy of culture as a quest for meaning.

QUESTIONS POSED BY CLASSICAL THEORISTS

The twentieth-century marked the creation of mass society, the nature of which remains a subject of underlying debate. For such sociologists as Edward Shils (1975), mass society represents the broader and closer integration of "peripheral" populations into "the center," that zone of values and institutions with the most concentrated sacral powers. Shils and others endorse the claim of T. H. Marshall (1964) that modern history describes a path of progress in extending to the masses an expanding set of rights—from political to social and then economic ones. For the neo-Marxist "critical theorists" of the Frankfurt School, such as Max Horkheimer and Theodor Adorno (1993 [1944]), and other proponents of the "hermeneutics of suspicion," on the other hand, mass society operates as a form of exploitative manipulation of the masses, resting on a popular-culture industry that neutralizes possibilities for meaningful resistance by transforming subjects into passive consumers of regressive cultural products.

The most influential founding sociologists of the nineteenth-century laid the groundwork for this debate by interpreting the dizzying effects of societal transformation—of simultaneous global political, economic, industrial, scientific, religious, intellectual, and urban revolutions—in ways that emphasized both their promise and their dangers. Max Weber (1946, 1968 [1920]) discerned in these multiple transformations a process of "rationalization"—the achievement of technical mastery of the universe so that in principle all things were calculable, but at the tragic cost of "disenchantment," the loss of meaning. In a contrarian reading of the Weberian corpus, Donald Levine (1985) argues that in ways partly obscured by the stunted translation of Weber's texts into English, Weber conceived so many different types of "rationality" and "freedom" that he was able to entertain the possibility that rationality could actually expand the realm of freedom.

Émile Durkheim (1933, 1995) explored the promise and danger of industrial capitalism by focusing on the transformation of the *conscience collective* expressive of social organization based on "mechanical" solidarity into that expressive of social organization based on "organic" solidarity. Ideally, the specialized division of labor that characterizes modern industrial society should increase the level of social solidarity, despite the increasing individualism it creates. But instead, Durkheim (1951a) observed the alarming acceleration, in his time, of increase in the incidence of egoism and anomie—social-psychological pathologies indicated

82   MARK D. JACOBS AND LESTER R. KURTZ

by rates of suicide under different conditions of modernity. These pathological weakenings of solidarity Durkheim attributed, in a succession of different works (1933, 1951b, 1995), to such causes as obsolete institutions of socialization, a forced and unjust division of labor, and a lack of civic rituals.

Today's sociology of culture continues to draw on the traditions of Weber and Durkheim. Wendy Griswold explicates those two traditions: the Weberian approach, on the one hand, emphasizes how culture in the form of ideas and world images "shapes action by defining what people want and how they imagine they can get it. Cultural analysis focuses on the complex systems of ideas that shape individuals' motives for action" (1995, 25). The Durkheimian approach, on the other hand, explores how representations, rituals, and symbols concretize "collective consciousness." Relevant to the underlying research problem of measuring the relative benefits and harms of late modernity, Weber bequeaths to the sociology of culture one major subproblem: How, amid a general decline in meaning and cultural authority, is it possible to exercise critical-normative judgment about issues of public and civic consequence? Durkheim bequeaths another: how do we increase social solidarity amid the growing recognition of individual and group difference?

SEMANTIC TENSIONS IN THE SOCIOLOGY OF CULTURE

Culture may be provisionally defined as the constant making and remaking of meaning, the medium of lived experience expressive of practical dilemmas. The very concept of human rights is a cultural construct, as is the concept of culture itself.

Since the "cultural turn" in the late 1980s, culture has been the subject of the most intense sociological study. The Section on the Sociology of Culture of the American Sociological Association is the largest and fastest-growing section, whose continued vitality is presaged by its claiming the largest contingent of graduate student members. The subfield is still generating enough intellectual ferment to defy codification; the elements of culture are variously denoted as symbols, rituals, metaphors, schemas, templates, frames, classification systems, boundaries, practices, discourses, cognitions, narratives, performances, and semiotic codes, among others, not to mention values and norms. Rather than being a linearly accumulating corpus of knowledge, the subfield is unified by a set of semantic tensions. Since this same set of tensions is common to the sociology of human rights, it is instructive to review how the concept of culture mediates them. Without presuming to engage in systematic codification, these semantic tensions can be illustrated with reference to selected exemplary cultural analyses.

If, taking advantage of modern technology, immigrant families steadily maintain real-time communication with relatives left behind, visit them periodically, and keep alive the dream of returning "home," where is the geographical locus of the family? Given the prevalence of international monetary and population

CULTURE   83

flows, even the "local community" has gone global. Social organization is no longer local or global but a dynamic interplay of both. As Peggy Levitt (2005) demonstrates in her study of Pakistani Americans in New England, urban ethnography must now be multisited and transnational. Analogously, Diana Crane (2005) operationalizes "globalization" in a range of action spheres from governance to art markets as a multidirectional set of cultural flows involving a complex array of actors—individual and corporate; public, private, and civic; international, transnational, and regional; grouped and networked.

Is "the law" a body of doctrine, imbued with sacral force—the perfect example of a social fact—as Durkheim believed, or is it a negotiable set of behaviors and practices? Susan Silbey (2005) notes that the attitudes of ordinary citizens exhibit the same chasm that exists in legal scholarship between these two views. In interviews that she and Patricia Ewick conducted, people told stories about the different ways they oriented themselves to the law as it entered their everyday lives. Some orientations were essentialistic, respecting the law's transcendent impartiality and authority; others were constructed, regarding the law as a resource to be employed in interactions with others or something itself manipulable. Silbey insightfully observes that the very plurality of these orientations strengthens the stability of the law as an institution. What she calls "the cultural construction of legality" must embrace this plurality, since no one orientation can reflect all the varied ways that people actually experience the law, and the law would lose credibility if it had to exclusively match a single orientation.

In what ways does Jürgen Habermas's original ideal of a universal public sphere—a forum for critical-rational discussion of civic matters of greatest concern, free from the "steering mechanisms" of power and money—violate the very possibilities for communicative action Habermas intended to promote? Nancy Fraser (1992) argues that since, in practice, members of marginalized groups cannot participate equally in such a forum, the universal public sphere can only exist as a remotely conceivable utopian outcome of dialogue among particularistic public spheres, each consisting of peers whose voice more nearly commands equal respect. Michele Dillon (2005) demonstrates that, conversely, universal identifications can strengthen particularistic bonds, as in the case of gay Catholics whose devotion to the more general tenets of Catholicism, despite the church's intolerance of homosexuality, strengthens their allegiance to each other.

Why would Howard Becker, in his seminal study *Art Worlds* (1982), insist on viewing art from the perspective of the sociology of work? Don't artists primarily seek to create beauty, and isn't their activity different from any other kind of work, somehow transcendent? And isn't mundane work primarily motivated by the search to achieve maximum productive efficiency? Yet, as Becker documents, any form of artistic production involves the coordination of a varied and far-reaching division of labor, so the effectiveness of that coordination is a necessary condition for the production of the artwork. And as John Dewey (1980 [1934])—a major influence on Becker—explains, even the most mundane activity attains esthetic quality if it represents a "consummation" of experience through the resolution of tension. Instrumental activity, action governed primarily by a logic of utility, has the potential to be fully meaningful, while expressive activity, action governed primarily by a logic of meaning, can be nothing but humdrum. Either form of activity, to be fulfilling, must transform "experience" into "an experience." Rather than denoting different types of action, "expressive" and "instrumental" denote necessarily complementary qualities of any single activity.

How can individuals or groups challenge the powerful structures that appear to them as essentially unchangeable? How, for example, could members of art and poetry circles transform Japan from an authoritarian feudal society into a modern nation-state so suddenly under the Meiji Restoration in the second half of the nineteenth century? Eiko Ikegami (2005) offers a "public-centered" explanation. Drawing on the work of Harrison White, William Sewell, and others, she recognizes that structure exists as a multiplicity of networks, each carrying distinctive cultural schemas. "Publics" are sites (such as arts circles) where individuals from different networks physically interact, affording them the emergent opportunity to switch network identifications along with the associated schemas. Japanese artists could evade official prohibitions against political party formation by switching the nature of their associations, instantly creating a culture of national identification and a structure of political participation. Agency and structure are not antithetical but rather mutually constitutive, each enabling as well as constraining the other. Publics are central sites of cultural production and transformation. They offer a compelling example of how culture links micro-level subjectivities with macro-level structures and indeed of how culture is the very switch point of agency and structure (Jacobs and Spillman 2005).

Global and local, universalistic and particularistic, essential and constructed, instrumental and expressive, structure and agency—these semantic tensions describe the deep structure of the sociology of culture. They prove to be false dualisms, better treated as paradoxes, that require the contrasting terms to be held in suspension with each other. Cultural analysis aims to mediate semantic tensions—including in human rights conflicts.

Semantic Tensions in Human Rights Discourse

How do these semantic tensions find expression in the discourse of human rights—in such arenas as the media, UN agencies, and national and international courts and tribunals? How do these tensions shape human rights dilemmas, and what paradoxical strategies do they suggest for reenvisioning them? These tensions both reflect and act back upon the everyday lived experience of real human beings, including victims of human rights abuses and those who serve as their advocates. Although human rights struggles are often represented in the dominant media as a simple dialogue between a unified global center— the "international community"—and a nation on the periphery, a cultural lens helps bring out the multiplicity of human voices involved, as well as the power interests at play. The cultural flows of information and opinion are both bottom up and top down, as what Robert Benford and David Snow (2000) call a "framing contest" emerges in the public sphere.

What is to be done, for instance, if practices of a particular local culture are considered cruel, inhuman, or degrading according to principles propagated by the so-called international community, enforced by international agreements? Or if local governments must comply with transnational ultimatums about rights as conditions of participation in the global economy? The universal principles of human rights paradoxically include the right of indigenous cultures to protect their traditions, so a local government can defend its challenged practices by an appeal to its own traditions.

This paradox of universalism and particularism is inflected by tensions of essentialism and constructivism, as well as globalism and localism. Are standards of human rights essential to the nature of all humans or constructed by a political process dominated by the United States and Europe in violation of other cultural traditions? The dominant definition of human rights proffered by international institutions is often criticized as an imposition, which itself violates the rights of non-Western peoples to maintain their own values and practices. Shu-Ju Ada Cheng and Lester Kurtz argue that "Western-based rights discourse, rooted in the liberal individualist tradition, focuses mainly on civil and political rights. The principle of natural rights, the root of the human rights discourse, emphasizes individual dignity, well-being, and freedom" (1998, 1).

A partial way to resolve this dilemma is to reframe the universalizing process as also addressing particular interests, by representing a common set of agreed-upon rights and enforcement institutions in such a way that the various particular societies see them as legitimate from their own cultural perspectives (see Snow et al. 1986; Benford and Snow 2000). Abdullahi Ahmed An-Na'im too suggests that "people are more likely to observe normative propositions if they believe them to be sanctioned by their own cultural traditions" (1992, 20). If the right to free elections, for example, is advocated in a Muslim culture as a natural right within the tradition of the Qur'an and the teachings of the Prophet Muhammad, rather than in some Western parliamentary sense, it is more likely to resonate within the culture, as we saw happening in the Arab uprisings in Tunisia, Egypt, and elsewhere in 2011 (see Esposito and Voll 2001).

Claims about global, universalistic, essentialistic rights are not always expressions of Western cultural hegemony. Particularistic variations create divides not only among nations but also within them. It is important to note, as An-Na'im does, that even within a single society, "there are either actual or potential differences in perceptions and interpretations of cultural values and norms" (1992, 20). Dominant groups attempt to foster the impression of consensus about "cultural values and norms that are supportive of their own interests, proclaiming them to be the only valid view of that culture" (An-Na'im 1992, 69). Female genital mutilation, soundly criticized by international human rights activists, is more a matter of patriarchal interests in maintaining control over women in a particular population than a widely shared value within that population.

Human Rights in China

In the Chinese case, although government officials may reject Western allegations of human rights abuse with countercharges of cultural interference, millions of Chinese themselves have challenged the system through dissident movements demanding their rights that wax and wane over the decades.

Yet the People's Republic of China, while failing to protect individual liberties, has raised 1 billion people out of poverty in the past half century. While Chinese citizens may lack freedom of speech, their basic human needs are being met by the political system. This case provides an instructive example of the different cultural definitions of basic human rights, a major issue during the Cold War and now resurfacing in conflicts over human rights between China and the United States. Western rights activists, on the one hand, attack China for its refusal to protect political dissent, freedom of speech, and the ability to organize opposition political parties—basic rights as defined by the Western paradigm. On the other hand, the Chinese development project, often deliberately designed to prioritize economic development over individual freedoms, has pro-foundly changed the social and economic conditions of its citizens, with dramatic improvements in the standard of living, health, education, and general well-being of the nation's population.

When we look at cultural mediations of this dilemma, a number of possibilities emerge. First, a new global culture is under construction, with its increasing unity and diversity; we are conscious of both the global village in which we live and our own cultures, which sometimes butt up against the globalizing process—hence the emergence of fundamentalist movements that resist globalization by asserting their own countertruth, sometimes violently. The human rights movement itself is part of a dynamic process that involves confrontations and consultations between particular cultures and interests on many levels.

China's ambivalent embrace of the Internet illustrates how the process of globalization creates cultural flows in more than one direction. The Chinese government had to accept Google's search engine as a communication tool necessary for economic development. But Google threatened governmental control of the population by allowing its users to circumvent official censorship and to interact with each other as a virtual public. The government effectively forced Google to revise its global commitment to the free flow of information as a condition of doing business in China. Despite its technical ability to establish servers in Hong Kong and elsewhere around the entire globe, Google was confronted with a choice of accommodating China's censorship policy or losing that crucial market. The universal communication technology of globalization bent to the force of Chinese particularism.

Yet the virtual public created by the Internet has also frustrated the efforts of the Chinese government to resist the celebration of human rights as a globally shared value. The government was unable to repress either the local hero of discontent Liu Xiaobo or the news of his award of the 2010 Nobel Peace Prize. Instead, its attempt to do so backfired, causing negative fallout for China worldwide and an

CULTURE 87

avalanche of critical Internet communication within the country. Ying Chan, dean of Cheung Kong School of Journalism and Communication at Shantou University, followed the overwhelming unofficial response in China on her BlackBerry and laptop. "I was following the actions of these free-thinking strangers in real time without ever setting foot outside," she declared, in an act of resistance that made her local site global (Kurtz 2010).

The Occupy Movement

The Occupy Movement that first emerged (as Occupy Wall Street) in New York in the fall of 2011 offers another example of all the semantic tensions that animate human rights. It resulted from, and in turn produced, cultural flows moving in all directions around the world. Inspired by the "occupation" of Tahrir Square, half a world away, a few months earlier, encampments of protesters sprung up, first in New York and then in thousands of other sites around the world. These sites can easily be seen as examples of the "publics" described by Eiko Ikegami (2005), offering opportunities for the dramatic exercise of agency in transforming economic and political structures through the switching of network identifications and cultural schemas. Each encampment modeled the tension of universalism and particularism: there were no identified leaders, and all decisions were made in assemblies of the whole, with the expectation that the diverse participants would meld their particularistic interests into a collective stance. The slogan "We are the 99%"—signifying concern for widespread suffering and economic injustice in the midst of especially hard times—instantly evoked deep resonance in the encampments and beyond, even in the mainstream press.

It is too early to assess the impact of the movement. But the gatherings were not solely (or even primarily) instrumental in nature. As many observers found puzzling, the "occupiers" did not even issue lists of concrete, specific demands. The expressive objectives of the occupations were manifest: a mood of communion developed in and among the encampments. "Occupy" helped answer a major research problem about the quiescent public reaction to the axial financial crisis that has so exacerbated economic distress and inequality: where was the "piacular" ritual (or ritual of atonement) that Durkheim claimed was necessary to preserve collective solidarity in the face of a calamity of such magnitude (Jacobs 2012)? The protests—and the spirit of communion among the protesters—served the expressive function of providing just such a ritual. In Sjoberg, Gill, and Williams's (2001) definition of human rights as claims against organized power, "Occupy" is both an expressive and an instrumental example of the struggle for human rights.

Mahatma Gandhi and the Indian Independence Movement

Making explicit the play of semantic tensions also helps better explain the remarkable achievement of Mahatma Gandhi, often cited as the modern source of inspiration for human rights movements. Indeed, this form of cultural analysis suggests answers to research problems that have frustrated traditional political analysis. How could a frail, nonviolent man exercise such agency against the might of the British Empire? How could he so thoroughly reverse the flow of global/local influence? Was his world-changing activity politically instrumental or spiritually expressive?

Gandhi brought together a series of particularisms into a universal approach to the problem of rights, starting with the warrior and pacifist motifs that run through the world's religious and ethical traditions regarding the use of violence and force to address issues of injustice. The warrior believes it a sacred duty to fight, and the pacifist believes it just as important not to harm. Gandhi's nonviolent civil resister fights like the warrior but also like the pacifist, without doing harm (see Kurtz 2008). Similarly, he drew on multiple religious traditions—starting with the Hindu and Islamic—bringing these multiple traditional worlds together in a recipe for revolution. Gandhi had not read his own Bhagavad Gita, recited with his mother in the temple when he was growing up in India, until he went to study law in England. He combined Jesus's Sermon on the Mount with Hindu and Buddhist concepts of *ahimsa*, nonharmfulness, and the idea of nonattached action: do what is right without focusing on the act's consequences. He brought together East and West, North and South, as well as the spiritual and the political, and redefined power as something that grows not out of the barrel of a gun but from the collaborative noncooperation of a mobilized people.

The dramas of resistance and liberation that he presented on the world stage were also politically strategic. The cloth and boycott struck at the heart of a colonial structure based on the industrial revolution in textiles, the exploitation of raw materials, and global trade. His Salt March in 1930 was at once a religious procession and an act of political resistance that gathered increasing crowds and attention as he marched to the Indian Ocean to make salt, in defiance of a British monopoly over the necessities of daily life. Applying the terms of Ikegami's (2005) analysis to these mass gatherings, these events can be seen as "publics" and these dramatisms as the newly popular cultural schemas that emerge from them, constituting counterstructures to the structure of British colonialism.

Why a Cultural Analysis of Human Rights Is Essential

These cases of China, Occupy, and Gandhi suggest the value of the sociology of culture for understanding human rights. Since the concept of human rights is a cultural construct, human rights issues are inflected by the same set of semantic tensions as the culture concept itself. The sociology of culture thus recommends a method for studying human rights: to explicate—indeed, to weave into an exegetical deep structure—those various tensions. This helps us to see beneath the distortions that power and other forms of domination introduce into the discourse of human rights and to recognize the full multiplicity of interests and voices.

Therefore, cultural analysis also recommends practical strategies for addressing human rights issues. A semantic tension poses a paradox. The resolution of paradox always involves enlarging the problem frame to uncover the larger unity between the terms. Analytically and practically, it is a mistake to seek a one-dimensional solution rather than holding the contrasting terms in suspense. Thus, for example, an enlarged problem frame reveals the strategic advantage of stating universalistic claims in particularistic terms and particularistic claims in universalistic ones.

These reflections on cultural analysis of human rights issues also suggest ways to broaden the sociology of culture. Indeed, they suggest the need for an "esthetic conception of culture" (Jacobs and Hanrahan 2005). Like art itself, in such a conception culture has the capacity to hold difference in suspension and express a higher unity. Like art itself, it suggests grounds of normative evaluation even in the absence of measurable or objective standards. As Jaeger and Selznick (1964) explain in "A Normative Theory of Culture," a translation into sociological terms of Dewey's *Art as Experience*, culture can and should be evaluated according to its "human-centeredness." Like art itself, in this conception culture reenvisions the actually existing world. Great "masters" earn that status, as Dewey (1980 [1934], 301) observes, "precisely because they do not follow either models or rules but subdue both of these things to serve enlargement of personal experience."

This conception broadens the sociology of culture by adding a tradition emanating from Georg Simmel to the ones emanating from his contemporary peers Max Weber and Émile Durkheim. Simmel, trained as an esthetician, developed an approach to sociology focused on the interrelated forms of social interaction and objective culture. His approach anticipated the understanding of art as "feeling embodied in form" famously proposed by modern esthetician Suzanne Langer (1953). An esthetic conception of culture suggests ways of addressing the major problems bequeathed by Weber and Durkheim—to exercise evaluative judgment amid cultural disenchantment and to increase social solidarity amid the growing recognition of individual and group difference. In the balance of these problems hangs the future of human rights.

CHAPTER EIGHT

SCIENCE, KNOWLEDGE, AND TECHNOLOGY

Jennifer L. Croissant

The sociology of science, knowledge, and technology and its affiliated field of science and technology studies (STS) comprise a heterogeneous discipline (Hess 1997; Hackett et al. 2007) that embodies contradictory approaches to considerations of human rights. These contradictions emerge from the specific intellectual trajectories that shape the major approaches in the field and the legacy of theory and methodology that shapes inquiry in these areas.

WHAT'S GOING ON

There are two general intellectual orientations within the social studies of science and technology: institutional studies and knowledge studies. These are, of course, approximations that elide the cross-fertilizations and trafficking across the subfields. The study of technology, as technology, is situated uneasily within each of these research trajectories. The distinction between these orientations, which I problematize below, is based on what might be termed the "Mertonian exemption," where Merton's (1973) institutional sociology of knowledge largely exempted the content of scientific knowledge claims from sociological examination. Unlike Mannheim (1936), who did not exempt scientific knowledge from the problems of ideology, Merton also avoided the utopian ambivalence of Marx, for whom a true "science" would emerge in a noncapitalist society (Perelman 1978). Merton's legacy in institutional studies of science generally posits that in a democratic social order, scientific institutions informed by functioning social norms of communalism, disinterestedness, organized skepticism, and universalism would work for the betterment of humankind and be freed from ideologies that might derive from or justify forms of oppression. Science, in this perspective, both needs and is good for democracy, although capitalism can produce distorting "interests" that lead to limited research or outright fraud. The institutional approach has informed science policy, such as the formulation of responsible-conduct-of-research (RCR) guidelines or pedagogical resources (COSEPUP 1995), even if as an unacknowledged narrative or set of assumptions.

Within institutional studies, there are thriving subspecialties that examine science as an occupation and organization, studies of scientific disciplines, and surveys of the public understanding of science. Each of these intersects with questions of human rights on several levels in contemporary research agendas. In terms of studying science as an occupation, the determinants of successful scientific careers, issues of equity, and access to scientific networks are long-standing yet continuously productive research areas (DiPrete and Eirich 2006; Fox 2010). The methods here include quantitative survey work, analyses of curriculum vitae, and interviews and qualitative observational work on the socialization of scientists. Recent findings of particular interest to those interested in human rights include considerations of family and gender equity, mentoring, and related issues in access to scientific careers, which indicate that there are no unambiguous effects of issues such as childrearing on scientific productivity and that there are mixed results regarding organizational structure and institutional equity (see Roth and Sonnert 2011; Fox 2008; Smith-Doerr 2004).

The study of science at a global, institutional level indicates that the latetwentieth-century emergence of a common template of a functioning state, both on practical and symbolic levels, is connected to the adoption of a relatively standardized educational system and to the use of Western science as the global common denominator of policy (Drori et al. 2003). This is an expression of and facilitates science's global cultural authority. Despite differences (such as gender patterns by field of specialization or areas of emphasis between "hard" and "soft" sciences based on specific historical trajectories of nations), there are complex trends, highly dependent on the indicator selected, suggesting the continued spread of global institutional forms of science along with global models of human rights. For example, formerly communist states and states with lower current metrics of democratic participation have greater emphasis on the natural rather than social sciences, while more internationalist states with high levels of democratic participation both demonstrate expertise about and produce policy in support of social-science research (Drori et al. 2003, 202). These trends are not without contradictory impulses. There are also questions about the loose coupling between matters of national policy and the specific organization of science, and again between the organizations and the actual practices of scientists. This is a finer-grained set of distinctions than Merton's overall claims about the productive relationship between science and democracy.

At a less global or macroscopic scale, the study of the organization of scientific disciplines has been transformed by the availability of low-cost and simplified scientometric and bibliometric tools and data sets, which put quantitative assessment of scientific networks within reach of a broad range of scholars. Focusing on the information gleaned from formal scientific publications, such as citation patterns, coauthorship, institutional alliances, and

92 JENNIFER L. CROISSANT

funding sources, current research questions include the spatialization or development of geographic referents for scientific networks, ranging from field level (such as genomics or nanotechnology) to regional innovation system analysis (Leydesdorff and Schank 2008). The new bibliometrics analyze the structure of scientific networks as represented in the published scientific literature. For example, the structure of scientific consensus in controversies such as vaccination's noncorrelation with autism or the noncarcinogeneity of coffee is very dense and stable, unlike the continued public debate on these issues (Shwed and Bearman 2010). Work such as this, however, must remain agnostic as to the veracity of the consensus (because today's consensus can be upended by tomorrow's discoveries) and provides few mechanisms that explain the persistence of the controversy in the public sector. The relative closure of many kinds of controversies in the scientific literature may also show the constraints of the current regimes of proof, where the establishment of causality is strictly linked to statistical significance measures that make disproof easier than proof. To the extent that the invocation of "science" can be used to quell public debate (Ehrenfeld 2002), there is some concern that this kind of work can add to the appeal of technocracy as a political theory that substitutes administration for politics, as if the science itself were neutral. Such goals illustrate the power that the scientific register has in public discourse. The achievement of this power has yet to be sufficiently explained.

The gap between professional scientific discourse and public understanding of science has vexed scholars and policy-makers for a long time. Until innovations by scholars such as Irwin and Wynne (1996), which interrogate local knowledge in relation to formal scientific knowledge, and the uptake and coproduction of science by "lay experts" (Epstein 1998), the primary model of public understanding was a deficit model of inadequate literacy, primarily examined through surveys of "known" scientific knowledge and belief. The deficit model is, at least in scholarship, superseded by analyses that take local knowledges seriously and also recognize hybrid social roles.

The organization of knowledge at the interface of scientific communities and the public is also engaged in what might be called critical institutional studies, which examine the emergence and circulation of new knowledges, also attuned to questions of power, ideology, and social justice. While human rights, per se, are not a frequent key phrase, this kind of work, ranging from the historical to the contemporary ethnographic, engages the coproduction of knowledge, expertise, identity, and policy (Frickel and Moore 2006). For example, how do people engaged in local environmental-quality controversies seek out and produce scientific knowledge, and what are the responses by policy-makers to multiple knowledge claims? An important dimension to this is the increasing attention to gaps in knowledge, whether due to intentionally withheld information or "undone science." As scientific priorities are set through complex processes that often reflect entrenched interests, it is often difficult to get science done by or on behalf of a broad public interest not defined by a potential market share. And there are also problems of "willful ignorance," such as in the case of homeowners in post-Katrina Louisiana not wanting to assess the toxicology of their property as that knowledge would make it unsalable (Frickel and Vincent 2007). It is in these kinds of studies that the field moves from studies of the organization of science as an institution to an engagement with studies of the organization of science as a fluid body of knowledge.

Not to be excluded from the question of science and human rights are questions about the science of human rights and about access to science as a human right. As an example of the latter, questions about scientists' access to international data resources are framed as a human right with regard to their ability to participate in the international scientific community (Arzberger et al. 2004). Similarly, the United Nations presents an unstated definition of science in its articulation of property rights from scientific discovery and privileges "the freedom indispensable for scientific research" (UNHCR 1966). In the case of the former, establishing human rights violations can be an issue of establishing matters of fact (Orentlicher 1990), engaging epistemological questions about what counts as evidence, and exploring methodological questions about indices and measures. Finally, of course, the incorporation of human rights into human-subjects-protection protocols based on a model of autonomous human agents working under conditions of informed consent both protects human subjects and the legitimacy of scientific research and reinscribes that particular model of an individuated subject.

The role of science and scientists in human rights discourse has a long and complicated trajectory. For example, Barnett (1948) argued for the separation of science and human rights based on a traditional (modernist) separation of matters of fact from matters of value, rights being a matter of value. Moore (2008), however, outlines the ways in which scientists themselves have challenged that separation on personal and institutional levels, particularly around issues of militarization but more generally opening up discussion around the social responsibilities of science. While the contemporary RCR enterprise is currently focused on internal dynamics of scientific conduct, such as fraud, falsification, and plagiarism, it remains to be seen if this rapidly emerging field will move from procedural ethics and issues of research compliance and policy to engaging substantive, or "macro," ethics and issues of distributive justice, human rights, and social responsibility on a different scale and moral register (Herkert 2004). At worst, the RCR approach contributes to a laissez-faire approach to science policy and ethics. The policy-making process for science, particularly in setting research priorities, may lead to neglect of matters of broad human rights concern if they do not fit into market-driven solutions.

The laissez-faire approach is clearly central to a great deal of scholarship on technology (see Baumol 2002). This approach generally conflates economic "democracy" of free markets with ideas about social democracy and rights. These sorts of innovation studies (see Comin and Hobijn 2004) are focused on a specific model of economic development and growth. More nuanced studies (Weeramantry 1993) that problematize the social changes surrounding importing Western technology into new contexts (such as women losing

94 JENNIFER L. CROISSANT

land rights when industrial farm implements are imported) circulate as case studies and moral warnings but often do not impinge on the quantitative development models (and despite the emergence of alternative accounting systems, such as Waring 2003). As Adas (2006) argues, US development efforts are justified by assumptions about technological superiority and technological necessity. As technology is a presumed good, its negative impacts in new contexts are attributed to insufficient preparation on the part of recipients or cultural backwardness rather than to the inappropriateness of the new technologies and the required infrastructure and cultural changes needed to support their implementation.

Current research in technology and human rights has become infatuated with information and communication technology (ICT) and its role as a tool for economic development and the expansion of human rights. This orientation is embodied in "one-laptop-per-child" programs, which have been criticized as imperialist, irrelevant, and a distraction from pressing basic issues (Smith 2005). And while it is clear that ICTs have had a role in global social movement organization and mobilization, be it flash mobs organized by cell-phone users or the transmission of information to global news sources (Van Aelst and Walgrave 2002), it is not clear that they are the panacea for global development in that government tracking and content restrictions impinge on these network solutions (see Shirazi, Ngwenyama, and Morawczynski 2010).

CHALLENGES

Significant challenges to the human rights paradigm emerge from methodological and epistemological consequences of studies in the sociology of science, knowledge, and technology and STS. The challenges emerge from three primary orientations: The first is in the empirical standpoint of postcolonial scholars such as Vandana Shiva (1997), who maintain that the spread of Western knowledge regimes and their intertwined property regimes has intensified inequalities, led to ecological disasters, and decreased human rights. The second challenge emerges from traditional Marxist orientations that identify science and technology as the product of capitalism and thus unable to contribute to humane modes of existence (Aronowitz 1988).

The third, final challenge to the human rights paradigm emerges from nuanced poststructuralist scholarship, particularly actor-network theory (ANT) (Law and Hassard 1999; Latour 2007) and posthumanist and anti-Enlightenment paradigms, often informed by Haraway's "A Cyborg Manifesto" (1991) and feminist critiques of rights discourses (Brown 1995). In that it applies itself to both knowledge and technologies, the term "technoscience" emerges from studies in the social construction of technology and ANT and becomes an important signifier of the organized networks of innovation. ANT may be, arguably, mislabeled as a theory and more effectively understood as a methodology in which the relations among things are traced out and their properties become attributes related to their perception and use in networks. That is, as with other networks studies, it remains to be seen whether the network is explanatory or needs itself to be explained.

ANT and its convergence with ethnomethodological and poststructuralist methodologies together produce an agnosticism about the key terms "human" and "rights," which inform human rights discourse, as well as "science" and "technology." As an antiessentialist move, ANT eschews the attribution of properties to technologies and other nonhuman entities except as they are instantiated through the relations of the networks of humans and nonhuman actants. ANT has proven a valuable framework for posthuman scholarship in the way it shifts focus from considering innate properties of things to problematizing the attribution of properties of actants such as rights or agency as emergent properties semiotically and materially produced in relation to an overall network. Callon's (1986) study of scallops and their goals in a controversy over scallop fishing or Latour's "Sociology of a Door Closer" (Johnson 1988), which explores the delegation of human agency to objects such as speed bumps and automatic door closers, are examples of this approach.

In this light, human rights are problematic in that that the boundary between human and nonhuman is permeable and seen as culturally specific, as a product of networks of attribution and action. As Butler (1993) argues, the point of a critical poststructuralist approach is not to determine what, in her case, the body "really is" as either a discursive or material thing, whether it is cultural or natural, but to examine what is at stake in dragging it to one side or the other of the discursively produced nature-culture divide. Similarly, the dualisms of "technical" and "social" or "technical" and "political" are rendered problematic, examined as the outcome of network processes. ANT as a form of poststructuralist inquiry eschewing essential distinctions such as "social," "technological," "political," "scientific," and "human" or "nonhuman" has thus been convergent with innovative extensions of rights to nonhumans, such as animals. The second term in the phrase "human rights" is similarly challenged by scholars, particularly in that rights discourses generally represent a propertarian orientation that reinstantiates individualism and the role of the state as the guarantor of rights (Brown 1995). What becomes apparent in this loose configuration of approaches is a destabilization of both terms of the phrase "human rights," as well as ideas about science as a value-free or objective enterprise. Thus the question for the expansion of human rights becomes a question about what counts as human, whether or not rights are guarantors of (human) well-being, and what power structures and ideologies are reproduced with the expansion of discourses of (human) rights.

Conversely, a focus on human rights, broadly defined, may challenge the approaches to science, knowledge, and technology that do not problematize the current institutional configuration of science and its relation to capital and the state. For example, the "triple-helix" model (Etzkowitz 2003) of government-university-industry relations in innovation is instantiated in policy across international boundaries (e.g., Rivera Vargas 2010), takes for granted that this configuration is both necessary and sufficient for progress, and unproblematically assumes a specific model of intellectual property, economic growth, and neoliberal subjectivity.

Additionally, technoscience is expensive. The consequences of this range from disparities in health research favoring the wealthy (e.g., prioritizing heart disease research over research on infectious diseases) to the problems of the appropriation of intellectual property from so-called third-world countries. Much is assumed in the vision of Western technoscience as the epitome of human achievement and as the end point of international development (Adas 2006). Clearly Western technoscience is seen as problematic for postcolonial scholars such as Shiva (1997). And yet, evidence, measurement, and proof are important to numerous social movements, whether related to environmental justice, antiglobalization, or human rights organizations (see Orentlicher 1990).

There is thus probably no single "future" to which the intellectual orientations of the sociology of science, knowledge, and technology and STS point, except perhaps a hopeful heterogeneity. Science as a social institution holds great sway as an arbiter of public life, and science operates as a powerful register of discourse. Similarly, there is a great deal of ambivalence about access to technology as both a marker and a guarantor of rights. For those interested in promoting human welfare, science has always produced a great deal of ambivalence: its tools can be used either to sustain or resist forms of oppression or to argue for the expansion or contraction of rights (Croissant and Restivo 1995).

CHAPTER NINE

SOCIOLOGY OF LAW

Christopher N. J. Roberts

The biggest challenge for the sociological study of human rights can be posed in five words: What is a human right? Traditional intellectual divisions of labor typically have left this question for lawyers, philosophers, political scientists, and advocates—not sociologists. Evidence of custom, however, is not a sufficient reason for its preservation. As human rights have become an undeniable social force in contemporary life, increasing numbers of sociologists have undertaken their study. This is fitting. The sociological canon is in many respects tailor-made for examining the most complex and pressing contemporary human rights problems. After all, human rights at their most basic level are about people as they exist in society. Yet the standard approaches to human rights—most often rooted in law, politics, and philosophy—often conceive of human rights in a way that dislocates them from these social moorings. Such conceptions of human rights, therefore, are not well suited for sociological inquiry.

As the "pioneers" in the sociological field of human rights well know, offering a sociological definition of the human rights concept is a deceptively challenging task (e.g., Turner 1993, 1995; Rowland 1995; Connell 1995; Waters 1995; Barbalet 1995). This, however, is not a task to begin anew. Examining new categories of transnationalism, globalization, or international treaty making—the very places one would first think to look for an answer—provides much less guidance than one might assume. Instead, this chapter looks to several foundational debates within the subfield of the sociology of law. In fact, all the necessary pieces of a robust sociological framework for studying human rights already exist, and most of the groundwork has already been laid.

In selecting a sociological answer to the question posed at the outset of this chapter, there are three important preliminary considerations. First, there is the multiplicity issue. The multitude of distinct forms that human rights manifest can make it an extremely complicated topic of inquiry—particularly in the context of a social-scientific analysis where specificity and precision are essential. The great difficulty is that the same term invokes a multiplicity of "registers"—an incredible array of disparate definitions and an intractable range of conflicting foundational sources (Somers and Roberts 2008). The term "human rights" can be thought of as a "free-floating" or "empty" signifier—a concept that is constantly deployed, yet vague, highly variable, and stripped of context and specified meaning (Derrida 1978). For example, when the phrase "human rights" is invoked, it is entirely unclear whether it refers to the eighteenth-century French "rights of man and citizen," the fundamental right of citizenship Hannah Arendt discusses in the context of European statelessness, or the rights associated within the modern post–World War II international human rights regime. As a broad starting point for the study of human rights, a sociological definition or framework for studying rights should narrow the field of study to identify the object of study at a level that provides sufficient sociological meaning, yet still captures the breadth of the subject in all its guises and myriad forms.

Second, the definition must conceive of human rights in a way that is amenable to sociological inquiry. Common notions of human rights will often require some degree of empirical translation. Human rights, for example, share much with natural rights arguments based on supposed inherent human traits, fundamental laws of nature, religious principles, historical experience, morality, and so forth. The problem for sociology is that such natural rights concepts exist within a universe that is unassailable and unknowable. An individual's inherent dignity, for example, can never be drafted away by treaty, plundered by tyrants, or proven spurious by social scientists (no matter their methodological rigor). But it can be studied as a sociological entity, within a categorically precise sociological framework that will permit access to human rights in all of their guises on a sociological plane.

Finally, as a broad orientation the sociological study of human rights is much more than sociologists who just happen to be studying human rights. Indeed, there should be something unique and different about a sociological approach to the study of human rights that distinguishes it from other approaches rooted in law, philosophy, and political science, for example. But just being different from other disciplines does not justify the effort. It should shed new light on a particular aspect of the world or present new understandings that are not available through existing approaches. There must be a sociological advantage.

Although the topic of human rights is broader than what typically counts as "the law," the debates and central questions that have emerged within the sociology of law subfield help in constructing a sociological framework for the study of human rights by identifying the central concerns, critical divisions, fault lines, and disciplinary boundaries. A comprehensive overview of the entire subfield of the sociology of law is of course not possible here (for overviews, see Cotterrell 2007, 1418; Deflem 2008; Freeman 2006; Trevino 1996). This chapter focuses narrowly on the problems and implications raised by four key sociology-of-law debates surrounding (1) normativity versus objectivity, (2) sociological empiricism, (3) levels of analysis, and (4) order versus conflict.

The subfield of the sociology of law has provided a space for these disciplinary discussions to define the subfield while shaping the contours of the broader discipline. Looking to these debates provides guidance not only in addressing the essential "What is a human right?" question, but also in establishing a conceptual space for disciplinary dialogue and debate within the emergent human rights subfield. These debates show that, at its essence, human rights is a sociological concept, for any statement of rights is a statement of social relationships. This understanding of human rights is broad and best operates as a starting point for sociological analysis. Because an understanding of human rights as social relationships applies equally well to the rights concept, throughout this chapter the terms "rights" and "human rights" are used interchangeably.

THE DEBATES, PROBLEMS, AND IMPLICATIONS

PROBLEM #1 FOR THE SOCIOLOGICAL STUDY OF HUMAN RIGHTS

Human rights are inherently value-laden entities. Is there a place for the normative component within an epistemological context that favors scientific objectivity and value freedom?

The tensions surrounding this fact/value question are foundational in the sociology of the law and in the broader discipline as well. In their respective studies of the law, both Max Weber and Émile Durkheim sought to distinguish jurisprudential or normative studies of the law from its sociological or social-scientific study (Durkheim 1982). Other early sociologists presumed that a "sociology of law" was "logically" and "theoretically impossible" given the incompatible nature of sociological inquiry (a study of what is) and the study of the law (what ought to be) (Timasheff 1941, 233). More recently within the subfield of the sociology of law, scholars have engaged in intense debates over whether and how to keep normative inquiry separate from scientific objectivity in the study of the law. Scholars such as Donald Black have argued that a sociological approach must only focus on what is scientifically knowable, thus leaving the more normative concerns to philosophers and jurists. For Black, the "study of fact" as a scientific venture must, in sociology, "be distinguished from the study of value" (1972, 1093). Others, most notably Philip Selznick, have called for an approach in which underlying philosophical, jurisprudential, or policy aspirations are incorporated within the framework of the sociological study. In a series of spirited exchanges with Black, Selznick urged sociologists not to shrink away from the normative and more philosophical elements of the law, for distanced neutrality was not the most appropriate role (or goal) for sociologists of the law. Instead, they "should be ready to explore the meaning of legality itself, to assess its moral authority, and to clarify the role of social science in creating a society based on justice" (Selznick 1959, 124).

Though international human rights were not on the agenda for Black or Selznick, the fault lines between fact and value exhibited in these debates cannot be ignored. Interestingly, each side sacrifices in proportion to what it seeks to maintain. An objective scientific approach, for example, may attempt to maintain a value-free perspective by reducing rights to strictly empirical phenomena. But to completely divorce rights from their normativity threatens to alter an essential feature of the object under investigation. For it is precisely the normative element within rights that makes them distinct entities that possess social importance and causal power in the first place. Doing so dramatically alters an entire field of inquiry before it can be analyzed. It can be argued, in fact, that separating a right from its normativity alters the object of study so completely that it quite possibly is no longer a "right."

On the other hand, an approach that seeks to integrate the underlying normativity rests on a very shaky scientific foundation. An overly normative study might not even be "sociology," but might bleed into other categories, such as jurisprudence, philosophy, social activism, or some other endeavor altogether. So one way (among others) the tensions between fact and value play out is this: study rights as empirical facts and sacrifice an essential piece of their nature, or integrate the normative elements within the study and risk sacrificing the epistemological orientation that makes sociology, sociology. As discussed below, these two paths are not necessarily mutually exclusive—the best framework for the sociological study of rights is one that is faithful to the nature of the object of study but still amenable to social-scientific methods.

PROBLEM #2 FOR THE SOCIOLOGICAL STUDY OF HUMAN RIGHTS

Human rights are not empirical entities.

Even if one were to adopt Black's supposedly scientific and objective empirical approach—his "pure sociology of law" (1972, 1087)—there remains a major problem: the law (and certainly human rights) cannot be found in the empirical world. While at the conceptual level they are each very real, powerful, and thus a worthy (if not a necessary) aspect of sociological inquiry, no one has ever seen a human right or touched the law. They are nonempirical entities. For Black, "Every scientific idea requires a concrete empirical referent of some kind. A science can only order experience, and has no way of gaining access to nonempirical domains of knowledge" (1972, 1086).

The key question, then, for gaining access is how to identify the tangible, empirical indicators that represent these concepts. In this sense, the empirical difficulties that emerge for the sociological study of rights are no different from those for other sociological areas of study, such as race, gender, inequality, culture, the family, emotions, and the law. Defining the concept under investigation is the necessary first step of an empirical study, which in turn points to where such visible, empirical indicators reside. Black (1972, 1976), for instance, views the law in terms of behavior. This moves him out of the normative (and epistemologically alien) realms of jurisprudence and moral philosophy, for example, and into a venue in which the tangible indicators of the law—human action and interaction—can be studied sociologically. While human rights are much more than "behavior," it is similarly necessary to narrow the concept down to a meaningful range of phenomena that can then be examined empirically.

There is significant breadth in the approaches used in the sociology of law to locate, measure, assess, and understand such empirical indicators. Quantitative and qualitative research techniques, as well as positivist, interpretive, ethnographic, and historical approaches, are equally at home within the sociology of law. Whether a particular approach is more or less appropriate than another depends upon the research question(s) posed at the outset, the available data, and the nature of the object of study. But regardless of the particular methodological approach employed, it must place the object under investigation within a contextual frame of reference in which distinctions can be drawn among categorically like objects.

A sociological framework must therefore define human rights and identify the relevant empirical indicators. The definition must at once incorporate a broad spectrum of competing definitions, while being narrow enough to possess sociological meaning.

PROBLEM #3 FOR THE SOCIOLOGICAL STUDY OF HUMAN RIGHTS

It remains unclear what the appropriate analytic level for studying human rights is.

A key difficulty for defining human rights is that so much remains unknown about what they in fact are, how they operate, and where they do their work. This question concerning location of the concept and its empirical referents is a particularly knotty one that reveals another dimension of the multiplicity issue. Common understandings of human rights seem to imply that they reside simultaneously at a variety of conflicting levels. Human rights can be thought of as individual-level, state-level, global, or universal phenomena. So how does one define human rights so that the research framework does not assume away the very questions that researchers need to ask?

Human rights are often assumed to be a category of individual right. The individual notion of rights is captured well in the many colloquial expressions—for example, "right holder," "right bearer," or one's "bundle of rights"—that tend to imply that rights are exclusive to the individual and are possessed or owned, independently of other aspects of the social world. Rooting the concept within the individual, however, places the concept in a realm that is less amenable to sociological methods and social-scientific epistemologies. Sociological studies of the law have approached this problem by viewing individual actors not exclusively on their own terms but as they are constituted within a broader matrix of social relationships, interactions, and structures (Deflem 2008; Durkheim 1982; Edelman 2004; Sanders 1990). As Edelman writes, "Ideas, norms, and rituals evolve at the group or societal level and help to constitute individual identities, needs, preferences, and behaviors. Individual action cannot be understood apart from the social environment that gives meaning to that action" (2004, 186).

102   CHRISTOPHER N. J. ROBERTS

But at what level does "society" exist in the contemporary world? While the boundaries of law are often presumed to begin and end at the level of the state, new patterns of transnational activity—migration, NGO activity, and international legal and economic processes, to name a few examples—reflect new spheres of social action and identity formation that do not necessarily coincide with the political and geographic boundaries of the state.

Sociologists of the law such as Boyle (2007) suggest that researchers must now grapple with "multiple levels of analysis." Halliday and Osinsky, however, advise empirical researchers to "maintain a studied skepticism about excessive claims made of globalization and its impact" (2006, 466). These warnings are particularly relevant for the study of human rights. Common understandings of human rights are freighted with notions of internationalism, global norms, and universal truths (or, conversely, of individual nature, human dignity). From a sociological perspective, these vague though normatively and heuristically compelling statements about the nature of reality are just that—statements. In sociological terms, they are "social facts." To assume within the empirical research framework that human rights are indeed "universal" or "individual" is to accept an ontology that assumes away the importance of the very sociological indicators—that is, social relationships—that reveal the essence of the concept. A sociological framework should therefore receive human rights on this sociological plane—one, for example, that conceives of human rights as basic statements of social relationships.

PROBLEM #4 FOR THE SOCIOLOGICAL STUDY OF HUMAN RIGHTS

Should sociologists view human rights in terms of stability and shared norms or conflict and change?

A major sociological debate in the post–World War II period concerns competing ideas about how society operates. Structural-functionalist approaches view society as an integrated system comprising a series of subsystems. Although these ideas can be traced to nineteenth-century thinkers such as Auguste Comte and Durkheim, the rise of structural functionalism in the post–World War II sociological canon is perhaps most associated with Talcott Parsons. As a broad orientation, structural-functionalist ideas typically view the law in its capacity for social integration, focusing, for instance, on its ability to inform social values and consensual norms and to achieve social equilibrium (Trevino 1996, 333). Interestingly, a significant portion of the impact of structural-functionalist thought on the sociology of law can be attributed to the work of its critics. Conflict theorists such as Ralf Dahrendorf (1958) believe that the structural-functionalist approach, slanted in its focus on harmony, stability, and consensus, overlooks a key part of social reality—authority within a system not only is integrative but can also be divisive and coercive. Thus, conflict-model theorists argue that coercion and conflict should be studied as an important element of society in its capacity to both preserve the social order and facilitate social change (for examples of conflict-theoretical work in the sociology of law, see Quinney 1970; Chambliss 1964).

In the sociology of the law, each of these starting assumptions about how society operates has a marked effect on how the law is conceived. Austin Turk explains it this way: "If one assumes that social order is an expression of general agreement among the members of a population on how they should go about business of social life . . . then legality will probably be defined as a characteristic of norms which the people consider important enough to protect against the few who do not go along with the majority" (1969, 30). On the other hand, Turk writes, "if order is seen as largely a pattern of conflict among parties seeking to protect and improve their life chances . . . then legality becomes an attribute of whatever words and deeds are defined as legal by those able to use to their advantage the machinery for making and enforcing rules" (1969, 31–32). These starting assumptions about social order or social conflict therefore have a profound effect on the entire research program, influencing the questions posed, the data sought, the inferences made, and the theories developed. But despite their incredible influence, Turk argues, such assumptions in the sociological study of the law are often left implicit and unstated.

The existence of unspoken apriorities is particularly relevant in the study of human rights. It is a common assumption that human rights represent basic, shared values or that they embody statements of fundamental principles that will (when adhered to) provide stability and social harmony. These assumptions might lead to questions about how to honor, enforce, and protect individuals' human rights. This, in turn, might lead to an empirical focus on processes of integration, the spreading of shared norms around core human rights, and how to use the law to promote and enforce human rights laws and norms. These assumptions—quite prevalent in human rights research—are not in and of themselves incorrect. They do, however, present a very particularized view of the world.

Human rights ideas are never free from conflict and struggle. The very fact that human rights might be needed in the first place underscores the lack of shared norms. In fact, during the 1940s and 1950s, when the foundations of the modern international human rights regime was being created, the human rights concept spurred incredible opposition and resistance as imperial powers such as Great Britain and influential political factions in the United States feared that human rights would alter existing social relationships and hierarchies. Interestingly, during the same period, prominent professional organizations such as the American Bar Association, the American Anthropological Association, and the American Medical Association, as well as progressive thinkers like Hannah Arendt and Mohandas Gandhi—all for their own reasons—also rejected key ideas within the emerging human rights concept. This opposition has had lasting effects on the modern international human rights concept. But because of how the human rights concept is usually defined (and the a priori assumptions that lie within), these influential social struggles and conflicts over human rights have, to date, received very little notice (see Roberts, forthcoming).

This, however, is not at all to argue that a conflict perspective is the only appropriate approach to human rights. As Dahrendorf says, "We need for the explanation of sociological problems both the equilibrium and the conflict models of society; and it may well be that, in a philosophical sense, society has two faces of equal reality: one of stability, harmony, and consensus and one of change, conflict, and constraint" (1958, 127). Although conflict, opposition, and resistance should always be expected in the empirical field of human rights, over time, the outcomes of such struggles can become integrated into the social structures, institutions, practices, laws, and ideas that define a social order and hold it together. The very relationships that were once contested and opposed, over time may become accepted and naturalized (or, in rights parlance, self-evident, inherent, fundamental, and natural).

A sociological lens used to study the process in which social struggles transcend their existence as social action and become a structural entity known as "human rights" must be able to account for what keeps a society together and what moves it forward. It must therefore be able to account for cyclical processes of conflict and order, stasis and transformation, social struggles, and the naturalization of social relationships.

A SOCIOLOGICAL FRAMEWORK

The nebulous and indistinct nature of human rights presents a number of difficulties for their sociological study. But a number of the core issues that have emerged in the subfield of the sociology of law help to illuminate the disciplinary tensions, fault lines, and boundaries within which a sociological framework for the study of human rights must operate. The issues discussed in this chapter certainly are not the only relevant ones. They are, however, central concerns that sociologists interested in studying human rights cannot ignore. As mentioned above, the sociological idea that human rights are statements of social relationships represents a broad analytic orientation. It is a conceptual starting point, an analytic framework for their study that is grounded in sociological ideas as old as the discipline.

A sociological conception of human rights is a "thin" conception purposely devoid of the typical substantive and normative claims associated with human rights (e.g., which categories of rights are "core," whether positive rights are more "real" than natural rights, and so forth). It does not claim to know whether human rights exist and operate at a global, local, or national level, and it leaves open the possibility that human rights operate through processes of both conflict and consensus. It therefore allows researchers to answer such questions through empirical study rather than to assume them away in the definition.

The one issue not yet settled is how to deal with the inherent normativity of human rights. As soon as a definition is offered for what a human right is, the normativity problem discussed in problem #1 presents itself in full force. This is true when defining any social concept. Selecting any single definition over others is always a normative move that has political implications and social consequences. In this sociological framework, though, it is important to note that the normativity does not reside within the human rights concept (where it generally resides in scholarship). Implicit within such an approach is the acknowledgment that human rights, if implemented, have the potential to reshape (or solidify) existing social configurations. As such, human rights can be agents of sweeping change by extending recognition to new categories of social actors. Conversely, they can also be the servants of the status quo by transferring older social hierarchies into the language and structures of human rights. Indeed, within this framework human rights are not inherently good or bad. As representations of social relationships, they have been used to justify bringing an end to Jim Crow and colonialism. Ironically, they have also been used to support the continuance of Jim Crow and colonialism (Roberts, forthcoming). This is already a dramatic departure from the typical normative-heavy understanding of human rights. Human rights are certainly important causal forces. But how, where, and the extent to which they do their work are all empirical, not normative, questions.

The normative component that exists within this sociological framework resides within the idea of social relationships. The importance of social relationships, social embeddedness, and the individual's existence as a social being is taken as a given in sociology. This is what makes the discipline unique and its conception of human rights sociological and not something else. Within this normative, sociological framework that views human rights as statements of social relationships, unbiased, objective, empirical research can take place.

The sociological canon and the past debates within the sociology of law provide much guidance for those who wish to study the underlying sociality that inheres within rights. As a subfield, however, the sociology of human rights is not simply a lesser subunit of the sociology of law. For one, what counts as human rights is broader than even the broadest articulations of what "the law" is. But neither is it merely a diffuse or indistinct topic of study within the broader discipline. So if the sociology of human rights is worthy of being its own subfield, those who occupy this space must embrace the shared questions and burdens of the greater discipline while simultaneously contributing distinct modes of inquiry and categories of knowledge that are not otherwise possible.

This process is not free from conflict. As the debates that helped to define the sociology of the law illustrate, the development of new knowledge will at times challenge prevailing orthodoxies, stir new debates, and redefine the contours of accepted thought and practice. And this process will move the entire discipline along.

Already, the nascent subfield promises to resituate some of the assumed antinomic relationships between fact and value and order and conflict, for example. Each of these two dichotomies exists and operates not to the exclusion of the other but as a necessary and essential component of what makes human rights what they are. Within the present framework these quarrelling categories are now housed within the same analytic quarters to do their work together. So rather than replicating the intellectual divisions that are perhaps no longer as deep or as impassable as they once were, this framework for studying human rights aims to be an analytic counterpart to the reality it attempts to understand.

The new research techniques, innovative modes of thought, and intellectual relationships that will continue to emerge within this new area of study, however, are not exclusive to the field of human rights. The law and its sociological study exist within a very similar contextual space as human rights. By "sociologizing" human rights, the concept and its study become a new conceptual space for intra-disciplinary dialogue and debate.

As with all research programs, this framework is not in any way a final statement. Nor is it the only possible sociological approach. It is one among many possible others. This approach represents a particularized orientation for studying rights that other scholars can hopefully use for their own research while contributing their own insights, helping to refine it along the way. Human rights formation is an ongoing process—as new issues emerge and the parameters of existing social relationships inevitably shift, so too must the various social meanings of the human rights concept, as well as the various ways of studying it.

Chapter Ten

Religion

David V. Brewington

The sociology of religion poses a wide variety of questions about human rights. Here I focus on four families of questions:

1. What are the sociological foundations of human rights?
2. What is religion's status regarding violations of human rights?
3. How do religious and political institutions interact with respect to rights?
4. What is religious freedom's status as a human right?

These basic questions serve as an entry point into understanding how the sociology of religion addresses issues surrounding human rights. I elaborate on each question by discussing first the substantive question and then the level of reality or realities to which the question pertains and the social structures, actors, institutions, and processes relevant to it.

The most fundamental question the sociology of religion asks regarding human rights concerns its foundations. How, why, and where do human rights develop in history as idea and practice? What sociological factors play roles in this development? These questions recognize that human rights, like any other idea and practice, are not innate to the human condition. Human rights have a history situated in time, place, social structure, process, actor, and institution. Does religion play a role in this history?

A second important question the sociology of religion poses concerning human rights is how religion is involved in human rights violations. This question has two poles: Does religion as an institution have a role in advocating for human rights, and does it have a role in violations of human rights? Why, how, and when do religious actors, be they nation-states, organizations, or individuals, play a role in actions for human rights or violations of rights of humans?

Religion as an institution interacts with political institutions. At times this interaction directly concerns human rights practices and ideas. What shape does this interaction take? Do political institutions violate religious practices?

108 DAVID V. BREWINGTON

Do religious institutions and organizations interact with political institutions to bolster or minimize human rights practice?

Finally, the practice of religion and conscience is recognized as a fundamental human right in both international law and many national constitutions. What is religious liberty's status, then? What can we say about kinds and levels of religious-liberty violations? Where and when do they take place? What do religious organizations do in response to violations? What do they do to prevent violations? These questions will form this chapter's basis.

ORIGINS, ADVOCATES, VIOLATIONS, AND FRAMES

How has the sociology of religion accounted for origins of human rights? There are two senses in which religion as an institution is implicated in human rights foundations. The first sense is how, historically, human rights come to be in the first place, while the second sense is how human rights practices and ideals are disseminated.

SECULARIZATION AND HUMAN RIGHTS: A FOUNDATIONAL ACCOUNT

Sociologist of religion William Garrett (2001) provides an account of the origins of religious liberty and human rights and identifies secularization as the process responsible. Secularization, in simplest terms, is a decline of religious authority (Chaves 1994) through time. Garrett locates the beginning of secularization in institutional differentiation during the Papal Revolution of the eleventh to thirteenth centuries. Prior to this period, religious and political bodies were one and the same. This was the case in Europe with the Holy Roman emperor and also under William the Conqueror in Normandy and the English Isles.

In the mid eleventh century, Pope Gregory VII began to assert the power of God over the emperor's secular power in selecting churchmen for church offices. Known as the lay investiture, the pope felt that secular powers were exerting too much authority over the church, raising questions of religious integrity. Only God and his agents on earth should have the power to appoint men to church offices.

For Garrett this created an interesting problem for the papacy. How did a pope establish a novel claim to authority "when he lacked both an army and customary practice to lend credibility to his innovations" (2001, 295)? The answer is that the pope turned to legal authority, and this unleashed 150 years of research, development, and codification of canon law through a revival of Roman law and Stoic natural law. This extended act of legal codification for Garrett is the big bang of Western secularization because it "transformed the church into a corporation" (2001, 295), a body unto itself, and in turn created the need for the political body to do the same. Thus, in a dialectic of legal corporatizing, religious and political institutions of the West devolve out of each other as separate bodies.

Though much legal innovation occurred in the intervening centuries, what is important for Garrett as the second great movement of secularization is that the lawyers and scholars working out secular rules and laws endeavored to develop secularized legal foundations without resorting to religious grounds for political institutions. Substantively they were not successful, but they did succeed in convincing later scholars that nonreligious institutions needed to be grounded in secular rather than religious foundational theories. This secular foundational thrust culminated in the US colonies' specific solutions to issues of church and state: human rights law emerged as a wall forbidding the state to intervene in religious issues.

Garrett (2001, 322–327) finds the first appeals to unlimited guarantee of freedom of religion and conscience with Roger Williams and the settlement he founded in Rhode Island and with the Levellers serving in Oliver Cromwell's New Model Army, both in the 1640s, as well as with Isaac Backus, a Baptist minister who emerged out of the first Great Awakening in the colonies in the 1770s. Each of these developed understandings of religious rights in the face of "a similar set of religiously repressive social conditions" through distinctively religious understandings of an individual's capacities and duties to conscience. For Williams, it was only through a deeply free conscience that individuals could come to a right understanding of the Christian god. The Levellers came to their understanding of human rights through a belief that the Christian god granted each person an ownership of his or her own person. From this ownership all other rights were derived. Backus derived his rights framework from the idea that "all persons are born equally free and independent" (Garrett 2001, 327).

The religious origins of each of these early enunciations of comprehensive human rights derived from the sacred origins of individuals and were born in religious repression. Whereas the Levellers' ideas in the United Kingdom did not survive the demise of the movement, by Garrett's account the religious environment in the United States afforded the ideas of Williams and Backus a means of fermentation and dissemination to the masses. Baptist and Separatist sects were bursting at the seams with new converts after the Great Awakening of the 1730s and 1740s, and their clergy preached religious and other freedoms borne of their own religious persecution. This created a mass appeal for rights discourse that resonated later with Thomas Jefferson's more Lockean natural rights theories of equality and inalienable rights (Garrett 2001, 329).

The religious reasoning behind the American human rights tradition and political reasoning behind the natural law tradition found sufficient expression in the American context to effect resolution of what Garrett (2001, 330) regards as a significant sociological problem: how to build a secular state and keep it out of the business of religion while simultaneously keeping religion out of the business of the state. Religious reasoning behind freedom of conscience defined sacredness as a property of the human individual deriving directly from Christian divinity, while political reasoning defined the state as a secular entity divorced of religious foundations and connections. These lines of reasoning converged in the US Bill of Rights, legally institutionalizing human rights and serving as an

110 David V. Brewington

institutional model for human rights and religious liberty in subsequent constitutions and international instruments (see Gill 2008).

Religions as Carriers of Human Rights

Garrett's account provides a view of human rights foundations from a sociology-of-religion perspective. In addition to its importance in the foundation of human rights, religion has also been a prominent carrier of human rights ideas and practices. The origins of numerous transnational human rights advocacy campaigns can be traced to religious voices, and religiously minded individuals and religious organizations have often sustained these movements. An incomplete list of religious bodies and their campaigns includes, in the nineteenth century, the Quakers, Methodists, Unitarians, and Presbyterians' work in the antislavery movement in America and the United Kingdom (Keck and Sikkink 1998, 41–51; Chabbott 1999, 228; Rabben 2002, 8–12); the Woman's Christian Temperance Movement's involvement in the women's suffrage movement (Keck and Sikkink 1998, 54; Berkovitch 1999); the Calvinist Henry Dunant's campaign leading to the Geneva Conventions and the International Society of the Red Cross/Crescent (ICRC 1998; Finnemore 1999); and Christian missionaries' anti-foot-binding movement in China (Keck and Sikkink 1998, 59–66). In the twentieth century we see Protestant organizations and the Catholic Church pushing for the inclusion of human rights in the UN Charter and in the drafting of the Universal Declaration of Human Rights (UDHR) (Traer 1991, 173–185); the Catholic Church's efforts to highlight human rights atrocities in Chile under Augusto Pinochet and in East Timor under Suharto (Risse 2000, 193–195); the Catholic group Pax Romana and the Quaker UN Office advocating at the United Nations for the inclusion of conscientious objection as a human right (Hovey 1997); and Catholics and Protestants as one segment of the Jubilee 2000 movement to eliminate third-world debt (Lechner 2005).

It is evident from this list that religious organizations and individuals are tied to the human rights paradigm's development. But religion has not always been on the side of human rights.

Religious Violations of Human Rights?

While religious actors and social processes involving religion are foundational to human rights, examples exist of religion not acting as a human rights advocate. The actions of nineteen al-Qaeda hijackers on September 11, 2001, constitute the most sensational example of religious actors violating human rights in recent memory. Other less astounding examples abound. Members of the People's Temple, a new religious movement (NRM), murdered children

RELIGION 111

as part of a mass suicide (Hall 1987). Government authorities intervene when NRM leaders are accused of child molestation, which occurred with the People's Temple in the 1970s and the Branch Davidians in the 1990s (Hall 1987; Hall, Schuyler, and Trinh 2000).

Lest we think that human rights violations are the product of peripheral organizations, we should consider more mainstream religions and their roles in human rights abuses. The ongoing child-molestation claims made by Catholic parishioners against the Catholic Church (Berry 1992; Burkett and Bruni 1993; Hidalgo 2007; Shupe 1998; Shupe 2007) point to clear violations of children's rights. The advocacy activities of conservative evangelical Protestant organizations in pursuing antiabortion and "natural" marriage legislation are framed by some as violations of reproductive rights and civil liberties. It is possible that Hindus of the untouchable caste would regard their status by birth as a violation of their rights.

These examples illustrate that religion and its actors can be violators as much as they can be advocates of human rights. The same religious organization can utilize organizational capacities, theological precepts, and moral teachings to promote human rights and at the same time violate human rights. Sociologists of religion can greatly expand their research programs by examining human rights as a frame of reference.

How Do Religious and Political Institutions Interact?

The interaction of political and religious institutions is fundamental to considerations of human rights. A frequent subject for the sociology of religion is interaction of religion and state, which often concerns freedom of religious believers to practice their faith, especially where minority religions are concerned. It is instructive to reflect on how the secularization process can be utilized to understand how a state might be expected to treat religion within its territories. Martin (1978) begins with the historical frame in which a society enters secularization. This frame structures society's subsequent history such that a society's path from secularization and subsequent treatment of religion within its borders are dependent on the frame through which it enters secularization.

Martin strongly associates religious pluralism with democratic pluralism and religious monopoly with strong secularism, while considering the impact of the size of religious minorities. The nature of specific religions also plays a role. Catholicism is associated with strong political power in the monopoly situation, and in the minority situation Catholics stress their beliefs' universal aspects. Protestants are inclined toward individual achievement, inhibiting organic formations in both majority and minority situations. Martin associates Protestantism with intrinsic pluralism and democracy—salvation for all tends to produce tolerance, if unintentionally.

The path through which a state enters secularization frames the relationship between religion and state. We can see examples of this path dependence in

112   DAVID V. BREWINGTON

how national legal systems address religious issues. In France in 2010, the full-face veil was banned in public places (Ajrouch 2007; Haddad 2007; Read 2007; Wallerstein 2005b). Religious and immigration histories of the United States and France shape their responses to the veil (Ajrouch 2007; Read 2007).

NRMs are also the subject of much legal scrutiny. Scientology has encountered hostile legal systems in much of the West, including the United States, Germany, France, Spain, Canada, Belgium, Denmark, Greece, Ireland, Italy, and others. Typically the legal cases involving Scientology concern whether it should be designated as a religious organization and accrue benefits from that status, including tax exemptions. The German state went so far as to put Scientology on its list of extremist groups, which also includes neo-Nazi factions (Seiwert 1999; Seiwert 2003; Simon 2010; Taylor 2003).

Religion-state interactions do not always surround human rights conflicts. In the United States, a consortium of religious organizations joined together with allies in Congress to send the International Religious Freedom Act to President Bill Clinton in 1998. The bill was signed into law and mandated that religious freedom become one of the criteria through which the US State Department evaluates other states (Farr et al. 2009; Fore 2002; Gunn 2000; Mousin 2003; Pastor 2005; Wales 2002).

While the sociology of religion provides a contextual frame for understanding these controversies (i.e., that of Martin 1978), very seldom does sociology of religion address these issues through human rights frames. As before, opportunities for sociology of religion to consider these issues in human rights contexts are considerable.

RELIGIOUS FREEDOM AS A HUMAN RIGHT

Religious freedom is codified in the UDHR as follows: "Everyone has the right to freedom of thought, conscience and religion; this right includes freedom to change his religion or belief, and freedom, either alone or in community with others and in public or private, to manifest his religion or belief in teaching, practice, worship and observance" (UN 1948). Based on recent research by the PEW Forum on Religion and Public Life (2009), only 7 countries out of the 198 they examined, or 4 percent, had no constitutional protection for religious freedom. At the same time, the PEW report finds that for the 191 national constitutions that provide some level of protection of freedom of religion, 146 (74 percent) also include language that appears "to qualify or substantially contradict the concept of 'religious freedom'" (2009, 54). Only forty-four nations (22 percent) do not have contradictory or qualifying language circumscribing religious freedom. According to PEW's Government Restrictions Index, nearly 22 percent of all countries have high levels of restrictions, including China, Iran, and Saudi Arabia. Moderate levels of restriction are found in 18.2 percent of countries, including Ethiopia, France, Mexico, and Venezuela. More than 60 percent of states impose low levels of restrictions, such as Costa Rica, Poland, and Senegal.

The national government of 141 countries (71 percent) either fully respects religious freedom in practice or generally respects religious freedom in practice with exceptions in some locations. National governments in fifty-nine countries (29 percent) do not respect religious freedom in practice generally or at all. Countries in this latter category tend to be in the Middle East and North Africa or Asia-Pacific. However, European nations are not exemplars in religious freedom. Former communist countries tend to favor one state-recognized religion, and western European countries "have laws aimed at protecting citizens from what the government considers dangerous cults or sects" (PEW 2009, 15).

While these national participation measures are important, they omit a piece of the religious-freedom story. This is the realm of not-for-profit advocacy organizations that work within national and international jurisdictions to call attention to religious-freedom issues. The PEW Research Center is a recent organization in a long tradition. Two early formal human rights international nongovernmental organizations (INGOs) dedicated to religious liberty are the International Religious Liberty Association, founded in 1893, and the International Association for Religious Freedom, founded in 1900.

Scholarly research on religious-liberty INGOs is unfortunately scant, but some of it provides an interesting comparison with other types of human rights advocacy. Religious-liberty INGOs are far more likely to be religious than all other human rights INGOs (Brewington 2005). They are less likely to have consultative status with the United Nations than INGOs for children's, women's, or people's rights. In absolute numbers, there were far fewer religious-liberty INGOs than children's, women's, or people's rights INGOs as of 1994 (Brewington 2005). Despite being one of the first formally organized human rights areas, religious liberty is less institutionalized in the UN system, the size of the population is relatively smaller than "younger" rights, and these organizations are much more likely to have religious origins than all other human rights INGOs. Religious-rights advocates are of predominantly three types: secular with a universalistic approach (freedom of religion is advocated for all humans), religious with a universalistic approach, and religious with a particularistic approach (freedom of religion is advanced for a particular faith) (Brewington 2011). The latter type of human rights organization is fairly rare in human rights advocacy. These early findings suggest some puzzles to which scholars of the sociology of religion and globalization need to pay more attention (see Brewington 2011).

Levels of Reality, Social Structures, Actors, Institutions, and Processes

Multiple levels of reality are implicated in questions that sociology of religion asks of human rights. Much of the focus is on national levels, however, and historically these questions have been asked of specific national contexts—the United States and western European states. There are two main reasons for this. First, sociology as a discipline and sociology of religion as a subdiscipline are

114 DAVID V. BREWINGTON

historically embedded in the West. The mythic founders in sociology—Weber, Marx, Durkheim, and Simmel—were all interested in religious questions as they observed the social, structural, and cultural changes around them in the context of the emergence of the modern era in Europe and the United States. When these and later authors referred to society, they were typically conflating US and European national societies, which became the default subject of study. Second, national governments are the actors held "responsible" for the rights of the people living within their territorial boundaries. Constitutional protections of rights are extended by states to the inhabitants of their national territories.

There are many relevant social structures at play in approaches that sociology of religion takes toward human rights. In most studies, the individual and the state are the most relevant actors. The individual, who possesses rights, and the state, as the entity that both protects and violates rights of its residents, are taken for granted by most sociologists and sociologists of religion as involved actors. Group or collective rights are also implicated in how sociologists of religion address human rights. By virtue of its being religious community, a group sometimes asserts rights as necessary for it to practice its faith. Proselytism, or an active effort to change a person's faith, is one practice that is often viewed as a violation of a religious group's collective rights. At the same time, most international human rights instruments provide for the right to conversion—to change one's belief. Assertions of collective rights and individual rights, especially regarding religious rights, can be quite controversial (Thomas 2004; Thomas 2001).

Religion as an institution is also implicated in the answers put forth by sociologists of religion to questions outlined above. A corollary is that religion as an institution is one among many institutions at play in national society. With respect to human rights, religion as an institution especially interacts with the national polity—the system of government, laws, and norms enacted within a specified territory.

Religious organizations, comprised of practitioners or political advocates, constitute actors of interest in the sociologist of religion's research. These actors are worshipers' organizations, secular or religious NGOs advocating for religious liberty, or religious NGOs advocating for human rights in general. International governmental organizations, especially the United Nations, are the target of much human rights advocacy.

The global level of reality is increasingly of interest to sociologists of religion studying human rights. Global processes, including the accelerating flows of information, ideas, norms, models, people, and materials, structure the phenomena of human rights of interest to sociologists of religion.

WHAT CAN THE HUMAN RIGHTS PARADIGM LEARN FROM WORK IN SOCIOLOGY OF RELIGION?

The sociological study of religion in general and its specific analysis of human rights in particular do offer some important lessons for studying human rights.

The first lesson concerns the ambivalent disposition of religion toward human rights. Religious actors and processes can be a catalyst simultaneously for the expansion of the human rights paradigm and for the promotion of human rights violators. This is not to say that these occur concurrently, but through history one religious actor may be a human rights advocate in one context and complicit in violations in another.

The philosopher Jacque Maritain (1952, 110–111), one of the principle architects of the UDHR, said that human rights ideology was indeed like a civic or secular religion. Others, in the tradition of Émile Durkheim, have examined human rights as a "cult of the individual" (Elliott 2007, 2008). We do not have to go as far as these scholars and claim that human rights ideology has religious properties, but the religious dimensions of human rights in its foundations and implementations suggest that the sociologist of religion should have several points of advice for scholars of human rights. Religion, as a realm of texts and discourse, is subject to the contexts in which it is interpreted, and interpretation is mutable. Human rights scholars should be sensitive to and understand how human rights ideology changes over time and is interpreted contextually.

A second offering from scholars of the sociology of religion would be that human rights scholars should be sensitive to the fact that human rights ideology is contested, as is religion, precisely because it is mutable in its interpretations, especially in an era of globalization (Beyer 2001; Beyer 2006; Robertson 1992). One example concerns Islamic members of the UN Human Rights Commission who have put forward resolutions seeking to define criticism of religion as a violation of practitioners' rights. Critics immediately point out that this is itself a violation of the right to free speech. Neoinstitutional sociological approaches to human rights point out that conflicting claims are expected with the global expansion of human rights (Elliott 2008; Elliott 2007; W. H. Thomas 2004; J. Thomas 2001): rights claims can overlap in ways that produce controversy and contestation.

A final offering that sociologists of religion would make to scholars of human rights is to remind them that however universal human rights might seem, they are in fact products of particular histories. While it would be simplistic to label the current conception of human rights as "Western," there is still truth to the claim, and interpreters of human rights do indeed criticize them as being of Western origin (Ishay 2004a).

Sociologist of religion and globalization Roland Robertson (1992) has captured much of these cautions in his work on globalization as a process whereby the particular becomes universal and the universal becomes particular. Simply put, human rights ideology is a particularistic product of a particular culture promulgated as a universal (i.e., as applying to all humans globally). This universal ideology is then received in particularistic ways—it is interpreted vis-à-vis the local context it is being situated within. While freedom of religion is conceived of as a universal human right, its local application is context specific. Thus, even while the US and French constitutions espouse freedom of religion as

116 DAVID V. BREWINGTON

a citizen's right, the historical relationship between religion and state conditions the practice and regulation of religious liberty. As we saw earlier in the French context, the full-face veil that some Muslim women wear has been banned in public spaces. This coheres with the French context in which religious symbols are not as welcomed in public life as in US contexts.

WHAT CAN THE SOCIOLOGY OF RELIGION LEARN FROM HUMAN RIGHTS SCHOLARSHIP?

The sociology of religion has much to learn from human rights scholarship. One branch of human rights scholarship approaches its subject matter from a neoinstitutional or world-polity approach (Boli and Thomas 1999; Lechner and Boli 2005; Powell and DiMaggio 1991; Thomas 1987). Simply put, neoinstitutional scholars take culture very seriously and promote a definition that goes deeper than conventional notions of culture. The environment in which social entities find themselves is filled with rules, norms, and models. Entities in this environment do not act; they enact. These rules, norms, and models are the culture to which neoinstitutionalists pay attention because they structure what and how entities enact within a given environment. Human rights scholars in this tradition would interpret the fact that 96 percent of all national constitutions have some stated protection for religious liberty as suggesting that they are enacting globally accessible norms that imply there better be at least some lip-service to religious freedom.

A popular approach in sociology of religion in the last twenty to twenty-five years is that of the rational-choice tradition, which is sensitive to the manner in which actors behave in their own self-interest. While interest maximization is undoubtedly a factor, it leaves out a great deal of sociologically interesting material to which neoinstitutional approaches are sensitive. From where did the idea of religious liberty come? From where do the individual's preferences for one religion over another come? In short, if sociologists of religion pay attention chiefly to interest maximization, they miss capturing key factors in their explanations of religious phenomena.

Sociology of religion can also learn from human rights scholars to pay more attention to issues of globalization. While a number of sociologists of religion, such as Robertson, Peter Beyer, and Jose Casanova, certainly take the global level seriously, it seems that human rights scholars are ahead in studying how globalization as a process is important to human rights study. Neoinstitutional scholars are among those who study human rights as a global process, but international relations scholars such as Keck and Sikkink (1998), Hafner-Burton and Tsutsui (2005), and Florini et al. (2000) were also at the forefront in studying human rights advocates in global contexts.

What Is the Future?

Where should the sociology of religion go in researching human rights? My hope, as a scholar of religion, human rights, and globalization, is that the sociology of religion will expand its understanding of human rights by taking the global level of reality more seriously and that it will feed other subdisciplines (e.g., social movements, organizations) by fleshing out the special nature of religion with respect to human rights: it is a progenitor of human rights but can be both advocate and violator of them. In light of what sociologists of religion might advise human rights scholars, it is my hope that the human rights paradigm will explore itself reflexively and understand that it is itself a source of ongoing controversy.

CHAPTER ELEVEN

ECONOMIC SOCIOLOGY

Clarence Y. H. Lo

The field of economic sociology examines how economic institutions and elites operate in the global context and what social inequalities are produced thereby. Economic sociology (otherwise known as the field of economy and society) focuses on a critique of models of rational self-interest, commonly used to explain economic phenomena. To many in the discipline of economics, rational self-interest models of microeconomic behavior provide a workable blueprint of an economy that can produce growth and efficiency without coercion, thereby justifying free markets and private, for-profit ownership of businesses (Friedman 1962). The field of economic sociology advocates an alternate vision, which has insisted that rational self-interest models ignore cultural and social factors that can be powerful explanations of economic life. With its view of economic, cultural, and social factors, economic sociology is well positioned to inform knowledge of human rights

THEORETICAL CRITIQUES OF MARKETS IN ECONOMIC SOCIOLOGY

In its critique of market individualism, economic sociology draws insights from organizational theory, which says that businesses in reality do not rationally choose the best policy from the available options. Rather, firms "satisfice" (Simon 1947), picking the first satisfactory solution. Searching for more information to find a better solution is avoided, since it entails significant costs for the firm. What is defined as "satisfactory" is socially and culturally determined, highly variable and context dependent, and thus a fitting subject for sociologists.

The New Institutionalism (Powell and DiMaggio 1991), which analyzes economies as social institutions, also goes beyond rational optimalization as an explanation and argues that cultural processes lead organizations and their policies to resemble each other. Instead of pursuing optimally effective policies, organizations develop policies as rituals or because of their

ECONOMIC SOCIOLOGY 119

symbolic dimensions and in relation to professional groups or more powerful or esteemed organizations.

Economic sociologists have pointed to other limitations of conceptualizing the economy as propertied individual actors maximizing self-interest. Even when individual decision-making is the unit to be analyzed, many economic sociologists argue that trust, sympathy, and morality are the lynchpins of economic life, a prerequisite before rational self-interest can begin to function—a perspective shared by no one other than Adam Smith ([2002] 1759). Although individual ownership of physical and money capital was fundamental to industrial society, Bourdieu (1984) argues that different forms of capital, social capital and cultural capital, are now important in the perpetuation of class position. Economic sociologists have examined the varied forms of cultural capital for social classes in different contexts (Lamont 2000).

Network analysts have contributed to economic sociology by adopting as their unit of analysis not individual maximizers but rather social relations, such as patterns of networks, to explain phenomena, for instance, successful job searches (Granovetter 1973). In technical and bureaucratic settings, the right to participate in decisions is contested by networks of actors that form to gain participation on a particular issue. In government, consultations with technical officials through such networks develop as an alternative to the intervention of elected representatives (Callon, Lascoumes, and Barthe 2009). Putnam (2000) argues, following Tocqueville's (1960 [1835]) analysis of nineteenth-century America, that the social relations of civic life are the foundation of American prosperity. In short, economic activity is best studied not as a rational choice abstracted from society but rather as action embedded in social relations, institutions, and culture (Polanyi 1944).

Thus, economic sociologists have pointed out that market models have been conceptually limited and have constructed inadequate explanations ignoring sociocultural factors. These same weaknesses, as will be evident below, have led economic sociologists to raise significant questions about the ability of markets to produce efficiently, yield economic growth, and provide for the well-being of workers, consumers, and society. Economic sociology has provided the values, standards, evaluative processes, and underlying causal factors by which market behavior and its outcomes have been judged and can be further criticized.

ECONOMIC SOCIOLOGY'S FINDINGS

Much of economic sociology casts doubt on the notion that market forces alone are capable of guiding the economy, let alone ordering society. Leading scholars in the field of economy and society have demonstrated that active governance and policy-making, by political leaders and economic elites, have been crucial factors of economic life since the beginning of the Industrial Revolution (Hobsbawm 1962; Krugman 2007).

120 CLARENCE Y. H. LO

Scholarship in the field of economy and society has demonstrated that the unparalleled prosperity after World War II in the United States and the rest of the capitalist world has been the result not of free markets but rather of government intervention. In the United States, the continuation of the New Deal from the 1930s brought about an acceptance of Keynesian fiscal policy (Lekachman 1966). In Europe, government takeovers of some industries led to a mixed economy, social democracy, and an elaborated welfare state. Labor unions were an integral part of the postwar boom, giving their blessing to technical advances in productivity in the United States and holding formal power on industry councils ("codetermination") in Germany, Sweden, and other western European nations (Hollingsworth et al 1994).

However, after 1973, higher oil prices destabilized global financial flows, as inflation disrupted Keynesian fiscal policy. Stagnant standards of living and youth unemployment upset political establishments, as did the earlier rise of the civil rights, antiwar, students', and women's movements around the world, complicating the task of legitimizing governments and their economic policies (Mishra 1984).

The field of economic sociology has analyzed the origins and implementation of, and the opposition to, the governmental market-privatization policies, which were the reaction to the economic turmoil after 1973. Deregulating airlines and banking, reducing nondefense spending, turning over government functions of prisons and education to private corporations, weakening environmental and consumer regulations, and other free market policies were promulgated by business interest groups and right-wing political parties around 1980. Among the most prominent implementers of such policies were US President Ronald Reagan and Prime Minister Margaret Thatcher in England (Harvey 2005).

The implementation of market privatization (also known as neoliberalism, or the Washington Consensus) necessitated government budget and service cutbacks, which in turn required changes in political organizations, processes, and rules, such as executive centralization (Steinmo, Thelen, and Longstreth 1992). Similar policies establishing markets and private business ownership were adopted by the Augusto Pinochet regime in Chile and elsewhere in Latin America (Centeno and Cohen 2010), as well as in the former Soviet Union and in Eastern Europe (Lo 2008). Such regimes increased economic inequalities between workers and those who managed large businesses and owned significant blocks of stock. For workers and retirees, neoliberal policies disrupted the security and subsidies that had offered some protection against economic adversities (Esping-Andersen 1999), thereby negatively affecting human rights.

Although market privatization has led to some signs of prosperity, such as increases in stock prices, asset values, and high-end consumption, critics have pointed out that such signs are indicative of speculative bubbles, which in the past have invariably burst (Kindleberger and Alibler 2005), with disastrous results for the human rights of populations. A prime example was the Tulip mania, in which bourgeois families spent huge sums for imported tulip bulbs that later collapsed in value in 1637. Later bubbles included the Roaring Twenties,

Economic Sociology 121

leading to the Great Depression. In the 1970s and 1980s, the widespread marketing of high-yield ("junk") bonds, pioneered by Michael Milkin and the firm Drexel Burnham Lambert, financed a wave of corporate mergers and takeovers. The junk-bond boom and bust resulted in high fees and profits for Wall Street firms but layoffs and plant closings as well. In Harrison and Bluestone's (1988) words, the "casino society" had produced a lack of productive investments that had deindustrialized the United States (Perrucci and Perrucci 2009), putting at risk the basic rights of populations.

Comparative historical analysis has been the methodology of choice for economic sociologists. The work of Esping-Andersen (1999) on different types of welfare states is cross-national quantitative research. The work of Skocpol (1992) is based on carefully documented studies comparing leading cases across time and key nations. The latest work by economic sociologists on the 2008 financial meltdown, collected in *Markets on Trial: The Economic Sociology of the U.S. Financial Crisis* (Lounsbury and Hirsch 2010), effectively uses a case-study methodology to argue that the 2008 crisis can be understood only if the economy is seen not as an effectively functioning free market but rather as a social institution that became a risky gamble because of inadequate government regulation.

This latest work in economic sociology thus continues the theoretical and practical critique of free markets. Theoretically, the market is not seen as intrinsically rational but rather as premised on social characteristics such as confidence (Swedberg 2010). The mortgage-securities markets that collapsed in 2008 were not free of government but rather were creatures of government entities like Fannie Mae that had greatly expanded housing-mortgage lending (Fligstein and Goldstein 2010). Government policy such as the Graham Leach Bliley Act of 1999 created a plethora of nonbank institutions that were minimally regulated and hence could rapidly increase subprime loans and repackage them as sound investments (Campbell 2010). Social institutions, financial and regulatory, sustained a perception that the mortgage markets could be trusted to rationally handle any risk that arose.

Contributions of Economic Sociology to Historical Analysis of Human Rights

The field of economic sociology, aided by its use of historical comparative methodology, seeks to comprehend how various types of human rights have been advanced in different economic formations in historical periods throughout world history.

Philosophers and theorists of human rights, such as the French Enlightenment thinkers and Immanuel Kant, have emphasized the universal nature of rights across all humanity, regardless of national borders or the stage of societal development. Economic sociology has added the specificity of a historical and practical dimension to our understanding of human rights. The context of economic life at

122   CLARENCE Y. H. LO

a particular place in time affects which rights are salient and how those rights are conceptualized. Sociologists have generated knowledge about the economic contexts from which specific rights are articulated, thereby contributing to grounded theorizing about human rights.

Economic sociology directly relates key historical developments of commerce, industry, and modernization to transformations in the thinking about human rights, as well as the actualization of specific rights in constitutions and laws and in everyday economic practice and norms. Many scholars have contributed to the analysis of the historical construction of rights from the beginning of early modern Europe.

Karl Polanyi (1944) argued that with the first stirrings of the commercial transformation of the English countryside, populations struggled to have their traditional statuses and rights preserved and recognized. T. H. Marshall (1964) argued that the Industrial Revolution in the nineteenth century had gradually but inextricably led to the progressive winning of different types of rights. Civil rights, such as free speech and the right to security of person and property against despotic governments, were won by democratic revolutions, such as in the United States in 1776 and France in 1789. Political rights (expanding voting to include middle-class men and then most other male citizens) occurred in the late nineteenth century. By the first half of the twentieth century, political rights were being used in elections to win economic and social rights, including accident, unemployment, and old-age insurance. These gains led to campaigns for extension of the right to vote to women and broadening the conceptualization of social and economic rights to include better housing, free public education, and health care.

In the context of American prosperity between the end of World War II through 1973, the increasing importance of Marshall's socioeconomic rights figures prominently in a key philosophical text of the time on equality and rights, John Rawls's A *Theory of Justice* (1971). Rawls emphasized the importance of individual liberty, the civil rights about which Marshall wrote. Rawls also argued that social arrangements are just only insofar as the condition of the worst off is improved; Rawls thereby included Marshall's economic rights in his thinking about justice. When Rawls sketched a possible economic system that would be consistent with his principles of justice, the system was a social democracy, a society that was politically democratic with regulated, privately owned businesses and a public sector for investment in social programs, the type of society in Europe that economic sociologists were studying to counterpose against the free market-model.

The first oil-price spike of 1973, in the name of the rights of oil-producing nations, put the world, economic sociologists included, on notice that the global character of the economy shapes human rights, for better or worse. A robust literature on transnational corporations emerged. Wallerstein (1976) argued that the structure of the contemporary world-system could be traced back to the "modern" world-system of 1450. William Appleman Williams (1962) and his students critiqued US market policies such as free trade, the open door, and the consequent imposing of regimes by the United States on former Spanish colonies by demonstrating that such policies in the US sphere of influence violated the American principles of democracy and human rights, even though US presidents justified those policies with the rhetoric of American freedoms. Williams's analysis of US "imperial anticolonialism" foreshadowed the work of later scholars of the postcolonial condition (Hardt and Negri 2000). By the end of the twentieth century, there was an outpouring of academic writing on the issue of "globalism" and its relation to democratic and human rights (Held 2004).

As a result of the growing academic interest in global inequalities, scholars interested in economy and society have explored new definitions of human rights, apart from American conceptions of electoral democracy and business freedom, which would be more relevant to those in the impoverished Global South. Sen (1992) revisits Rawls's (1971) discussion of which rights in the constellation should be primary to focus on defining what kind of equality would be most important to address in the developing world. Sen argues that more fundamental than equalities of wealth and income are equalities in the capabilities of individuals to accomplish a variety of ends. Health-care rights and public-health measures are necessary to enable the population to work and go on to raise further issues of rights of livelihood. Sen enables us to better comprehend how campaigns for public health in developing areas are crucial for the realization of a range of human rights.

The globalization of the economy has led to human rights issues that have transcended not only geographic borders but the narrow borders of conceptualization of rights as economic rights for labor. Narrow issues of distribution of material goods have spilled over into new definitions of political and social rights demanded by the feminist, antiwar, environmental, and black-consciousness movements (Laclau and Mouffe 1985), which have raised economic issues of equality and sustainability in ways different from earlier trade unions and old left political parties.

Fraser and Honneth (2003) argue that a basic right is for groups to be positively recognized so that group members can participate in a full range of interactions, without barriers or stigmatization. To be accomplished, recognition must include participation in democratic institutions. The democratic elitism of the periodic election of leaders must be replaced with a deeper and more inclusive participatory democracy (Fung and Wright 2003).

Racial-justice, feminist, environmental, and other social movements have increased recognition and participation of subordinate groups around the world. Global social movements, exemplified by world social forums (Chase-Dunn and Reese 2010), global feminisms (Naples and Desai 2002), environmental justice movements, and the movement for climate justice, put new definitions of human rights squarely on the bargaining table. At the same time the advance of economic globalism challenges the centrality of the state, national politics, and the entire system of sovereignty that arose with the Treaty of Westphalia (1648), which ended the Thirty Years' War in Europe.

Fraser (2009) argues that with a globalized economy, issues of justice and human rights cannot be effectively handled by nation-states, which can only alter policies within their borders. The key questions include who the global actors are and what standards of justice should be applied. Global social movements have been, and will continue to be, active players in the ongoing process of defining human rights.

Thus, human rights are not solely and narrowly an issue of economic rights; human rights require participatory politics to form a collective will whereby com-munities of citizens engage in the processes of learning to implement human rights by changing the rules in institutions (Bowles and Gintis 1986). Human rights cannot only be gauged by the metrics of individual equality, for a fundamental human right is to determine public policies collectively. Levine (1999) argues for going beyond individual egalitarianism to advocate the value of democratic political rights used to cooperatively guide the sources of economic productivity in a society.

The recent work of Margaret Somers (2008) in *Genealogies of Citizenship* reprises previous historical investigations of economic sociologists and goes on to show how the themes that form the basis for research in the field of economic sociology— namely, the critique of markets and the establishment of the theoretical primacy of grounded societal institutions—can sharpen the conceptualization of human rights and citizenship rights. The development of market liberalism into a dominant ideology over the past 170 years has reduced the concept of rights to mere freedom from state intervention, making remaining rights contractual, activated only if individuals are successful in market exchanges in obtaining the resources needed to activate their rights.

For Somers, contemporary events provide searing episodes of how the practical and ideological primacy of the market can lead to the abridgements of citizenship and hence human rights. American conservatives have argued that rights to the good life should only be extended to those individuals who prove themselves worthy through participation in work and the labor market (the "responsibility crusade"); conversely, those individuals who are morally failures through their own free decision are undeserving (the "perversity thesis"). The poor and black residents of New Orleans, whose marginal participation in the economy afforded them neither means of transportation nor social respect, remained in the city as a shocking example of how basic human rights have been contractualized, afforded only to those who succeed in markets.

Somers argues for a fuller definition of citizenship as a basic human right that would be grounded not in market relations, as in neoliberalism, but rather in the social relations that economic sociologists see as more important than market relationships. For Somers, citizenship rights require social inclusion, the recognition of groups in society as worthy members of a community who, as Somers puts it, have the "right to have rights." Human rights, then, are fundamentally constituted by society and crucially depend on the strength of institutions in civil society as opposed to the state or the market.

REDEFINITION OF ECONOMIC SOCIOLOGY WITHIN A HUMAN RIGHTS PARADIGM

Economic sociology thus contributes to the human rights perspective by historicizing and specifying the particular human rights that have shaped economic life in the progression from an agrarian society, through mercantilism and the stages of the Industrial Revolution, to advanced capitalism and a global economy. Conversely, a human rights perspective can contribute to economic sociology by prompting research into how different ideals of human rights come to influence specific debates in economic policy, as well as the actual policies themselves.

Rearticulated concepts of human rights and standards of justice challenge some of the ideologies that justify inequalities, such as racial hierarchy, market exchange, and the sanctity of property rights enshrined in the modern corporation. Ideologies of racial domination, as Omi and Winant (1994) point out, are continually reformulated due to the stirrings of social movements. The collision of human rights principles and racial and ethnic hierarchy produces new hybrid forms of discourse characteristic of governance institutions in the age that Hardt and Negri (2000) characterize as postcolonial empire. Similarly, a human rights perspective can contribute to economic sociology by exploring the conflicts between human rights and the fundamentals of the capitalist economy, such as private property and markets. These conflicts result in changing temporary compromises or "fixes" that can be studied as Omi and Winant studied racial formations.

Equality and other human rights contend with property rights to form a series of compromises, among them the notion of "fairness." Fairness leads to reforms that are considerably less sweeping than a drive for full equality. Notions of fairness or "equity," rather than equality, exemplify the development of hybrid concepts of rights that may be found, for example, in global discussions where advocates of women's equality collided with those who sought to rearticulate inequalities.

Equality of rights and the economic condition for women has been advanced through the UN Convention on the Elimination of All Forms of Discrimination against Women (1979) and at UN-sponsored forums such as the Fourth World Conference on Women held in Beijing in 1995. There, representatives from areas with traditional religious views argued that universalistic definitions of equality need to be tempered with national customs as to what is proper. Full equality of educational and economic opportunity, so the argument went, was not realistic and should be replaced with equity as a more modest goal (Facio and Morgan 2009).

Human rights discourses, in addition to operating at the global level, also permeate local contexts. Human rights discourses constitute knowledge used in institutions such as the media, popular culture, law, and professional and academic disciplines (Powell and DiMaggio 1991). Elster (1992) establishes a theoretical framework that can be used to analyze how different concepts of equality and justice are applied in the knowledge, culture, and routines of specific institutions. As Glenn (2002) points out, the civil, political, and economic rights theorized by Marshall (1964) are contested and altered in their application to educational institutions and other forms of civic life in local communities.

The conflicts between human rights such as universal equality and contrary principles that support property rights and markets have produced hybrid concepts about equity and fairness in many institutions. In US federal courts, the hybridities between the class-based discourse of property rights and the popular discourse of economic rights were articulated in a series of legal compromises in the early twentieth century. The doctrines of court majorities responded to political debates couched in terms of long-standing American rights and new definitions of those rights stemming from the claims of social movements. Court decisions led to further commentary by politicians and social movements (Friedman 2002). The notion that the rights of small producers were violated by monopolistic agreements among large companies spawned political rhetoric, even more litigation, and eventually the legal doctrine of ruinous competition—that price cutting among producers could become cutthroat and hence destructive for the common person as well. Another legal doctrine of the time was the "rule of reason," articulated by justices such as Edward Douglass White, Oliver Wendell Holmes, and Louis Brandeis, who argued that the rights of small producers should not sweep away all trusts and all their restraints of trade; some restraints were reasonable and therefore permissible under the Sherman Antitrust Act (Hovenkamp 1991; Peritz 1996).

Legal discourses affect political speech in Congress and in presidential campaigns, such as the election of 1912 (Sklar 1988), and vice versa. New temporary resolutions of the tensions between two contrary grand principles, human rights and property rights, originate in one area of the public sphere and reverberate through others. Hybridities can begin in the discourse in one discipline, such as the law, and travel to spawn other hybridities in another discipline, such as political theory. The human rights perspective has given rise to major works in economic and political sociology that detail the legal, political, and regulatory consequences of conflicts between human versus business rights. The resulting regulations that were passed and administered were crucial for the rise of the large industrial corporation (Peritz 1996) and the development of a global economic system of advanced capitalism (Sassen 2006b).

As I argue in my new book (Lo, forthcoming), through a discourse interwoven with conflicting rights, Americans developed a sense of what was fair, or "equitable," on the market. Some argued that markets were fair; they just had to be left alone. Some argued that injustices of the market were so glaring that they could only be made fair through reform pushed through by government power. Such was the debate following the Great Recession of 2008.

New Possibilities for Economic Sociology and Human Rights Realization

The ebb and flow of hybrid rights and justice discourses has animated debates over economic reforms. Economic sociology that is focused on human rights can identify, analyze, legitimize, and promulgate new concepts of rights, thereby contributing to the success of reform. For example, many of the leading empirical works in the field of economic sociology have already sought, quite explicitly, to advance different types of human rights—democratic political and participatory rights (Etzioni 1988, 2009), economic security (Esping-Andersen 1999), women's rights (Walby 2009), individual opportunity (Giddens 1998), and social democracy.

Many arguments for policies to advance human rights are grounded in an economic-sociology critique of markets, such as the failure of markets to deal adequately with externalities or provide economic security (Esping-Andersen 1999). Langewoort (1996) argues that the widespread failure of individuals to behave rationally during investment booms necessitates the US federal government's taking on additional responsibilities to see to it that small investors are protected. During periods of speculative fervor, individuals are prone to judge the present situation in light of recent gains, attributing upside profit to skill rather than luck. Regulation is needed, Langewoort argues, to save us from our own behavior in markets, which is irrational despite what the models claim.

In the area of labor rights, Margaret Weir (1992) argues that political rhetoric and processes in Congress led to the concretization of specific employment rights. Following the 2008 recession, the AFL-CIO used a new language of rights when it argued for employees' right to sick leave as an extension of the right to free association. In addition, labor used rights-based arguments to advocate for the Employee Free Choice Act, which would give unions additional opportunities to organize workplaces through gathering signatures rather than gaining votes in an election (Clawson 2003).

The emergent ways in which rights are defined have greatly impacted the success of movements to gain credit rights. Credit rights can be defined as the right of an individual woman to be fairly considered for loans or, alternatively, as the right of a depositor to benefit from a proper fiduciary relationship with the local bank to whom she has entrusted her money. It was the latter definition of rights that led to the successful passage of the Community Reinvestment Act of 1977 (Krippner 2010). Economic sociology, using conceptions of human rights as an analytic tool, can discover which definitions of rights have actually led to reforms that have most advanced the cause of human rights.

Discussion Questions

Chapter 1: Medical Sociology

1. What are examples of evidence of unequal distribution of health?
2. How may voting rights improve human rights to health care?
3. The authors contend that the spread of biomedicalization invited exploitation. How? How may individuals and groups employ human rights to challenge this exploitation?
4. The authors state that a national health-care policy, by itself, will not make health care a human right. What other factors are needed? What roles do human rights play?

Chapter 2: Crime, Law, and Deviance

1. If government can be viewed as a perpetrator of human rights abuses, what avenues are available to overcome those abuses and change government policies and practices?
2. How may activists use human rights to battle legacies of discriminatory abuses achieved through legal systems?
3. The author points out that human rights scholars can learn from sociologists of crime on how to approach human rights abuses as a collective harm. Can you apply this approach to a contemporary situation of human rights violations of a social group?
4. The author states that selection of leaders of weak countries for criminal prosecution reflects, to some degree, international power differences. If a leader of a hegemonic country was tried for a war crime, how would international power differences change?

Chapter 3: Education

1. What evidence exists to support the notion that "education is necessary and central to the development of a state and its people"?

DISCUSSION QUESTIONS 129

2. There have been three predominant approaches to studying education sociologically. What are these three approaches, and how do they inform a human rights sociology of education?
3. The authors state that what is needed is a "globalized curriculum grounded in human rights education." What does this mean? What might it look like?
4. After reading this chapter, what is the purpose of schooling? What could be the purpose of schooling? What should be the purpose of schooling?

CHAPTER 4: FAMILY

1. Why do you think sociologists are so interested in studying the changes in the American family?
2. How would families *not* experiencing precarity benefit from a human rights approach to family life?
3. Thinking from a human rights perspective, why might families be changing?
4. The family is a place where people may lack basic needs due to budget shortfalls. How can human rights respond to this situation?

CHAPTER 5: ORGANIZATIONS, OCCUPATIONS, AND WORK

1. Benson identifies five foundational puzzles that students of human rights and organization must grapple with. Which two puzzles do you think are most important? And why?
2. Why should organizational sociologists concern themselves with human rights? Why should human rights scholars concern themselves with the insights of organizational sociologists?
3. What is "emancipatory work" according to Benson? Why does it matter in the discussion of organizations, occupations, work, and human rights?
4. What six steps does Benson suggest for reconstructing the field in more human rights orientation?
5. Are there different social organizations that might produce more human rights?

CHAPTER 6: POLITICAL SOCIOLOGY

1. As you become familiar with human rights treaties, do you find duties and obligations articulated in those treaties?
2. Of the five theories of political sociology that deal with human rights, which one is most useful for explaining genocide? Why?

130 DISCUSSION QUESTIONS

3. The author concludes by stating that "the politics of fighting human rights abuses will no longer be built from within countries alone." Of the five theories, which do you believe can provide most insights from political sociology for future human rights scholarship?
4. When identifying power constellations, what actors and institutions does a world polity approach name?

CHAPTER 7: CULTURE

1. We often talk about how culture causes human rights conflict. Jacobs and Kurtz remind us that it is also possible for culture to mediate tensions in human rights conflict. How do you think this can happen in practice?
2. How do you see publics uniting, in spite of difference, because of their unity?
3. Laws are constructed by society. How can we construct laws that acknowledge a human rights society?
4. How can work be reconfigured to acknowledge human rights? How are publics contributing to this change?
5. How can human rights protect agency and facilitate structures that honor culture?

CHAPTER 8: SCIENCE, KNOWLEDGE, AND TECHNOLOGY

1. Describe the two general intellectual traditions within the social studies of science and technology.
2. According to the chapter, why is there a disconnect between professional scientific discourse and the public understanding of science? What are the implication of this gap?
3. What is the role of science in the pursuit of human rights?
4. What three challenges does the author propose in the merging of human rights concerns and the scholarship on science and technology?

CHAPTER 9: SOCIOLOGY OF LAW

1. The author points out that rights are social. What is a common social relationship that is foundational to human rights practices?
2. What is a predominant indicator of a human right?
3. Given intangible qualities of human rights and law, are human rights and law more important to some social groups? How could that be?
4. The author reminds us that rights are often thought of as inalienable. How may a sociological study of law demonstrate value of a human right denied to vulnerable individuals?

CHAPTER 10: RELIGION

1. What challenges to the *universality* of human rights are uncovered by considering religion?
2. Human rights violations occur in the name of religion. The news gives us examples regularly. How can society respond? How can we as individuals respond?
3. How is religion related to human dignity?
4. While religion and human rights could be an amazing example of symbiosis in institutions, they are frequently in tension and struggle. How can religion and human rights—two institutions in society—better support each other for the well-being of all?

CHAPTER 11: ECONOMIC SOCIOLOGY

1. How might human rights organizations in civil society and governance inform and influence policy-making?
2. This chapter points to many examples of markets and economic policy denying human rights. How might markets and policies facilitate human rights?
3. What new policies might emerge if economic policy were informed by human rights? Think locally and globally.
4. Many Americans have a greater aversion to economic equality than economic inequality. How might a human rights lens encourage Americans to be open to economic equality—or even a lesser degree of economic inequality?

Acronyms

AFL-CIO	American Federation of Labor and Congress of Industrial Organizations
ANT	actor network theory
ASA	American Sociological Association
CA	conversation analysis
CBSM	collective behavior and social movements
CEDAW	Convention on the Elimination of All Forms of Discrimination against Women
CUS	community and urban sociology
DOMA	Defense of Marriage Act
EM	ethnomethodology
EPI	Economic Policy Institute
FGC	female genital cutting
fMRI	functional magnetic resonance imaging
HRW	Human Rights Watch
ICANN	Internet Corporation for Assigned Names and Numbers
ICC	International Criminal Court
ICCPR	International Covenant on Civil and Political Rights
ICESCR	International Covenant on Economic, Social, and Cultural Rights
ICJ	International Court of Justice
ICT	information and communication technology
ICTY	International Criminal Tribunal for the Former Yugoslavia
ILO	International Labour Organization
IMF	International Monetary Fund
INGO	international nongovernmental organization
IRAF	International Association for Religious Freedom
IRLA	International Religious Liberty Association
LGBT	lesbian, gay, bisexual, and transgender
LIS	Luxembourg Income Study
MCA	membership categorization analysis
MSM	men who have sex with men
NAACP	National Association for the Advancement of Colored People

NAFTA	North American Free Trade Agreement
NELP	National Employment Law Project
NGO	nongovernmental organization
NHSL	National Health and Social Life
NIA	National Institute on Aging
NICHD	National Institute of Child Health and Human Development
NSF	National Science Foundation
OECD	Organization for Economic Cooperation and Development
PDHRE	People's Decade for Human Rights Education
PET	positron emission tomography
PISA	Programme for International Student Assessment
SA	sequential analysis
SALC	sociology of age and the life course
SKAT	science, knowledge, and technology
SSP	social structure and personality
STD	sexually transmitted disease
STI	sexually transmitted infection
STS	science and technology studies
SWS	Sociologists for Women in Society
TAN	transnational advocacy network
TANF	Temporary Aid to Needy Families
TINA	there is no alternative
TVA	Tennessee Valley Authority
UDHR	Universal Declaration of Human Rights
UN	United Nations
UNCRC	United Nations Convention on the Rights of the Child
UNESCO	United Nations Educational, Scientific, and Cultural Organization
UNICEF	United Nations International Children's Emergency Fund
WHO	World Health Organization
WSF	World Social Forum
WTO	World Trade Organization
WWII	World War II

BIBLIOGRAPHY

A., E. 1950a. "Grace Abbot and Hull House 1908–1921. Part 1." *Social Service Review* 24: 374–394.
———. 1950b. "Grace Abbot and Hull House 1908–1921. Part 2." *Social Service Review* 24: 493–518.
Abbot, Andrew. 1988. *The System of Professions: An Essay on the Division of Expert Labor.* Chicago: University of Chicago Press.
———. 2001. "Self-Similar Social Structures." In *Chaos of Disciplines*, 157–196. Chicago: University of Chicago Press.
Abolafia, Mitchell. 2001. *Making Markets: Opportunism and Restraint on Wall Street.* Cambridge, MA: Harvard University Press.
Abraham, David. 2009. "Doing Justice on Two Fronts: The Liberal Dilemma in Immigration." *Ethnic and Racial Studies* 33, no. 6: 968–985.
Abraham, John. 2010. "Pharmaceuticalization of Society in Context: Theoretical, Empirical and Health Dimensions." *Sociology* 44, no. 4: 603–622.
Abramovitz, Mimi. 1998. "Social Work and Social Reform: An Arena of Struggle." *Social Work* 43: 512–526.
Achenbaum, Andrew W. 1978. *Old Age in the New Land: The American Experience since 1790.* Baltimore: Johns Hopkins University Press.
———. 2009. "A Metahistorical Perspective on Theories of Aging." In *Handbook of Theories of Aging*, edited by V.L. Bengston, D. Gans, N. M. Putney, and M. Silverstein. 2nd ed. New York: Springer Publishing.
Acker, Joan. 2006. "Inequality Regimes: Gender, Class and Race in Organizations." *Gender and Society* 20: 441–464.
Ackerly, B. A. 2008. *Universal Human Rights in a World of Difference.* New York: Cambridge University Press.
Ackerly, Brooke A., and Bina D'Costa. 2005. "Transnational Feminism: Political Strategies and Theoretical Resources." Working paper, Australian National University Department of International Relations.
Adam, Barry D. 1998. "Theorizing Homophobia." *Sexualities* 1: 387–404.
Adam, Barry D., Dan Willem Duyvendak, and André Krouwel. 1999. *The Global Emergence of Gay and Lesbian Politics: National Imprints of a Worldwide Movement.* Philadelphia: Temple University Press.
Adams, Carol. 1990. *The Sexual Politics of Meat.* New York: Continuum Press.
Adams, Guy, and Danny Balfour. 1998. *Unmasking Administrative Evil.* Thousand Oaks, CA: Sage.
———. 2004. "Human Rights, the Moral Vacuum of Modern Organizations, and Administrative Evil." In *Human Rights and the Moral Responsibilities of Corporate and Public Sector Organizations*, edited by Tom Campbell and Seamus Miller, 205–221. New York: Kluwer Academic Publishers.
Adams, Vincanne. 1998. "Suffering the Winds of Lhasa: Politicized Bodies, Human Rights, Cultural Difference, and Humanism in Tibet." *Medical Anthropology Quarterly* 12: 74–102.
———. 2010. "Against Global Health? Arbitrating Science, Non-Science, and Nonsense through Health." In *Against Health: How Health Became the New Morality*, edited by Jonathan M. Metzl and Anna Kirkland, 40–58. New York: New York University Press.
Adas, Michael. 2006. *Dominance by Design: Technological Imperatives and America's Civilizing Mission.* Cambridge, MA: Harvard University Press.
Addams, Jane. 1999. *Twenty Years at Hull House.* New York: Signet Classics.
Adelson, Joseph. 2001. "Sex among the Americans." In *Speaking of Sexuality: Interdisciplinary Readings*, edited by J. Kenneth Davidson Sr. and Nelwyn B. Moore, 57–63. Los Angeles: Roxbury Publishing.

BIBLIOGRAPHY   135

Adeola, F. O. 1994. "Environmental Hazards, Health, and Racial Inequity in Hazardous Waste Distribution." *Environment and Behavior* 26: 99–126.

———. 2000a. "Cross-National Environmental Injustice and Human Rights Issues: A Review of Evidence in the Developing World." *American Behavioral Scientist* 43: 686–706.

———. 2000b. "Endangered Community, Enduring People: Toxic Contamination, Health and Adaptive Responses in a Local Context." *Environment and Behavior* 32: 209–249.

———. 2001. "Environmental Injustice and Human Rights Abuse: The States, MNCs, and Repression of Minority Groups in the World System." *Human Ecology Review* 8: 39–59.

———. 2004. "Environmentalism and Risk Perception: Empirical Analysis of Black and White Differentials and Convergence." *Society and Natural Resources* 17: 911–939.

———. 2009. "From Colonialism to Internal Colonialism and Crude Socioenvironmental Injustice: Anatomy of Violent Conflicts in the Niger Delta of Nigeria." In *Environmental Justice in the New Millennium: Global Perspectives on Race, Ethnicity, and Human Rights*, edited by F. C. Steady, 135–163. New York: Palgrave Macmillan.

———. 2011. *Hazardous Wastes, Industrial Disasters, and Environmental Health Risk: Local and Global Environmental Struggles*. New York: Palgrave Macmillan.

Adikari, Y., and J. Yoshitani. 2009. *Global Trends in Water-Related Disasters: An Insight for Policymakers*. Paris: UNESCO.

Adkins, Daniel E., and Stephen Vaisey. 2009. "Toward a Unified Stratification Theory: Structure, Genome, and Status across Human Societies." *Sociological Theory* 27: 99–121.

Adkins, Daniel E., Victor Wang, and Glen H. Elder Jr. 2008. "Stress Processes and Trajectories of Depressive Symptoms in Early Life: Gendered Development." *Advances in Life Course Research* 13: 107–136.

Adkins, W. 2003. "The Social Construction of Disability: A Theoretical Perspective." Paper presented at the annual meeting for the American Sociological Association, Atlanta, Georgia, 1–31.

Adler, Patricia A., and Peter Adler. 2011. *The Tender Cut: Inside the Hidden World of Self-Injury*. New York: New York University Press.

Adorno, T. 2003. "Education after Auschwitz." In *Can One Live after Auschwitz? A Philosophical Reader*, edited by R. Tiedemann, 19–33. Stanford, CA: Stanford University Press.

AFL-CIO. 2005. "The Silent War: The Assault on Workers' Freedom to Choose a Union and Bargain Collectively in the United States." Issue Brief. AFL-CIO. September. http://www.aflcio.org/joinaunion/how/upload/vatw_issuebrief.pdf.

Agyeman, J. 2005. *Sustainable Communities and the Challenge of Environmental Justice*. New York: New York University Press.

Ajrouch, Kristine J. 2007. "Global Contexts and the Veil: Muslim Integration in the United States and France." *Sociology of Religion* 68: 321–325.

Alba, R., and V. Nee. 1997. "Rethinking Assimilation Theory for a New Era of Immigration." *International Migration Review* 31: 826–874.

Albritton, Robert B. 2005. "Thailand in 2004: The 'Crisis in the South.'" *Asian Survey* 45: 166–173.

Aldrich, Howard E. 1999. *Organizations Evolving*. London: Sage.

Alexander, D. 2006. "Globalization of Disaster: Trends, Problems and Dilemmas." *Journal of International Affairs* 59: 1–22.

Alexander, Jeffrey. 2006. *The Civil Sphere*. New York: Oxford University Press.

———. 2010. "Power, Politics, and the Civil Sphere." In *Handbook of Politics: State and Society in Global Perspective*, edited by K. T. Leicht and J. C. Jenkins, 111–126. Heidelberg and New York: Springer Science and Business Media.

Alexander, Jeffrey C. 2004. "On the Social Construction of Moral Universals: The 'Holocaust' from War Crime to Trauma Drama." In *Cultural Trauma and Collective Identity*, edited by J. C. Alexander et al., 196–263. Berkeley: University of California Press.

Alexander, Jeffrey C., Ron Eyerman, Bernard Giesen, Neil J. Smelser, and Piotr Sztompka. 2004. *Cultural Trauma and Collective Identity*. Berkeley: University of California Press.

Alexander, M. Jacqui, and Chandra Talpade Mohanty. 1997. "Introduction." In *Feminist Genealogies, Colonial Legacies, Democratic Future*, edited by M. Jacqui Alexander and Chandra Talpade Mohanty, xiii–xlii. New York: Routledge.

Allegretto, Sylvia A. 2011. "The State of Working America's Wealth, 2011: Through Volatility and Turmoil, the Gap Widens." Economic Policy Institute, State of Working America. http://www.epi.org/page/-/BriefingPaper292.pdf?nocdn=1 (accessed March 23, 2011).

Allen, Beverly. 1996. *Rape Warfare: The Hidden Genocide in Bosnia-Herzegovina and Croatia*. Minneapolis: University of Minnesota Press.

136 BIBLIOGRAPHY

Allman, Paula. 2001. *Critical Education against Global Capitalism: Karl Marx and Revolutionary Critical Education*. Westport, CT: Bergin and Garvey.

———. 2007. *On Marx: An Introduction to the Revolutionary Intellect of Karl Marx*. Rotterdam: Sense Publishers.

Allport, G. W. 1954. *The Nature of Prejudice*. Reading, MA: Addison-Wesley.

Altbach, Philip G., and Patti Peterson. 1971. "Before Berkeley: Historical Perspectives on American Student Activism." *Annals of the American Academy of Political and Social Science* 395: 1–14.

Altenbaugh, Richard J. 1990. *Education for Struggle: The American Labor Colleges of the 1920s and 1930s*. Philadelphia: Temple University Press.

Alvarez-Jimenez, Alberto. 2009. "The WTO Appellate Body's Decision-Making Process." *Journal of International Economics Law* 12, no. 2: 289–331.

Alvesson, Mats, and Hugh Willmott, eds. 1992. *Critical Management Studies*. London: Sage.

———. 2003. *Studying Management Critically*. London: Sage Publications.

Alwin, Duane F., Scott M. Hofer, and Ryan J. McCammon. 2006. "Modeling the Effects of Time: Integrating Demographic and Developmental Perspectives." In *Handbook of Aging and the Social Sciences*, edited by R. H. Binstock and L. K. George, 20–41. 6th ed. Amsterdam: Elsevier.

American Civil Liberties Union (ACLU). 2010. "President Obama Signs Bill Reducing Sentencing Disparities." ACLU. http://www.aclu.org/drug-law-reform/president-obama-signs-bill-reducing-cocaine-sentencing-disparity (accessed October 18, 2011).

American Sociological Association (ASA). 2011. "Animals and Society Section." ASA. www2.asanet.org/sectionanimals (accessed March 1, 2011).

Amirthalingam, Kumaraligam. 2005. "Women's Rights, International Norms, and Domestic Violence: Asian Perspectives." *Human Rights Quarterly* 27: 683–708.

Amnesty International. 2010. *Amnesty International Report 2010*. London: Amnesty International British Section.

An Na'im, Abdullahi Ahmed. 1992. "Toward a Cross-Cultural Approach to Defining International Standards of Human Rights: The Meaning of Cruel, Inhuman or Degrading Treatment or Punishment." In *Human Rights in Cross-Cultural Perspectives*, edited by Abdullahi Ahmed An-Na'im, 19–43. Philadelphia: University of Pennsylvania Press.

———. 2001. "Human Rights." In *The Blackwell Companion to Sociology*, edited by Judith Blau, 86–99. Malden, MA: Blackwell.

Ancheta, Angelo N. 1998. "Race, Rights, and the Asian American Experience." *Journal of Asian American Studies* 1: 293–297.

Anderson, Benedict. 2006 [1983]. *Imagined Communities: Reflections on the Origin and Spread of Nationalism*. London: Verso, New Left Books.

Anderson, Elijah. 1994. *Code of the Street*. New York: W. W. Norton.

———. 2000. *Code of the Street: Decency, Violence, and the Moral Life of the Inner City*. New York: W. W. Norton.

———. 2011. *The Cosmopolitan Canopy: Race and Civility in Everyday Life*. New York: W. W. Norton.

Anderson, Leon, and David A. Snow. 2001. "Inequality and the Self: Exploring Connections from an Interactionist Perspective." *Symbolic Interaction* 24: 395–406.

Anderson, Margo, and Stephen Fienberg. 2001. *Who Counts: The Politics of Census-Taking in Contemporary America*. New York: Russell Sage Foundation.

Andersson, Matthew A., and Colleen S. Conley. 2008. "Expecting to Heal through Self-Expression: A Perceived Control Theory of Writing and Health." *Health Psychology Review* 2: 138–162.

Anghie, Antony. 1970. "On the Measurement of Inequality." *Journal of Economic Theory* 2: 244–263.

———. 2005. *Imperialism, Sovereignty and the Making of International Law*. Cambridge, UK: Cambridge University Press.

Annette, John. 2005. "Character, Civic Renewal and Service Learning for Democratic Citizenship in Higher Education." *British Journal of Educational Studies* 53: 326–340.

Anoushirvani, S. 2010. "The Future of the International Criminal Court: The Long Road to Legitimacy Begins with the Trial of Thomas Lubanga Dyilo." *Pace International Law Review* 22: 213–239.

Antrobus, Peggy. 2004. *The Global Women's Movement: Origins, Issues, and Strategies*. London: Zed Books.

Apocada, C. 2007. "The Whole World Could Be Watching." *Journal of Human Rights* 6: 147–164.

Archibugi, Daniele. 2008. *The Global Commonwealth of Citizens*. Princeton, NJ: Princeton University Press.

Arena, Jay. 2010. "The Contested Terrains of Public Sociology: Theoretical and Practical Lessons from the Movement to Defend Public Housing in Pre- and Post-Katrina New Orleans." *Societies without Borders* 5: 103–125.

Aries, Philippe. 1962. *Centuries of Childhood*. New York: Vintage.

Bibliography 137

Arington, Michele. 1991. "English Only Laws and Direct Legislation: The Battle in the States over Language Minority Rights." *Journal of Law and Politics* 7: 325–352.

Armstrong, Susan J., and Richard G. Botzler, eds. 2008. *The Animal Ethics Reader.* 2nd ed. London and New York: Routledge.

Aronowitz, Stanley. 1988. *Science as Power: Discourse and Ideology in Modern Society.* Minneapolis: University of Minnesota Press.

Arum, Richard. 2011. *Academically Adrift: Limited Learning on College Campuses.* Chicago: University of Chicago Press.

Arzberger, Peter, Peter Schroeder, Anne Beaulieu, Geof Bowker, Kathleen Casey, Leif Laaksonen, David Moorman, Paul Uhlir, and Paul Wouters. 2004. "An International Framework to Promote Access to Data." *Science* 303, no. 5665: 1777–1778.

Asch, A. 2001. "Disability, Bioethics, and Human Rights." In *Handbook of Disability Studies,* edited by G. L. Albrecht, K. D. Seelman, and M. Bury, 297–326. Thousand Oaks, CA: Sage.

Asencio, Marysol. 2009. *Latina/o Sexualities: Probing Powers, Passions, Practices, and Policies.* New Brunswick, NJ: Rutgers University Press.

Ashar, Sameer. 2003. "Immigration Enforcement and Subordination: The Consequences of Racial Profiling after September 11." *Immigration and National Law Review* 23: 545–560.

Atkin, C. K., K. Neuendorf, and S. McDermott. 1983. "The Role of Alcohol Advertising in Excessive and Hazardous Drinking." *Journal of Drug Education* 13: 313–325.

Atkinson, A. B. 1970. "On the Measurement of Inequality." *Journal of Economic Theory* 2: 244–263.

Atkinson, Anthony B. 1975. *The Economics of Inequality.* London: Oxford.

Atterton, Peter, and Matthew Calarco, eds. 2004. *Animal Philosophy: Ethics and Identity.* New York: Continuum.

Aylward, Carol A. 2010. "Intersectionality: Crossing the Theoretical and Praxis Divide." *Journal of Critical Race Inquiry* 1: 1–48.

Baars, Jan, Dale Dannefer, Chris Philipson, and Alan Walker. 2006. *Aging, Globalization, and Inequality: The New Critical Gerontology.* Amityville, NY: Baywood Publishing Company.

Babugura, Agnes A. 2008. "Vulnerability of Children and Youth in Drought Disasters: A Case Study of Botswana." *Children, Youth, and Environments* 18, no. 1: 126–157.

Baca, Maxine Zinn, and Bonnie Thornton Dill. 1994. "Difference and Domination." In *Women of Color in U.S. Society.* Philadelphia: Temple University Press.

———. 1996. "Theorizing Difference from Multiracial Feminism." *Feminist Studies* 22: 321–331.

Baden, Sally, and Anne Marie Goetz. 1997. "Who Needs [Sex] When You Can Have [Gender]? Conflicting Discourses on Gender at Beijing." In *Women, International Development, and Politics,* edited by Kathleen Staudt, 37–58. Philadelphia: Temple University Press.

Bagemihl, Bruce. 2000. *Biological Exuberance: Animal Homosexuality and Natural Diversity.* New York: St. Martin's Press.

Bailey, Christopher. 2004. "'Informed Choice' to 'Social Hygiene': Government Control of Smoking in the US." *Journal of American Studies* 38, no. 1: 41–65.

Baker, Carrie N. 2007. *The Women's Movement against Sexual Harassment.* New York: Cambridge University Press.

Bakker, J. I. (Hans). 1993. *Toward a Just Civilization: Gandhi.* Toronto: Canadian Scholars' Press.

———. 2010a. "Theory, Role of." In *Encyclopedia of Case Study Research,* edited by Albert J. Mills, Gabrielle Durepos, and Elden Wiebe, 930–932. Los Angeles, CA: Sage.

———. 2010b. "Deference versus Democracy in Traditional and Modern Bureaucracy: A Refinement of Max Weber's Ideal Type Model." In *Society, History and the Global Condition of Humanity,* edited by Zaheer Baber and Joseph M. Bryant, 105–128. Lanham, MD: Lexington Publishers.

Bales, Kevin, and Ron Soodalter. 2009. *The Slave Next Door: Human Trafficking and Slavery in America Today.* Berkeley: University of California Press.

Ballatine, Jeannie H. and Joan Z. Spade. 2011. *Schools and Society: A Sociological Approach to Education.* 4th Edition. Thousand Oaks, CA: Sage Publications.

Baltrušaityt·e, G. 2010. "Psychiatry and the Mental Patient: An Uneasy Relationship." *Culture and Society* 1. http://culturesociety.vdu.lt/wp-content/uploads/2010/11/G.-Baltrusaityte-Psychiatry-and-the-Mental-Patient-An-Uneasy-Relationship1.pdf (accessed January 22, 2012).

Bandy, Joe, and Jackie Smith. 2005. *Coalitions across Borders: Transnational Protest and the Neoliberal Order.* Lanham, MD: Rowman & Littlefield.

Barak, Gregg, ed. 1991. *Crimes by the Capitalist State: An Introduction to State Criminality.* Albany: State University of New York Press.

Barbalet, J. M. 1995. "Symposium: Human Rights and the Sociological Project (a Social Emotions Theory of Basic Rights)." *Australian and New Zealand Journal of Sociology* 31: 36–42.

138 Bibliography

Barbotte, E., F. Guillemin, and N. Chau. 2002. "Prevalence of Impairments, Disabilities, Handicaps and Quality of Life in the General Population: A Review of Recent Literature." *Bulletin of the World Health Organization* 79: 1047–1055.

Barham P. 1992. *Closing the Asylum*. London: Penguin Books.

Barnes, C. 1996. "Theories of Disability and the Origins of the Oppression of Disabled People." In *Disability and Society: Emerging Issues and Insights*, edited by L. Barton, 43–60. London: Longman.

Barnes, C., and G. Mercer. 2010. *Exploring Disability*. 2nd ed. Cambridge, UK: Polity Press.

Barnett, H. G. 1948. "On Science and Human Rights." *American Anthropologist* 50, no. 2: 352–355.

Baron, James N. 1984. "Organizational Perspectives on Stratification." *Annual Review of Sociology* 10: 37–69.

Barry, John, and K. Woods. 2009. "The Environment." In *Human Rights: Politics and Practice*, edited by M. Goodhart, 316–333. London: Oxford University Press.

Basch, Linda, Nina Glick Schiller, and Cristina Szanton Blanc. 1994. *Nations Unbound: Transnational Projects, Postcolonial Predicaments, and Deterritorialized Nation-States*. Routledge: London.

Bashford, Alison, and Phillipa Levine, eds. 2010. *The Oxford Handbook of the History of Eugenics*. Oxford: Oxford University Press.

Bass, Gary J. 2000. *Stay the Hand of Vengeance: The Politics of War Crimes Tribunals*. Princeton, NJ: Princeton University Press.

Basu, Amrita, ed. 2010. *Women's Movements in the Global Era: The Power of Local Feminisms*. Boulder, CO: Westview Press.

Batliwala, S. 2007. "Taking the Power Out of Empowerment—an Experiential Account." *Development in Practice* 17: 557–565.

Battersby, P., and J. M. Siracusa. 2009. *Globalization and Human Security*. Lanham, MD: Rowman & Littlefield.

Battle, Juan. 2009. *Black Sexualities: Probing Powers, Passions, Practices, and Policies*. New Brunswick, NJ: Rutgers University Press.

Bauböck, Rainer. 2009. "Global Justice, Freedom of Movement, and Democratic Citizenship." *European Journal of Sociology* 50: 1–31.

Bauman, Zygmunt. 1989. *Modernity and the Holocaust*. Ithaca, NY: New York University Press.

———. 2001. "Wars of the Globalization Era." *European Journal of Social Theory* 4: 11–28.

Baumer, Eric. 1994. "Poverty, Crack and Crime: A Cross-City Analysis." *Journal of Research in Crime and Delinquency* 31: 311–327.

Baumol, William J. 2002. *The Free-Market Innovation Machine: Analyzing the Grown Miracle of Capitalism*. Princeton, NJ: Princeton University Press.

Baxi, Upendra. 2002. *The Future of Human Rights*. New Delhi: Oxford University Press.

Baxter, David. 1989. "Marx, Lukes and Human Rights." *Social Theory and Practice* 15, no. 3: 355–373.

Bearman, Peter S., and Hannah Bruckner. 2001. "Promising the Future: Virginity Pledges and First Intercourse." *American Journal of Sociology* 106: 859–912.

Beating, J. 1993. "Technological Impacts on Human Rights: Models of Development, Science and Technology, and Human Rights." In *The Impact of Technology on Human Rights: Global Case Studies*, edited by C. G. Weeramantry. Tokyo, Japan: United Nations Press. http://unu.edu/unupress/unubooks/uu08ie/uu08ie00.htm (accessed November 12, 2010).

Beaver, Kevin M. 2008. "Nonshared Environmental Influences on Adolescent Delinquent Involvement and Adult Criminal Behavior." *Criminology* 46, no. 2: 341–369.

Beck, Ulrich. 1996. "Risk Society and the Provident State." In *Risk, Environment, and Modernity*, edited by S. Lash, B. Szersynski, and B. Wynne, 27–43. Thousand Oaks, CA: Sage.

———. 1999. *World Risk Society*. Malden, MA: Polity Press.

———. 2007a. *Cosmopolitan Europe*. Cambridge, UK: Polity Press.

———. 2007b. *World at Risk*. Malden, MA: Polity Press.

Beck, Ulrich, and Natan Sznaider. 2006. "Unpacking Cosmopolitanism for the Social Sciences." *British Journal of Sociology* 57, no. 1: 1–23.

Becker, Anne E. 1994. "Nurturing and Negligence: Working on Others' Bodies in Fiji." In *Embodiment and Experience: The Existential Ground of Culture and Self*, edited by Thomas J. Csordas, 100–115. Cambridge, UK: Cambridge University Press.

Becker, Howard S. 1963. *Outsiders: Studies in the Sociology of Deviance*. New York: The Free Press.

———. 1967. "Whose Side Are We On?" *Social Problems* 14: 239–247.

———. 1982. *Art Worlds*. Berkeley: University of California Press.

Beckett, Katherine, and Steve Herbert. 2009. *Banished: The New Social Control in Urban America*. New York: Oxford University Press.

Beckett, Katherine, Kris Nyrop, Lori Pfingst, and Melissa Bowen. 2005. "Drug Use, Drug Possession Arrests, and the Question of Race: Lessons from Seattle." *Social Problems* 52, no. 3: 419–441.

BIBLIOGRAPHY   139

Beckoff, Marc. 2002. *Minding Animals: Awareness, Emotions, and Heart*. New York: Oxford.
Beetham, David. 1995. "What Future for Economic and Social Rights?" *Political Studies* 43: 41–60.
Behar, Ruth. 1997. *The Vulnerable Observer: Anthropology that Breaks Your Heart*. Boston: Beacon Press.
Bell, Daniel. 1978 [1976]. *The Cultural Contradictions of Capitalism*. New York: Basic Books, Harper.
———. 2000. *East Meets West: Human Rights and Democracy in East Asia*. Princeton, NJ: Princeton University Press.
Bell, L. A. 1997. "Theoretical Foundations for Social Justice Education." In *Teaching for Diversity and Social Justice: A Sourcebook*, edited by M. Adams, L. A. Bell, and P. Griffin, 3–15. New York: Routledge.
Beneke, Timothy. 1983. *Men on Rape: What They Have to Say about Sexual Violence*. New York: St. Martin's Press.
Benford, Robert D., and David A. Snow. 2000. "Framing Processes and Social Movements." *Annual Review of Sociology* 26: 611–639.
Bengston, Vern L., Daphna Gans, Norella M. Putney, and Merril Silverstein, eds. 2009a. *Handbook of Theories of Aging*. 2nd ed. New York: Springer Publishing.
———. 2009b. "Theories about Age and Aging." In *Handbook of Theories of Aging*, edited by Vern L. Bengston, Daphna Gans, Norella M. Putney, and Merril Silverstein, 3–24. 2nd ed. New York: Springer Publishing.
Benhabib, Seyla, and Judith Resnick. 2009. "Introduction: Citizenship and Migration Theory Engendered." In *Migrations and Mobilities: Citizenship, Borders, and Gender*, edited by Seyla Benhabib and Judith Resnik, 1–46. New York: New York University Press.
Bennett, Angela. 2006. *The Geneva Convention*. Charleston, SC: History Press.
Bennett, Michael, and Juan Battle. 2001. "'We Can See Them, but We Can't Hear Them': LGBT Members of African American Families." In *Queer Families, Queer Politics: Challenging Culture and the State*, edited by Mary Bernstein and Renate Reimann, 53–67. New York: Columbia University Press.
Benoit, Cecelia, Dena Carroll, and Munaza Chaudhry. 2003. "In Search of a Healing Place: Aboriginal Women in Vancouver's Downtown Eastside." *Social Science and Medicine* 56: 821–833.
Benson, J. Kenneth. 1975. "The Interorganizational Network as a Political Economy." *Administrative Science Quarterly* 20: 229–249.
———. 1977. "Innovation and Crisis in Organizational Analysis." *Sociological Quarterly* 18: 3–16.
———. 1982. "A Framework for Policy Analysis." In *Interorganizational Coordination: Theory, Research, and Implementation*, edited by David L. Rogers and David A. Whetten, 137–176. Ames: Iowa State University Press.
———. 1983. "Paradigm and Praxis in Organizational Analysis." In *Research on Organizational Behavior*, edited by Barry Staw and L. L. Cummings, 33–56. Annual Series 5. Greenwich, CT: JAI Press.
Beresford, P., and A. Wilson. 2002. "Genes Spell Danger: Mental Health Service Users/Survivors, Bioethics and Control." *Disability and Society* 17: 541–553.
Berger, Joseph, Bernard P. Cohen, and Morris Zelditch Jr. 1966. "Status Characteristics and Expectation States." In *Sociological Theories in Progress*, edited by Joseph Berger, Morris Zelditch Jr., and Bo Anderson, 1:29–46. Boston: Houghton Mifflin.
Berger, Peter, and Thomas Luckmann. 1966. *The Social Construction of Reality*. Garden City, NY: Anchor.
Berkovitch, Nitza. 1999. *From Motherhood to Citizenship: Women's Rights and International Organizations*. Baltimore: Johns Hopkins University Press.
Berlant, Lauren, and Michael Warner. 1998. "Sex in Public." *Critical Inquiry* 24: 547–566.
Bernard, L. L. 1945. "The Teaching of Sociology in the United States in the Last Fifty Years." *American Journal of Sociology* 50: 534–548.
Bernerjee, D. 2008. "Environmental Rights." In *The Leading Rogue State: The U.S. and Human Rights*, edited by Judith Blau et al., 163–172. Boulder, CO: Paradigm Publishers.
Bernstein, Basil. 1970. "Education Cannot Compensate for Society." *New Society* 387: 344–347.
———. 1977. *Class, Codes, and Control*. Vol. 3: *Towards a Theory of Educational Transmissions*. London: Routledge and Kegan Paul.
———. 1990. *Class, Codes, and Control*. Vol. 4: *The Structuring of Pedagogic Discourse*. London: Routledge.
———. 1996. *Pedagogy, Symbolic Control, and Identity: Theory, Research, Critique*. London: Taylor and Francis. Bernstein, Irving. 1960a. *The Lean Years: A History of the American Worker, 1920–1933*. Boston: Houghton Mifflin.
———. 1960b. "Union Growth and Structural Cycles." In *Labor and Trade Unionism*, edited by W. Galenson and S. M. Lipset, 73–89. New York: Wiley.
———. 1970. *The Turbulent Years: A History of the American Worker, 1933–1941*. Boston: Houghton Mifflin.
Bernstein, Mary. 2004. "Paths to Homophobia." *Sexuality Research and Social Policy* 1: 41–55.

140 BIBLIOGRAPHY

———. 2005. "Identity Politics." *Annual Review of Sociology* 31: 47–74.

Bernstein, Mary, and Constance Kostelac. 2002. "Lavender and Blue: Attitudes about Homosexuality and Behavior toward Lesbians and Gay Men among Police Officers." *Journal of Contemporary Criminal Justice* 18: 302–328.

Bernstein, Mary, Constance Kostelac, and Emily Gaarder. 2003. "Understanding 'Heterosexism': Applying Theories of Racial Prejudice to Homophobia Using Data from a Southwestern Police Department." *Race, Gender and Class* 10: 54–74.

Bernstein, Mary, and Renate Reimann, eds. 2001. *Queer Families, Queer Politics: Challenging Culture and the State.* New York: Columbia University Press.

Berry, J. G., and W. H. Jones. 1991. "Situational and Dispositional Components of Reaction towards Persons with Disabilities." *Journal of Social Psychology* 131: 673–684.

Berry, Jason. 1992. *Lead Us Not into Temptation: Catholic Priests and the Sexual Abuse of Children.* New York: Doubleday.

Bertman, Martin. 2004. "The Theoretical Instability and Practical Progress of Human Rights." *International Journal of Human Rights* 8, no. 1: 89–99.

Best, Joel. 2007. *Social Problems.* New York: W. W. Norton and Company.

Best, Steve, and Anthony J. Nocella II. 2004. *Terrorists or Freedom Fighters? Reflections on the Liberation of Animals.* New York: Lantern Books.

Bevc, Christine, Brent K. Marshall, and J. Stephen Picou. 2007. "Environmental Justice and Toxic Exposure: Toward a Spatial Model of Physical Health and Psychological Well-Being." *Social Science Research* 37: 48–67.

Bevington, Douglas, and Chris Dixon. 2005. "Movement-Relevant Theory: Rethinking Social Movement Scholarship and Activism." *Social Movement Studies* 4, no. 3: 185–208.

Beyer, Peter. 2001. *Religion in the Process of Globalization.* Würzburg, Germany: Ergon.

———. 2006. *Religions in Global Society.* London and New York: Routledge.

Beyrer, Chris. 1998. "Burma and Cambodia: Human Rights, Social Disruption, and the Spread of HIV/AIDS." *Health and Human Rights* 2: 84–97.

Bhabha, Homi K. 2004. *RC Series Bundle: The Location of Culture.* 2nd ed. London: Routledge.

Bhattacharji, Preeti. 2009. *Uighurs and China's Xinjiang Region.* Washington, DC: Council on Foreign Relations. http://www.cfr.org/china/uighurs-chinas-xinjiang-region/p16870 (accessed September 30, 2011).

Bhattacharyya, A., P. K. Pattanaik, and Y. Xu. 2011. "Choice, Internal Consistency and Rationality." *Economics and Philosophy* 27, no. 2 (July): 123–149.

Biblarz, Timothy J., and Adrian E. Raftery. 1999. "Family Structure, Educational Attainment, and Socioeconomic Success: Rethinking the 'Pathology of Matriarchy.'" *American Journal of Sociology* 105: 321–365.

Bierne, Piers. 2009. *Confronting Animal Abuse: Law, Criminology, and Human-Animal Relationships.* Lanham, MD: Rowman & Littlefield.

Bigelow, J. 1831. *Elements of Technology.* Boston: Hilliard, Gray, Little and Wilkins.

Bilder, Richard B. 2006. "The Role of Apology in International Law and Diplomacy." *Virginia Journal of International Law* 46: 433–473.

Billson, Janet Mancini. 2008. "Focus Groups in the Context of International Development: In Pursuit of the Millennium Development Goals." In *International Clinical Sociology,* edited by Jan Marie Fritz, 188–207. New York: Springer.

Bilton, C. 2007. *Management and Creativity: From Creative Industries to Creative Management.* Malden, MA: Blackwell.

Binion, Gayle. 1995. "Human Rights: A Feminist Perspective." *Human Rights Quarterly* 17: 509–526.

Binstock, Robert H. 2007. "The Doomsters Are Wrong: What's Needed Are Policies Aimed at Several Generations." *AARP Bulletin* 48, no. 3: 33.

Binstock, Robert H., Linda K. George, Stephen J. Cutler, Jon Hendricks, and James H. Schultz. 2006. *Handbook of Aging and the Social Sciences.* Amsterdam: Elsevier.

———. 2011. *Handbook of Aging and the Social Sciences.* Amsterdam: Elsevier.

Binstock, Robert H., and Stephen G. Post. 1991. *Too Old for Health Care? Controversies in Medicine, Law, Economics, and Ethics.* 6th ed. Baltimore: Johns Hopkins University Press.

Bird, Chloe E., Peter Conrad, and Allen M. Fremont. 2000. "Medical Sociology at the Millennium." In *Handbook of Medical Sociology,* edited by Chloe E. Bird, Peter Conrad, and Allen M. Fremont, 1–10. 5th ed. Upper Saddle River, NJ: Prentice Hall.

Birren, J. E., ed. 1959. *Handbook of Aging and the Individual: Psychological and Biological Aspects.* Chicago: University of Chicago Press.

Black, Donald. 1972. "The Boundaries of Legal Sociology." *Yale Law Journal* 81, no. 6: 1086–1100.

———. 1976. *The Behavior of the Law.* New York: Academic Press.

BIBLIOGRAPHY   141

Black, R. S., and L. Pretes. 2007. "Victims and Victors: Representation of Physical Disability on the Silver Screen." *Research and Practice for Persons with Severe Disabilities* 32: 66–83.

Black, Timothy. 2010. *When a Heart Turns Rock Solid: The Lives of Three Puerto Rican Brothers on and off the Streets*. New York: Vintage.

Blair, T., and M. Minkler. 2009. "Participatory Action Research with Older Adults: Key Principles in Practice." *Gerontologist* 49: 651–662.

Blau, J., and A. Moncada. 2005. *Human Rights: Beyond the Liberal Vision*. Lanham, MD: Rowman & Littlefield.

———. 2006. *Justice in the United States: Human Rights and the U.S. Constitution*. London: Rowman & Littlefield.

———. 2007a. "It Ought to Be a Crime: Criminalizing Human Rights Violations." *Sociological Forum* 22: 364–371.

———. 2007b. "Sociologizing Human Rights: Reply to John Hagan and Ron Levi." *Sociological Forum* 22: 381–384.

———. 2009. *Human Rights: A Primer*. Boulder, CO: Paradigm Publishers.

Blau, Judith. 2005. "Don't Blink Now: It's the Transition to the Second World System." *Contemporary Sociology* 34, no. 1: 7–9.

———. 2006. "Why Should Human Rights Be Important to Sociologists?" Sociologists Without Borders. http://www.sociologistswithoutborders.org/president.html (accessed September 5, 2012).

———. 2010. Personal communication with J. M. Fritz. December 24.

———. 2011. "Human Rights Cities: The Transformation of Communities, or Simply Treading Water?" In *Essentials of Community Intervention*, edited by J. M. Fritz and J. Rheaume, draft chapter. The Netherlands: Springer.

Blau, Judith, David Brunsma, Alberto Moncada, and Catherine Zimmer, eds. 2008. *The Leading Rogue State*. Boulder, CO: Paradigm Publishers.

Blau, Judith, and Mark Frezzo, eds. 2011. *Sociology and Human Rights: A Bill of Rights for the Twenty-First Century*. Newbury Park, CA: Pine Forge Press.

Blau, Judith, and Marina Karides. 2008. *The World and US Social Forums: Another World Is Possible and Necessary*. Leiden: Brill Publishers.

Blau, Judith, and Keri Iyall Smith. 2006. *Public Sociologies Reader*. Lanham, MD: Rowman & Littlefield.

Blau, P. M. 1974. "Presidential Address: Parameters of Social Structure." *American Sociological Review* 39: 615–635.

Blau, Peter M., and Richard Schoenherr. 1971. *The Structure of Organizations*. New York: Basic Books.

Blauner, Robert. 1964. *Alienation and Freedom: The Factory Worker and His Industry*. Chicago: University of Chicago Press.

Bloom, Samuel. W. 2000. "The Institutionalization of Medical Sociology in the United States, 1920–1980." In *Handbook of Medical Sociology*, edited by Chloe E. Bird, Peter Conrad, and Allen M. Fremont, 11–31. 5th ed. Upper Saddle River, NJ: Prentice Hall.

Bluestone, Barry, and Bennett Harrison. 1982. *The Deindustrialization of America: Plant Closings, Community Abandonment, and the Dismantling of Basic Industry*. New York: Basic Books.

Blum, T. 1984. "Problem Drinking or Problem Thinking? Patterns of Abuse in Sociological Research." *Journal of Drug Issues* 14: 655–665.

Blumberg, Rae Lesser. 2004. "Extending Lenski's Schema to Hold Up Both Halves of the Sky—a Theory-Guided Way of Conceptualizing Agrarian Societies that Illuminates a Puzzle about Gender Stratification." *Sociological Theory* 22: 278–291.

Blumenson, Eric, and Eva S. Neilsen. 2002. "How to Construct an Underclass, or How the War on Drugs Became a War on Education." NELLCO Legal Scholarship Repository. http://lsr.nellco.org/suffolk_fp/1 (accessed September 2011).

Blute, Marion. 2006. "Gene-Culture Coevolutionary Games." *Social Forces* 85: 145–149.

———. 2010. *Darwinian Sociocultural Evolution: Evolutionary Solutions to Dilemmas in Cultural and Social Theory*. Cambridge, UK: Cambridge University Press.

Boardman, Jason D., Casely L. Blalock, and Fred C. Pampel. 2010. "Trends in the Genetic Influences on Smoking." *Journal of Health and Social Behavior* 51: 108–123.

Bob, Clifford, ed. 2005. *The Marketing of Rebellion: Insurgents, Media, and International Activism*. Cambridge, UK: Cambridge University Press.

———. 2009. *The International Struggle for New Human Rights*. Philadelphia: University of Pennsylvania Press.

Boersema, D. 2011. *Philosophy of Human Rights: Theory and Practice*. Boulder, CO: Westview Press.

Bogason, Peter. 2006. "The Democratic Prospects of Network Governance." *American Review of Public Administration* 36, no. 1: 3–18.

142 BIBLIOGRAPHY

Bogle, Kathleen. 2008. *Hooking Up: Sex, Dating, and Relationships on Campus*. New York: New York University Press.

Boli, John, and George M. Thomas. 1997. "World Culture and the World Polity: A Century of International Non-Governmental Organization." *American Sociological Review* 62, no. 2: 171–190.

———. 1999. *Constructing World Culture: International Nongovernmental Organizations since 1875*. Stanford, CA: Stanford University Press.

Bond, Johanna E. 2003. "International Intersectionality: Theoretical and Pragmatic Exploration of Women's International Human Rights Violations." *Emory Law Journal* 52: 71–187.

Bonilla-Silva, Eduardo. 2003. *Racism without Racists: Color-Blind Racism and the Persistence of Racial Inequality in the United States*. Lanham, MD: Rowman & Littlefield Publishers.

———. 2008. "'Look, a Negro': Reflections on the Human Rights Approach to Racial Inequality." In *Globalization and America*, edited by A. J. Hattery, D. G. Embrick, and E. Smith, 9–22. Lanham, MD: Rowman & Littlefield Publishers.

Bonilla-Silva, Eduardo, and Sarah Mayorga. 2009. "*Si Me Permiter Hablar*: Limitations of the Human Rights Tradition to Address Racial Inequality." *Societies without Borders* 4: 366–382.

Bonnell, Victoria E. 1980. "The Uses of Theory, Concepts and Comparison in Historical Scholarship." *Comparative Study of Society and History* 22: 156–173.

Bonnin, Debbie. 1995. "Road to Beijing." *Agenda* 27: 74–77.

Bookchin, Murray. 1982. *The Ecology of Freedom: The Emergence and Dissolution of Hierarchy*. Palo Alto, CA: Cheshire Books.

Booth, Alan, Douglas A. Granger, and Elizabeth A. Shirtcliff. 2008. "Gender- and Age-Related Differences in the Association between Social Relationship Quality and Trait Levels of Salivary Cortisol." *Journal of Research on Adolescence* 18: 239–260.

Booth, Aland, D. Johnson, and Douglas Granger. 2005. "Testosterone, Marital Quality, and Role Overload." *Journal of Marriage and the Family* 67: 483–498.

Border Network for Human Rights (BNHR). 2003. *Two—US/Mexico Border Reports*. BNHR. http://www.bnhr.org/reports/u-s-mexico-border-reports-2000-2005 (accessed July 17, 2012).

Bordo, Susan. 2004. *Unbearable Weight: Feminism, Western Culture, and the Body*. Berkeley: University of California Press.

Borjas, George. 2004. "Increasing the Supply of Labor through Immigration: Measuring the Impact on Native-Born Workers." Center for Immigration Studies. http://www.cis.org/LaborSupply-Immigration EffectsNatives (accessed July 17, 2012).

Bottomore, T. B. 1963. *Karl Marx: Early Writings*. New York: McGraw-Hill.

Bottomore, Tom. 1985. *Theories of Modern Capitalism*. London: Allen & Unwin.

Bouilloud, J.-P. 2010. Personal communication with J. M. Fritz. December 13 and 15.

Bourdieu, Pierre. 1973. "Cultural Reproduction and Social Reproduction." In *Knowledge, Education, and Cultural Change*, edited by Richard Brown, 71–112. London: Tavistock.

———. 1977. *Outline of a Theory of Practice*. Cambridge, UK: Cambridge University Press.

———. 1984. *Distinction: A Social Critique of the Judgment of Taste*. Translated by Richard Nice. London: Routledge and Kegan Paul.

———. 1998. *Acts of Resistance: Against the Tyranny of the Market*. Translated by Richard Nice. New York: The New Press.

Bourdieu, Pierre, and Loic J. D. Wacquant. 1992. *An Invitation to Reflexive Sociology*. Chicago: University of Chicago Press.

Bourgois, Philippe. 1990. "Confronting the Ethics of Ethnography: Lessons from Fieldwork in Central America." In *Ethnographic Fieldwork: An Anthropological Reader*, edited by Antonius C. G. M. Robben and Jeffery A. Sluka. Malden, MA: Blackwell Publishing.

Bourgois, Philippe, and Jeff Schonberg. 2009. *Righteous Dopefiend*. Berkeley: University of California Press.

Bowles, Samuel, and Herbert Gintis. 1976. *Schooling in Capitalist America: Educational Reform and the Contradictions of Economic Life*. London: Routledge and Kegan Paul.

———. 1986. *Democracy and Capitalism: Property, Community, and the Contradictions of Modern Social Thought*. New York: Basic Books.

Boyer, Ernst. 1997. *Scholarship Reconsidered: Priorities of the Professorate*. San Francisco: Jossey-Bass.

Boyle, Elizabeth Heger. 2002. *Female Genital Cutting: Cultural Conflict in the Global Community*. Baltimore: Johns Hopkins University Press.

———. 2007. "Processes of Legislative Globalization." In *Encyclopedia of Law and Society: American and Global Perspectives*, edited by David Scott Clark, 661–665. Thousand Oaks, CA: Sage Publications.

———. 2009. "The Cost of Rights or the Right Cost? The Impact of Global Economic and Human Rights Policies on Child Well-Being since 1989." NSF Grant, Law and Social Science Program.

BIBLIOGRAPHY   143

Boyle, Elizabeth Heger, and Amelia Corl. 2010. "Law and Culture in a Global Context: The Practice of Female Genital Cutting." *Annual Review of Law and Social Science* 6: 195–215.

Brabant, Sarah Callaway. 2008. "Clinical Sociology and Bereavement." In *International Clinical Sociology*, edited by Jan Marie Fritz, 97–114. New York: Springer.

Brabeck, Kalina, and Qingwen Xu. 2010. "The Impact of Detention and Deportation on Latino Immigrant Children and Families: A Quantitative Exploration." *Hispanic Journal of Behavioral Sciences* 32: 341–361.

Brackett, Jeffrey R. 1907. "Contribution to Symposium on How Should Sociology Be Taught—As a College or University Course?" *American Journal of Sociology* 12: 602–603.

Bradshaw, W., D. Roseborough, and M. Armour. 2006. "Recovery from Severe Mental Illness: The Lived Experience of the Initial Phase of Treatment." *International Journal of Psychosocial Rehabilitation* 10: 123–131.

Branch, A. 2007. "Uganda's Civil War and the Politics of ICC Intervention." *Ethics and International Affairs* 21: 179–198.

Branningan, Augustine, and Kelly H. Hardwick. 2003. "Genocide and General Theory." In *Control Theories of Crime and Delinquency*, edited by Chester L. Britt and R. Michael, 109–131. New Brunswick, NJ: Transaction.

Brass, Martin. 2011. *Labour Regime Change in the Twenty-First Century*. Leiden, The Netherlands: Brill.

Braverman, Harry. 1974. *Labor and Monopoly Capital*. New York: Monthly Review Press.

Brenkert, George G. 1986. "Marx and Human Rights." *Journal of the History of Philosophy* 24, no. 1: 55–77.

Brenner, Neil, Peter Marcuse, and Margit Mayer, eds. 2012. *Cities for People, Not for Profit: Critical Urban Theory and the Right to the City*. New York: Routledge.

Brewer, Marilynn. 1997. "The Social Psychology of Intergroup Relations: Can Research Inform Practice?" *Journal of Social Issues* 53: 197–211.

Brewer, Rose. 1993. "Theorizing Race, Class and Gender: The New Scholarship of Black Feminist Intellectuals and Black Women's Labor." In *Theorizing Black Feminisms: The Visionary Pragmatism of Black Women*, edited by Stanlie M. James and Abena P. A. Busia, 13–30. New York: Routledge.

Brewington, David V. 2005. "Late to the Party: Organizing Religious Human Rights." Paper presented at the annual meeting of the American Sociological Association, Philadelphia, Pennsylvania.

———. 2011. "International Associations at the Nexus of Globalization, Religion, and Human Rights." PhD diss., Emory University, Atlanta.

Brewster, Karin L., and Ronald R. Rindfuss. 1990. "Homophobia and Homosociality: An Analysis of Boundary Maintenance." *Sociological Quarterly* 31: 423–439.

———. 2000. "Fertility and Women's Employment in Industrialized Nations." *Annual Review of Sociology* 26: 271–296.

Brice, Arthur. 2010. "Mexico Asks for Probe into Teen's Shooting Death by U.S. Border Agent." CNN News. June 10. http://articles.cnn.com/2010-06-08/us/texas.border.patrol.shooting_1_ciudad-juarez-fbi-agent?_s=PM:US (accessed March 23, 2011).

Briggs, Laura. 1998. "Discourses of 'Forced Sterilization' in Puerto Rico: The Problem with the Speaking Subaltern." *Differences* 10, no. 2: 30–66.

Brinkmann, Svend. 2010. "Human Vulnerabilities: Toward a Theory of Rights for Qualitative Researchers." In *Qualitative Inquiry and Human Rights*, edited by Norman Denzin and Michael Giardina, 82–99. Walnut Creek, CA: Left Coast Press.

Britton, Dana M. 2003. *At Work in the Iron Cage: The Prison as Gendered Organization*. New York: New York University Press.

Brod, H. 1987. *The Making of Masculinities: The New Men's Studies*. Boston, MA: Allen and Unwin.

Brody, David. 1960. *Steelworkers in America: The Nonunion Era*. Cambridge, MA: Harvard University Press.

———. 1965. *Labor in Crisis: The Steel Strike of 1919*. Philadelphia: Lippincott.

———. 1979. "The Old Labor History and the New: In Search of an American Working Class." *Labor History* 20: 111–126.

———. 2001. "Labour Rights as Human Rights: A Reality Check." *British Journal of Industrial Relations* 39: 601–605.

Broido, E. M. 2000. "The Development of Social Justice Allies during College: A Phenomenological Investigation." *Journal of College Student Development* 41: 3–17.

Bronshtein, I. N., and K. A. Semendyayev. 1985. *Handbook of Mathematics*. English translation edited by K. A. Hirsch. Leipzig edition. Based on the original 1945 Russian edition and the 1957 translation into German. New York: Van Nostrand Reinhold.

Brown, B. S. 2011. *Research Handbook on International Criminal Law*. Northampton, MA: Edward Elgar Publishing.

Brown, Lester R. 2009. *Plan B 4.0: Mobilizing to Save Civilization*. New York: W. W. Norton.

144 BIBLIOGRAPHY

Brown, Phil. 2000. "Popular Epidemiology and Toxic Waste Contamination: Lay and Professional Ways of Knowing." In *Perspectives in Medical Sociology*, edited by Phil Brown, 157–181. Prospect Heights, IL: Waveland Press.

Brown, Phil, and Edwin J. Mikkelsen. 1990. *No Safe Place: Toxic Waste, Leukemia, and Community Action*. Berkeley: University of California Press.

Brown, Roger, and Andrew Gilman. 1960. "The Pronouns of Power and Solidarity." In *Style in Language*, edited by Thomas A. Sebeok, 253–276. Cambridge, MA: MIT Press.

Brown, Stephen. 2003. "The Problem with Marx on Rights." *Journal of Human Rights* 2, no. 4: 517–522.

Brown, Tony N., Sherrill L. Sellers, Kendrick T. Brown, and James S. Jackson. 1999. "Race, Ethnicity, and Culture in the Sociology of Mental Health." In *Handbook of the Sociology of Mental Health*, edited by Carol S. Aneshensel and J. C. Phelan, 167–182. New York: Springer.

Brown, Wendy. 1995. *States of Injury*. Princeton, NJ: Princeton University Press.

Browning, Christopher R. 1998. *Ordinary Men: Police Battalion 101 and the Final Solution in Poland*. 2nd ed. New York: HarperCollins.

Brownlie, I. 2008. *Principles of Public International Law*. 7th ed. Oxford: Oxford University Press.

Brubaker, R. 1996. *Nationalism Reframed: Nationhood and the National Question in the New Europe*. Cambridge, UK: Cambridge University Press.

Brubaker, Rogers, Mara Lovemen, and Peter Stamatov. 2004. "Ethnicity as Cognition." *Theory and Society* 33: 31–64.

Brubaker, William Rogers. 1990. "Immigration, Citizenship, and the Nation-State in France and Germany: A Comparative Historical Analysis." *International Sociology* 5, no. 4: 379–407.

Brückner, H., and K. U. Mayer. 2005. "De-Standardization of the Life Course: What It Might Mean? And if It Means Anything, whether It Actually Took Place." In *The Structure of the Life Course: Standardized? Individualized? Differentiated?*, edited by R. Macmillan, 27–54. Advances in Life Course Research 9. Amsterdam: JAI Elsevier.

Brunnhölzl, Karl. 2007. "'Introduction' to Nagarjuna." In *In Praise of Dharmadhātu*, edited and translated by Karl Brunnhölzl, 21–55. Ithaca, NY: Snow Lion Publications.

Brunsson, Nils. 1985. *The Irrational Organization*. New York: John Wiley.

Brush, Lisa D. 2002. *Gender and Governance*. Lanham, MD: AltaMira Press.

Bryant, Rachel, and Robin Shura. 2010. "A Life Course of Human Rights? The 'Rising Sun' of Medical Decision-Making over the Life Course." Paper presented at the annual meeting of the American Sociological Association, Atlanta, Georgia, August 16, 2010.

Bucholz, Kathleen, and Lee Robins. 1989. "Sociological Research on Alcohol Use, Problems, and Policy." *Annual Review of Sociology* 15: 163–186.

Bullard, R. D. 1993. *Confronting Environmental Racism: Voices from the Grassroots*. Cambridge, MA: South End Press.

———. 2000. *Dumping in Dixie: Race, Class, and Environmental Quality*. Boulder, CO: Westview Press.

———. 2005. *The Quest for Environmental Justice: Human Rights and the Politics of Pollution*. San Francisco: Sierra Club Books.

Bullard, Robert D., and Beverly Wright, eds. 2009. *Race, Place, and Environmental Justice after Hurricane Katrina*. Boulder, CO: Westview Press.

Bulmer, Martin. 1984. *The Chicago School of Sociology: Institutionalization, Diversity, and the Rise of Sociological Research*. Chicago: University of Chicago Press.

Bumpass, L., and J. Sweet. 1989. *Children's Experience in Single-Parent Families: Implications of Cohabitation and Marital Transitions*. Madison: University of Wisconsin, Center for Demography and Ecology.

Bunch, Charlotte. 1990. "Women's Rights as Human Rights: Toward a Re-Vision of Human Rights." *Human Rights Quarterly* 12: 486–498.

Bunch, Charlotte, and Susana Fried. 1996. "Beijing '95: Moving Women's Human Rights from Margin to Center." *Signs* 22: 200–204.

Bunch, Charlotte, and Niamh Reilly. 1994. *Demanding Accountability: The Global Campaign and Vienna Tribunal for Women's Human Rights*. Rutgers, NJ: Center for Women's Global Leadership and the United Nations Development Fund for Women.

Burawoy, Michael. 1983. "Between the Labor Process and the State: The Changing Face of Factory Regimes under Advanced Capitalism." *American Sociological Review* 48: 587–605.

———. 2004. "Public Sociologies: Contradictions, Dilemmas and Possibilities." *Social Forces* 82, no. 4: 1603–1618.

———. 2005. "For Public Sociology." *American Sociological Review* 70: 4–28.

———. 2006. "A Public Sociology for Human Rights." Introduction to *Public Sociologies Reader*, edited by Judith Blau and Keri Iyall Smith, 1–18. Lanham, MD: Rowman & Littlefield.

———. 2007. "Evaluating 'No Child Left Behind.'" *The Nation*. http://www.thenation.com/doc/20070521/darling-hammond (accessed May 19, 2009).

Burawoy, Michael, and Janos Lukács. 1992. *The Radiant Past: Ideology and Reality in Hungary's Road to Capitalism*. Chicago: University of Chicago Press.

Burchardt, T. 2004. "Capabilities and Disability: The Capabilities Framework and the Social Model of Disability." *Disability and Society* 19: 735–751.

Bureau of Labor Statistics. 2011. "Union Members Summary." Bureau of Labor Statistics, U.S. Department of Labor. http://www.bls.gov/news.release/union2.nr0.htm (accessed January 21, 2011).

Burgers, Jan Herman. 1992. "The Road to San Francisco: The Revival of the Human Rights Idea in the Twentieth Century." *Human Rights Quarterly* 14: 447–477.

Burke, Mary C. 2010. "Transforming Gender: Medicine, Body Politics, and the Transgender Rights Movement." PhD diss., University of Connecticut, Storrs.

Burke, Roland. 2010. *Decolonization and the Evolution of International Human Rights*. Philadelphia: University of Pennsylvania Press.

Burkett, Elinor, and Frank Bruni. 1993. *A Gospel of Shame: Children, Sexual Abuse and the Catholic Church*. New York: Viking.

Burris, Beverly H. 1993. *Technocracy at Work*. Albany: State University of New York Press.

Burton, Linda. 1990. "Teenage Childbearing as an Alternative Life-Course Strategy in Multi-Generational Black Families." *Human Nature* 1: 58–81.

Burton, Linda, Eduardo Bonilla-Silva, Victor Ray, Rose Buckelew, and Elizabeth H. Freeman. 2010. "Critical Race Theories, Colorism, and the Decade's Research on Families of Color." *Journal of Marriage and Family* 72: 440–459.

Busfield, J. 1996. *Men, Women and Madness: Understanding Gender and Mental Disorder*. London: Macmillan Press.

Bush, Melanie, and Deborah Little. 2009. "Teaching towards Praxis and Political Engagement." In *Engaging Social Justice: Critical Studies of 21st Century Social Transformation*, edited by David Fasenfest, 9–36. Leiden, the Netherlands: Brill.

Bush, Roderick. 2000. *We Are Not What We Seem: Black Nationalism and Class Struggle in the American Century*. New York: New York University Press.

———. 2009. *The End of White World Supremacy: Black Internationalism and the Problem of the Color Line*. Philadelphia: Temple University Press.

Bustamante, Jorge A. 1972. "The Wetback as Deviant: An Application of Labeling Theory." *American Journal of Sociology* 77: 706–718.

Butin, Daniel. 2010. *Service-Learning in Theory and Practice: The Future of Engagement in Higher Education*. New York: Palgrave.

Butler, Judith. 1990. *Gender Trouble: Feminism and the Subversion of Identity*. New York: Routledge.

———. 1993. *Bodies that Matter: On the Discursive Limits of "Sex."* New York: Routledge.

Butler, R. 2002 [1972]. *Why Survive? Being Old in America*. Baltimore: Johns Hopkins.

Button, Graham, ed. 1993. *Technology in Working Order: Studies of Work, Interaction and Technology*. London: Routledge.

Button, Graham, Jeff Coulter, John R. E. Lee, and Wes Sharrock. 1995. *Computers, Minds and Conduct*. Cambridge, UK: Polity Press.

Button, Tanya M. M., Michael C. Stallings, Soo Hyun Rhee, Robin P. Corley, Jason D. Boardman, and John K. Hewitt. 2009. "Perceived Peer Delinquency and the Genetic Predisposition for Substance Dependence Vulnerability." *Drug and Alcohol Dependence* 100: 1–8.

Buvinic, Mayra. 1998. "Women in Poverty: A New Global Underclass." Women in Politics. http://www.onlinewomeninpolitics.org/beijing12/womeninpoverty.pdf (accessed April 11, 2011).

Bynum, Thomas. 2009. "'We Must March Forward!': Juanita Jackson and the Origins of the NAACP Youth Movement." *Journal of African American History* 94: 487–508.

Caetano, R. 1984. "Self-Reported Intoxication among Hispanics in Northern California." *Journal of Studies of Alcohol and Alcoholism* 45: 349–354.

———. 1987. "Acculturation and Attitudes towards Appropriate Drinking among US Hispanics." *Alcohol and Alcoholism* 22: 427–433.

Cagatay, Nilufer. 2001. *Trade, Gender, and Poverty*. New York: United Nations Development Program.

Cahill, Sean. 2009. "The Disproportionate Impact of Antigay Family Policies on Black and Latino Same-Sex Couple Households." *Journal of African American Studies* 13: 219–250.

Caldwell, John C. 2006. *Demographic Transition Theory*. Dordrecht, The Netherlands: Springer.

Calhoun, Craig, ed. 2007. *Sociology in America: A History*. Chicago: University of Chicago Press.

146 BIBLIOGRAPHY

California Legislature. Senate. 1943. *The Report of Joint Fact-Finding Committee on Un-American Activities in California*. Internet Archive. http://www.archive.org/details/reportofjointfac00calirich (accessed December 21, 2011).

Callahan, D. 1987. *Setting Limits: Medical Goals in an Aging Society*. New York: Simon and Schuster.

Callon, Michel. 1986. "Some Elements of a Sociology of Translation: Domestication of Scallops and the Fisherman of St. Brieuc Bay." In *Power, Action, and Belief: A New Sociology of Knowledge?*, edited by J. Law, 196–223. London: Routledge.

Callon, Michel, Pierre Lascoumes, and Yannick Barthe. 2009. *Acting in an Uncertain World: An Essay on Technical Democracy*. Translated by Graham Burchell. Cambridge, MA: MIT Press.

Callon, Michel, and Jean-Pierre Vignolle. 1975. "Breaking Down the Organization: Local Conflicts and Societal Systems of Action." *Social Science Information* 16, no. 2: 147–167.

Campbell, John. 2011. "Neoliberalism in Crisis: Regulatory Roots of the U.S. Financial Meltdown." In *Markets on Trial: The Economic Sociology of the U.S. Financial Crisis*, edited by Michael Lounsbury and Paul M. Hirsch, 65–102. Research in the Sociology of Organizations 30A. London: Emerald Group Publishing.

Campbell-Lendrum, Diarmid, and Majula Lusti-Narasimhan. 2009. "Taking the Heat out of the Population and Climate Change." World Health Organization. http://www.who.int/bulletin/volumes/87/11/09-072652/en/index.html (accessed August 21, 2012).

Cancian, Francesca M., and Steven L. Gordon. 1988. "Changing Emotion Norms in Marriage: Love and Anger in U.S. Women's Magazines since 1900." *Gender and Society* 2: 308–342.

Cantor, Daniel, and Juliet Schor. 1987. *Tunnel Vision: Labor, the World Economy, and Central America*. Boston: South End Press.

Caprioli, Mary. 2001. "Gendered Conflict." *Journal of Peace Research* 37, no. 1: 51–68.

Carlton-Ford, Steve. 2010. "Major Armed Conflicts, Militarization, and Life Chances: A Pooled Time Series Analysis." *Armed Forces and Society* 36: 864–889.

Carpenter, M. 2000. "'It's a Small World': Mental Health Policy under Welfare Capitalism since 1945." *Sociology of Health and Illness* 22: 602–620.

Carson, Rachel. 1962. *Silent Spring*. Boston: Houghton and Mifflin Press.

Casebeer, Kenneth M. 1989. "Drafting Wagner's Act: Leon Keyserling and the Pre-Committee Drafts of the Labor Disputes Act and the National Labor Relations Act." *Industrial Relations Law Journal* 11: 73–131.

Cassese, Antonio A., Guido G. Acquaviva, Mary D. Fan, and Alex A. Whiting. 2011. *International Criminal Law: Cases and Commentary*. Oxford: Oxford University Press.

Castel, R. 1988. *The Regulation of Madness: The Origins of Incarceration in France*. Oxford: Blackwell.

Castells, Manuel. 2000. *The Information Age: Economy, Society and Culture*. Vol. 1: *The Rise of the Network Society*. 2nd ed. Cambridge, UK: Cambridge University Press.

Cavanagh, Shannon E. 2007. "The Social Construction of Romantic Relationships in Adolescence: Examining the Role of Peer Networks, Gender, and Race." *Sociological Inquiry* 77: 572–600.

Centeno, Miguel Angel, and Joseph N. Cohen. 2010. *Global Capitalism: A Sociological Perspective*. Cambridge, MA: Polity.

Centers for Disease Control (CDC). 2011. "Tobacco Use: Targeting the Nation's Leading Killer." CDC. http://www.cdc.gov/chronicdisease/resources/publications/AAG/osh.htm (accessed January 1, 2011).

Cerna, Christina M. 1995. "East Asian Approaches to Human Rights: Proceedings of the Annual Meeting." *American Society of International Law* 89: 152–157.

Cerulo, Karen A. 2007. "The Forum Mailbag." *Sociological Forum* 22: 555–565.

Césaire, Aimé. 2001. *Discourse on Colonialism*. New York: Monthly Review Press.

Chabbott, Collette. 1999. "Development INGOs." In *Constructing World Culture: International Nongovernmental Organizations since 1875*, edited by J. Boli and G. M. Thomas. Stanford, CA: Stanford University Press.

Chambliss, William J. 1964. "A Sociological Analysis of the Law of Vagrancy." *Social Problems* 12, no. 1: 67–77.

———. 1989. "State Organized Crime." *Criminology* 27: 183–208.

Chandler, Alfred D., Jr. 1962. *Strategy and Structure: Chapters in the History of the American Industrial Enterprise*. Cambridge, MA: MIT Press.

———. 1977. *The Visible Hand: The Managerial Revolution in American Business*. Cambridge, MA: Harvard University Press.

Chapel Hill and Carrboro Human Rights Center. 2011. http://www.humanrightscities.org (accessed May 24, 2011).

Chapkis, Wendy. 2000. "Power and Control in the Commercial Sex Trade." In *Sex for Sale: Prostitution, Pornography, and the Sex Industry*, edited by Ronald Weitzer, 181–202. New York: Routledge.

BIBLIOGRAPHY 147

Charlton, Sue Ellen, Jana Everett, and Kathleen Staudt. 1989. *Women, the State, and Development*. Albany: State University of New York Press.

Chase-Dunn, Christopher. 2005. "Social Evolution and the Future of World Society." *Journal of World-Systems Research* 11: 171–192.

Chase-Dunn, Christopher, Robert A. Hanneman, Richard Niemeyer, Christine Petit, and Ellen Reese. 2007. "The Contours of Solidarity and Division among Global Movements." *International Journal of Peace Studies* 12, no. 2: 1–16.

Chaves, Mark. 1994. "Secularization as Declining Religious Authority." *Social Forces* 72: 749–774.

Chavez, Leo R. 2008. *The Latino Threat: Constructing Immigrants, Citizens, and the Nation*. Stanford, CA: Stanford University Press.

Cheng, Shu-Ju Ada, and Lester R. Kurtz. 1998. "Third World Voices Redefining Peace." *Peace Review* 10 (March): 5–12. Available at http://works.bepress.com/lester_kurtz/7 (accessed January 20, 2012).

Cherlin, Andrew. 2008. "Public Display: The Picture-Perfect American Family? These Days, It Doesn't Exist." *Washington Post*. September 7, B1.

Chew, Sing. 1997. "For Nature: Deep Greening World Systems Analysis of the 21st Century." *Journal of World-Systems Research* 3, no. 3: 381–402.

———. 2001. *World Ecological Degradation: Accumulation, Urbanization, and Deforestation: 3000 BC–AD 2000*. New York: Altamira Press.

Child, J. 1972. "Organization Structure, Environment, and Performance: The Role of Strategic Choice." *Sociology* 6: 1–22.

Chiquiar, Daniel, and Gordon H. Hanson. 2005. "International Migration, Self-Selection, and the Distribution of Wages: Evidence from Mexico and the United States." *Journal of Political Economy* 113: 239–281.

Chirayath, Heidi T. 2007. "Difficult, Dysfunctional, and Drug-Dependent: Structure and Agency in Physician Perceptions of Indigent Patients." *Social Theory and Health* 5, no. 1: 30–52.

Chiswick, Barry, and Michael Wenz. 2005. "The Linguistic and Economic Adjustment of Soviet Jewish Immigrants in the United States, 1980 to 2000." IZA DP No. 1726. Institute for the Study of Labor. ftp://repec.iza.org/RePEc/Discussionpaper/dp1238.pdf (accessed July 17, 2012).

Chiswick, Barry R. 1988. "Illegal Immigration and Immigration Control." *Journal of Economic Perspectives* 2, no. 3 (summer): 101–115.

Chomsky, Noam, and Edward S. Herman. 1979. *The Political Economy of Human Rights: The Washington Connection and Third World Fascism*. Boston: South End Press.

Chomsky, Noam, Ralph Nader, Immanuel Wallerstein, Richard C. Lewontin, and Richard Ohmann. 1998. *The Cold War and the University: Toward an Intellectual History of the Postwar Years*. New York: The New Press.

Chow, Esther Ngan-ling. 1996. "Making Waves, Moving Mountains: Reflections on Beijing '95 and Beyond." *Signs* 22: 185–192.

Christakis, Nicholas A., and James H. Fowler. 2009. *Connected: The Surprising Power of Social Networks and How They Shape Our Lives*. New York: Simon and Schuster.

Chudacoff, H. 1989. *How Old Are You? Age Consciousness in America*. Princeton, NJ: Princeton University Press.

Ciganda, Daniel, Alain Gagnon, and Eric Tenkorang. 2010. "Child and Young Adult Headed Households in the Context of the AIDS Epidemic in Zimbabwe, 1988–2006." PSC Discussion Papers Series 24, no. 4: 1–17.

City of Eugene. 2011a. "Equity and Human Rights." City of Eugene. http://www.eugene-or.gov/diversity (accessed May 26, 2011).

———. 2011b. "Sustainable Eugene." City of Eugene. http://www.eugene-or.gov/sustainability (accessed May 26, 2011).

Clanton, Gordon. 1989. "Jealousy in American Culture, 1945–1975: Reflections from Popular Culture." In *The Sociology of Emotions: Original Essays and Research Papers*, edited by D. D. Franks and E. D. McCarthy, 179–193. Greenwich, CT: JAI Press.

Clapham, Andrew. 2007. *Human Rights: A Very Short Introduction*. New York: Oxford University Press.

Clapp, J. 2001. *Toxic Exports: The Transfer of Hazardous Wastes from Rich to Poor Countries*. Ithaca, NY: Cornell University Press.

Clark, Adele E., Laura Mamo, Jennifer R. Fishman, Janet Shim, and Jennifer Fosket. 2003. "Biomedicalization: Technoscientific Transformations of Health, Illness and U.S. Biomedicine." *American Sociological Review* 68, no. 2: 161–194.

Clark, Candace. 1990. "Emotions and Micropolitics in Everyday Life: Some Patterns and Paradoxes of 'Place.'" In *Research Agendas in the Sociology of Emotions*, edited by T. D. Kemper, 305–333. Albany: State University of New York Press.

148 BIBLIOGRAPHY

Clark, Cindy Dell. 2010. *A Younger Voice: Doing Child-Centered Qualitative Research*. New York: Oxford University Press.

Clark-Ibáñez, Marisol. 2007. "Inner-City Children in Sharper Focus: Sociology of Childhood and Photo-Elicitation Interviews." In *Visual Research Methods: Image, Society, and Representation*, edited by Gregory C. Stanczak, 167–196. Thousand Oaks, CA: Sage Publications.

Clarke, Lee. 2006. *Worst Cases: Terror and Catastrophe in the Popular Imagination*. Chicago: University of Chicago Press.

Clawson, Dan. 1980. *Bureaucracy and the Labor Process*. New York: Monthly Review Press.

———. 2003. *The Next Upsurge: Labor and the New Social Movements*. Ithaca, NY: ILR Press.

Clayton, Mark. 2011. "Fukushima Meltdown Could Be Template for Nuclear Terrorism, Study Says." *Christian Science Monitor*. June 7.

Clegg, Stewart. 1989. *Frameworks of Power*. London: Sage.

———. 1990. *Modern Organization: Organization Studies in the Postmodern World*. London: Sage.

Clegg, Stewart, and Winton Higgins. 1987. "Against the Current: Organizational Sociology and Socialism." *Organization Studies* 8: 201–221.

Cohany, Sharon, and Emy Sok. 2007. *Trends in Labor Force Participation of Married Mothers of Infants*. Washington, DC: Bureau of Labor Statistics.

Cohen, Beth. 2007. *Case Closed: Holocaust Survivors in Postwar America*. New Brunswick, NJ: Rutgers University Press.

Cohen, Carl. 1986. "The Case for the Use of Animals in Biomedical Research." *New England Journal of Medicine* 315: 865–870.

Cohen, Cathy. 1999. *The Boundaries of Blackness: AIDS and the Breakdown of Black Politics*. Chicago: University of Chicago Press.

Cohen, Stanley. 2001. *States of Denial: Knowing about Atrocities and Suffering*. Cambridge, UK: Polity Press.

Cohn, Marjorie. 2001. "The World Trade Organization: Elevating Property Interests above Human Rights." *Georgia Journal of International and Comparative Law* 29: 427–440.

Cole, W. M. 2005. "Sovereignty Relinquished? Explaining Commitment to the International Human Rights Covenants, 1966–1999." *American Sociological Review* 70: 472–495.

Coleman, James. 1964. *Introduction to Mathematical Sociology*. New York: The Free Press.

———. 1990. *Foundations of Social Theory*. Cambridge, MA: Belknap Press.

———. 2006. *The Criminal Elite*. New York: Worth Publishers.

Coleman, Matthew. 2007. "Immigration Geopolitics beyond the Mexico-U.S. Border." *Antipode* 39: 54–76.

Colker, R. 2005. *The Disability Pendulum the First Decade of the Americans with Disabilities Act*. New York: New York University Press.

Collett, Jessica L., and Omar Lizardo. 2009. "A Power-Control Theory of Gender and Religiosity." *Journal for the Scientific Study of Religion* 48: 213–231.

Collins, Patricia Hill. 1990. *Black Feminist Thought: Knowledge, Consciousness, and the Politics of Empowerment*. New York: Routledge, Chapman and Hall.

———. 1993. "Toward a New Vision: Race, Class, and Gender as Categories of Analysis and Connection." *Race, Sex and Class* 1: 25–45.

———. 1994. "Shifting the Center: Race, Class, and Feminist Theorizing about Motherhood." In *Representations of Motherhood*, edited by Donna Basin and Margaret Honey, 56–74. New Haven, CT: Yale University Press.

———. 2005. *Black Sexual Politics*. New York: Routledge.

Collins, Randall. 1974. "Three Faces of Cruelty: Towards a Comparative Sociology of Violence." *Theory and Society* 1, no. 4 (winter): 415–440.

———. 1975. *Conflict Sociology: Toward an Explanatory Science*. New York: Academic Press.

———. 1990. "Stratification, Emotional Energy, and the Transient Emotions." In *Research Agendas in the Sociology of Emotions*, edited by T. D. Kemper, 27–57. Albany: State University of New York Press.

———. 1998. *The Sociology of Philosophies: A Global Theory of Intellectual Change*. Cambridge, MA: Belknap Press.

———. 2008. *Violence*. Princeton, NJ: Princeton University Press.

Coltraine, Scott, and Michelle Adams. 2008. *Gender and Families*. Lanham, MD: AltaMira Press.

Columbia Law School Human Rights Institute and International Association of Official Human Rights Agencies (IAOHRA). 2010. *State and Local Human Rights Agencies: Recommendations for Advancing Opportunity and Equality through an International Human Rights Framework*. New York: Columbia Law School Human Rights Institute and IAOHRA.

Comin, Diego, and Bart Hobijn. 2004. "Cross-Country Technology Adoption: Making the Theories Face the Facts." *Journal of Monetary Economics* 51: 39–83.

BIBLIOGRAPHY 149

Committee on Science, Engineering, and Public Policy (COSEPUP). 1995. *On Being a Scientist: Responsible Conduct in Research*. Washington, DC: National Academy Press.

Committee on the Elimination of Racial Discrimination. 2000. "General Recommendation 25, Gender Related Dimensions of Racial Discrimination." University of Minnesota, Human Rights Library. http:// www1.umn.edu/humanrts/gencomm/genrexxv.htm (accessed September 6, 2012).

Commons, John, Ulrich Bonnell Phillips, Eugene Allen Gilmore, and John B. Andrews, eds. 1910–1911. *A Documentary History of American Industrial Society*. 11 vols. Cleveland, OH: Arthur Clark Company.

———. 1918–1935. *History of Labor in the United States*. 4 vols. New York: Macmillan.

Compa, Lance. 2000. *Unfair Advantage: Workers' Freedom of Association in the United States under International Human Rights Standards*. Ithaca, NY: ILR Press.

Comte, Auguste. 1970. *Introduction to Positive Philosophy*. Indianapolis: Bobbs Merrill.

Conley, Dalton, Kate W. Strully, and Neil G. Bennett. 2003. *The Starting Gate: Birth Weight and Life Chances*. Berkeley: University of California Press.

Conley, Dalton. 2011. *You May Ask Yourself: An Introduction to Thinking Like a Sociologist*. Second Edition. New York, NY: W. W. Norton.

Connell, Raeyn. 1987. *Gender and Power: Society, the Person, and Sexual Politics*. Stanford, CA: Stanford University Press.

———. 1995. "Symposium: Human Rights and the Sociological Project (Sociology and Human Rights)." *Australian and New Zealand Journal of Sociology* 31: 25–29.

———. 2005. *Masculinities*. Berkeley: University of California Press.

Conrad, Peter. 2000. "Medicalization, Genetics and Human Problems." In *Handbook of Medical Sociology*, edited by Chloe E. Bird, Peter Conrad, and Allen M. Fremont, 322–333. 5th ed. Upper Saddle River, NJ: Prentice Hall.

———. 2007. *Medicalization of Society: On the Transformation of Human Conditions into Treatable Disorders*. Baltimore: Johns Hopkins University Press.

Conrad, Peter, and Joseph Schneider. 1992. *Deviance and Medicalization: From Badness to Sickness*. Philadelphia: Temple University Press.

Cook, Daniel T., and John Wall, eds. 2011. *Children and Armed Conflict*. Hampshire, UK: Palgrave Macmillan.

Cook, J. A., and E. R. Wright. 1995. "Medical Sociology and the Study of Severe Mental Illness: Reflections on Past Accomplishments and Directions for Future Research." *Journal of Health and Social Behaviour* 35: 95–114.

Cooley, Charles Horton. 1964 [1902]. *Human Nature and the Social Order*. New York: Schocken Books.

Cooney, Mark. 1997. "From Warre to Tyranny: Lethal Conflict and the State." *American Sociological Review* 62: 316–338.

Coontz, S. 1992. *The Way We Never Were: American Families and the Nostalgia Trap*. New York: Basic Books.

———. 1997. *The Way We Really Are: Coming to Terms with America's Changing Families*. New York: Basic Books.

Coosmans, F., F. Grunfeld, and M. T. Kamminga. 2010. "Methods of Human Rights Research: A Primer." *Human Rights Quarterly* 32: 179–186.

Cornfield, Daniel B. 1989. *Becoming a Mighty Voice: Conflict and Change in the United Furniture Workers of America*. New York: Russell Sage.

Corrêa, S., and V. Muntarbhorn. 2007. "The Yogyakarta Principles on the Application of International Human Rights Law in Relation to Sexual Orientation and Gender Identity." The Yogyakarta Principles. http://www.yogyakartaprinciples.org/principles_en.htm (accessed July 21, 2010).

Corsaro, William A. 2005. *The Sociology of Childhood*. Newbury Park, CA: Pine Forge Press.

Corsaro, William A., and Laura Fingerson. 2003. "Development and Socialization in Childhood." In *Handbook of Social Psychology*, edited by John Delamater, 125–156. New York: Kluwer.

Cotterrell, Roger. 2007. "Sociology of Law." In *Encyclopedia of Law and Society: American and Global Perspectives*, edited by David Scott Clark, 1413–1419. Thousand Oaks, CA: Sage Publications.

Coulter, Jeff. 1979. *The Social Construction of Mind: Studies in Ethnomethodology and Linguistic Philosophy*. Totowa, NJ: Rowman & Littlefield.

———. 1982. "Remarks on the Conceptualization of Social Structure." *Philosophy of the Social Sciences* 12: 33–46.

———. 1989. *Mind in Action*. Atlantic Highlands, NJ: Humanities Press International.

Coulter, Jeff, and Wes Sharrock. 2007. *Brain, Mind, and Human Behaviour in Contemporary Cognitive Science: Critical Assessments of the Philosophy of Psychology*. Lewiston, NY: Edwin Mellen.

Council of Europe. 2011. http://www.coe.int (accessed May 24, 2011).

150 BIBLIOGRAPHY

Council of Europe Congress of Local and Regional Authorities. 2010. "The Role of Local and Regional Authorities in the Implementation of Human Rights." Draft Resolution, Congress of Local and Regional Authorities, 18th Session, Strasbourg, France, March 1.

Courant, Richard. 1937 [1934]. *Differential and Integral Calculus.* Translated by E. J. McShane. 2 vols. New York: Wiley.

Courtwright, David. 2001. *Forces of Habit: Drugs and the Making of the Modern World.* Cambridge, MA: Harvard University Press.

Cousins, S. 1989. "Culture and Selfhood in Japan and the U.S." *Journal of Personality and Social Psychology* 56: 124–131.

Cox, Laurence, and Cristina Flesher Fominaya. 2009. "Movement Knowledge: What Do We Know, How Do We Create Knowledge and What Do We Do with It?" *Interface: A Journal for and about Social Movements* 1, no. 1: 1–20.

Cox, Laurence, and Alf Gunvald Nilsen. 2007. "Social Movements Research and the 'Movement of Movements': Studying Resistance to Neoliberal Globalisation." *Sociology Compass* 1, no. 2: 424–442.

Cox, Oliver Cromwell. 1948. *Caste, Class, and Race: A Study in Social Dynamics.* New York: Monthly Review Press.

Crane, Diana. 2005. "Democracy and Globalization in the Global Economy." In *The Blackwell Companion to the Sociology of Culture,* edited by Mark D. Jacobs and Nancy Weiss Hanrahan. 412–427. Malden, MA: Blackwell.

Craven, Matthew C. R. 1995. *The International Covenant on Economic, Social, and Cultural Rights: A Perspective on Its Development.* Oxford: Oxford University Press.

Crenshaw, Kimberlé. 1991. "Mapping the Margins: Intersectionality, Identity Politics, and Violence against Women of Color." *Stanford Law Review* 43: 1241–1299.

Cress, Daniel M., and David A. Snow. 1996. "Mobilization at the Margins: Resources, Benefactors, and the Viability of Homeless Social Movement Organizations." *American Sociological Review* 61: 1089–1109.

———. 2000. "The Outcomes of Homeless Mobilization: The Influence of Organization, Disruption, Political Mediation, and Framing." *American Journal of Sociology* 105: 1063–1104.

Crimmins, Eileen M. 1993. "Demography: The Past 30 Years, the Present, and the Future." *Demography* 30, no. 4: 571–594.

Crocker, Jennifer. 2002. "Contingencies of Self-Worth: Implications for Self-Regulation and Psychological Vulnerability." *Self and Identity* 1: 143–149.

Croissant, Jennifer, and Sal Restivo. 1995. "Technoscience or Tyrannoscience Rex: Science and Progressive Thought." In *Ecologies of Knowledge,* edited by Susan Leigh Star, 39–87. Albany: State University of New York Press.

Crompton, Tom, and Tim Kasser. 2009. *Meeting Environmental Challenges: The Role of Human Identity.* Devon, UK: Green Books (World Wildlife Fund).

Crooms, Lisa. 1997. "Indivisible Rights and Intersectional Identities or 'What Do Women's Rights Have to Do with the Race Convention?'" *Howard Law Journal* 40: 620–640.

Crosnoe, Robert. 2011. *Fitting In, Standing Out: Navigating the Social Challenges of High School to Get an Education.* New York: Cambridge University Press.

Crosnoe, Robert, and Glen H. Elder Jr. 2004. "From Childhood to the Later Years: Pathways of Human Development." *Research on Aging* 26, no. 6: 623–654.

Croteau, David, William Hoynes, and Charlotte Ryan. 2005. *Rhyming Hope and History: Activists, Academics, and Social Movement Scholarship.* Minneapolis: University of Minnesota Press.

Cummins, E. E. 1936. "Workers' Education in the United States." *Social Forces* 14: 597–605.

Cunningham, W. P., and M. A. Cunningham. 2008. *Principles of Environmental Science: Inquiry and Applications.* New York: McGraw-Hill.

Currah, Paisley, Richard M. Juang, and Shannon Price Minter. 2006. *Transgender Rights.* Minneapolis: University of Minnesota Press.

Currie, Elliot. 1994. *Reckoning: Drugs, the Cities, and the American Future.* New York: Hill and Wang.

Cutler, J. Elbert. 1907. "Contribution to Symposium on How Should Sociology Be Taught as a College or University Course." *American Journal of Sociology* 12: 604–606.

Cyert, Richard, and James March. 1963. *A Behavioral Theory of the Firm.* 2nd ed. Malden, MA: Wiley-Blackwell.

Czarniawska, Barbara. 1997. *Narrating the Organization: Dramas of Institutional Identity.* Chicago: University of Chicago Press.

D'Cunha, J. 2005. "Claim and Celebrate Women Migrants' Human Rights through CEDAW: The Case of Women Migrant Workers, a UNIFEM Briefing Paper." United Nations Entity for Gender Equality and the Empowerment of Women. http://www.unwomen-eseasia.org/projects/migrant/mig_pub.htm (accessed July 17, 2012).

Dabbs, J. M., Jr., and M. G. Dabbs. 2000. *Heroes, Rogues, and Lovers: Testosterone and Behavior.* New York: McGraw-Hill.

Dagum, Camilo. 1983. "Income Inequality Measures." In *Encyclopedia of Statistical Sciences*, edited by Samuel Kotz, Norman L. Johnson, and Campbell B. Read, 4:34–40. New York: Wiley.

Dahrendorf, Ralf. 1958. "Out of Utopia: Toward a Reorientation of Sociological Analysis." *American Journal of Sociology* 64, no. 2: 115–127.

Dalai Lama and Paul Eckman. 2008. *Emotional Awareness: Overcoming the Obstacles to Psychological Balance and Compassion.* Foreword by Daniel Goleman. New York: Times Books, Henry Holt and Co.

Dallaire, Bernadette, Michael McCubbin, Paul Morin, and David Cohen. 2000. "Civil Commitment Due to Mental Illness and Dangerousness: The Union of Law and Psychiatry within a Treatment-Control System." *Sociology of Health and Illness* 22: 679–699.

Daniels, Roger. 2004. *Guarding the Golden Door: American Immigration Policy and Immigrants since 1882.* New York: Hill and Wang.

Dannefer, Dale. 1984. "Adult Development and Social Theory: A Paradigmatic Reappraisal." *American Sociological Review* 49: 1.

———. 2010. "Age, the Life Course, and the Sociological Imagination: Prospects for Theory." In *Handbook of Aging and the Social Sciences*, edited by R. Binstock and L. George, 3–16. New York: Academic.

Dannefer, Dale, and P. Uhlenberg. 1999. "Paths of the Life Course: A Typology." In *Handbook of Theories of Aging*, edited by V. Bengston and K. W. Schaie, 306–327. New York: Springer.

Dannefer, Dale, and Chris Phillipson, eds. 2010. *International Handbook of Social Gerontology.* London: Sage.

Dannefer, Dale, and Robin Shura. 2007. "The Second Demographic Transition, Aging Families, and the Aging of the Institutionalized Life Course." In *Social Structures: Demographic Changes and the Well-Being of Older Persons*, edited by K. Warner Schaie and Peter Uhlenberg, 212–229. New York: Springer.

———. 2009. "Experience, Social Structure and Later Life: Meaning and Old Age in an Aging Society." In *International Handbook of Population Aging*, edited by P. Uhlenberg, 747–755. Dordrecht, the Netherlands: Springer.

Danto, Arthur C. 1967. "Philosophy of Science, Problems of." In *Encyclopedia of Philosophy*, edited by Paul Edwards, 6:296–300. New York: Macmillan.

Davidson, Alastair. 2010. "History, Human Rights and the Left." *Thesis Eleven* 100: 106–116.

Davis, Gerald F., Doug McAdam, W. Richard Scott, and Mayer N. Zald, eds. 2005. *Social Movements and Organization Theory.* Cambridge, UK: Cambridge University Press.

Davis, Jeff, and Daniel Were. 2008. "A Longitudinal Study of the Effects of Uncertainty on Reproductive Behaviors." *Human Nature* 19: 426–452.

Davis, Kingsley, and Wilbert E. Moore. 1945. "Some Principles of Stratification." *American Sociological Review* 10: 242–249.

De Genova, Nicholas. 2005. "In Re: Rodriguez." In *The Oxford Encyclopedia of Latinos and Latinas in the United States*, edited by S. Oboler and D. J. González, 2:380–382. New York: Oxford University Press.

De Haas, H. 2010. "Migration and Development: A Theoretical Perspective." *International Migration Review* 44: 227–264.

De Souza, Roger-Mark, J. S. Williams, and F. A. B. Meyerson. 2003. "Critical Links: Population, Health, and Environment." *Population Bulletin* 58: 1–43.

De Than, C., and E. Shorts. 2003. *International Criminal Law and Human Rights.* London: Sweet and Maxwell.

Deci, Edward L., and Richard M. Ryan. 2000. "The 'What' and 'Why' of Goal Pursuits: Human Needs and the Self-Determination of Behavior." *Psychological Inquiry* 11: 227–268.

Deegan, Mary Jo. 1988. *Jane Addams and the Men of the Chicago School, 1892–1918.* New Brunswick, NJ: Transaction Publishers.

———. 2002. *Race, Hull House, and the University of Chicago: A New Conscience against Ancient Evils.* Westport, CT: Praeger.

Deflem, Mathieu. 2008. *Sociology of Law: Visions of a Scholarly Tradition.* Cambridge, UK: Cambridge University Press.

Deflem, Mathieu, and Stephen Chicoine. 2011. "The Sociological Discourse on Human Rights: Lessons from the Sociology of Human Rights." *Development and Society* 40, no. 1 (June): 101–115.

Delanty, Gerard. 2009. *The Cosmopolitan Imagination.* New York: Cambridge University Press.

Della Porta, Donatella, Massimillano Andretta, Lorenzo Mosca, and Herbert Reiter. 2006. *Globalization from Below: Transnational Activists and Protest Networks.* Minneapolis: University of Minnesota Press.

DeMartino, George. 2010. "On Marxism, Institutionalism and the Problem of Labor Exploitation." *Rethinking Marxism* 22, no. 4: 524–530.

152 BIBLIOGRAPHY

Denning, Michael. 1998. *The Cultural Front: The Laboring of American Culture in the Twentieth Century.* New York: Verso Books.

Denzin, Norman. 1997. *Interpretative Ethnography: Ethnographic Practices for the 21st Century.* Thousand Oaks, CA: Sage.

———. 2010. *The Qualitative Manifesto: A Call to Arms.* Walnut Creek, CA: Left Coast Press.

Denzin, Norman, and Michael D. Giardina. 2010. *Qualitative Inquiry and Human Rights.* Walnut Creek, CA: Left Coast Press.

Department of Homeland Security (DHS). 2009. "Immigration Statistics." DHS. http://www.dhs.gov/files/ statistics/immigration.shtm (accessed January 31, 2011).

———. 2010. "Immigration Enforcement Actions: 2009." DHS. http://www.dhs.gov/xlibrary/assets/statistics/publications/enforcement_ar_2009.pdf (accessed October 12, 2010).

Department of Justice. 2010. "Crime in the United States, 2009." Federal Bureau of Investigation. http://www2.fbi.gov/ucr/cius2009/arrests/index.html (accessed January 1, 2011).

Derrida, Jacques. 1978. *Writing and Difference.* London: Routledge and Kegan Paul.

———. 2004. "The Animal that I Am." In *Animal Philosophy: Essential Readings in Continental Thought,* edited by Peter Allerton and Matthew Calarco: 113–128. New York: Continuum.

Desai, Manisha. 2002. "Transnational Solidarity: Women's Agency, Structural Adjustment, and Globalization." In *Women's Activism and Globalization: Linking Local Struggles and Transnational Politics,* edited by N. Naples and M. Desai, 15–33. New York: Routledge.

———. 2005. "Transnationalism: The Face of Feminist Politics Post-Beijing." *International Social Science Journal* 57: 319–330.

DeSouza, Roger-Mark, John S. Williams, and Frederick A. B. Meyerson. 2003. *Critical Links: Population, Health, and the Environment.* Population Resource Bureau. http://www.prb.org/Publications/PopulationBulletins/2003/CriticalLinksPopulationHealthandtheEnvironmentPDF340KB.aspx.

———. 2006. "From Autonomies to Solidarities: Transnational Feminist Practices." In *Handbook of Gender and Women's Studies,* edited by Kathy Davis, Mary Evans, and Judith Lorber, 459–470. Thousand Oaks, CA: Sage Publications.

DeVault, Marjorie. 2007. "Knowledge from the Field." In *Sociology in America: A History,* edited by Craig Calhoun, 155–182. Chicago: University of Chicago Press.

Devinatz, Victor G. 2003. "U.S. Labor and Industrial Relations Historiography: A Review Essay." In *Work in America: An Encyclopedia of History, Policy and Society,* edited by Carl E. Van Horn and Herbert A. Schaffner, xxvii–xxxviii. Santa Barbara, CA: ABC-CLIO.

Devine, Patricia G. 1989. "Stereotypes and Prejudice: Their Automatic and Controlled Components." *Journal of Personality and Social Psychology* 56: 5–18.

Dewey, J. 1922. *Human Nature and Conduct.* New York: Holt.

———. 1980 [1934]. *Art as Experience.* Reprint. New York: Perigree.

———. 1985. *The Later Works, 1925–1953.* Vol. 6. Carbondale: Southern Illinois University Press.

Dhamoon, Rita. 2010. *Identity/Difference Politics: How Difference Is Produced, and Why It Matters.* Vancouver: University of British Columbia.

Diamond, Lisa. 2006. "Careful What You Ask For: Reconsidering Feminist Epistemology and Autobiographical Narrative in Research on Sexual Identity Development." *Signs* 31: 471–491.

Diaz-McConnell, Eileen. 2011. "An 'Incredible Number of Latinos and Asians': Media Representations of Racial and Ethnic Population Change in Atlanta, Georgia." In "Latino/as and the Media," special issue, *Latino Studies* 9, no. 2/3: 177–197.

Dill, Bonnie Thornton. 1983. "Race, Class, and Gender: Prospects for an All-Inclusive Sisterhood." *Feminist Studies* 9: 131–150.

Dillon, Michele. 2005. "Sexuality and Religion: Negotiating Identity Differences." In *The Blackwell Companion to the Sociology of Culture,* edited Mark D. Jacobs and Nancy Weiss Hanrahan, 220–233. Malden, MA: Blackwell.

DiMaggio, Paul, and Walter W. Powell. 1983. "The Iron Cage Revisited: Institutional Isomorphism and Collective Rationality in Organizational Fields." *American Sociological Review* 48: 147–160.

DiMauro, Diane. 1995. *Sexuality Research in the United States: An Assessment of the Social and Behavioral Sciences.* New York: Social Sciences Research Council.

DiPrete, Thomas, and Gregory M. Eirich. 2006. "Cumulative Advantage as a Mechanism for Inequality: A Review of Theoretical and Empirical Developments." *Annual Review of Sociology* 32: 271–297.

Dixit, Raman. 2010. "Naxalite Movement in India: The State's Response." *Journal of Defense Studies* 4, no. 2: http://www.idsa.in/jds/4_2_2010_NaxaliteMovementinIndia_rdixit (accessed July 17, 2012).

Dixon, D., and L. Maher. 2002. "Anh Hai: Policing, Culture, and Social Exclusion in a Street Heroin Market." *Policing and Society* 12, no. 2: 93–110.

BIBLIOGRAPHY 153

Dobbin, Frank. 1994. *Forging Industrial Policy: The United States, Britain, and France in the Railway Age*. Cambridge, UK: Cambridge University Press.

———. 2005. "Comparative and Historical Perspectives in Economic Sociology." In *The Handbook of Economic Sociology*, edited by Neil Smelser and Richard Swedberg, 26–48. 2nd ed. Princeton, NJ: Princeton University Press and Russell Sage Foundation.

Dolgon, Corey, and Chris Baker. 2010. *Social Problems: A Service Learning Approach*. Thousand Oaks, CA: Sage Publications.

Dolgon, Corey, and Mary Chayko. 2010. *Pioneers of Public Sociology: 30 Years of Humanity and Society*. New York: Sloan Publishing.

Dolgon, Corey, Mavis Morton, Tim Maher, and James Pennell. 2012. "Civic Engagement and Public Sociology: Two 'Movements' in Search of a Mission." *Journal of Applied Social Science* 6, no. 1: 5–30.

Domhoff, G. William. 2005. "Power at the Local Level: Growth Coalition Theory." University of Santa Cruz Sociology Department. http://sociology.ucsc.edu/whorulesamerica/local/growth_coalition_theory. html (accessed May 29, 2011).

Donaldson, L. 1987. "Strategy and Structural Adjustment to Regain Fit and Performance: In Defence of Contingency Theory." *Journal of Management Studies* 24, no. 1: 1–24.

Donnelly, Jack. 1982. "Human Rights and Human Dignity: An Analytic Critique of Non-Western Conceptions of Human Rights." *American Political Science Review* 76, no. 2: 303–316.

———. 1985. *The Concept of Human Rights*. London: St. Martin's Press.

———. 2003. *Universal Human Rights in Theory and Practice*. 2nd ed. Ithaca, NY: Cornell University Press.

———. 2006. *International Human Rights*. Boulder, CO: Westview Press.

———. 2007. "The Relative Universality of Human Rights." *Human Rights Quarterly* 28: 281–306.

Donoho, Douglas Lee. 1990–1991. "Relativism versus Universalism in Human Rights: The Search for Meaningful Standards." *Stanford Journal of International Law* 27: 345–391.

Donovan, Josephine, and Carol Adams, eds. 1995. *Animals and Women: Feminist Theoretical Explorations*. Durham, NC: Duke University Press.

———, eds. 2007. *The Feminist Care Tradition in Animal Ethics*. New York: Columbia University Press.

Douglas, Karen Manges, and Rogelio Sáenz. 2010. "The Making of 'Americans': Old Boundaries, New Realities." In *Teaching and Studying the Americas: Cultural Influences from Colonialism to the Present*, edited by A. B. Pinn, C. F. Levander, and M. O. Emerson, 139–156. New York: Palgrave Macmillan.

Douglas, M., and A. Wildavsky. 1982. *Risk and Culture: An Essay on the Selection of Technological and Environmental Dangers*. Berkeley: University of California Press.

Dowd, Jacquelyn Hall. 1993. *Revolt against Chivalry*. New York: Columbia University Press.

Dowse, L. 2001. "Contesting Practices, Challenging Codes: Self Advocacy, Disability Politics and the Social Model." *Disability and Society* 16: 123–141.

Doyal, Lesley. 1995. *What Makes Women Sick: Gender and the Political Economy of Health*. London: Macmillan.

———. 2001. "Sex, Gender, and Health: The Need for a New Approach." *British Medical Journal* (November 3): 323–331.

Dreby, Joanna. 2010. *Divided by Borders*. Berkeley: University of California Press.

Dreier, J. 2004. "Decision Theory and Morality." In *The Oxford Handbook of Rationality*, edited by A. Mele and P. Rawling, 156–181. Oxford: Oxford University Press.

Dreier, Peter, John Mollenkopf, and Todd Swanstrom. 2005. *Place Matters: Metropolitics for the Twenty-First Century*. 2nd ed. Lawrence: University Press of Kansas.

Drew, Paul, and John Heritage, eds. 2006. *Conversation Analysis*. 4 vols. London: Sage.

Drori, Gili, John Meyer, Francisco Ramirez, and Evan Schofer. 2003. *Science in the Modern World Polity: Institutionalization and Globalization*. Palo Alto, CA: Stanford University Press.

Drucker, Peter. 2000. *Different Rainbows*. London: Gay Men's Press.

DuBois, W. E. B. 1983. *Dusk of Dawn: An Essay toward an Autobiography of a Race Concept*. Piscataway, NJ: Transaction Publishers.

———. 2010 [1899]. *The Philadelphia Negro*. New York: Cosimo Classics.

Dudley-Marling, C. 2004. "The Social Construction of Learning Disabilities." *Journal of Learning Disabilities* 37: 482–489.

Dumas, Alex, and Bryan S. Turner. 2007. "The Life-Extension Project: A Sociological Critique." *Health Sociology Review* 16: 5–17.

Dunaway, Wilma A., ed. 2003. *Emerging Issues in the 21st Century World-System*. Vol. 2: *New Theoretical Directions for the 21st Century World System*. Westport, CT: Praeger Publishers.

Duncan-Andrade, Jeffrey, and Ernest Morrell. 2008. *The Art of Critical Pedagogy: Possibilities for Moving from Theory to Practice in Urban Schools*. New York: Peter Lang.

154 BIBLIOGRAPHY

Dunn, Timothy J. 2001. "Border Militarization via Drug and Immigration Enforcement: Human Rights Implications." *Social Justice* 28: 7–30.

———. 2009. *Blockading the Border and Human Rights: The El Paso Operation that Remade Immigration Enforcement*. Austin: University of Texas Press.

Dunn, Timothy J., Ana Maria Aragones, and George Shivers. 2005. "Recent Mexican Migration in the Rural Delmarva Peninsula: Human Rights versus Citizenship Rights in a Local Context." In *New Destinations: Mexican Immigration in the United States*, edited by V. Zúñiga and R. Hernández-León, 155–183. New York: Russell Sage.

Durand, Jorge, William Kandel, Emilio A. Parrado, and Douglas S. Massey. 1996. "International Migration and Development in Mexican Communities." *Demography* 33: 249–264.

Durkheim, Émile. 1915. *L'Allemagne au-desus de tout: la mentalite allemande et la guerre*. Paris: A. Colin.

———. 1951a. *The Division of Labor in Society*. New York: The Free Press.

———. 1951b [1933]. *Suicide*. New York: The Free Press.

———. 1956. *Education and Sociology*. New York: The Free Press.

———. 1962. *Moral Education*. New York: The Free Press.

———. 1964 [1893]. *The Division of Labour in Society*. Translated by George Simpson. New York: The Free Press.

———. 1977. *The Evolution of Educational Thought*. Translated by Peter Collins. London: Routledge and Kegan Paul.

———. 1982. *The Rules of the Sociological Method*, edited by Steven Lukes. New York: The Free Press.

———. 1995. *Elementary Forms of Religious Life*. New York: The Free Press.

Duster, Troy. 1997. "Pattern, Purpose and Race in the Drug War." In *Crack in America: Demon Drugs and Social Justice*, edited by Craig Reinarman and Harry Levine, 260–287. Berkeley: University of California Press.

———. 2003. *Backdoor to Eugenics*. New York: Routledge.

———. 2005. "Race and Reification in Science." *Science* 307: 1050–1051.

Earl, Jennifer, and Katrina Kimport. 2011. *Digitally Enabled Social Change: Activism in the Internet Age*. Cambridge, MA: MIT Press.

Eaton, W.W. 1980. "A Formal Theory of Selection for Schizophrenia." *American Journal of Sociology* 86: 149–158.

Eckel, Jan. 2009. "Utopie der Moral, Kalkül der Macht: Menschenrechte in der globalen Politiknach 1945." *Archiv für Sozialgeschichte* 49: 437–484.

Economic Policy Institute (EPI). 2011. "Income Inequality: It Wasn't Always This Way." EPI. http://www.epi.org/economic_snapshots/entry/income_inequality_it_wasnt_always_this_way (accessed February 9, 2011).

Economist, The. 2006. "Asia: A Specter Haunting India: India's Naxalites." *The Economist* 380, no. 8491: 52.

Edelman, Lauren B. 2004. "Rivers of Law and Contested Terrain: A Law and Society Approach to Economic Rationality." *Law and Society Review* 38, no. 2: 181–198.

Edin, Kathryn, and Maria Kefalas. 2005. *Promises I Can Keep: Why Poor Women Put Motherhood before Marriage*. Berkeley: University of California Press.

Edin, Kathryn, Laura Lein, and Christopher Jencks. 1997. *Making Ends Meet: How Single Mothers Survive Welfare and Low-Wage Work*. New York: Russell Sage Foundation.

Edwards, Bob, and John D. McCarthy. 1992. "Social Movement Schools." *Sociological Forum* 7: 541–550.

Edwards, C., S. Staniszweska, and N. Crichton. 2004. "Investigation of the Ways in Which Patients' Reports of Their Satisfaction with Healthcare Are Constructed." *Sociology of Health and Illness* 26: 159–183.

Edwards, K. E. 2006. "Aspiring Social Justice Ally Identity Development: A Conceptual Model." *NASPA Journal* 43: 39–60.

Edwards, Richard. 1979. *Contested Terrain: The Transformation of the Workplace in the Twentieth Century*. New York: Basic Books.

Egan, Patrick J., and Kenneth Sherrill. 2009. *California's Proposition 8: What Happened, and What Does the Future Hold?* San Francisco: Evelyn and Walter Haas Jr. Fund and the National Gay and Lesbian Task Force Policy Institute.

Ehrenfeld, David. 2002. "The Cow Tipping Point." *Harper's* 305: 13–20.

Eisenstein, Hester. 1983. *Contemporary Feminist Thought*. Boston: G. K. Hall.

Elder, Glen H., Jr. 1999 [1974]. *Children of the Great Depression: Social Change in Life Experience*. 25th anniv. ed. Boulder, CO: Westview Press.

Elder, Glen H., Jr., Elizabeth Colerick Clipp, J. Scott Brown, Leslie R. Martin, and Howard S. Friedman. 2009. "The Life-Long Mortality Risks of World War II Experiences." *Research on Aging* 30, no. 4: 391–412.

Elias, Norbert. 1978. *The Civilizing Process*. New York: Urizen.

Elliott, Michael. 2007. "Human Rights and the Triumph of the Individual in World Culture." *Cultural Sociology* 1: 343–363.

———. 2008. "A Cult of the Individual for a Global Society: The Development and Worldwide Expansion of Human Rights Ideology." PhD diss., Emory University, Atlanta.

Elliott, Richard, Joanne Csete, Evan Wood, and Thomas Kerr. 2005. "Harm Reduction, HIV/AIDS, and the Human Rights Challenge to Global Drug Control Policy." *Health and Human Rights* 8, no. 2: 104–138.

Ellis, Lee. 2001. "The Biosocial Female Choice Theory of Social Stratification." *Social Biology* 48: 298–320.

———. 2004. "Sex, Status, and Criminality: A Theoretical Nexus." *Social Biology* 51: 144–165.

Ellis, Lee, Scott Hershberber, Evelyn Field, and Scott Wersinger. 2008. *Sex Differences: Summarizing More Than a Century of Scientific Research*. London: Psychology Press.

Ellwood, Charles A. 1907. "How Should Sociology Be Taught as a College or University Subject?" *American Journal of Sociology* 12: 588–606.

Elster, J. 1989. *Nuts and Bolts for the Social Sciences*. Cambridge, UK: Cambridge University Press.

———. 1992. *Local Justice: How Institutions Allocate Scarce Goods and Necessary Burdens*. New York: Russell Sage Foundation.

———. 2007. *Explaining Social Behavior: More Nuts and Bolts for the Social Sciences*. Cambridge, UK: Cambridge University Press.

Ely, Richard T. 1886. *The Labor Movement in America*. New York: Thomas Y. Crowell.

Ember, Carol R., and Melvin Ember. 1994. "War, Socialization, and Impersonal Violence: A Cross Cultural Study." *Journal of Conflict Resolution* 38: 620–646.

Emerson, Rupert. 1975. "The Fate of Human Rights in the Third World." *World Politics* 27: 201–226.

End Corporal Punishment. http://www.endcorporalpunishment.org.

Engels, Friedrich. 1847. "The Principles of Communism." Marxists Internet Archive. http://www.marxists .org/archive/marx/works/1847/11/prin-com.htm (accessed July 17, 2012).

England, Paula. 2005. "Gender Inequality in Labor Markets: The Role of Motherhood and Segregation." *Social Politics* 12: 264–288.

Engles, Eric. 2008. "Human Rights According to Marxism." *Guild Practitioner* 65, no. 249: 249–256.

Enloe, Cynthia. 1990. *Bananas, Beaches, and Bases: Making Feminist Sense of International Politics*. Berkeley: University of California Press.

———. 2000. *Maneuvers: The International Politics of Militarizing Women's Lives*. Berkeley: University of California Press.

———. 2007. *Globalization and Militarism: Feminists Make the Link*. Boulder, CO: Rowman & Littlefield.

Epstein, L., and J. Knight. 1998. *The Choices Justices Make*. Washington, DC: Congressional Quarterly.

Epstein, Steven. 1998. *Impure Science: AIDS, Activism, and the Politics of Knowledge*. Berkeley: University of California Press.

Ericksen, Julia A., with Sally A. Steffen. 2001. *Kiss and Tell: Surveying Sex in the Twentieth Century*. Cambridge, MA: Harvard University Press.

Erikson, Kai. 1994. *A New Species of Trouble: Explorations in Disaster, Trauma and Community*. New York: W. W. Norton.

Ermann, M. David, and Richard J. Lundman, eds. 2002. *Corporate and Governmental Deviance: Problems of Organizational Behavior in Contemporary Society*. New York: Oxford University Press.

Ervin-Tripp, Susan. 1972. "On Sociolinguistic Rules: Alternation and Co-Occurrence." In *Directions in Sociolinguistics: The Ethnography of Communication*, edited by John J. Gumperz and Dell Hymes, 213–250. New York: Holt, Rinehart and Winston.

Eschbach, Karl, J. Hagan, N. Rodriguez, R. Hernandez-Leon, and S. Bailey. 1999. "Death at the Border." *International Migration Review* 33: 430–454.

Escober, Arturo. 2006. "Difference and Conflict in the Struggle over Natural Resources: A Political Ecology Framework." *Development* 49: 6–13.

Esping-Andersen, G. 1994. "Welfare States and the Economy." In *The Handbook of Economic Sociology*, edited by N. J. Smelser and R. Swedberg, 711–732. Princeton, NJ: Princeton University Press.

Esping-Andersen, Gøsta. 1999. *Social Foundations of Postindustrial Economies*. Oxford and New York: Oxford University Press.

Esposito, John L., and John O. Voll. 2001. "Islam and Democracy." *Humanities* 22 (November/December). http://www.neh.gov/news/humanities/2001-11/islam.html (accessed January 20, 2012).

Estes, C. L., S. Goldberg, S. Shostack, K. Linkins, and R. Beard. 2006. "Implications of Welfare Reform for the Elderly: A Case Study of Provider, Advocate, and Consumer Perspectives." *Journal of Aging and Social Policy* 19, no. 1: 41–63.

Etzioni, Amatai. 1961. *A Comparative Analysis of Complex Organizations*. Glencoe, IL: Free Press.

156 BIBLIOGRAPHY

———. 1988. *The Moral Dimension: Toward a New Economics*. New York: The Free Press.

———. 2009. "Minorities and the National Ethos." *Politics* 29, no. 2 (June): 100–110.

Etzkowitz, Henry. 2003. "Innovation in Innovation: The Triple Helix of University-Industry-Government Relations." *Social Science Information* 42, no. 3: 293–338.

Eugene Human Rights City Project. 2011. http://www.humanrightscity.com (accessed May 26, 2011).

Eurobarometer. 2010. "Mental Health. Part One: Report." Special Eurobarometer 345/Eurobarometer 73.2. http://ec.europa.eu/health/mental_health/docs/ebs_345_en.pdf (accessed April 20, 2011).

Evans, Derek G. 2007. "Human Rights: Four Generations of Practice and Development." In *Educating for Human Rights and Global Citizenship*, edited by A. Abdi and L. Shultz, 1–12. Albany: State University of New York Press.

Evans, N. J., J. L. Assadi, and T. K. Herriott. 2005. "Encouraging the Development of Disability Allies." *New Directions for Student Services* 110: 67–79.

Evans, Tony. 2001a. "If Democracy, Then Human Rights?" *Third World Quarterly* 22: 623–642.

———. 2001b. *The Politics of Human Rights*. London: Pluto Press.

Ewen, Lynda Ann. 1991. "Coming Home: A Sociological Journey." In *Radical Sociologists and the Movement: Experiences, Lessons, and Legacies*, edited by Martin Oppenheimer, Martin J. Murray, and Rhonda F. Levine, 140–157. Philadelphia: Temple University Press.

Facio, Alda, and Martha I. Morgan. 2009. "Morgan Symposium on the Gender of Constitutional and Human Rights Law: Equity or Equality for Women? Understanding CEDAW's Equality Principles." *Alabama Law Review* 60: 1133.

Fakhoury, W., and S. Priebe. 2002. "The Process of Deinstitutionalization: An International Overview." *Current Opinion in Psychiatry* 15: 187–192.

Fals-Borda, Orlando. 1988. *Knowledge and People's Power*. New Delhi: Indian Social Institute.

Fanon, Frantz. 2005. *The Wretched of the Earth*. New York: Grove Press.

———. 2008. *Black Skin, White Masks*. Revised. New York: Grove Press.

Fantasia, Rick. 1988. *Cultures of Solidarity: Consciousness, Action, and Contemporary American Workers*. Berkeley: University of California Press.

Fararo, Thomas J. 1973. *Mathematical Sociology: An Introduction to Fundamentals*. New York: Wiley.

———. 1989. *The Meaning of General Theoretical Sociology: Tradition and Formalization*. Cambridge, UK: Cambridge University Press.

Farmer, Paul. 2003. *Pathologies of Power: Health, Human Rights, and the New War on the Poor*. Berkeley: University of California Press.

———. 2010. *Partner to the Poor: A Paul Farmer Reader*. Berkeley: University of California Press.

———. 2011. *Haiti after the Earthquake*. New York: Public Affairs.

Farnall, O., and K. A. Smith. 1999. "Reactions to People with Disabilities: Personal Contact versus Viewing of Specific Media Portrayal." *Journalism and Mass Communication Quarterly* 76: 659–672.

Farr, Thomas F., Richard W. Garnett IV, T. Jeremy Gunn, and William L. Saunders. 2009. "Religious Liberties: The International Religious Freedom Act." *Houston Journal of International Law* 31: 469–514.

Fasenfest, David. 2009. *Engaging Social Justice: Critical Studies of 21st Century Social Transformation*. Leiden, the Netherlands: Brill.

Faugeron, C., and M. Kokoreff. 1999. "Les practiques sociales des drogues: elements por una mise en perspective des recherché en France." *Societes Contemporaines* 36: 5–17.

Fausto-Sterling, Anne. 2000a. "The Five Sexes Revisited." *Sciences* 40: 18–23.

———. 2000b. *Sexing the Body: Gender Politics and the Construction of Sexuality*. New York: Basic Books.

Feagin, Joe R. 2006. *Systemic Racism: A Theory of Oppression*. New York: Routledge.

———. 2010. *The White Racial Frame: Centuries of Racial Framing and Counter-Framing*. New York: Routledge.

Feagin, Joe R., and Hernan Vera. 2008. *Liberation Sociology*. 2nd ed. Boulder, CO: Paradigm Publishers.

Feher, Ferenc, Agnes Heller, and Gyorgy Markus. 1986. *Dictatorship over Needs: An Analysis of Soviet Societies*. Oxford: Basil Blackwell.

Fehr, E., and S. Gächter. 2002. "Altruistic Punishment in Humans." *Nature* 415: 137–140.

Fein, Helen. 1979. *Accounting for Genocide*. Chicago: University of Chicago Press.

Fenster, T., ed. 1999. *Gender, Planning and Human Rights*. London and New York: Routledge.

Ferguson, J. 1994. *The Anti-Politics Machine: Development, Depoliticization, and Bureaucratic Power in Lesotho*. Minneapolis: University of Minnesota Press.

Ferguson, Kathy E. 1991. "Interpretation and Genealogy in Feminism." *Signs: Journal of Women in Culture and Society* 16: 322–339.

Ferraris, Maurizio. 1996 [1988]. *History of Hermeneutics*. Translated by Luca Somigli. Atlantic Highlands, NJ: Humanities Press International.

BIBLIOGRAPHY 157

Ferree, Myra Marx, and Tetyana Pudrovska. 2006. "Transnational Feminist NGOs on the Web: Networks and Identities in the Global North and South." In *Global Feminism: Transnational Women's Activism, Organizing, and Human Rights*, edited by Myra Marx Ferree and Aili Mari Tripp, 247–274. New York: New York University Press.

Ferree, Myra Marx, and Aili Mari Tripp. 2006. *Global Feminism: Transnational Women's Activism, Organizing, and Human Rights*. New York: New York University Press.

Fieder, M., and S. Huber. 2007. "The Effects of Sex and Childlessness on the Association between Status and Reproductive Output in Modern Society." *Evolution and Human Behavior* 28: 392–398.

Field, Les W. 1994. "Review: Who Are the Indians? Reconceptualizing Indigenous Identity, Resistance, and the Role of Social Science in Latin America." *Latin American Research Review* 29: 237–248.

Fields, Belden. 2010. "Human Rights Theory, Criteria, Boundaries, and Complexities." In *Qualitative Inquiry and Human Rights*, edited by Norman Denzin and Michael Giardina, 66–81. Walnut Creek, CA: Left Coast Press.

Fillmore, K. M. 1987a. "Prevalence, Incidence and Chronicity of Drinking Patterns and Problems among Men as a Function of Age: A Longitudinal and Cohort Analysis." *British Journal of Addiction* 82: 77–83.

———. 1987b. "Women's Drinking across the Adult Life Course as Compared to Men's: A Longitudinal and Cohort Analysis." *British Journal of Addiction* 82: 801–811.

Fine, Gary Alan. 1993. "The Sad Demise, Mysterious Disappearance, and Glorious Triumph of Symbolic Interactionism." *Annual Review of Sociology* 19: 61–87.

———. 1995. *A Second Chicago School: The Development of a Postwar American Sociology*. Chicago: University of Chicago Press.

Fink, Leon. 2003. *The Mayan of Morganton*. Chapel Hill: University of North Carolina Press.

Finnegan, Amy, Adam R. Saltsman, and Shelley K. White. 2010. "Negotiating Politics and Culture: The Utility of Human Rights for Activist Organizing in the United States." *Journal of Human Rights Practice* 2, no. 3: 307–333.

Finnemore, Martha. 1999. "Rules of War and Wars of Rules: The International Red Cross and the Restraint of State Violence." In *Constructing World Culture: International Nongovernmental Organizations since 1875*, edited by J. Boli and G. M. Thomas, 149–168. Stanford, CA: Stanford University Press.

Firebaugh, Glenn. 1999. "Empirics of World Income Inequality." *American Journal of Sociology* 104: 1597–1630.

Firth, Roderick. 1952. "Ethical Absolutism and the Ideal Observer." *Philosophy and Phenomenological Research* 12: 317–345.

Fish, Stanley. 2008. *Save the World on Your Own Time*. New York: Oxford University Press.

Fitzgerald, Amy, Linda Kalof, and Thomas Dietz. 2009. "Slaughterhouses and Increased Crime Rates: An Empirical Analysis of Spillover from 'The Jungle' into the Surrounding Community." *Organization and Environment* 22: 158–184.

Fitzgerald, John. 2010. "Images of the Desire for Drugs." *Health Sociology Review* 19, no. 2: 205–217.

Fix, Michael, and Wendy Zimmermann. 2001. "All under One Roof: Mixed-Status Families in an Era of Reform." *International Migration Review* 35: 397–419.

Flacks, Richard. 2004. "Knowledge for What? Thoughts on the State of Social Movement Studies." In *Rethinking Social Movements: Structure, Culture, Emotion*, edited by J. Goodwin and J. Jasper, 135–155. Lanham, MD: Rowman & Littlefield.

———. 2005. "The Question of Relevance in Social Movement Studies." In *Rhyming Hope and History: Activists, Academics, and Social Movement Scholarship*, edited by David Croteau, William Hoynes, and Charlotte Ryan, 3–19. Minneapolis: University of Minnesota Press.

Fleischer, D. A., and F. Zames. 2001. *The Disability Rights Movement: From Charity to Confrontation*. Philadelphia: Temple University Press.

Fligstein, Neil. 2001. *The Architecture of Markets: An Economic Sociology of Twentieth Century Capitalist Societies*. Princeton, NJ, and Oxford, UK: Princeton University Press.

Fligstein, Neil, and Adam Goldstein. 2010. "The Anatomy of the Mortgage Securitization Crisis." In *Markets on Trial: The Economic Sociology of the U.S. Financial Crisis*, edited by Michael Lounsbury and Paul M. Hirsch, 20–70. Research in the Sociology of Organizations 30A. London: Emerald Group Publishing.

Flippen, Chenoa Anne. 2004. "Unequal Returns to Housing Investments? A Study of Real Housing Appreciation among Black, White, and Hispanic Households." *Social Forces* 82: 1523–1551.

Florini, Ann, Nihon Kokusai, Koryu Senta, and Carnegie Endowment for International Peace. 2000. *The Third Force: The Rise of Transnational Civil Society*. Tokyo: Japan Center for International Exchange, Washington Carnegie Endowment for International Peace, and Brookings Institution Press.

Fone, Byrne. 2000. *Homophobia: A History*. New York: Metropolitan Books.

158 BIBLIOGRAPHY

Foner, A. 1974. "Age Stratification and Age Conflict in Political Life." *American Sociological Review* 39, no. 2: 187–196.

Foner, Eric. 1984. "Why Is There No Socialism in the United States?" *History Workshop Journal* 17: 57–80.

Forbes, Catherine, Merran Evans, Nicholas Hastings, and Brian Peacock. 2011. *Statistical Distributions*. 4th ed. New York: Wiley.

Fore, Matthew L. 2002. "Shall Weigh Your God and You: Assessing the Imperialistic Implications of the International Religious Freedom Act in Muslim Countries." *Duke Law Journal* 52: 423–453.

Forman, Tyrone A., and Amanda E. Lewis. 2006. "Racial Apathy and Hurricane Katrina: The Social Anatomy of Prejudice in the Post–Civil Rights Era." *Du Bois Review: Social Science Research on Race* 3: 175–202.

Forsythe, David. 2000. *Human Rights in International Relations*. New York: Cambridge University Press.

———. 2007. *The Humanitarians*. New York: Cambridge.

Fortman, Bas de Gaay. 2011. *Political Economy of Human Rights: Rights, Realities and Realization*. London: Routledge.

Foster-Fishman, Pennie, Tiffany Jimenez, Maria Valenti, and Tasha Kelley. 2007. "Building the Next Generation of Leaders in the Disabilities Movement." *Disability and Society* 22: 341–356.

Foucault, Michel. 1978. *The History of Sexuality: An Introduction*. Vol. 1. New York: Vintage Books.

———. 1980. *Power/Knowledge*, edited by Colin Gordon, translated by Colin Gordon, Leo Marshall, John Mephan, and Kate Soper. New York: Pantheon Books.

———. 1995 [1971]. *Madness and Civilization: A History of Insanity in the Age of Reason*. London: Tavistock. Fox, Mary Frank. 1995. "From the President." *SWS Network News*, 2.

———. 2008. "Institutional Transformation and the Advancement of Women Faculty: The Case of Academic Science and Engineering." In *Higher Education: Handbook of Theory and Research*, edited by John C. Smart, 23: 73–103. New York: Springer.

———. 2010. "Women and Men Faculty in Academic Science and Engineering: Social-Organizational Indicators and Implications." *American Behavioral Scientist* 53, no. 7: 997–1012.

Francis, David, and Stephen Hester. 2004. *An Invitation to Ethnomethodology: Language, Society and Social Interaction*. London: Sage.

Franck, Thomas M. 2001. "Are Human Rights Universal?" *Foreign Affairs* 80: 191–204.

Frank, A. W. 1988. "Garfinkel's Deconstruction of Parsons's Plenum." *Discourse Analysis Research Group Newsletter* 4, no. 1: 5–8.

Frank, Andre G. 1991. *Third World War: A Political Economy of the Gulf War and New World Order*. Róbinson Rojas Archive. http://www.rrojasdatabank.info/agfrank/gulf_war.html (accessed July 17, 2012).

Frankenberg, Ruth. 1993. *White Women, Race Matters: The Social Construction of Whiteness*. London: Taylor and Francis.

Frankl, Viktor E. 1984 [1959]. *Man's Search for Meaning*. New York: Simon and Schuster.

Franklin, James C. 2008. "Shame on You: The Impact of Human Rights Criticism on Political Repression in Latin America." *International Studies Quarterly* 52: 187–211.

Franks, David. 2010. *Neurosociology: The Nexus between Neuroscience and Social Psychology*. New York: Springer.

Franks, David, and Thomas Smith. 2009. "A Neurosociological Perspective on Emotions. A Review Article by David Franks and Thomas Smith: Mind, Brain and Society: Toward a Neurosociology of Emotion." *Sociologie* 5: 244–256.

Fraser, Nancy. 1992. "Rethinking the Public Sphere: A Contribution to the Critique of Actually Existing Democracy." In *Habermas and the Public Sphere*, edited by Craig Calhoun, 109–142. Cambridge, MA: MIT Press.

———. 2009. *Scales of Justice: Reimagining Political Space in a Globalizing World*. New York: Columbia University Press.

Fraser, Nancy, and Axel Honneth. 2003. *Redistribution or Recognition: A Political-Philosophical Exchange*. Translated by Joel Golb, James Ingram, and Christiane Wilke. London: Verso.

Freedman, M. 2007. *Prime Time: How Baby Boomers Will Revolutionize Retirement and Transform America*. Cambridge, MA: Perseus Books.

Freeman, M. 2002. *Human Rights: An Interdisciplinary Approach*. Malden, MA: Blackwell Publishers.

Freeman, Marsha. 1999. "International Institutions and Gendered Justice." *Journal of International Affairs* 52: 513–533.

Freeman, Michael, ed. 2006. *Law and Sociology*. Oxford: Oxford University Press.

Freeman, R. B., and James L. Medoff. 1984. *What Do Unions Do?* New York: Basic Books.

Freese, Jeremy, and Brian Powell. 1999. "Sociobiology, Status, and Parental Investment in Sons and Daughters: Testing the Trivers-Willard Hypothesis." *American Journal of Sociology* 104: 1704–1743.

Freidson, Eliot. 1970. *Professional Dominance: The Social Structure of Medical Care*. New York: Atherton Press.
———. 2001. *Professionalism, the Third Logic*. Chicago: The Third Logic.
Freire, Paulo. 2000. *Pedagogy of the Oppressed*. New York: Continuum International.
Freire, Paulo, and Donald Macedo. 1987. *Literacy: Reading the Word and the World*. New York: Routledge.
Freudenburg, William R., and Robert Gramling. 2010. *Blowout: The BP Oil Disaster and the Future of Energy in America*. Cambridge, MA: MIT Press.
Freudenburg, William R., Robert B. Gramling, Shirley Laska, and Kai Erikson. 2009. *Catastrophe in the Making: The Engineering of Katrina and Disasters of Tomorrow*. Washington, DC: Island Press.
Frezzo, Mark. 2008. "Sociology, Human Rights, and the World Social Forum." *Societies without Borders* 3: 35–47.
———. 2011. "Sociology and Human Rights in the Post Development Era." *Sociology Compass* 5, no. 3: 203–214.
Frickel, Scott, and Kelly Moore, eds. 2006. *The New Political Sociology of Science: Institutions, Networks, and Power*. Madison: University of Wisconsin Press.
Frickel, Scott, and M. Bess Vincent. 2007. "Katrina, Contamination, and the Unintended Organization of Ignorance." *Technology in Society* 29: 181–188.
Friedkin, Noah E. 1998. *A Structural Theory of Social Influence*. Cambridge, UK: Cambridge University Press.
Friedländer, Saul. 2007. *Nazi Germany and the Jews, 1939–1945: The Years of Extermination*. New York: Harper.
Friedman, E. L. 1977. *Industry and Labour: Class Struggle at Work and Monopoly Capitalism, 18–35*. London: Macmillan Press.
Friedman, Elisabeth J. 1995. "Women's Human Rights: The Emergence of a Movement." In *Women's Rights, Human Rights: International Feminist Perspectives*, edited by Julia Peters and Andrea Wolper. New York: Routledge.
———. 2003. "Gendering the Agenda: The Impact of the Transnational Women's Rights Movement at the UN Conferences of the 1990s." *Women's Studies International Forum* 26: 313–331.
Friedman, Lawrence Meir. 2002. *American Law in the 20th Century*. New Haven, CT: Yale University Press.
Friedman, Milton. 1962. *Capitalism and Freedom*. Chicago: University of Chicago Press.
Friedman, Neil A. 1986. "A Human Rights Approach to the Labor Rights of Undocumented Workers." *California Law Review* 74, no. 5: 1715–1745.
Friedman, Thomas L. 2005. *The World Is Flat: A Brief History of the Twenty-First Century*. New York: Farrar, Straus and Giroux.
Friedrichs, David O. 2009. "On Resisting State Crime: Conceptual and Contextual Issues." *Social Justice* 36: 4–27.
Fritz, J. M. 1989. "Dean Winternitz, Clinical Sociology and the Julius Rosenwald Fund." *Clinical Sociology Review* 7: 17–27.
———. 1991. "The Emergency of American Clinical Sociology: The First Courses." *Clinical Sociology Review* 9: 15–26.
———. 2004. "Derriere la magie: models, approaches et theories de mediation [Behind the Magic: Mediation, Models, Approaches and Theories]." *Esprit Critique* 6. http://www.espritcritique.fr/0603/esp0603article01.pdf (accessed September 6, 2012).
———. 2005. "The Scholar-Practitioners: The Development of Clinical Sociology in the United States." In *Diverse Histories of American Sociology*, edited by A. J. Blasi, 40–56. Leiden, the Netherlands: Brill.
———. ed. 2008. *International Clinical Sociology*. New York: Springer.
———. 2010. "Special Education Mediation in the United States." In *People with Health Limitations in Modern Society*, edited by O. Dikova-Favorskaya, 268–285. Zhitomar, Ukraine: DZHIVIES.
Fritz, J. M., P. Bistak, and C. Auffrey. 2000. "The Bumpy Road to a Tobacco-Free Community: Lessons from Well City." *Sociological Practice* 2: 113–126.
Fritz, J. M., S. Doering, and F. Belgin Gumru. 2011. "Women, Peace, Security, and the National Action Plans." *Journal of Applied Social Science* 5, no. 1 (spring): 1–23.
Frost, Jennifer. 2001. *An Interracial Movement of the Poor: Community Organizing and the New Left in the 1960s*. New York: New York University Press.
Fry, C. L. 2007. "Demographic Transitions, Age, and Culture." In *Social Structures: Demographic Changes and the Well-Being of Older Persons*, edited by K. W. Schaie and P. Uhlenberg, 283–300. New York: Springer Publishing Co.
Fukumura, Yoko, and Martha Matsuoka. 2002. "Redefining Security: Okinawa Women's Resistance to U.S. Militarism." In *Women's Activism and Globalization: Linking Local Struggles and Transnational Politics*, edited by Nancy A. Naples and Manisha Desai, 239–263. New York: Routledge.

Fulcomer, David. 1947. "Some Newer Methods of Teaching Sociology." *Journal of Educational Sociology* 21: 154–162.

Fuller, Robert W. 2003. *Somebodies and Nobodies: Overcoming the Abuse of Rank.* Gabriola Island, BC: New Society Publishers.

Fuller, Robert W., and T. Scheff. 2009. "Bleeding Heart Liberals Proven Right: Too Much Inequality Harms a Society." *Huffington Post.* June 18.

Fung, Archon, and Erik Olin Wright. 2003. *Deepening Democracy: Institutional Innovations in Empowered Participatory Governance,* with contributions by Rebecca Neaera Abers et al. London: Verso.

Furstenberg, Frank. 2010. "On a New Schedule: Transitions to Adulthood and Family Change." *Transition to Adulthood* 20, no. 1: 68–87.

Gaer, Felice. 1998. "And Never the Twain Shall Meet? The Struggle to Establish Women's Rights as International Human Rights." In *The International Human Rights of Women: Instruments of Change,* edited by Carol Lockwood et al., 41–69. Washington, DC: American Bar Association Section of International Law and Practice.

Gaines, Atwood D. 2011. "Millennial Medical Anthropology: From There to Here and Beyond, or the Problem of Global Health." *Culture, Medicine and Psychiatry* 35, no. 1: 83–89.

Galbraith, John Kenneth. 1983. *The Anatomy of Power.* Boston: Houghton Mifflin.

Gallahue, Patrick. 2010. "Targeted Killing of Drug Lords: Traffickers as Members of Armed Opposition Groups and/or Direct Participants in Hostilities." *International Yearbook on Human Rights and Drug Policy* 1.

Galtung, Johan. 1996. *Peace by Peaceful Means.* Thousand Oaks, CA: Sage Publications.

Gamson, William A. 1988. "Review: [untitled]." *American Journal of Sociology* 94: 436–438.

———. 1992. *Talking Politics.* Cambridge, UK: Cambridge University Press.

Gamson, William A., and David S. Meyer. 1996. "Framing Political Opportunity." In *Comparative Perspectives in Social Movements: Political Opportunities, Mobilizing Structures, and Cultural Framings,* edited by Doug McAdam, John D. McCarthy, and Mayer N. Zald, 275–290. Cambridge, UK: Cambridge University Press.

Gandhi, Mahatma. 1993a. *The Collected Works of Mahatma Gandhi* (electronic book). New Delhi: Publications Division Government of India.

———. 1993b. *Gandhi and the Gita,* edited by. J. I. (Hans) Bakker. Toronto: Canadian Scholars' Press.

———. 1999. *The Collected Works of Mahatma Gandhi* (electronic book). 98 vols. New Delhi: Publications Division Government of India. http://www.gandhiserve.org/cwmg/cwmg.html (accessed January 20, 2012).

———. 2002. *The Essential Gandhi: An Anthology of His Writings on His Life, Work and Ideas.* New York: Vintage Publishers.

Gans, H. J. 1997. "Toward a Reconciliation of 'Assimilation' and 'Pluralism': The Interplay of Acculturation and Ethnic Retention." *International Migration Review* 31: 875–892.

Gardner, G., and T. Prugh. 2008. "Seeding the Sustainable Economy." In *State of the World: Innovations for Sustainable Economy,* edited by Linda Starke, 3–17. New York: W. W. Norton.

Garey, A. 1999. *Weaving Work and Motherhood.* Philadelphia, PA: Temple University Press.

Garfinkel, Harold. 1967. *Studies in Ethnomethodology.* Englewood Cliffs, NJ: Prentice Hall.

———, ed. 1986. *Ethnomethodological Studies of Work.* London: Routledge and Kegan Paul.

———. 2002. *Ethnomethodology's Program: Working Out Durkheim's Aphorism,* edited and introduced by Anne Warfield Rawls. Lanham, MD: Rowman & Littlefield.

———. 2006. *Seeing Sociologically: The Routine Grounds of Social Action,* edited and introduced by Anne Warfield Rawls. Boulder, CO: Paradigm.

———. 2008. *Toward a Sociological Theory of Information,* edited and introduced by Anne Warfield Rawls. Boulder, CO: Paradigm.

Garfinkel, Harold, and Harvey Sacks. 1970. "On Formal Structures of Practical Action." In *Theoretical Sociology: Perspectives and Developments,* edited by J. C. McKinney and E. A. Tiryakian, 338–366. New York: Appleton-Century-Crofts.

Garfinkel, Harold, and D. Lawrence Wieder. 1992. "Two Incommensurable, Asymmetrically Alternate Technologies of Social Analysis." In *Text in Context: Contributions to Ethnomethodology,* edited by Graham Watson and Robert M. Seiler, 175–206. Newbury Park, CA: Sage.

Gargano, G. 2008. "Art and Science in Italian Clinical Sociology." In *International Clinical Sociology,* edited by J. M. Fritz, 153–169. New York: Springer.

Garland, David. 1990. *Punishment in Modern Society.* Chicago: University of Chicago Press.

Garnett, Richard A. 1988. "The Study of War in American Sociology: An Analysis of Selected Journals, 1936–1988." *American Sociologist* 19: 270–282.

Garrett, William R. 2001. "Religion, Law, and the Human Condition." In *Religion in the Process of Globalization,* edited by Peter Beyer, 289–340. Würzburg: Ergon.

BIBLIOGRAPHY   161

Garroutte, Eva M. 2001. "The Racial Formation of American Indians: Negotiating Legitimate Identities within Tribal and Federal Law." *American Indian Quarterly* 25, no. 2: 224–239.

———. 2003. *Real Indians: Identity and the Survival of Native America*. Los Angeles: University of California Press.

Gaston, Alonso, Noel Anderson, Celina Su, and Jeanne Theoharis. 2009. *Our Schools Suck: Students Talk Back to a Segregated Nation on the Failures of Urban Education*. New York: New York University Press.

Gaulejac, V. de. 2008. "On the Origins of Clinical Sociology in France: Some Milestones." In *International Clinical Sociology*, edited by J. M. Fritz, 54–71. New York: Springer.

———. 2010. Personal communication with J. M. Fritz. December 15.

Gavey, N., K. McPhillips, and M. Doherty. 2001. "'If It's Not On, It's Not On'—or Is It? Discursive Constraints on Women's Condom Use." *Gender and Society* 15: 917–934.

Gecas, Viktor. 1991. "The Self-Concept as a Basis for a Theory of Motivation." In *The Self-Society Dynamic*, edited by Judith A. Howard and Peter L. Callero, 171–185. Cambridge, UK: Cambridge University Press.

Gecas, Viktor, and Peter Burke. 1995. "Self and Identity." In *Sociological Perspectives on Social Psychology*, edited by Karen S. Cook, Gary Alan Fine, and James T. House, 156–173. Boston: Allyn and Bacon.

Geiger, Roger. 1986. *To Advance Relevant Knowledge: The Growth of American Research Universities, 1900–1940*. Oxford: Oxford University Press.

Gendron, Richard, and G. William Domhoff. 2008. *The Leftmost City: Power and Progressive Politics in Santa Cruz*. Boulder, CO: Westview Press.

Gerhardt, U. 1989. *Ideas about Illness: An Intellectual and Political History of Medical Sociology*. New York: New York University Press.

Gerstenfeld, Phylis, Diana Grant, and Chau-Pu Chiang. 2003. "Hate Online: A Content Analysis of Extremist Internet Sites." *Analyses of Social Issues and Public Policy* 3: 29–44.

Ghosh, B. 1992. "Migration-Development Linkages: Some Specific Issues and Practical Policy Measures." *International Migration* 30: 423–452.

GID Reform Advocates. 2008. "GID Reform Advocates." Transgender Forum. http://www.transgender.org/gird (accessed November 11, 2011).

Giddens, Anthony. 1985. *The Nation-State and Violence*. Cambridge, UK: Polity Press.

———. 1998. *The Third Way: The Renewal of Social Democracy*. Cambridge, UK: Polity Press.

———. 1999. *Runaway World*. London: Profile Books.

———. 2009. *The Politics of Climate Change*. Malden, MA: Polity Press.

Giesen, Bernhard. 2004. *Triumph or Trauma*. Boulder, CO: Paradigm.

Gill, Aisha K., and Anitha Sundari. 2011. *Forced Marriage: Introducing a Social Justice and Human Rights Perspective*. Boston: Zed Books.

Gill, Anthony James. 2008. *The Political Origins of Religious Liberty*. Cambridge, UK, and New York: Cambridge University Press.

Gill, D. A., and J. S. Picou. 1998. "Technological Disasters and Chronic Community Stress." *Society and Natural Resources* 11: 795–815.

Gill, E. 2002. "Unlocking the Iron Cage: Human Agency and Social Organization." *Studies in Symbolic Interaction* 25: 109–128.

Gillum, R. F. 2005. "Religiosity and the Validity of Self-Reported Smoking: The Third National Health and Nutritional Examination Survey." *Review of Religious Research* 47, no. 2: 190–196.

Ginsberg, Morris. 1942. "The Individualist Basis of International Law and Morals: The Presidential Address." *Proceedings of the Aristotelian Society* 43: i–xxvi.

Ginsburg, Tom. 2009. "The Clash of Commitments at the International Criminal Court." *Chicago Journal of International Law* 9, no. 2: 499–514.

Giroux, Henry. 1983a. "Theories of Reproduction and Resistance in the New Sociology of Education: A Critical Analysis." *Harvard Educational Review* 55: 257–293.

———. 1983b. *Theories and Resistance in Education*. South Hadley, MA: Bergin and Garvey.

———. 1997. *Pedagogy and the Politics of Hope: Theory, Culture, and Schooling*. Boulder, CO: Westview.

Glazebrook, Susan. 2009. "Human Rights and the Environment." *Victoria University Wellington Law Review* 40: 293–350.

Glazebrook, Trish, and Anthony Kola-Olusanya. 2011. "Justice, Conflict, Capital and Care: Oil in the Niger Delta." *Environmental Ethics* 33, no. 2: 163–184.

Glenn, Evelyn Nakano. 1999. "The Social Construction and Institutionalization of Gender and Race: An Integrative Framework." In *Revisiting Gender*, edited by Myra Marx Ferree, Judith Lorber, and Beth B. Hess, 3–43. New York: Sage.

162 BIBLIOGRAPHY

———. 2002. *Unequal Freedom: How Race and Gender Shaped American Citizenship and Labor*. Cambridge, MA: Harvard University Press.

Gluck, Sherna Berger, with Maylei Blackwell, Sharon Cotrell, and Karen S. Harper. 1997. "Whose Feminism, Whose History? Reflections on Excavating the History of (the) U.S. Women's Movement(s)." In *Community Activism and Feminist Politics: Organizing across Race, Gender, and Class*, edited by Nancy A. Naples, 31–56. New York: Routledge.

Goffman, Erving. 1955. "On Face-Work: An Analysis of Ritual Elements in Social Interaction." *Psychiatry* 18, no. 3: 213–231.

———. 1956a. "The Nature of Deference and Demeanor." *American Anthropologist* 58, no. 3: 473–502.

———. 1956b. "Embarrassment and Social Organization." *American Journal of Sociology* 62, no. 3: 264–271.

———. 1959. *The Presentation of Self in Everyday Life*. 1st ed. Garden City, NY: Anchor.

———. 1961. *Asylums: Essays on the Social Situation of Mental Patients and Other Inmates*. New York: Anchor Books.

———. 1963. *Stigma: Notes on the Management of Spoiled Identity*. Englewood Cliffs, NJ: Prentice Hall.

———. 1979. *Gender Advertisements*. New York: HarperCollins.

———. 1986. *Frame Analysis: An Essay on the Organization of Experience*. Boston: Northeastern University Press.

Golash-Boza, Tanya. 2009. "The Immigration Industrial Complex: Why We Enforce Immigration Policies Destined to Fail." *Sociology Compass* 3: 295–309.

———. 2011. *Immigration Nation: Raids, Detentions, and Deportations in Post-9/11 America*. Boulder, CO: Paradigm Publishers.

Goldberg, David Theo. 1990. *Anatomy of Racism*. Minneapolis: University of Minnesota Press.

Goldberg, Walter. 1986. Personal communication.

Goldfield, Michael. 1987. *The Decline of Organized Labor in the United States*. Chicago: University of Chicago Press.

———. 1989. "Worker Insurgency, Radical Organization, and New Deal Labor Legislation." *American Political Science Review* 83: 1257–1282.

Goldfrank, Walter L. 2000. "Paradigm Regained? The Rules of Wallerstein's World-System Method." *Journal of World-Systems Research* 6, no. 2: 150–195.

Goldfrank, Walter L., David Goodman, and Andrew Szasz. 1999. *Ecology and the World System*. Westport, CT: Greenwood Press.

Goldring, Luin. 1998. "The Power of Status in Transnational Social Fields." In *Transnationalism from Below*, edited by Michael Smith and Luis Guarnizo, 165–195. London: Transaction Publishers.

Goldsmith, Jack, and Stephen D. Krasner. 2003. "The Limits of Idealism." *Daedalus* 132: 47–63.

Goldstein, Joseph, Burke Marshall, and Jack Schwartz. 1976. *The My Lai Massacre and Its Cover-Up: Beyond the Reach of Law? The Peers Commission Report with a Supplement and an Introductory Essay on the Limits of Law*. New York: The Free Press.

Goldstein, Joshua S. 2001. *War and Gender: How Gender Shapes the War System and Vice Versa*. Cambridge, UK: Cambridge University Press.

Goldstone, Jack. 2001. "Towards a Fourth Generation of Revolutionary Theory." *Annual Review of Political Science* 4: 139–187.

Goldthorpe, J. 2007. *On Sociology*. Stanford, CA: Stanford University Press.

Gonzales, Roberto G. 2011. "Learning to Be Illegal." *American Sociological Review* 76: 602–619.

González-López, Gloria. 2005. *Erotic Journeys: Mexican Immigrants and Their Sex Lives*. Berkeley: University of California Press.

Goodale, Mark. 2009. *Surrendering to Utopia: Anthropology of Human Rights*. Stanford, CA: Stanford University Press.

Goode, William J. 1978. *The Celebration of Heroes: Prestige as a Control System*. Berkeley: University of California Press.

Goodhard, Michael. 2003. "Origins and Universality in the Human Rights Debates: Cultural Essentialism and the Challenge of Globalization." *Human Rights Quarterly* 25: 935–964.

Goodwin, Glenn. 1987. "Humanistic Sociology and the Craft of Teaching." *Teaching Sociology* 15, no. 1: 19.

Goodwin, Jeff. 2001. *No Other Way Out*. New York: Cambridge University Press.

Goodwin, Jeff, and James M. Jasper. 2004. *Rethinking Social Movements: Structure, Meaning, and Emotion*. Lanham, MD: Rowman & Littlefield.

Goodyear-Smith, F., and S. Buetow. 2001. "Power Issues in the Doctor-Patient Relationship." *Health Care Analysis* 9: 449–462.

Goonesekere, Savitri. 2000. "Human Rights as a Foundation for Family Law Reform." *International Journal of Children's Rights* 8: 83–99.

BIBLIOGRAPHY **163**

Gordon, B. O., and K. E. Rosenblum. 2001. "Bringing Disability into the Sociological Frame: A Comparison of Disability with Race, Sex, and Sexual Orientation Statuses." *Disability and Society* 16: 5–19.

Gordon, Milton. 1964. *Assimilation in American Life*. New York: Oxford University Press.

Gordon, N., J. Swanson, and J. Buttigieg. 2000. "Is the Struggle for Human Rights a Struggle for Emancipation?" *Rethinking Marxism* 12, no. 3: 1–22.

Gordon, Steven L. 1981. "The Sociology of Sentiments and Emotions." In *Social Psychology: Sociological Perspectives*, edited by M. Rosenberg and R. H. Turner, 562–592. New York: Basic Books.

———. 1989a. "Institutions and Impulsive Orientations in Selectively Appropriating Emotions to Self." In *The Sociology of Emotions: Original Essays and Research Papers*, edited by D. D. Franks and E. D. McCarthy, 115–135. Greenwich, CT: JAI Press.

———. 1989b. "The Socialization of Children's Emotions: Emotional Culture, Competence, and Exposure." In *Children's Understanding of Emotion*, edited by C. Saarni and P. L. Harris, 319–349. Cambridge, UK: Cambridge University Press.

———. 1990. "Social Structural Effects on Emotions." In *Research Agendas in the Sociology of Emotions*, edited by T. D. Kemper, 180–203. Albany: State University of New York Press.

Gottfried, Heidi. 2012. *Gender, Work, and Economy: Unpacking the Global Economy*. Cambridge, UK: Polity Press.

Gould, K. A. 2009. "Technological Change and the Environment." In *Twenty Lessons in Environmental Sociology*, edited by K. A. Gould and T. L. Lewis, 95–106. New York: Oxford University Press.

Gould, Stephen Jay. 1981. *The Mismeasure of Man*. New York: Norton.

Gouldner, A. 1955. "Explorations in Applied Social Science." *Social Problems* 3: 169–181.

Government Accountability Office (GAO). 2005. *Denial of Federal Benefits*. GAO-05-238. GAO. http://www.gao.gov/new.items/d05238.pdf (accessed January 1, 2011).

Gramsci, Antonio. 1971. *Selections from the Prison Notebooks*. New York: International Publishers Co.

———. 1982. *Selections from the Prison Notebooks*. London: Lawrence and Wishart.

Gran, Brian K. 2008. "Public or Private Management? A Comparative Analysis of Social Policies in Europe." *Sociology Compass* 2: 1–29.

———. 2010a. "A Comparative-Historical Analysis of Children's Rights." NSF Grant, Law and Social Science Program.

———. 2010b. "Comparing Children's Rights: Introducing the Children's Rights Index." *International Journal of Children's Rights* 18, no. 1: 1–17.

———. 2011. "The Roles of Independent Children's Rights Institutions in Implementing the CRC." In *Children's Rights: From 20th Century Visions to 21st Century Implementation?*, 219–237. Surrey, UK: Ashgate Publishing Group.

Gran, Brian K., and Dawn M. Aliberti. 2003. "The Office of Children's Ombudsperson: Children's Rights and Social-Policy Innovation." *International Journal of the Sociology of Law* 31, no. 2: 89–106.

Grande, Sandy. 2004. *Red Pedagogy: Native American Social and Political Thought*. Lanham, MD: Rowman & Littlefield.

Granovetter, Mark S. 1973. "The Strength of Weak Ties." *American Journal of Sociology* 78: 1360–1380.

Gready, P. 2008. "Rights-Based Approaches to Development: What Is the Value-Added?" *Development in Practice*. http://www.developmentinpractice.org/journals/rights-based-approaches-development-what-value-added (accessed July 17, 2012).

Greenberg, David F. 1988. *The Construction of Homosexuality*. Chicago: University of Chicago Press.

Grewal, Inderpal, and Caren Kaplan, eds. 1994. *Scattered Hegemonies: Postmodernity and Transnational Feminist Practices*. Minneapolis: University of Minnesota Press.

———. 2000. "Postcolonial Studies and Transnational Feminist Practices." *Jouvert: A Journal of Postcolonial Studies* 5. http://social.chass.ncsu.edu/jouvert/v5i1/con51.htm (accessed September 6, 2012).

Griffin, Larry J., Michael Wallace, and Beth A. Rubin. 1986. "Capitalist Resistance to the Organization of Labor before the New Deal: Why? How? Success?" *American Sociological Review* 51: 147–167.

Griswold, Wendy. 1995. *Cultures and Societies in a Changing World*. Los Angeles: Sage Pine Forge.

Grosfoguel, Ramon. 2008. "Transmodernity, Border Thinking, and Global Coloniality." *Eurozine*. http://www.eurozine.com/articles/2008-07-04-grosfoguel-en.html (accessed January 1, 2011).

Gross, James A. 2009. "Takin' It to the Man: Human Rights at the American Workplace." In *Human Rights in Labor and Employment Relations: International and Domestic Perspectives*, edited James A. Gross and Lance Compa, 13–41. Urbana-Champaign, IL: Labor and Employment Relations Association.

Gross, James A., and Lance Compa. 2009. "Introduction." In *Human Rights in Labor and Employment Relations: International and Domestic Perspectives*, edited James A. Gross and Lance Compa, 1–11. Urbana-Champaign, IL: Labor and Employment Relations Association.

BIBLIOGRAPHY

Grossberg, Lawrence. 1992. *We Gotta Get Out of This Place: Popular Conservatism and Postmodern Culture*. 1st ed. London: Routledge.

Grouzet, Frederick M. E., Tim Kasser, Aaron Ahuvia, José Miguel Fernandez-Dols, Youngmee Kim, Sing Lau, Richard M. Ryan, Shaun Saunders, Peter Schmuck, and Kennon M. Sheldon. 2005. "The Structure of Goal Contents across 15 Cultures." *Journal of Personality and Social Psychology* 89: 800–816.

Grue, L. 2010. "Eugenics and Euthanasia—Then and Now." *Scandinavian Journal of Disability Research* 12: 33–45.

Grundmann, Reiner, and Nico Stehr. 2012. *Experts: The Knowledge and Power of Expertise*. London: Rutledge.

Guardian. 2010. "Xinjiang Riots: One Year On, Uighur and Han Fears Still Run Deep." *Guardian*, July 4. http://www.guardian.co.uk/world/2010/jul/05/xianjiang-riots-security-uighur-han (accessed September 6, 2012).

Guarnizo, Luis, Alejandro Portes, and William Haller. 2003. "Assimilation and Transnationalism: Determinants of Transnational Political Action among Contemporary Migrants." *American Journal of Sociology* 108: 1211–1248.

Guarnizo, Luis, and Michael Peter Smith. 1998. "The Locations of Transnationalism." In *Transnationalism from Below*, edited by Michael Smith and Luis Guarnizo. London: Transaction Publishers.

Gubrium, Jaber. 1997. *Living and Dying and Murray Manor*. Charlottesville: University Press of Virginia.

Gubrium, Jaber, and James A. Holstein. 2012. "Don't Argue with the Members." *American Sociologist* 43, no. 1 (March): 85–98.

Guillen, M. F. 2001. *The Limits of Convergence: Globalization and Organizational Change in Argentina, South Korea, and Spain*. Princeton, NJ: Princeton University Press.

Gunn, T. Jeremy. 2000. "A Preliminary Response to Criticisms of the International Religious Freedom Act of 1998." *Brigham Young University Education and Law Journal* 841–865.

Guo, Guang, Glen H. Elder, Tianji Cai, and Nathan Hamilton. 2009. "Gene-Environment Interactions: Peers' Alcohol Use Moderates Genetic Contribution to Adolescent Drinking Behavior." *Social Science Research* 38: 213–224.

Guo, Guang, Michael Roettger, and Tianji Cai. 2008. "The Integration of Genetic Propensities into Social Control Models of Delinquency and Violence among Male Youths." *American Sociological Review* 73: 543–568.

Guo, Guang, and Yuying Tong. 2006. "Age at First Sexual Intercourse, Genes, and Social and Demographic Context: Evidence from Twins and the Dopamine D4 Receptor Gene." *Demography* 43: 747–769.

Guo, Guang, Yuying Tong, and Tianji Cai. 2008. "Gene by Social-Context Interactions for Number of Sexual Partners among White Male Youths: Genetics-Informed Sociology." *American Journal of Sociology* 114: 36–66.

Guskin, Jane, and David Wilson. 2007. *The Politics of Immigration: Questions and Answers*. New York: St. Martin's Press.

Gutman, A., and D. Thompson. 2004. *Why Deliberative Democracy?* Princeton, NJ: Princeton University Press.

Gutman, Herbert G. 1961. "Trouble on the Railroads in 1873–1874: Prelude to the 1877 Crisis?" *Labor History* 2: 215–235.

———. 1962. "Reconstruction in Ohio: Negroes in the Hocking Valley Coal Mines in 1873 and 1874." *Labor History* 3: 243–264.

———. 1976. *Work, Culture, and Society in Industrializing America: Essays in American Working Class and Social History*. New York: Alfred A. Knopf.

Gwangju Metropolitan City, Republic of Korea. 2011. *The Vision of Gwangju as a Human Rights City: The Action Plan and Gwangju Human Rights Index*. Gwangju, Republic of Korea: Gwangju Metropolitan City.

Gwangju World Human Rights Cities Forum. 2011. "Gwangju Declaration." Human Rights Cities. http:// humanrightscity.net/eng/subpage.php?pagecode=020301 (accessed July 17, 2012).

Habermas, Jürgen. 1979. *Communication and the Evolution of Society*. Boston: Beacon Press.

———. 1981. *The Theory of Communicative Action*. Vol. 1: *Reason and the Rationalization of Society*. Translated by Thomas McCarthy. Boston: Beacon Press.

———. 1989 [1981]. *The Theory of Communicative Action*. Vol. 2: *Lifeworld and System: A Critique of Functionalist Realism*. Translated by Thomas McCarthy. Boston: Beacon Press.

———. 1995. "Reconciliation through the Public Use of Reason: Remarks on John Rawls' Political Liberalism." *Journal of Philosophy* 92: 109–131.

BIBLIOGRAPHY   165

Hackett, Edward J., Olga Amsterdamska, Michael Lynch, and Judy Wajcman, eds. 2007. *The Handbook of Science and Technology Studies*. 3rd ed. Cambridge, MA: MIT Press.

Hackworth, Jason. 2007. *The Neoliberal City: Governance, Ideology, and Development in American Urbanism*. Ithaca, NY: Cornell University Press.

Haddad, Yvonne Yazbeck. 2007. "The Post-9/11 Hijab as Icon." *Sociology of Religion* 68: 253–267.

Hafner-Burton, Emilie. 2005. "Right or Robust? The Sensitive Nature of Repression to Globalization." *Journal of Peace Research* 42: 679–698.

———. 2008. "'Sticks and Stones': Naming and Shaming the Human Rights Enforcement Problem." *International Organization* 62 (fall): 689–716.

———. 2009. *Forced to Be Good: Why Trade Agreements Boost Human Rights*. Ithaca, NY: Cornell University Press.

Hafner-Burton, Emilie M., and Alexander H. Montgomery. 2008. "Power Positions: International Organizations, Social Networks, and Conflict." *Journal of Conflict Resolution* 54, no. 2: 213–242.

Hafner-Burton, Emilie M., and Kiyoteru Tsutsui. 2005. "Human Rights in a Globalizing World: The Paradox of Empty Promises." *American Journal of Sociology* 110: 1373–1411.

Hafner-Burton, Emilie M., Kiyoteru Tsutsui, and John W. Meyer. 2008. "International Human Rights Law and the Politics of Legitimation: Repressive States and Human Rights Treaties." *International Sociology* 23, no. 1: 115–141.

Hagan, John. 1994. *Crime and Disrepute*. Thousand Oaks, CA: Pine Forge Press.

———. 2003. *Justice in the Balkans*. Chicago: University of Chicago Press.

Hagan, John, and Scott Greer. 2002. "Making War Criminal." *Criminology* 40: 231–264.

Hagan, John, and Sanja Kutnjak. 2006. "War Crimes, Democracy, and the Rule of Law in Belgrade, the Former Yugoslavia, and Beyond." *Annals of the American Academy of Political and Social Science* 605: 130–51.

Hagan, John, and Ron Levi. 2005. "Crimes of War and the Force of Law." *Social Forces* 3: 1499–1534.

———. 2007. "Justiciability as Field Effect: When Sociology Meets Human Rights." *Sociological Forum* 22: 372–384.

Hagan, John, and Ruth Peterson. 1995. "Criminal Inequality in America." In *Crime and Inequality*, edited by John Hagan and Ruth D. Peterson, 14–36. Stanford, CA: Stanford University Press.

Hagan, John, and Wenona Rymond-Richmond. 2008. "The Collective Dynamics of Racial Dehumanization and Genocidal Victimization in Darfur." *American Sociological Review* 6: 875–902.

———. 2009. *Darfur and the Crime of Genocide*. Cambridge, UK: Cambridge University Press.

Hagan, John, Wenona Rymond-Richmond, and Patricia Parker. 2005. "The Criminology of Genocide: The Death and Rape of Darfur." *Criminology* 43: 525–561.

Hagan, John, Heather Schoenfeld, and Alberto Palloni. 2006. "The Science of Human Rights, War Crimes and Humanitarian Emergencies." *Annual Review of Sociology* 32: 329–350.

Hagestad, Gunhild O. 2008. "The Book-Ends: Emerging Perspectives on Children and Old People." In *Families and Social Policy: Intergenerational Solidarity in European Welfare States*, edited by C. Saraceno, 20–37. London: Edward Elgar Publishing.

Hagestad, Gunhild O., and Peter Uhlenberg. 2005. "The Social Separation of Old and Young: A Root of Ageism." *Journal of Social Issues* 61: 343–360.

———. 2006. "Should We Be Concerned about Age Segregation? Some Theoretical and Empirical Explorations." *Research on Aging* 28: 638–653.

———. 2007. "The Impact of Demographic Changes on Relations between Age Groups and Generations: A Comparative Perspective." In *Social Structures: Demographic Changes and the Well-Being of Older Persons*, edited by K. W. Schaie and P. Uhlenberg, 239–261. New York: Springer Publishing Co.

Hagestad, Gunhild O., and Dale Dannefer. 2001. "Concepts and Theories of Aging: Beyond Microfication in Social Science Approaches." In *Handbook of Aging and Social Sciences*, edited by R. Binstock and L. George. 5th ed. San Diego: Academic Press.

Haiken, Elizabeth. 1999. *Venus Envy: A History of Cosmetic Surgery*. Baltimore: Johns Hopkins University Press.

Halbwachs, Maurice. 1992. *On Collective Memory*. Chicago: University of Chicago Press.

Hall, G. B., and G. Nelson. 1996. "Social Networks, Social Support, Personal Empowerment, and the Adaptation of Psychiatric Consumers: Survivors: Path Analytic Models." *Social Science and Medicine* 43: 1743–1754.

Hall, John R. 1987. *Gone from the Promised Land: Jonestown in American Cultural History*. New Brunswick, NJ: Transaction Books.

Hall, John R., Philip Daniel Schuyler, and Sylvaine Trinh. 2000. *Apocalypse Observed: Religious Movements and Violence in North America, Europe, and Japan*. London and New York: Routledge.

166 BIBLIOGRAPHY

Hall, Peter A., and D. Soskice, eds. 2001. *Varieties of Capitalism: The Institutional Foundations of Comparative Advantage*. Oxford: Oxford University Press.

Hall, Peter M. 1987. "Interactionism and the Study of Social Organization." *Sociological Quarterly* 28, no. 1: 1–22.

Hall, Peter M., and Patrick J. W. McGinty. 1997. "Policy as the Transformation of Intentions." *Sociological Quarterly* 38: 439–467.

Hall, S., C. Critcher, T. Jefferson, J. Clarke, and B. Roberts. 1978. *Policing the Crisis: Mugging, the State, and Law and Order*. London: Macmillan.

Hall, Stuart. 1986. "Gramsci's Relevance for the Study of Race and Ethnicity." *Journal of Communication Inquiry* 10: 5–27.

Hall, Stuart, and Paul Du Gay. 1996. *Questions of Cultural Identity*. Thousand Oaks, CA: Sage.

Hall, Thomas. 2002. "World-Systems Analysis and Globalization Directions for the Twenty-First Century." *Research in Political Sociology* 11: 81–22.

Hall, Thomas D., and James V. Fenelon. 2009. *Indigenous Peoples and Globalization: Resistance and Revitalization*. Boulder, CO: Paradigm Publishers.

Haller, B., B. Dorries, and J. Rahn. 2006. "Media Labeling versus the US Disability Community Identity: A Study of Shifting Cultural Language." *Disability and Society* 21: 61–75.

Halliday, Terence C., and Pavel Osinsky. 2006. "Globalization of Law." *Annual Review of Sociology* 32: 447–470.

Hamilton, Laura, Simon Cheng, and Brian Powell. 2007. "Adoptive Parents, Adaptive Parents: Evaluating the Importance of Biological Ties for Parental Investment." *American Sociological Review* 72: 95–116.

Hammond, Michael. 2004. "The Enhancement Imperative and Group Dynamics in the Emergence of Religion and Ascriptive Inequality." *Advances in Group Processes* 21: 167–188.

Haney, Lynn. 2000. "Feminist State Theory: Applications to Jurisprudence, Criminology, and the Welfare State." *Annual Review of Sociology* 26: 641–666.

Hannan, Michael, and John Freeman. 1977. "The Population Ecology of Organizations." *American Journal of Sociology* 82: 929–964.

Hao, Lingxin, and Suet-ling Pong. 2008. "The Role of School in Upward Mobility of Disadvantaged Immigrants' Children." *Annals of the American Academy of Political and Social Sciences* 620, no. 1: 62–89.

Haraway, Donna. 1991. "A Cyborg Manifesto: Science, Technology, and Socialist-Feminism in the Late Twentieth Century." In *Simians, Cyborgs and Women: The Reinvention of Nature*, 149–181. New York; Routledge.

Harding, David J. 2007. "Cultural Context, Sexual Behavior, and Romantic Relationships in Disadvantage." *American Sociological Review* 72: 341–364.

Harding, Sandra. 2003. "How Standpoint Methodology Informs Philosophy of Social Science." In *The Blackwell Guide to the Philosophy of the Social Sciences*, edited by Stephen P. Turner and Paul A. Roth, 291–310. Malden, MA: Blackwell Publishing.

Harding, Sandra, and K. Norberg. 2005. "New Feminist Approaches to Social Science Methodologies: An Introduction." *Signs: Journal of Women in Culture and Society* 30: 2009–2015.

Hardt, Michael, and Antonio Negri. 2000. *Empire*. Cambridge, MA: Harvard University Press.

———. 2009. *Commonwealth*. Cambridge, MA: Belknap Press.

Hare, Richard M. 1981. *Moral Thinking: Its Levels, Method, and Point*. Oxford, UK: Clarendon Press.

Harmon, Katherine. 2009. "Deaths from Avoidable Medical Error More Than Double in Past Decade, Investigation Shows." *Scientific American*. http://www.scientificamerican.com/blog/post.cfm?id=deaths-from-avoidable-medical-error-2009-08-10 (accessed January 1, 2011).

Harper, A. Breeze, ed. 2010. *Sistah Vegan: Black Female Vegans Speak on Food, Identity, Health, and Society*. New York: Lantern Books.

Harris, Angela. 1990. "Race and Essentialism in Feminist Legal Theory." *Stanford Law Review* 42: 581–616.

Harrison, Bennett, and Barry Bluestone. 1988. *The Great U-Turn: Corporate Restructuring and the Polarizing of America*. New York: Basic Books.

Hartman, Chester, and Gregory Squires. 2009. *The Integration Debate: Competing Futures for American Cities*. New York: Routledge.

Harvey, David. 2005. *A Brief History of Neoliberalism*. New York: Oxford University Press.

———. 2008. "The Right to the City." *New Left Review* 53: 23–40.

Hastings, N. A. J., and J. B. Peacock. 1974. *Statistical Distributions*. London: Butterworths.

Hattery, Angela. 2001. *Women, Work, and Family: Balancing and Weaving*. Thousand Oaks, CA: Sage Publications.

———. 2009. *Intimate Partner Violence*. Lanham, MD: Rowman & Littlefield.

BIBLIOGRAPHY 167

Hattery, Angela, and Earl Smith. 2006. "Teaching Public Sociologies." In *Public Sociologies Reader*, edited by Judith Blau and Keri E. Iyall Smith, 265–280. New York: Rowman & Littlefield.

———. 2007. *African American Families*. Thousand Oaks, CA: Sage Publishers.

Haugen, Hans M. 2008. "Human Rights and Technology—a Conflictual Relationship? Assessing Private Research and the Right to Adequate Food." *Journal of Human Rights* 7: 224–244.

Hayden, Tom. 2006. *Radical Nomad: C. Wright Mills and His Times*. Boulder, CO: Paradigm Publishers.

Hayner, Priscilla B. 2001. *Unspeakable Truths: Confronting State Terror and Atrocity*. London: Routledge.

Haynes, J. 2008. *Development Studies*. Malden, MA: Polity.

Hayward, T. 2005. *Constitutional Environmental Rights*. Oxford: Oxford University Press.

Hays, Sharon. 2003. *Flat Broke with Children*. New York: Oxford University Press.

Headrick, D. R. 2010. *Power over Peoples: Technology, Environments, and Western Imperialism, 1400 to the Present*. Princeton, NJ: Princeton University Press.

Heberer, Patricia, and Jürgen Matthäus, eds. 2008. *Atrocities on Trial*. Lincoln: University of Nebraska Press.

Hedström, P., and R. Swedberg. 1998. *Social Mechanisms. An Analytical Approach to Social Theory*. Cambridge, UK: Cambridge University Press.

Heinz, Walter R. 2003. "From Work Trajectories to Negotiated Careers: The Contingent Work Life Course." In *Handbook of the Life Course*, edited by Jeylan T. Mortimer and Michael J. Shanahan, 185–204. New York: Kluwer.

Held, David. 1995. *Democracy and the Global Order: From the Modern State to Cosmopolitan Governance*. Stanford, CA: Stanford University Press.

———. 2004. *Global Covenant: The Social Democratic Alternative to the Washington Consensus*. Cambridge, UK: Polity Press.

———. 2010. *Cosmopolitanism*. Cambridge, UK: Polity Press.

Hendawi, Hamza. 2011. "Egypt: Internet Down, Counterterror Unit Up." *Press-Register*, January 28. http://www.3news.co.nz/Egypt-internet-down-counterterror-unit-up/tabid/417/articleID/196288/Default .aspx (accessed September 6, 2012).

Henderson, Conway W. 1991. "Conditions Affecting the Use of Political Repression." *Journal of Conflict Resolution* 35: 120–142.

———. 1993. "Population Pressures and Political Repression." *Social Science Quarterly* 74: 322–333.

Herd, D. 1985. "Migration, Cultural Transformation, and the Rise of Black Liver Cirrhosis Mortality." *British Journal of Addiction* 80: 397–410.

———. 1988a. "A Review of Drinking Patterns and Alcohol Problems among US Blacks." Report of the Secretary's Task Force on Black and Minority Health. *Chemical Dependency and Diabetes* 7: 7–140. Washington, DC: U.S. Government Printing Office.

———. 1988b. "The Epidemiology of Drinking Patterns and Alcohol Problems among US Blacks." In *Alcohol Use among U.S. Ethnic Minorities*, edited by D. Spiegler, D. Tate, S. Aitken, and C. Christian, 3–51. Rockville, MD: National Institute on Alcohol Abuse and Alcoholism.

Herdt, Gilbert. 1994. *Third Sex, Third Gender*. New York: Zone Books.

———. 1997. *Same Sex, Different Cultures: Exploring Gay and Lesbian Lives*. Oxford: Westview.

Herek, Gregory M., and Kevin T. Berrill. 1992. *Hate Crimes: Confronting Violence against Lesbians and Gay Men*. Newbury Park, CA: Sage Publications.

Herek, Gregory M., and John P. Capitanio. 1996. "'Some of My Best Friends': Intergroup Contact, Concealable Stigma, and Heterosexuals' Attitudes toward Gay Men and Lesbians." *Personality and Social Psychology Bulletin* 22: 412–424.

Herek, Gregory M., and Eric K. Glunt. 1993. "Interpersonal Contact and Heterosexuals' Attitudes toward Gay Men: Results from a National Survey." *Journal of Sex Research* 30: 239–244.

Herkert, J. R. 2004. "Microethics, Macroethics, and Professional Engineering Societies." In *Emerging Technologies and Ethical Issues in Engineering*, edited by National Academy of Engineering, 107–114. Washington, DC: National Academies Press.

Hernan, R. E. 2010. *This Borrowed Earth: Lessons from the 15 Worst Environmental Disasters around the World*. New York: Palgrave Macmillan.

Hershock, Peter D. 2000. "Dramatic Intervention: Human Rights from a Buddhist Perspective." *Philosophy East and West* 50: 9–33.

Hertel, Shareen, and Kathryn Libal. 2011. *Human Rights in the United States: Beyond Exceptionalism*. New York: Cambridge University Press.

Hess, David J. 1997. *Science Studies: An Advanced Introduction*. New York: New York University Press.

Hesse-Biber, Sharlene Nagy. 2006. *The Cult of Thinness*. New York: Oxford University Press.

Hester, Stephen. 2009. "Ethnomethodology: Respecifying the Problem of Social Order." In *Encountering the Everyday: An Introduction to the Sociologies of the Unnoticed*, edited by Michael Hviid Jacobsen, 234–256. Basingstoke, UK: Palgrave Macmillan.

168 BIBLIOGRAPHY

Hester, Stephen, and Peter Eglin, eds. 1997a. *Culture in Action: Studies in Membership Categorization Analysis*. Washington, DC: International Institute for Ethnomethodology and Conversation Analysis and University Press of America.

———. 1997b. "Membership Categorization Analysis: An Introduction." In *Culture in Action: Studies in Membership Categorization Analysis*, edited by Stephen Hester and Peter Eglin, 1–23. Washington, DC: International Institute for Ethnomethodology and Conversation Analysis and University Press of America.

———. 1997c. "Conclusion: Membership Categorization Analysis and Sociology." In *Culture in Action: Studies in Membership Categorization Analysis*, edited by Stephen Hester and Peter Eglin, 153–163. Washington, DC: International Institute for Ethnomethodology and Conversation Analysis and University Press of America.

Hewitt, Lyndi. 2008. "Feminists and the Forum: Is It Worth the Effort?" *Societies without Borders* 3: 118–135.

———. 2009. *The Politics of Transnational Feminist Discourse: Framing across Differences, Building Solidarities*. PhD diss., Vanderbilt University, Nashville, Tennessee.

Heydebrand, Wolf. 1977. "Organizational Contradictions in Public Bureaucracies, toward a Marxian Theory of Organizations." *Sociological Quarterly* 18, no. 1: 83–107.

———. 1983. "Technocratic Corporatism: Toward a Theory of Occupational and Organizational Transformation." In *Organizational Theory and Public Policy*, edited by Richard Hall and Robert Quinn, 93–114. Beverly Hills, CA: Sage.

Heyman, Josiah. 2002. "U.S. Immigration Officers of Mexican Ancestry as Mexican Americans, Citizens, and Immigration Police." *Current Anthropology* 43: 479–507.

———. 2010. "Human Rights and Social Justice Briefing 1: Arizona's Immigration Law—S.B. 1070." Society for Applied Anthropology. http://www.sfaa.net/committees/humanrights/AZImmigrationLawSB1070.pdf (accessed July 17, 2012).

Hidalgo, Myra L. 2007. *Sexual Abuse and the Culture of Catholicism: How Priests and Nuns Become Perpetrators*. New York: Haworth Maltreatment and Trauma Press.

Higgins, E. Tory. 1987. "Self-Discrepancy: A Theory Relating Self and Affect." *Psychological Review* 94: 319–340.

Hill, Herman. 1993. "The CIA in National and International Labor Movements. Review of *Compromised Campus: The Collaboration of Universities with the Intelligence Community, 1945–1955*, by Sigmund Diamond." *International Journal of Politics* 6: 405–407.

Hill, Jane H. 2008. *The Everyday Language of White Racism*. Malden, MA: Wiley-Blackwell.

Hinde, Andrew. 1998. *Demographic Methods*. London: Oxford University Press.

Hinton, Alexander L., and Kevin L. O'Neill. 2009. *Genocide: Truth, Memory, and Representation*. Durham, NC: Duke University Press.

Hinze, Susan W., Jielu Lin, and Tanetta Andersson. 2011. "Can We Capture the Intersections? Older Black Women, Education, and Health." *Women's Health Issues* 22, no. 1 (January): e91–e98.

Hinze, Susan W., Noah J. Webster, Heidi T. Chirayath, and Joshua H. Tamayo-Sarver. 2009. "Hurt Running from Police? No Chance of (Pain) Relief: The Social Construction of Deserving Patients in Emergency Departments." *Research in the Sociology of Health Care* 27: 235–261.

Hirschman, A. O. 1983. "Morality and the Social Sciences: A Durable Tension." In *Social Science as Moral Inquiry*, edited by N. Hann et al., 21–32. New York: Columbia University Press.

Hiskes, Richard P. 2010. "The Relational Foundations of Emergent Human Rights: From Thomas Hobbes to the Human Right to Water." *Zeitschrift für Menschenrechte [Journal for Human Rights]* 4, no. 2: 127–146.

Hitlin, Steven, and Jane A. Piliavin. 2004. "Values: A Review of Recent Research and Theory." *Annual Review of Sociology* 30: 359–393.

Hitt, L., ed. 2002. *Human Rights: Great Speeches in History*. San Diego, CA: Greenhaven Press.

Hlaing, Kyaw Y. 2004. "Myanmar in 2003: Frustration and Despair?" *Asian Survey* 44: 87–92.

———. 2005. "Myanmar in 2004: Another Year of Uncertainty." *Asian Survey* 45: 174–179.

Hoang, Nghia. 2009. "The 'Asian Values' Perspective of Human Rights: A Challenge to Universal Human Rights." Social Science Research Network. http://ssrn.com/abstract=1405436 (accessed July 17, 2012).

Hobhouse, L. T. 1922. *The Elements of Social Justice*. London: G. Allen and Unwin.

Hobsbawm, Eric J. 1962. *The Age of Revolution: Europe 1789–1848*. London: Weidenfeld and Nicolson.

———. 1964. *Labouring Men: Studies in the History of Labour*. London: Weidenfeld and Nicolson.

Hochschild, Arlie. 1979. "Emotion Work, Feeling Rules, and Social Structure." *American Journal of Sociology* 85: 551–575.

———. 1983. *The Managed Heart: Commercialization of Human Feeling*. Berkeley: University of California Press.

BIBLIOGRAPHY 169

Hockenberry, J. 1995. *Moving Violations: War Zones, Wheelchairs, and Declarations of Independence.* New York: Hyperion.

Hoffman Plastic Compounds, Inc. v. NLRB. 2002. 122 S. Ct. 1275.

Hoffman, John P. 2006. "Extracurricular Activities, Athletic Participation, and Adolescent Alcohol Use: Gender-Differentiated and School-Contextual Effects." *Journal of Health and Social Behavior* 47, no. 3: 275–290.

Holland, J., C. Ramazanoglu, S. Sharpe, and R. Thomson. 1998. *The Male in the Head: Young People, Heterosexuality and Power.* London: The Tufnell.

Hollingshead, A. B., and F. C. Redlich. 1958. *Social Class and Mental Illness.* New York: Wiley.

Hollingsworth, J. Rogers, Philippe C. Schmitter, and Wolfgang Streeck, eds. 1994. *Governing Capitalist Economies: Performance and Control of Economic Sectors.* New York: Oxford University Press.

Holmes, Malcolm D. 2008. *Race and Police Brutality: Roots of an Urban Dilemma.* Albany: State University of New York Press.

Holstein, James A., and Jaber F. Gubrium. 1999. *The Self We Live By: Narrative Identity in a Postmodern World.* 1st ed. New York: Oxford University Press.

———, eds. 2003. *Inner Lives and Social Worlds: Readings in Social Psychology.* New York: Oxford University Press.

Homans, George C. 1974. *Social Behavior: Its Elementary Forms.* Rev. ed. New York: Harcourt, Brace, Jovanovich.

Hopcroft, Rosemary L. 2005. "Parental Status and Differential Investment in Sons and Daughters: Trivers-Willard Revisited." *Social Forces* 83: 169–193.

———. 2008. "Darwinian Conflict Theory: Alternative Theory or Unifying Paradigm for Sociology?" In *The New Evolutionary Science: Human Nature, Social Behavior and Social Change,* edited by Heinz-Jürgen Niedenzu, Tamás Meleghy, and Peter Meyer. Boulder, CO: Paradigm Publishers.

———. 2009. "Gender Inequality in Interaction: An Evolutionary Account." *Social Forces* 87: 1845–1872.

Hopcroft, Rosemary L., and Dana Burr Bradley. 2007. "The Sex Difference in Depression across 29 Countries." *Social Forces* 85: 1483–1507.

Hopgood, Stephen. 2006. *Keepers of the Flame.* Ithaca, NY: Cornell University Press.

Horkheimer, Max, and Theodor W. Adorno. 1993 [1944]. *Dialectic of Enlightenment.* Translated by John Cumming. New York: Continuum.

Hornburg, Alf. 1998. "Ecosystems and World Systems: Accumulation as an Ecological Process." *Journal of World-Systems Research* 4, no. 2: 169–177.

Horne, Christine. 2004. "Values and Evolutionary Psychology." *Sociological Theory* 22: 477–503.

Horne, Sharon, and Melanie J. Zimmer-Gembeck. 2005. "Female Sexual Subjectivity and Well-Being: Comparing Late Adolescents with Different Sexual Experiences." *Sexuality Research and Social Policy* 2: 25–40.

Horowitz, Louis Irving. 1980. *Taking Lives: Genocide and State Power.* New Brunswick, NJ: Transaction Books.

———. 2002. *Tanking Lives: Genocide and State Power.* 5th ed. New Brunswick, NJ: Transaction.

Horton, Hayward Derrick. 1999. "Critical Demography: The Paradigm of the Future?" *Sociological Forum* 14, no. 3: 363–367.

Hosken, Fran P. 1993. *The Hosken Report: Genital and Sexual Mutilation of Females.* 4th ed. Lexington, MA: Women's International Network News.

House, J. S. 1981. "Social Structure and Personality." In *Social Psychology, Sociological Perspectives,* edited by M. Rosenberg and R. H. Turner, 525–561. New York: Basic Books.

House, James S. 1977. "The Three Faces of Social Psychology." *Sociometry* 40: 161–177.

House, James S., James M. Lepkowski, Ann M. Kinney, Richard P. Mero, Ronald C. Kessler, and A. Regula Herzog. 1994. "The Social Stratification of Aging and Health." *Journal of Health and Social Behavior* 35: 213–234.

Hovenkamp, Herbert. 1991. *Enterprise and American Law, 1836–1937.* Cambridge, MA: Harvard University Press.

Hovey, Michael W. 1997. "Interceding at the United Nations: The Human Right of Conscientious Objection." In *Transnational Social Movements and Global Politics: Solidarity beyond the State,* edited by J. Smith, C. Chatfield, and R. Pagnucco. Syracuse, NY: Syracuse University Press.

Hovil, L., and E. Werker. 2005. "Portrait of a Failed Rebellion: An Account of Rational, Sub-Optimal Violence in Western Uganda." *Rationality and Society* 17: 5–34.

Howard, Jay. 2010. "2009 Hans O. Mauksch Address: Where Are We and How Did We Get Here? A Brief Examination of the Past, Present and Future of the Teaching and Learning Movement in Sociology." *Teaching Sociology* 38: 81–92.

170 BIBLIOGRAPHY

Howard, Judith, and Carolyn Allen. 1996. "Reflections on the Fourth World Conference on Women and NGO Forum '95: Introduction." *Signs* 22: 181–185.

Howard, Rhoda E. 1985. "Legitimacy and Class Rule in Commonwealth Africa: Constitutionalism and the Rule of Law." *Third World Quarterly* 7, no. 2: 323–347.

———. 1995. *Human Rights and the Search for Community*. Boulder, CO: Westview Press.

Howard, Rhoda E., and Jack Donnelly. 1986. "Human Dignity, Human Rights and Political Regimes." *American Political Science Review* 80: 801–817.

Huber, Evelyn, and John Stephens. 2001. *Development and Crisis of the Welfare State*. Chicago: University of Chicago Press.

Huber, Joan. 2007. *On the Origins of Gender Inequality*. Boulder, CO: Paradigm Publishers.

Huda, S. 2006. "Sex Trafficking in South Asia." *International Journal of Gynecology and Obstetrics* 94: 374–381.

Hughes, Everett C. 1963. "Good People and Dirty Work." In *The Other Side*, edited by Howard Becker, 23–36. New York: The Free Press.

———. 1971. *The Sociological Eye: Selected Papers*. Chicago: Aldine-Atherton.

Hughes, Jason. 2003. *Learning to Smoke: Tobacco Use in the West*. Chicago: University of Chicago Press.

Hughes, John A., Peter J. Martin, and W. W. Sharrock. 1995. *Understanding Classical Sociology: Marx, Weber, Durkheim*. London: Sage.

Hughes, John A., and W. W. Sharrock. 2007. *Theory and Methods in Sociology: An Introduction to Sociological Thinking and Practice*. Basingstoke, UK: Palgrave Macmillan.

Hughs, Alex, and Ann Witz. 1997. "Feminism and the Matter of Bodies: From de Beauvoir to Butler." *Body and Society* 3: 47–60.

Huizinga, Johann. 2006 [1919]. *The Autumn of the Middle Ages*. Translated by Rodney J. Payton and Ulrich Mammitzsch. Chicago: University of Chicago Press.

Hulko, Wendy. 2009. "The Time- and Context-Contingent Nature of Intersectionality and Interlocking Oppressions." *Affilia: Journal of Women and Social Work* 24: 44–55.

Human Rights Watch (HRW). 2000. "Racial Disparities in the War on Drugs." HRW. http://www.hrw.org/legacy/reports/2000/usa/Rcedrg00.htm#P54_1086 (accessed January 1, 2011).

———. 2010. *World Report*. New York: HRW.

Hunt, Lynn. 2007. *Inventing Human Rights: A History*. New York: W. W. Norton and Co.

Huntington, Samuel. 1991. *The Third Wave*. Norman: University of Oklahoma Press.

Husak, Douglas. 2003. "The Criminalization of Drug Use." *Sociological Forum* 18, no. 3: 503–513.

Hutchinson, Phil, Rupert Read, and Wes Sharrock. 2008. *There Is No Such Thing as a Social Science: In Defence of Peter Winch*. Aldershot, UK: Ashgate.

Hynes, Patricia, Michele Lamb, Damien Short, and Matthew Waites. 2010. "Sociology and Human Rights: Confrontations, Evasions and New Engagements." *International Journal of Human Rights* 14, no. 6: 811–832.

Hynie, M., and J. E. Lydon. 1995. "Women's Perceptions of Female Contraceptive Behavior: Experimental Evidence of the Sexual Double Standard." *Psychology of Women Quarterly* 19: 563–581.

Ignatiev, N. 1995. *How the Irish Became White*. New York: Routledge.

Ikegami, Eiko. 2005. "Bringing Culture into Macrostructural Analysis in Historical Sociology." *Poetics* 33: 15–32.

Illich, Ivan. 1971. *Deschooling Society*. London: Calder and Boyars.

Inglehart, Ronald. 1977. *The Silent Revolution Changing Values and Political Styles among Western Publics*. Princeton, NJ: Princeton University Press.

Inglehart, Ronald, and Wayne E. Baker. 2000. "Modernization, Cultural Change, and the Persistence of Traditional Values." *American Sociological Review* 65, no. 1: 19–51.

Ingraham, Chrys. 2008. *White Weddings: Romancing Heterosexuality in Popular Culture*. New York: Routledge.

International Criminal Court (ICC). 2011. "Rome Statute." ICC. http://www.icc-cpi.int/Menus/ICC/Legal+Texts+and+Tools/Official+Journal/Rome+Statute.htm (accessed August 15, 2012).

International Federation of Red Cross and Red Crescent Societies. 2004. *World Disaster Report: Focus on Community Resilience*. Bloomfield, CT: Kumarian Press.

International Gay and Lesbian Human Rights Commission (IGLHRC). 2011. "Our Issues." IGLHRC. http://www.iglhrc.org/cgi-bin/iowa/theme/1.html (accessed November 11, 2011).

International Labour Office. 1973. Minimum Age Convention. http://www.ilocarib.org.tt/projects/cariblex/conventions_6.shtml (accessed September 6, 2012).

Irvine, Janice M. 2002. *Talk about Sex: The Battles over Sex Education in the United States*. Berkeley: University of California Press.

Irwin, Alan, and Brian Wynne, eds. 1996. *Misunderstanding Science? The Public Reconstruction of Science and Technology*. Cambridge, UK: Cambridge University Press.

BIBLIOGRAPHY 171

Ishay, Micheline R., ed. 1997. *The Human Rights Reader: Major Political Essays, Speeches, and Documents from the Bible to the Present*. New York: Routledge.

———. 2004a. *The History of Human Rights: From Ancient Times to the Globalization Era*. Berkeley: University of California Press.

———. 2004b. "What Are Human Rights? Six Historical Controversies." *Journal of Human Rights* 3: 359–371.

Israel, Jonathan. 2011. *Democratic Enlightenment: Philosophy, Revolution, and Human Rights*. Oxford: Oxford University Press.

Ito, Mizuko, Sonja Baumer, Matteo Bittanti, Danah Boyd, Rachel Cody, Becky Herr-Stephenson, Heather A. Horst, Patricia G. Lange, Dilan Mahendran, Katynka Z. Martinez, C. J. Pascoe, Dan Perkel, Laura Robinson, Christo Sims, and Lisa Tripp, with Judd Antin, Megan Finn, Arthur Law, Annie Manion, Sarai Mitnick, David Scholssberg, and Sarita Yardi. 2009. *Hanging Out, Messing Around, and Geeking Out*. Cambridge, MA: Massachusetts Institute of Technology Press.

Jacobs, David, Zenchao Qian, Jason T. Carmichael, and Stephanie L. Kent. 2007. "Who Survives on Death Row? An Individual and Contextual Analysis." *American Sociological Review* 72: 610–632.

Jacobs, Mark D. 2012. "Financial Crises as Symbols and Rituals." In *The Oxford Handbook of the Sociology of Finance*, edited by Karin Knorr Cetina and Alex Preda. New York: Oxford University Press.

Jacobs, Mark D., and Nancy Weiss Hanrahan. 2005. Introduction to *The Blackwell Companion to the Sociology of Culture*, edited by Mark D. Jacobs and Nancy Weiss Hanrahan. Malden, MA: Blackwell.

Jacobs, Mark D., and Lyn Spillman. 2005. "Cultural Sociology at the Crossroads of the Discipline." *Poetics* 33: 1–14.

Jaeger, Gertrude, and Philip Selznick. 1964. "A Normative Theory of Culture." *American Sociological Review* 29: 653–669.

Jain, D. 2005. *Women, Development, and the UN: A Sixty-Year Quest for Equality and Justice*. Bloomington: Indiana University Press.

Jalata, Asafa. 2005. "State Terrorism and Globalization: The Cases of Ethiopia and Sudan." *International Journal of Comparative Sociology* 46, no. 1–2: 79–102.

———. 2008. "Struggling for Social Justice in the Capitalist World System: The Cases of African Americans, Oromos, and Southern and Western Sudanese." *Social Identities* 14, no. 3: 363–388.

James, Helen. 2006. "Myanmar in 2005: In a Holding Pattern." *Asian Survey* 46: 162–167.

Jamieson, Dale. 2003. *Morality's Progress: Essays on Humans, Other Animals, and the Rest of Nature*. London: Oxford University Press.

Janoski, Thomas. 1998. *Citizenship and Civil Society*. New York: Cambridge University Press.

Jasper, James. 1997. *The Art of Moral Protest: Culture, Biography, and Creativity in Social Movements*. Chicago: University of Chicago Press.

———. 2004. "A Strategic Approach to Collective Action: Looking for Agency in Social Movement Choices." *Mobilization* 9, no. 1: 1–16.

Jasso, Guillermina. 1978. "On the Justice of Earnings: A New Specification of the Justice Evaluation Function." *American Journal of Sociology* 83: 1398–1419.

———. 1980. "A New Theory of Distributive Justice." *American Sociological Review* 45: 3–32.

———. 1988a. "Distributive-Justice Effects of Employment and Earnings on Marital Cohesiveness: An Empirical Test of Theoretical Predictions." In *Status Generalization: New Theory and Research*, edited by Murray Webster and Martha Foschi, 123–162 (references, 490–493). Stanford, CA: Stanford University Press.

———. 1988b. "Principles of Theoretical Analysis." *Sociological Theory* 6: 1–20.

———. 1990. "Methods for the Theoretical and Empirical Analysis of Comparison Processes." *Sociological Methodology* 20: 369–419.

———. 2001. "Studying Status: An Integrated Framework." *American Sociological Review* 66: 96–124.

———. 2008. "A New Unified Theory of Sociobehavioral Forces." *European Sociological Review* 24: 411–434.

———. 2009. "A New Model of Wage Determination and Wage Inequality." *Rationality and Society* 21: 113–168.

———. 2010. "Linking Individuals and Societies." *Journal of Mathematical Sociology* 34: 1–51.

Jasso, Guillermina, and Samuel Kotz. 2007. "A New Continuous Distribution and Two New Families of Distributions Based on the Exponential." *Statistica Neerlandica* 61: 305–328.

———. 2008. "Two Types of Inequality: Inequality between Persons and Inequality between Subgroups." *Sociological Methods and Research* 37: 31–74.

Jayasree, A. K. 2004. "Searching for Justice for Body and Self in a Coercive Environment: Sex Work in Kerala, India." *Reproductive Health Matters* 12: 58–67.

Jayyusi, Lena. 1984. *Categorization and the Moral Order*. London: Routledge and Kegan Paul.

172 BIBLIOGRAPHY

———. 1991. "Values and Moral Judgment: Communicative Praxis as a Moral Order." In *Ethnomethodology and the Human Sciences*, edited by Graham Button, 227–251. Cambridge, UK: Cambridge University Press.

Jenkins, Alan, and Kevin Shawn Hsu. 2008. "American Ideals and Human Rights: Findings from New Public Opinion Research by the Opportunity Agenda." *Fordham Law Review* 77, no. 2: 439–458.

Jenkins, J. Craig. 1983. "Resource Mobilization Theory and the Study of Social Movements." *Annual Review of Sociology* 9: 527–553.

Jenkins, J. Craig, and Craig Eckert. 1986. "Channeling Black Insurgency: Elite Patronage and the Development of the Civil Rights Movement." *American Sociological Review* 51: 812–830.

Jensen, Gary. 2007. *The Path of the Devil: Early Modern Witch Hunts*. Lanham, MD: Rowman & Littlefield.

Jessop, Robert D. 2002. *The Future of the Capitalist State*. Cambridge, MA: Polity.

Jo, Moon Ho. 1984. "The Putative Political Complacency of Asian Americans." *Political Psychology* 5: 583–605.

Joachim, Jutta. 2003. "Framing Issues and Seizing Opportunities: Women's Rights and the UN." *International Studies Quarterly* 47: 247–274.

Joas, Hans. 2000. *The Genesis of Values*. Cambridge, UK: Polity Press.

———. 2003. *War and Modernity*. Cambridge, UK: Polity Press.

Jochnick, Chris. 1999. "Confronting the Impunity of Non-State Actors: New Fields for the Promotion of Human Rights." *Human Rights Quarterly* 21, no. 1: 56–79.

Johansen, Bruce. 2003. *The Dirty Dozen: Toxic Chemicals in the Earth's Future*. Westport, CT: Praeger.

Johnson, C., and T. Forsyth. 2002. "In the Eyes of the State: Negotiating a 'Rights-Based Approach' to Forest Conservation in Thailand." *World Development* 20: 1591–1605.

Johnson, E. Patrick. 2003. *Appropriating Blackness: Performance and the Politics of Authenticity*. Durham, NC: Duke University Press.

Johnson, Eric A., and Eric H. Monkkonen, eds. 1996. *The Civilization of Crime*. Urbana: University of Illinois Press.

Johnson, Heather Beth. 2006. *The American Dream and the Power of Wealth: Choosing Schools and Inheriting Inequality in the Land of Opportunity*. New York: Routledge.

Johnson, J. 2001. "In-depth Interviewing." In *Handbook of Interview Research: Context and Method*, edited by Jay Gubrium and James Holstein, 103–119. Thousand Oaks, CA: Sage.

Johnson, Jim (aka Bruno Latour). 1988. "Mixing Humans and Nonhumans Together: The Sociology of a Door-Closer." *Social Problems* 35, no. 3: 298–310.

Johnson, Norman L., and Samuel Kotz. 1969–1972. *Distributions in Statistics*. 4 vols. New York: Wiley.

Johnson, Norman L., Samuel Kotz, and N. Balakrishnan. 1994. *Continuous Univariate Distributions*. Vol. 1. 2nd ed. New York: Wiley.

———. 1995. *Continuous Univariate Distributions*. Vol. 2. 2nd ed. New York: Wiley.

Johnson, Victoria. 2011. "Everyday Rituals of the Master Race: Fascism, Stratification, and the Fluidity of 'Animal' Domination." In *Critical Theory and Animal Liberation*, edited by John Sanbonmatsu, 203–218. Lanham, MD: Rowman & Littlefield.

Johnston, Barbara R. 1995. "Human Rights and the Environment." *Human Ecology* 23: 111–123.

Johnston, Hank, and Bert Klandermans, eds. 1995. *Social Movements and Culture*. Minneapolis: University of Minnesota Press.

Johnston, Hank, and John A. Noakes, eds. 2005. *Frames of Protest: Social Movements and the Framing Perspective*. Lanham, MD: Rowman & Littlefield Publishers.

Jordan, Kathleen Casey. 1997. "The Effect of Disclosure on the Professional Life of Lesbian Police Officers." PhD diss., City University of New York.

Jordan-Zachary, Julia S. 2007. "Am I a Black Woman or a Woman Who Is Black? A Few Thoughts on the Meaning of Intersectionality." *Politics and Gender* 3: 254–263.

Jorgensen, Anja, and Dennis Smith. 2009. "The Chicago School of Sociology: Survival in the Urban Jungle." In *Encountering the Everyday: An Introduction to the Sociologies of the Unnoticed*, edited by Michael Hviid Jacobsen, 45–69. New York: Macmillan.

Jorgenson, Andrew. 2003. "Consumption and Environmental Degradation: A Cross-National Analysis of the Ecological Footprint." *Social Problems* 50, no. 3: 374–394.

Joseph, Paul. 1993. *Peace Politics: The United States between the Old and New World Orders*. Philadelphia: Temple University Press.

Jost, Timothy S. 2003. *Disentitlement? The Threats Facing Our Public Health Care Programs and a Rights-Based Response*. Oxford: Oxford University Press.

Jotkowitz, A., S. Glick, and B. Gesundheit. 2008. "A Case against Justified Non-Voluntary Active Euthanasia (The Groningen Protocol)." *American Journal of Bioethics* 8: 23–26.

Juris, Jeffrey. 2008. *Networking Futures*. Durham, NC: Duke University Press.

BIBLIOGRAPHY 173

Kaiser Family Foundation. 2002. *Sex Smarts Survey: Gender Roles*. Menlo Park, CA: Kaiser Family Foundation.
Kalberg, Stephen. 1994. *Max Weber's Comparative-Historical Sociology*. Chicago: University of Chicago Press.
——. 2011. Introduction to *The Protestant Ethic and the Spirit of Capitalism* by Max Weber. Translated by Stephen Kalberg. Rev. 1920 ed. New York: Oxford University Press.
Kaldor, Mary. 1999. *New and Old Wars: Organized Violence in a Global Era*. Stanford, CA: Stanford University Press.
——. 2003. *Global Civil Society: An Answer to War*. Cambridge, UK: Polity Press.
Kang, Miliann. 2003. "The Managed Hand: The Commercialization of Bodies and Emotions in Korean Immigrant-Owned Nail Salons." *Gender and Society* 17: 820–839.
Kant, Immanuel. 1933 [1788]. *Critique of Practical Reason*. Upper Saddle River, NJ: Prentice Hall.
——. 1939. *Perpetual Peace*. New York: Columbia University Press.
Kapur, Ratna. 2002. "The Tragedy of Victimization Rhetoric: Resurrecting the 'Native' Subject in International/Post-Colonial Feminist Legal Politics." *Harvard Law School Human Rights Journal of Law* 15: 1–38.
——. 2005. *Erotic Justice: Law and the New Politics of Postcolonialism*. London: Glasshouse Press.
Kara, Karel. 1968. "On the Marxist Theory of War and Peace." *Journal of Peace Research* 5: 1–27.
Karger, Howard. 1989. "The Common and Conflicting Goals of Labor and Social Work." *Administration in Social Work* 13: 1–17.
Karp, David. 1996. *Speaking of Sadness: Depression, Disconnection, and the Meanings of Illness*. New York: Oxford University Press.
Karpik, Lucien. 1977. "Technological Capitalism." In *Critical Issues in Organizations*, edited by S. Clegg and D. Dunkerley, 41–71. London: Routledge and Kegan Paul.
Karstedt, Susanne. 2007. "Human Rights." In *The Blackwell Encyclopedia of Sociology*, edited by George Ritzer, 2182–2185. Malden, MA: Blackwell Publishing.
——. 2011. "Human Rights." In *The Concise Encyclopedia of Sociology*, edited by George Ritzer and J. Michael Ryan, 294–295. Malden, MA: Wiley-Blackwell.
Kasinitz, Philip, Mary Waters, John H. Mollenkopf, and Jennifer Holdaway. 2009. *Inheriting the City: The Children of Immigrants Come of Age*. New York: Russell Sage Foundation.
Kass, Leon R. 1971. "The New Biology: What Price Relieving Man's Estate?" *Science* 174: 779–788.
Kasser, Tim. 2011. "Cultural Values and the Well-Being of Future Generations: A Cross-National Study." *Journal of Cross-Cultural Psychology* 42, no. 2 (March): 206–215.
Katsui, H., and J. Kumpuvuori. 2008. "Human Rights Based Approach to Disability in Development in Uganda: A Way to Fill the Gap between Political and Social Spaces?" *Scandinavian Journal of Disability Research* 10: 227–236.
Katz, Jonathan. 2007. *The Invention of Heterosexuality*. Chicago: University of Chicago Press.
Kausikan, Bilahari. 1995. "An East Asian Approach to Human Rights." *Buffalo Journal of International Law* 2: 263–283.
Kautsky, Karl. 1931. *Bolshevism at a Deadlock*. London: G. Allen and Unwin.
Keck, Margaret E., and Kathryn Sikkink. 1998. *Activists beyond Borders: Advocacy Networks in International Politics*. Ithaca, NY: Cornell University Press.
Keith, Michael, and Steve Pile. 1993. *Place and the Politics of Identity*. London: Psychology Press.
Keller, C., and M. Siegrist. 2010. "Psychological Resources and Attitudes toward People with Physical Disabilities." *Journal of Applied Social Psychology* 40: 389–401.
Kelman, Herbert C., and V. Lee Hamilton. 2002. "The My Lai Massacre: Crimes of Obedience and Sanctioned Massacres." In *Corporate and Governmental Deviance: Problems of Organizational Behavior in Contemporary Society*, edited by M. David Ermann and Richard J. Lundman, 195–221. Oxford: Oxford University Press.
Kempadoo, Kamala, ed. 2005. *Trafficking and Prostitution Reconsidered: New Perspectives on Migration, Sex Work, and Human Rights*. Boulder, CO: Paradigm Publishers.
Kemper, Theodore D. 1990. "Social Relations and Emotions: A Structural Approach." In *Research Agendas in the Sociology of Emotions*, edited by T. D. Kemper, 207–237. Albany: State University of New York Press.
Kemper, Theodore D., and Randall Collins. 1990. "Dimensions of Microinteraction." *American Journal of Sociology* 93: 32–68.
Kendall, Maurice G. 1943. *The Advanced Theory of Statistics*. Vol. 1: *Distribution Theory*. Original 2-vol. ed. London: Charles Griffin.
Kendall, Maurice G., and Alan Stuart. 1958. *The Advanced Theory of Statistics*. Vol. 1: *Distribution Theory*. First 3-vol. ed. New York: Hafner.
Kendler, Kenneth S., Sara Jaffee, and Dan Romer, eds. 2010. *The Dynamic Genome and Mental Health: The Role of Genes and Environments in Development*. Oxford: Oxford University Press.

174 BIBLIOGRAPHY

Kennedy, David. 2002. "Boundaries in the Field of Human Rights: The International Human Rights Movement: Part of the Problem?" *Harvard Law School Human Rights Journal* 15: 101–25.

Kessler R. C., and J. McLeod. 1984. "Sex Differences in Vulnerability to Undesirable Life Events." *American Sociological Review* 49: 620–631.

Kessler, Suzanne J. 1990. *Lessons from the Intersexed*. New Brunswick, NJ: Rutgers University Press.

Kestnbaum, Meyer. 2009. "The Sociology of War and the Military." *Annual Review of Sociology* 35: 235–254.

Khalili-Borna, C. A. 2007. "Technological Advancement and International Human Rights: Is Science Improving Human Life or Perpetuating Human Rights Violations?" *Michigan Journal of International Law* 29: 95–125.

Kick, Edward, and Andrew Jorgenson. 2003. "Globalization and the Environment." *Journal of World-Systems Research* 9, no. 2: 195–203.

Kikuzawa, Saeko, Sigrun Olafsdottir, and Bernice Pescosolido. 2008. "Similar Pressures, Different Contexts: Public Attitudes toward Government Intervention for Health Care in 21 Nations." *Journal of Health and Social Behavior* 49: 385–399.

Kilbourne, Jean. 1999. *Deadly Persuasion: Why Women and Girls Must Fight the Addictive Power of Advertising*. New York: The Free Press.

Kim, Hyun Sik. 2011. "Consequences of Parental Divorce for Child Development." *American Sociological Review* 76, no. 3: 487–511.

Kimeldorf, Howard. 1991. "Bringing Unions Back In (or Why We Need a New Old Labor History)." *Labor History* 32: 91–103.

Kimeldorf, Howard, and Judith Stepan-Norris. 1992. "Historical Studies of Labor Movements in the United States." *Annual Review of Sociology* 18: 495–517.

Kimmel, Michael S. 2001. "The Kindest Un-Cut: Feminism, Judaism, and My Son's Foreskin." *Tikkun* 16, no. 1. http://www.cirp.org/pages/cultural/kimmel1/ (accessed September 6, 2012).

———. 2005. *Manhood in America: A Cultural History*. New York: Oxford University Press.

Kincaid, Jamaica. 2000. *A Small Place*. 1st ed. New York: Farrar, Straus and Giroux.

Kincheloe, Joe, and Peter McLaren. 1994. "Rethinking Critical Theory and Qualitative Research." In *Handbook of Qualitative Research*, edited by Norman Denzin and Yvonna Lincoln, 138–157. Thousand Oaks, CA: Sage.

Kindleberger, Charles Poor, and Robert Z. Aliber. 2005. *Manias, Panics and Crashes: A History of Financial Crises*. Hoboken, NJ: John Wiley and Sons.

King, Deborah K. 1988. "Multiple Jeopardy, Multiple Consciousnesses: The Context of a Black Feminist Ideology." *Signs: Journal of Women in Culture and Society* 14: 42–72.

King, Martin Luther, Jr. 1986. "If the Negro Wins, Labor Wins." In *A Testament of Hope: The Essential Writings and Speeches of Martin Luther King, Jr.*, edited by James M. Washington. New York: HarperCollins.

Kingsbury, Benedict, Nico Krisch, and Richard Stewart. 2005. "The Emergence of Global Administrative Law." *Law and Contemporary Problems* 68: 15–61.

Kinney, Eleanor D., and Brian Alexander Clark. 2004. "Provisions for Health and Health Care in the Constitutions of the Countries of the World." *Cornell International Law Journal* 37: 285–355.

Kinsey, Alfred, Wardell B. Pomeroy, and Clyde E. Martin. 1948. *Sexual Behavior in the Human Male*. Philadelphia: W. B. Saunders Company.

Kiser, Edgar, and Howard T. Welser. 2010. "The Relationship between Theory and History in Revolutionary Biology: A Model for Historical Sociology?" Unpublished manuscript, University of Washington.

Kitano, Harry H. L. 1988. "Asian Americans and Alcohol: The Chinese, Japanese, Koreans and Filipinos in Los Angeles." In *Alcohol Use among U.S. Ethnic Minorities*, edited by D. Spiegler, D. Tate, S. Aitken, and C. Christian, 373–382. Rockville, MD: National Institute on Alcohol Abuse and Alcoholism.

Kitschelt, Herbert P. 1986. "Political Opportunity Structures and Political Protest: Anti-Nuclear Movements in Four Democracies." *British Journal of Political Science* 16, no. 1: 57–85.

Klandermans, Bert, and Suzanne Staggenborg, eds. 2002. *Methods of Social Movement Research*. Minneapolis: University of Minnesota Press.

Klare, Karl E. 1978. "Judicial Deradicalization of the Wagner Act and the Origins of Modern Legal Consciousness, 1937–1941." *Minnesota Law Review* 62: 265.

Kleiber, Christian, and Samuel Kotz. 2003. *Statistical Size Distributions in Economics and Actuarial Sciences*. Hoboken, NJ: Wiley.

Knights, David, and Hugh Wilmott, eds. 1990. *Labour Process Theory*. London: Macmillan.

Knoke, D., and E. O. Laumann. 1987. *The Organizational State: Social Choice in National Policy Domains*. Madison: University of Wisconsin Press.

BIBLIOGRAPHY   175

Koch, T. 2004. "The Difference that Difference Makes: Bioethics and the Challenge of 'Disability.'" *Journal of Medicine and Philosophy* 29: 697–716.

Kohler, Hans-Peter, J. L. Rodgers, and Kaare Christensen. 1999. "Is Fertility Behavior in Our Genes? Findings from a Danish Twin Study." *Population and Development Review* 25: 253–288.

———. 2002. "Between Nurture and Nature: The Shifting Determinants of Female Fertility in Danish Twin Cohorts." *Social Biology* 49: 218–248.

Kohli, M., and J. W. Meyer. 1986. "Social Structure and Social Construction of Life Stages." *Human Development* 29, no. 3: 145–149.

Kohli, Martin. 1986. "Social Organization and Subjective Construction of the Life Course." In *Human Development and the Life Course*, edited by A. Sorensen, F. Weinert, and L. Sherrod, 271–292. Cambridge, MA: Harvard University Press.

———. 2007. "The Institutionalization of the Life Course: Looking Back to Look Ahead." *Research in Human Development* 4, no. 3–4: 253–271.

Kohn, Melvin L. 1981. "Social Class and Schizophrenia: A Critical Review and a Reformulation." In *The Sociology of Mental Illness: Basic Studies*, edited by O. Grusky and Pollner M. Holt, 127–143. New York: Rinehart and Winston.

Kohn, Melvin L., and Carmi Schooler. 1983. *Work and Personality: An Inquiry into the Impact of Social Stratification*. Norwood, NJ: Ablex Publishing Corporation.

Kohn, Melvin L., Kazimierz M. Slomczynski, Krystyna Janicka, Valeri Khmelko, Bogdan W. Mach, Vladimir Paniotto, Wojciech Zaborowski, Roberto Gutierrez, and Cory Heyman. 1997. "Social Structure and Personality under Conditions of Radical Social Change: A Comparative Analysis of Poland and Ukraine." *American Sociological Review* 62: 614–638.

Kohn, P. M., and R. G. Smart. 1987. "Wine, Women and Suspiciousness and Advertising." *Journal Studies of Alcohol and Drugs* 48: 161–166.

Kolakowski, Leszek. 1983. "Marxism and Human Rights." *Daedalus* 112, no. 4: 81–92.

Kolben, Kevin. 2010. "Labor Rights as Human Rights?" *Virginia Journal of International Law* 50: 449–484.

Komarovsky, Mirra. 1951. "Editorial: Teaching College Sociology." *Social Forces* 30: 252–256.

Koo, Jeong-Woo, and Francisco O. Ramirez. 2009. "National Incorporation of Global Human Rights: Worldwide Adoptions of National Human Rights Institutions, 1966–2004." *Social Forces* 87: 1321–1354.

Korgen, Kathleen, and Jonathan White. 2010. *The Engaged Sociologist: Connecting the Classroom to the Community*. 3rd ed. Thousand Oaks, CA: Pine Forge.

Kornbluh, Joyce. 1987. *A New Deal for Workers' Education: The Workers' Service Program, 1933–1942*. Urbana: University of Illinois Press.

Korpi, Walter. 1983. *The Democratic Class Struggle*. London: Routledge and Kegan Paul.

Kostecki, Marian, and Krzysztof Mrela. 1984. "Collective Solidarity in Poland's Powdered Society." *Critical Sociology* 12: 131–141.

Koven, Seth, and Sonya Michel, eds. 1993. *Mothers of a New World: Maternalist Politics and the Origins of Welfare States*. New York: Routledge.

Krahe, B., and C. Altwasser. 2006. "Changing Negative Attitudes towards Persons with Physical Disabilities: An Experimental Intervention." *Journal of Community and Applied Social Psychology* 16: 59–69.

Krain, Matthew, and Anne Nurse. 2004. "Teaching Human Rights through Service Learning." *Human Rights Quarterly* 26: 189–207.

Krieger, Nancy. 2000. "Discrimination and Health." In *Social Epidemiology*, edited by L. Berkman and I. Kawachi, 36–75. Oxford: Oxford University Press.

———. 2011. *Epidemiology and the People's Health*. Oxford: Oxford University Press.

Krieger, Nancy, D. L. Rowley, A. A. Herman, B. Avery, and M. T. Philips. 1993. "Racism, Sexism and Social Class: Implications for Studies of Health, Disease, and Well-Being." *American Journal of Preventive Medicine* 9: 82–122.

Krieger, Nancy, and Stephen Sidney. 1997. "Prevalence and Health Implications of Anti-Gay Discrimination: A Study of Black and White Women and Men in the Cardia Cohort." *International Journal of Health Services* 27, no. 1: 157–176.

Krieger, Nancy, Pamela D. Waterman, Cathy Hartman, Lisa M. Bates, Anne M. Stoddard, Margaret M. Quinn, Glorian Sorensen, and Elizabeth M. Barbeau. 2006. "Social Hazards on the Job: Workplace Abuse, Sexual Harassment, and Racial Discrimination—a Study of Black, Latino, and White Low-Income Women and Men Workers in the United States." *International Journal of Health Services* 36: 51–85.

Kriesi, Hanspeter. 2004. "Political Context and Opportunity." In *The Blackwell Companion to Social Movements*, edited by David A. Snow, Sarah A. Soule, and Hanspeter Kreisi, 67–90. Oxford, UK: Blackwell.

176 BIBLIOGRAPHY

Kreisler, Harry. 2005. "Lakhdar Brahimi Interview: Conversations with History; Institute of International Studies. UC Berkeley." Institute of International Studies. April 5. http://globetrotter.berkeley.edu/people5/Brahimi/brahimi-con4.html.

Krippner, Greta. 2010. "Democracy of Credit: Transformations in Economic Citizenship." Paper presented at the annual meeting of the American Sociological Association, Atlanta, Georgia, August.

Kristoff, Nicholas. 2010. "Our Banana Republic." *New York Times*. November 6. http://www.nytimes.com/2010/11/07/opinion/07kristof.html (accessed December 18, 2010).

Krog, Antjie. 2010. "In the Name of Human Rights: I Say (How) You (Should) Speak (before I Listen)." In *Qualitative Inquiry and Human Rights*, edited by Norman Denzin and Michael Giardina, 66–81. Walnut Creek, CA: Left Coast Press.

Krugman, Paul R. 2007. *The Conscience of a Liberal*. New York: W. W. Norton and Co.

Kuhn, Thomas S. 1996. *The Structure of Scientific Revolutions*. Chicago: University of Chicago Press.

Kulick, Don. 1998. *Travesti: Sex, Gender, and Culture among Brazilian Transgendered Prostitutes*. Chicago: University of Chicago Press.

Kunioka, Todd T., and Karen M. McCurdy. 2006. "Relocation and Internment: Civil Rights Lessons from World War II." *PS: Political Science and Politics* 39: 503–511.

Kurashige, Scott. 2002. "Detroit and the Legacy of Vincent Chin." *Amerasia Journal* 28: 51–55.

Kuroiwa, Yoko, and Maykel Verkuyten. 2008. "Narratives and the Constitutions of Common Identity: The Karen in Burma." *Identities: Global Studies in Power and Culture* 15: 391–412.

Kurtz, Lester R. 2008. "Gandhi and His Legacies." *Encyclopedia of Violence, Peace and Conflict*, edited by Lester R. Kurtz, 837–851. 2nd ed. Amsterdam: Elsevier.

———. 2010. "Repression's Paradox in China." OpenDemocracy. November 17. http://www.opendemocracy.net/lester-r-kurtz/repression's-paradox-in-china (accessed January 20, 2012).

———. 2012. *Gods in the Global Village*. Los Angeles: Sage Pine Forge.

Laclau, Ernesto, and Chantal Mouffe. 1985. *Hegemony and Socialist Strategy: Towards a Radical Democratic Politics*. Translated by Winston Moore and Paul Cammack. London: Verso.

Lamb, H. R. 1998. "Mental Hospitals and Deinstitutionalization." In *Encyclopedia of Mental Health*, edited by H. S. Friedman, 2: 665–676. San Diego: Academic Press.

Lamont, Michèle. 2000. *The Dignity of Working Men: Morality and the Boundaries of Race, Class, and Immigration*. Cambridge, MA: Harvard University Press.

Landry, Bart. 2007. *Race, Gender, and Class: Theory and Methods of Analysis*. Upper Saddle River, NJ: Pearson.

Landsman, Stephen. 2005. *Crimes of the Holocaust: The Law Confronts Hard Cases*. Philadelphia: University of Pennsylvania Press.

Langer, Suzanne K. 1953. *Feeling and Form: A Theory of Art*. New York: Scribner.

Langevoort, Donald C. 1996. "Selling Hope, Selling Risk: Some Lessons for Law from Behavioral Economics about Stockbrokers and Sophisticated Customers." *California Law Review* 84: 627.

Langlois, Anthony J. 2002. "Human Rights: The Globalization and Fragmentation of Moral Discourse." *Review of International Studies* 28, no. 3: 479–496.

Lareau, Annette. 2003. *Unequal Childhoods: Class, Race, and Family Life*. Berkeley: University of California Press.

Larson, Heidi. 1999. "Voices of Pacific Youth: Video Research as a Tool for Youth Expression." *Visual Sociology* 14: 163–172.

Laslett, John H. M. 1970. *Labor and the Left: A Study of Socialist and Radical Influences in the American Labor Movement*. New York: Basic Books.

Laslett, John H. M., and Seymour Martin Lipset, eds. 1974. *Failure of a Dream? Essays on the History of American Socialism*. Garden City, NY: Doubleday.

Latour, Bruno. 2007. *Reassembling the Social*. New York: Oxford University Press.

Laumann, Edward O., John H. Gagnon, Robert T. Michael, and Stuart Michaels. 2000. *The Social Organization of Sexuality: Sexual Practices in the United States*.

Lauren, Paul Gordon. 1998. *The Evolution of International Human Rights: Visions Seen*. Philadelphia: University of Pennsylvania Press.

———. 2008. "History and Human Rights: People and Forces in Paradoxical Interaction." *Journal of Human Rights* 7: 91–103.

LaVeist, Thomas A. 2002. "Segregation, Poverty and Empowerment: Health Consequences for African Americans." In *Race, Ethnicity and Health*, edited by Thomas A. LaVeist, 76–96. San Francisco: Jossey-Bass.

Law, Joan, and John Hassard, eds. 1999. *Actor Network Theory and After*. Oxford and Keele, UK: Blackwell and the Sociological Review.

Leary, Virginia A. 1996. "The Paradox of Workers' Rights as Human Rights." In *Human Rights, Labor Rights, and International Trade,* edited by Lance A. Compa and Stephen F. Diamond. Philadelphia: University of Pennsylvania Press.

Leasher, M. K., C. E. Miller, and M. P. Gooden. 2009. "Rater Effects and Attitudinal Barriers Affecting People with Disabilities in Personnel Selection." *Journal of Applied Social Psychology* 39: 2236–2274.

Lebovic, James H., and Erik Voeten. 2006. "The Politics of Shame: The Condemnation of Country Human Rights Practices in the UNHCR." *International Studies Quarterly* 50, no. 4: 861–888.

Lebowitz, Michael. 2010. "Socialism: The Goal, the Paths and the Compass. The Bullet. Socialist Project." *E-Bulletin* 315 (February 20).

Lechner, Frank. 2005. "Religious Rejections of Globalization and Their Directions." In *Religion in Global Civil Society,* edited by M. Juergensmeyer. Oxford: Oxford University Press.

Lechner, Frank, and John Boli. 2005. *World Culture: Origins and Consequences.* Malden, MA: Blackwell Publishing.

Lee, Alfred McClung. 1973. *Toward Humanist Sociology.* Englewood-Cliffs, NJ: Prentice Hall.

———. 1979. "The Services of Clinical Sociology." *American Behavioral Scientist* 22: 487–511.

Lee, Angela Y. 2001. "The Mere Exposure Effect: An Uncertainty Reduction Explanation Revisited." *Personality and Social Psychology Bulletin* 27: 1255–1266.

Lee, Everett S. 1966. "A Theory of Migration." *Demography* 3: 47–57.

Lefebvre, Henri. 1968. *The Sociology of Marx.* Translated by Norbert Guterman. New York: Pantheon Books.

———. 1971. *Everyday Life in the Modern World.* Translated by Sacha Rabinovitch. New York: Harper and Row.

Lefort, Claude. 1986. "Politics and Human Rights." In *The Political Forms of Modern Society* 239. http://www.geocities.com/~johngray/impl13.htm (accessed September 6, 2012).

Leibovitz, Joseph. 2007. "Faultline Citizenship: Ethnonational Politics, Minority Mobilisation, and Governance in the Israeli 'Mixed Cities' of Haifa and Tel Aviv–Jaffa." *Ethnopolitics* 6: 235–263.

Leigh, Gillian, and Robin Gerrish. 1986. "Attitudes toward Alcoholism in Volunteer Therapist Aides: Do They Change?" *Drug and Alcohol Dependence* 17, no. 4: 381–390.

Leik, Robert K., and Barbara F. Meeker. 1975. *Mathematical Sociology.* Englewood Cliffs, NJ: Prentice Hall.

Lekachman, Robert. 1966. *The Age of Keynes.* New York: Random House.

Lembcke, Jerry. 1984. "Labor and Education: Portland Labor College, 1921–1929." *Oregon Historical Quarterly* 85: 117–134.

Lemus, Maria, Kimberly Stanton, and John Walsh. 2005. "Colombia: A Vicious Cycle of Drugs and War." In *Drugs and Democracy in Latin America,* edited by Eileen Rosin and Coletta Youngers, 112–120. Boulder, CO: Lynne Rienner Publishers.

Lengerman, Patricia, and Jill Niebrugge-Brantley. 1998. *The Women Founders: Sociology and Social Theory, 1830–1930.* Boston, MA: McGraw-Hill.

———. 2002. "Back to the Future: Settlement Sociology, 1885–1930." *American Sociologist* 33: 5–20.

———. 2007. "Thrice Told: Narratives of Sociology's Relation to Social Work." In *Sociology in America,* edited by Craig Calhoun, 63–114. Chicago: University of Chicago Press.

Lenin, Vladimir I. 1939. *Imperialism, the Highest Stage of Capitalism.* New York: International Publishers.

———. 2007. *The State and Revolution.* Synergy International of the Americas.

Lenski, Gerhard. 1966. *Power and Privilege: A Theory of Social Stratification.* New York: McGraw-Hill.

———. 2005. *Ecological-Evolutionary Theory: Principles and Applications.* Boulder, CO, and London: Paradigm Publishers.

Lenski, Gerhard, and Patrick Nolan. 2005. "Trajectories of Development among Third World Societies." In *Evolutionary Theory: Principles and Applications,* edited by Gerhard Lenski, 187–201. Boulder, CO: Paradigm Publishers.

Lenzer, Gertrud, and Brian K. Gran. 2011. "Rights and the Role of Family Engagement in Child Welfare: An International Treaties Perspective on Family's Rights, Parents' Rights, and Children's Rights." In "Taking Child and Family Rights Seriously: Family Engagement and Its Evidence in Child Welfare," special issue, *Child Welfare* 90, no. 4: 157–179.

Lerner, S. 2010. *Sacrifice Zones: The Frontlines of Toxic Chemical Exposure in the United States.* Cambridge, MA: MIT Press.

Levels, M., J. Dronkers, and G. Kraaykamp. 2008. "Educational Achievement of Immigrants in Western Countries: Origin, Destination, and Community Effects on Mathematical Performance." *American Sociological Review* 73, no. 5: 835–853.

Levine, Donald Nathan. 1985. "Rationality and Freedom: Inveterate Multivocals." In *The Flight from Ambiguity: Essays in Social and Cultural Theory,* 142–178. Chicago: University of Chicago Press.

178 BIBLIOGRAPHY

Levine, J. 2002. *Harmful to Minors: The Perils of Protecting Children from Sex.* Minneapolis: University of Minnesota Press.

Levine, Judith A., Clifton R. Emery, and Harold Pollack. 2007. "The Well-Being of Children Born to Teen Mothers." *Journal of Marriage and Family* 69 (February): 105–122.

Levit, Nancy. 2002. "Theorizing the Connections among Systems of Subordination." *University of Missouri– Kansas City Law Review* 77: 227–249.

Levitt, Peggy. 2001. *Transnational Villagers.* Berkeley: University of California Press.

———. 2005. "Building Bridges: What Migration Scholarship and Cultural Sociology Have to Say to Each Other." *Poetics* 33: 49–62.

Levitt, Peggy, and Sally Merry. 2009. "Vernacularization on the Ground: Local Uses of Global Women's Rights in Peru, China, India and the United States." *Global Networks* 9, no. 4: 441–461.

Levy, Daniel, and Natan Sznaider. 2006. "Sovereignty Transformed: A Sociology of Human Rights." *British Journal of Sociology* 57: 657–676.

Lewack, Howard. 1953. *Campus Rebels: A Brief History of the Student League for Industrial Democracy.* New York: Student League for Industrial Democracy.

Lewis, L. 2009a. "Introduction: Mental Health and Human Rights: Social Policy and Sociological Perspectives." *Social Policy and Society* 8: 211–214.

———. 2009b. "Politics of Recognition: What Can a Human Rights Perspective Contribute to Understanding Users' Experiences of Involvement in Mental Health Services?" *Social Policy and Society* 8: 257–274.

Lewis, Tammy. 2004. "Service Learning for Social Change? Lessons from a Liberal Arts College." *Teaching Sociology* 32: 94–108.

Leydesdorff, L., and T. Schank. 2008. "Dynamic Animations of Journal Maps: Indicators of Structural Change and Interdisciplinary Developments." *Journal of the American Society for Information Science and Technology* 59, no. 11: 1810–1818.

Liao, Tim Futing. 2006. "Measuring and Analyzing Class Inequality with the Gini Index Informed by Model-Based Clustering." *Sociological Methodology* 36: 201–224.

Lichtenstein, B. 2003. "Stigma as a Barrier to Treatment of Sexually Transmitted Infection in the American Deep South: Issues of Race, Gender, and Poverty." *Social Science & Medicine* 57: 2435–2445.

Liebow, Elliot. 1993. *Tell Them Who I Am: The Lives of Homeless Women.* New York: Penguin.

———. 2003. *Tally's Corner: A Study of Negro Streetcorner Men.* 2nd ed. New York: Rowman & Littlefield.

Liebowitz, Deborah. 2008. *Respect, Protect, and Fulfill: Raising the Bar on Women's Rights in San Francisco.* San Francisco: Women's Institute for Leadership Development for Human Rights.

Light, Donald W. 2001. "Comparative Models of Health Care Systems." In *The Sociology of Health and Illness: Critical Perspectives,* edited by Peter Conrad, 464–479. 6th ed. New York: Worth Publishers.

Lindenberg, S. 2006a. "Rational Choice Theory." In *International Encyclopedia of Economic Sociology,* edited by J. Beckert and M. Zafirovski, 548–552. New York: Routledge.

———. 2006b. "Social Rationality." In *International Encyclopedia of Economic Sociology,* edited by J. Beckert and M. Zafirovski, 16–618. New York: Routledge.

Lindsay, Jo. 2009. "Young Australians and the Staging of Intoxification and Self-Control." *Journal of Youth Studies* 12, no. 4: 371–384.

Link, B. G., B. Dohrenwend, and A. Skodol. 1986. "Socioeconomic Status and Schizophrenia: Noisome Occupational Characteristics as a Risk Factor." *American Sociological Review* 51: 242–258.

Link, B. G., E. L. Struening, M. Rahav, J. C. Phelan, and L. Nuttbrock. 1997. "On Stigma and Its Consequences: Evidence from a Longitudinal Study of Men with Dual Diagnosis of Mental Illness and Substance Abuse." *Journal of Health and Social Behavior* 38: 177–190.

Link, Bruce, and Jo Phelan. 1995. "Social Conditions and Fundamental Causes of Illness." *Journal of Health and Social Behavior* (extra issue) 35: 80–94.

———. 2001. "Conceptualizing Stigma." *Annual Review of Sociology* 27: 363–385.

———. 2010. "Social Conditions as Fundamental Causes of Health Inequalities." In *Handbook of Medical Sociology,* edited by Chloe Bird, Peter Conrad, Allen Fremont, and Stephan Timmermans, 3–17. 6th ed. Nashville, TN: Vanderbilt University Press.

Linzey, Andrew. 2009. *The Link between Animal Abuse and Human Violence.* East Sussex, UK: Sussex Academic Press.

Lippett, R., J. Watson, and B. Westley. 1958. *The Dynamics of Planned Change.* New York: Harcourt, Brace and World.

Lippman, Abby. 1991. "Prenatal Genetic Testing and Screening: Constructing Needs and Reinforcing Tendencies." *American Journal of Law and Society* 17: 15–50.

Lipset, Seymour Martin. 1960. "The Political Process in Trade Unions: A Theoretical Statement." In *Labor and Trade Unionism*, edited by W. Galenson and S. M. Lipset. New York: Wiley.

———. 1981. *Political Man*. Baltimore: John Hopkins University Press.

Lipsitz, George. 2006. *The Possessive Investment in Whiteness: How White People Profit from Identity Politics*. Philadelphia: Temple University Press.

Lipton, M. 1980. "Migration from Rural Areas of Poor Countries: The Impact on Rural Productivity and Income Distribution." *World Development* 8: 1–24.

Lisborg, Russell, S. 1993. "Migrant Remittances and Development." *International Migration* 31: 267–287.

Little, David. 1991. *Varieties of Social Explanation*. Boulder, CO: Westview.

———. 1999. "Review: Rethinking Human Rights: A Review Essay on Religion, Relativism, and Other Matters." *Journal of Religious Ethics* 27: 149–177.

Lo, Clarence Y. H. 2008. "State Capitalism." In *International Encyclopedia of the Social Sciences*, edited by William A. Darity Jr. 2nd ed. Detroit, MI: Macmillan Reference.

———. Forthcoming. *Politics of Justice for Corporate Wrongdoing—Equality, Market Fairness, and Retribution in Enron and Beyond*.

Locke, J. 1970 [1689]. *Two Treatises of Government*. Cambridge, UK: Cambridge University Press.

Lockwood, Elizabeth, Daniel Barstow Magraw, Margaret Faith Spring, and S. I. Strong. 1998. *The International Human Rights of Women: Instruments of Change*. Washington, DC: American Bar Association Section of International Law and Practice.

Loe, Meika. 2006. *The Rise of Viagra: How the Little Blue Pill Changed Sex in America*. New York: New York University Press.

Logan, John R., and Harvey L. Molotch. 2007. *Urban Fortunes: The Political Economy of Place*. 2nd ed. Berkeley: University of California Press.

London, L. 2008. "What Is a Human Rights–Based Approach to Health and Does It Matter?" *Health and Human Rights* 10: 65–80.

Long, A. B. 2008. "Introducing the New and Improved Americans with Disabilities Act: Assessing the ADA Amendments Act of 2008." *Northwestern University Law Review Colloquy* 103: 217–229.

Longmore, P. K. 2003. *Why I Burned My Book and Other Essays on Disability*. Philadelphia: Temple University Press.

López, Ian Haney. 2006. *White by Law: The Legal Construction of Race*. Rev. and updated 10th anniv. ed. New York: New York University Press.

Lopez, Iris. 1993. "Agency and Constraint: Sterilization and Reproductive Freedom among Puerto Rican Women in New York City." *Urban Anthropology* 22: 299–323.

———. 2008. *Matters of Choice: Puerto Rican Women's Struggle for Reproductive Freedom*. New Brunswick, NJ: Rutgers University Press.

Lorber, Judith. 2002. *Gender and the Construction of Illness*. Lanham, MD: AltaMira Press.

Lorber, Judith, and Lisa Jean Moore. 2002. *Gender and the Social Construction of Illness*. Newbury Park, CA: Sage Publications.

———. 2007. *Gendered Bodies: Feminist Perspectives*. New York: Oxford.

Los Angeles Times. 2011. "Mexico under Siege: The Drug War at Our Doorstop." *Los Angeles Times*. http://projects.latimes.com/mexico-drug-war (accessed January 1, 2011).

Lounsbury, Michael, and Paul M. Hirsch, eds. 2010. *Markets on Trial: The Economic Sociology of the U.S. Financial Crisis*. Research in the Sociology of Organizations 30A. London: Emerald Group Publishing.

Low, Petra. 2010. "Devastating Natural Disasters Continue Steady Rise." *Vital Signs: Global Trends that Shape Our Future* (March): 38–41.

Ludvig, Alice. 2006. "'Differences between Women' Intersecting Voices in a Female Narrative." *European Journal of Women's Studies* 13: 245–258.

Lukács, Georg. 1971. *History and Class Consciousness: Studies in Marxist Dialectics*. Translated by Rodney Livingstone. Cambridge, MA: MIT Press.

Luker, Kristin. 2006. *When Sex Goes to School: Warring Views on Sex and Sex Education since the Sixties*. New York: W. W. Norton.

Lukes, Steven. 1972. *Émile Durkheim: His Life and Work*. New York: Harper and Row Publishers.

———. 2005 [1974]. *Power: A Radical View*. Houndsmill, UK: Palgrave Macmillan.

Lupton, D. 1999. *Risk*. New York: Routledge.

Lynch, Michael. 1996. "Ethnomethodology." In *The Social Science Encyclopaedia*, edited by Adam Kuper and Jessica Kuper, 266–267. 2nd ed. London: Routledge.

Lynch, Michael, and Wes Sharrock, eds. 2003. *Harold Garfinkel*. 4 vols. Sage Masters in Modern Social Thought Series. London: Sage.

Lynd, Robert S. 1939. *Knowledge for What? The Place of the Social Sciences in American Culture*. Princeton, NJ: Princeton University Press.

180 BIBLIOGRAPHY

Lynd, Robert S., and Helen Merrell Lynd. 1929. *Middletown: A Study in Modern American Culture.* New York: Harcourt, Brace and World.

Maas, Peter. 2009. *Crude World: The Violent Twilight of Oil.* New York: Alfred Knopf.

Mackelprang, R. W., and R. D. Mackelprang. 2005. "Historical and Contemporary Issues in End-of-Life Decisions: Implications for Social Work." *Social Work* 40: 315–324.

MacKinnon, Catherine. 1993. "On Torture: A Feminist Perspective on Human Rights." In *Human Rights in the Twenty-First Century: A Global Challenge,* edited by Kathleen E. Mahoney and Paul Mahoney. Boston: Springer Publishing.

MacLean, Vicky, and Joyce Williams. 2009. "US Settlement Sociology in the Progressive Era: Neighborhood Guilds, Feminist Pragmatism and the Social Gospel." Paper presented at the annual meeting for the American Sociological Association, San Francisco, California.

Macy, M. W., and A. Flache. 1995. "Beyond Rationality in Models of Choice." *Annual Review of Sociology* 21: 73–91.

Mahler, Sarah. 1998. "Theoretical and Empirical Contributions toward a Research Agenda for Transnationalism." In *Transnationalism from Below,* edited by Michael Smith and Luis Guarnizo. London: Transaction Publishers.

Mahoney, Jack. 2006. *The Challenge of Human Rights: Origin, Development and Significance.* Malden, MA: Wiley-Blackwell.

Maier-Katkin, Daniel, Daniel P. Mears, and Thomas J. Bernard. 2011. "Toward a Criminology of Crimes against Humanity." *Theoretical Criminology* 13: 227–255.

Maira, Sunaina. 2004. "Youth Culture, Citizenship and Globalization: South Asian Muslim Youth in the United States after September 11th." *Comparative Studies of South Asia, Africa and the Middle East* 24: 219–231.

Maldonado-Torres, Nelson. 2007. "On the Coloniality of Being." *Cultural Studies* 21, no. 2–3: 240–270.

Malešević, Siniša. 2010. *The Sociology of War and Violence.* Cambridge, UK: Cambridge University Press.

Mallett, Robin K., Timothy D. Wilson, and Daniel T. Gilbert. 2008. "Expect the Unexpected: Failure to Anticipate Similarities Leads to an Intergroup Forecasting Error." *Journal of Personality and Social Psychology* 94: 265–277.

Mallinder, Louise. 2008. *Amnesties, Human Rights and Political Transitions.* Oxford: Hart.

Mamo, Laura. 2007. *Queering Reproduction: Achieving Pregnancy in the Age of Technoscience.* Durham, NC: Duke University Press.

Maney, Gregory M. 2011. "Of Praxis and Prejudice: Enhancing Scholarship and Empowering Activists through Movement-Based Research." Plenary address, Collective Behavior and Social Movements Workshop, Las Vegas, Nevada.

Mann, Abby. 1961. "Judgment at Nuremberg Script—Dialogue Transcript." Drew's Script-O-Rama. http://www.script-o-rama.com/movie_scripts/j/judgment-at-nuremburg-script-transcript.html (accessed July 20, 2012).

Mann, Jonathan M. 1996. "Health and Human Rights." *British Medical Journal* 312: 924.

Mann, Michael. 1987. "War and Social Theory: Into Battle with Classes, Nations and States." In *Sociology of War and Peace,* edited by Colin Creighton and Martin Shaw. Dobbs Ferry, NY: Sheridan House.

———. 1988. *States, War and Capitalism: Studies in Political Sociology.* Oxford: Blackwell.

Mannheim, Karl. 1936. *Ideology and Utopia.* London: Routledge.

Mansbridge, Jane. 1994. "Feminism and the Forms of Freedom." In *Critical Studies in Organization and Bureaucracy,* edited by Frank Fischer and Carmen Sirianni, 544–543. Rev. ed. Philadelphia: Temple University Press.

Manza, Jeff, and Christopher Uggen. 2006. *Locked Out: Felon Disenfranchisement and American Democracy.* New York: Oxford University Press.

March, James G., and Johan P. Olsen. 1984. "The New Institutionalism: Organizational Factors in Political Life." *American Political Science Review* 78, no. 3: 734–749.

March, James G., and Herbert Simon. 1958. *Organizations.* New York: Wiley.

———. 1976. *Ambiguity and Choice in Organizations.* Bergen, Norway: Universitetsforlaget.

Margolis, Eric. 1999. "Class Pictures: Representations of Race, Gender and Ability in a Century of School Photography." *Visual Sociology* 14, no. 1: 7–38.

Marković, Mihailo. 1974. *From Affluence to Praxis.* Ann Arbor: University of Michigan Press.

Marks, Stephen P., and Kathleen A. Modrowski. 2008. *Human Rights Cities: Civic Engagement for Societal Development.* New York: UN-HABITAT and PDHRE.

Marmot, Michael G. 2004. *The Status Syndrome: How Your Social Standing Directly Affects Your Health and Life Expectancy.* London: Bloomsbury.

Marriage Project. 2010. *When Marriage Disappears: The New Middle America.* Charlottesville, VA: Institute for American Values.

BIBLIOGRAPHY 181

Marshall, Brent K., and J. Steven Picou. 2008. "Post-Normal Science, Precautionary Principle and Worst Cases: The Challenge of Twenty-First Century Catastrophes." *Sociological Inquiry* 78: 230–247.

Marshall, S. L. A. 1947. *Men against Fire: The Problem of Battle Command.* New York: Morrow.

Marshall, T. H. (Thomas Humphrey). 1964. *Class, Citizenship, and Social Development.* Garden City, NY: Doubleday.

Martin, David. 1978. *A General Theory of Secularization.* New York: Harper and Row.

Martin, Karin A. 1996. *Puberty, Sexuality, and the Self: Boys and Girls at Adolescence.* New York: Routledge.

Martin, Patricia Yancey. 2004. "Gender as Social Institution." *Social Forces*, 82(4): 1,249–1,273.

Martino, George. 2000. *Global Economy, Global Justice: Theoretical Objections and Policy Alternatives to Neo-Liberalism.* New York: Routledge.

Marx Ferree, Myra, and Aili Mari Tripp, eds. 2006. *Global Feminism: Transnational Women's Activism, Organizing, and Human Rights.* New York and London: New York University Press.

Marx, Karl. 1843a. "On the Jewish Question." Marxists Internet Archive. http://www.marxists.org/archive/marx/works/1844/jewish-question (accessed July 18, 2012).

———. 1843b. "Introduction to a Contribution to the Critique of Hegel's Philosophy of Right." Marxists Internet Archive. http://www.marxists.org/archive/marx/works/1843/critique-hpr/intro.htm (accessed July 18, 2012).

———. 1956. *The Holy Family.* Moscow: Foreign Language Publishing House.

———. 1967 [1867]. *Capital: A Critique of Political Economy.* Vol. 1: *The Process of Capitalist Production.* New York: International Publishers.

———. 1978 [1844]. "Economic and Philosophic Manuscripts of 1844." In *The Marx-Engels Reader*, edited by Robert C. Tucker, 56–67. New York: W. W. Norton.

Marx, Karl, and Friedrich Engels. 1848. *The Communist Manifesto.* http://www.anu.edu.au/polsci/marx/classics/manifesto.html (accessed September 5, 2012).

———. 1976 [1846]. *The German Ideology.* Moscow: Progress Publishers.

Mason-Schrock, Douglas. 1996. "Transsexuals' Narrative Construction of the 'True Self.'" *Social Psychology Quarterly* 59: 176–192.

Massey, Douglas S. 1988. "Economic Development and International Migration in Comparative Perspective." *Population and Development Review* 14: 383–413.

———. 2004. "Segregation and Stratification: A Biosocial Perspective." *Du Bois Review: Social Science Research on Race* 1: 7–25.

Massey, Douglas, and Nancy Denton. 1993. *American Apartheid: Segregation and the Making of the Underclass.* Cambridge, MA: Harvard University Press.

Massey, Douglas, Jorge Durand, and Nolan J. Malone. 2002. *Beyond Smoke and Mirrors: Mexican Immigration in an Era of Economic Integration.* New York: Russell Sage Foundation.

Massey, Douglas, and Rene Zenteno. 2000. "A Validation of the Ethnosurvey: The Case of Mexico-U.S. Migration." *International Migration Review* 34: 766–793.

Matcha, Duane A. 2003. *Health Care Systems of the Developed World: How the United States' System Remains an Outlier.* Westport, CT: Praeger.

Matsueda, Ross. 2006. "Differential Social Organization, Collective Action, and Crime." *Crime, Law, and Social Change* 46: 3–33.

Matsueda, Ross, Derek A. Kreager, and David Huizinga. 2006. "Deterring Delinquents: A Rational Choice Model of Theft and Violence." *American Sociological Review* 71: 95–122.

Matthews, N. 2009. "Contesting Representations of Disabled Children in Picture-Books: Visibility, the Body and the Social Model of Disability." *Children's Geographies* 7: 37–49.

Matthus, Jürgen. 2009. *Approaching an Auschwitz Survivor: Holocaust Testimony and Its Transformations.* New York: Oxford University Press.

Mayer, Karl Ulrich, and W. Müller. 1986. "The State and the Structure of the Life Course." In *Human Development and the Life Course: Multidisciplinary Perspectives*, edited by A. B. Sorensen, F. E. Weinert, and L. R. Sherrod, 217–245. Hillsdale, NJ: Lawrence Erlbaum Associates.

Mayer, Karl Ulrich. 2009. "New Directions in Life Course Research." *Annual Review of Sociology* 35: 413–433.

Maynard, Douglas W., and Stephen E. Clayman. 1991. "The Diversity of Ethnomethodology." *Annual Review of Sociology* 17: 385–418.

Mayo, E. 1933. *The Human Problems of an Industrial Civilization.* New York: Macmillan.

Mazower, Mark. 2004. "The Strange Triumph of Human Rights, 1933–1950." *Historical Journal* 47: 379–398.

Mazur, Allan. 2004. *Biosociology of Dominance and Deference.* Lanham, MD: Rowman & Littlefield.

Mazur, Allan, and A. Booth. 1998. "Testosterone and Dominance in Men." *Behavioral and Brain Sciences* 21: 353–363.

182 BIBLIOGRAPHY

McAdam, Doug. 1982. *Political Process and the Development of Black Insurgency, 1930–1970*. Chicago: University of Chicago Press.

———. 1994. "Social Movements and Culture." In *Ideology and Identity in Contemporary Social Movements*, edited by Joseph R. Gusfield, Hank Johnston, and Enrique Laraña, 36–57. Philadelphia: Temple University Press.

———. 1999. *Political Process and Black Insurgency, 1930–1970*. 2nd ed. Chicago: University of Chicago Press.

McAdam, Doug, John D. McCarthy, and Mayer N. Zald. 1996. *Comparative Perspectives on Social Movements: Political Opportunities, Mobilizing Structures, and Cultural Framings*. Cambridge, UK: Cambridge University Press.

McAdoo, Harriette P. 1998. "African-American Families." In *Ethnic Families in America: Patterns and Variations*, edited by Charles H. Mindel, Robert W. Haberstein, and Roosevelt Wright Jr. Upper Saddle River, NJ: Prentice Hall.

McCall, Leslie. 2001. *Complex Inequality: Gender, Class and Race in the New Economy*. New York: Routledge.

———. 2005. "The Complexity of Intersectionality." *Signs* 30: 1771–1800.

McCammon, Holly J. 1990. "Legal Limits on Labor Militancy: U.S. Labor Law and the Right to Strike since the New Deal." *Social Problems* 37: 206–229.

———. 2001. "Stirring Up Suffrage Sentiment: The Formation of the State Woman Suffrage Organizations, 1866–1914." *Social Forces* 80: 449–480.

———. 2012. *A More Just Verdict: The U.S. Women's Jury Movements and Strategic Adaptation*. New York: Cambridge University Press.

McCammon, Holly J., Soma Chaudhuri, Lyndi Hewitt, Courtney Sanders Muse, Harmony D. Newman, Carrie Lee Smith, and Teresa M. Terrell. 2008. "Becoming Full Citizens: The U.S. Women's Jury Rights Campaigns, the Pace of Reform, and Strategic Adaptation." *American Journal of Sociology* 113: 1104–1148.

McCammon, Holly J., Courtney Sanders Muse, Harmony D. Newman, and Teresa M. Terrell. 2007. "Movement Framing and Discursive Opportunity Structures: The Political Successes of the U.S. Women's Jury Movements." *American Sociological Review* 72: 725–749.

McCarthy, John D., and Mayer N. Zald. 1977. "Resource Mobilization and Social Movements: A Partial Theory." *American Sociological Review* 82: 1212–1241.

McClain, Linda. 1994. "Rights and Responsibilities." *Duke Law Journal* 43, no. 5: 989–1088.

McConnell, Eileen Diaz. 2011. "An 'Incredible Number of Latinos and Asians': Media Representations of Racial and Ethnic Population Change in Atlanta, Georgia." In "Latino/as and the Media," special issue, *Latino Studies* 9 (summer/autumn): 177–197.

McDew, Charles. 1966. "Spiritual and Moral Aspects of the Student Nonviolent Struggle in the South." In *The New Student Left*, edited by Mitchell Cohen and Dennis Hale, 51–57. Boston, MA: Beacon Press.

McFarland, Sam. 2010. "Personality and Support for Human Rights: A Review and Test of a Structural Model." *Journal of Personality* 78: 1–29.

McIntyre, Alice. 1997. *Making Meaning of Whiteness: Exploring Racial Identity with White Teachers*. Albany: State University of New York Press.

McIntyre, Richard P. 2003. "Globalism, Human Rights and the Problem of Individualism." *Human Rights and Human Welfare* 3, no. 1: 1–14.

———. 2008. *Are Worker Rights Human Rights?* Ann Arbor: University of Michigan Press.

McKinlay, John B. 1974. "A Case for Refocusing Upstream: The Political Economy of Illness." Reprinted in *The Sociology of Health and Illness: Critical Perspectives*, edited by Peter Conrad, 519–529. 5th ed. New York: Worth Publishers.

———. 1996. "Some Contributions from the Social System to Gender Inequalities in Heart Disease." *Journal of Health and Social Behavior* 37: 1–26.

McKinney, Kathleen, and Carla Howery. 2006. "Teaching and Learning in Sociology: Past, Present and Future." In *21st Century Sociology: A Reference Handbook*, edited by Clifton D. Bryant and Dennis L. Peck, 2: 379–388. Thousand Oaks, CA: Sage.

McLaren, Peter. 1989. *Life in Schools: An Introduction to Critical Pedagogy in the Foundations of Education*. New York: Longman.

———. 1999. *Schooling as Ritual Performance*. London: Routledge.

———. 2005. *Capitalists and Conquerors: A Critical Pedagogy against Empire*. New York: Rowman & Littlefield.

McLaren, Peter, and Nathalia E. Jaramillo. 1999. "Medicine and Public Health, Ethics and Human Rights." In *Health and Human Rights: A Reader*, edited by Jonathan Mann, Michael A. Grodin, Sofia Gruskin, and George J. Annas, 439–452. New York: Routledge.

———. 2007. *Pedagogy and Praxis in the Age of Empire: Towards a New Humanism*. Rotterdam: Sense Publishers.

BIBLIOGRAPHY 183

McLeod, Jane D., and Kathryn J. Lively. 2003. "Social Structure and Personality." In *Handbook of Social Psychology*, edited by John DeLamater, 77–102. New York: Kluwer.

McNally, David. 2001. *Bodies of Meaning: Studies on Language, Labor and Liberation*. Albany: State University of New York Press.

McWhorter, John. 2011. "How the War on Drugs Is Destroying Black America." *Cato's Letter* 9, no. 1. http://www.cato.org/pubs/catosletter/catosletterv9n1.pdf.

Mead, George Herbert. 1934. *Mind, Self, and Society*. Chicago: University of Chicago Press.

———. 1967. *Mind, Self, and Society: From the Standpoint of a Social Behaviorist*. Chicago: University of Chicago Press.

———. 2008 [1918]. "Immanuel Kant on Peace and Democracy." In *Self, War and Society: George Herbert Mead's Macrosociology*, edited by Mary Jo Deegan, 159–174. New Brunswick, NJ: Transaction Publishers.

Mead, S., and M. E. Copeland. 2001. "What Recovery Means to Us: Consumers' Perspectives." In *The Tragedy of Great Power Politics*, edited by John J. Mearsheimer. New York: Norton.

Mearsheimer, John J. 2001. *The Tragedy of Great Power Politics*. New York: Norton.

Mechanic, David. 1997. "Muddling through Elegantly: Finding the Proper Balance in Rationing." *Health Affairs* 16: 83–92.

Mechanic, David, and Donna D. McAlpine. 2010. "Sociology of Health Care Reform: Building on Research and Analysis to Improve Health Care." *Journal of Health and Social Behavior* 51: S137–S159.

Mele, A., and P. Rawling. 2004. *The Oxford Handbook of Rationality*. Oxford: Oxford University Press.

Melucci, Alberto. 1989. *Nomads of the Present: Social Movements and Individual Needs in Contemporary Society*. Philadelphia: Temple University Press.

Mendez, Jennifer Bickham. 2005. *From the Revolution to the Maquiladoras: Gender, Labor, and Globalization in Nicaragua*. Durham, NC: Duke University Press.

Menjívar, Cecilia, and Leisy Abrego. 2009. "Parents and Children across Borders: Legal Instability and Intergenerational Relations in Guatemalan and Salvadoran Families." In *Across Generations: Immigrant Families in America*, edited by N. Foner, 160–189. New York: New York University Press.

Menon, Anu. 2010. *Human Rights in Action: San Francisco's Local Implementation of the United Nations' Women's Treaty (CEDAW)*. San Francisco: City and County of San Francisco, Department on the Status of Women.

Mental Health Advisory Team IV. 2006. "Operation Iraqi Freedom 05-07." Final Report of November 17. Office of the Surgeon, Multinational Force—Iraq, and Office of the Surgeon General, United States Army Medical Command.

Merenstein, Beth Frankel. 2008. *Immigrants and Modern Racism: Reproducing Inequality*. Boulder, CO: Lynne Rienner Publishers.

Merry, Sally Engle. 2006. *Human Rights and Gender Violence: Translating International Law into Local Justice*. Chicago: University of Chicago Press.

Merton, Robert K. 1938. "Social Structure and Anomie." *American Sociological Review* 3: 672–682.

———. 1968. *Social Theory and Social Structure*. New York: The Free Press.

———. 1973. *The Sociology of Science: Theoretical and Empirical Investigations*, edited by Norman Storer. Chicago: University of Chicago Press.

Mertus, Julie. 2007. "The Rejection of Human Rights Framings: The Case of LGBT Advocacy in the US." *Human Rights Quarterly* 29: 1036–1064.

Messner, Michael A. 1992. *Power at Play: Sports and the Problem of Masculinity*. Boston: Beacon Press.

Messner, Steven F., and Richard Rosenfeld. 2007. *Crime and the American Dream*. 4th ed. Belmont, CA: Wadsworth.

Mesthene, E. 2000. "The Role of Technology in Society." In *Technology and the Future*, edited by A. H. Teich, 61–70. 8th ed. New York: Bedford/St. Martin's.

Metzger, Barbara. 2007. "Towards an International Human Rights Regime during the Inter-War Years: The League of Nations' Combat of Traffic in Women and Children." In *Beyond Sovereignty: Britain, Empire and Transnationalism, 1880–1950*, edited by Kevin Grant, Philippa Levine, and Frank Trentmann. New York: Palgrave Macmillan.

Meyer, David S. 2004. "Protest and Political Opportunities." *Annual Review of Sociology* 30: 125–145.

Meyer, Jean-Baptiste. 2001. "Network Approach versus Brain Drain: Lessons from the Diaspora." *International Migration* 39: 1468–2435. doi.10.1111/1468-2435.00173.

Meyer, John W., John Boli, George Thomas, and Francisco Ramirez. 1997. "World Society and the Nation-State." *American Journal of Sociology* 103: 144–181.

Meyer, John W. 2010. "World Society, Institutional Theories and the Actor." *Annual Review of Sociology* 36: 1–20.

Meyer, John W., and Brian Rowan. 1977. "Institutionalized Organizations: Formal Structure as Myth and Ceremony." *American Journal of Sociology* 83, no. 2: 340–363.

184 BIBLIOGRAPHY

Meyer, Marshall W., and Lynn G. Zucker. 1989. *Permanently Failing Organizations*. Newbury Park, CA: Sage.

Meyer, William H. 1996. "Human Rights and MNCs: Theory versus Quantitative Analysis." *Human Rights Quarterly* 18: 368–397.

Michels, Robert. 1962 [1915]. *Political Parties*. New York: The Free Press.

Micklin, Michael, and Dudley L. Poston. 1995. *Continuities in Social Human Ecology*. New York: Plenum.

Middelstaedt, Emma. 2008. "Safeguarding the Rights of Sexual Minorities: Incremental and Legal Approaches to Enforcing International Human Rights Obligations." *Chicago Journal of International Law* 9: 353–386.

Midgley, Mary. 1995. *Beast and Man: The Roots of Human Nature*. London: Routledge.

Miech, R. A., A. Caspi, T. E. Moffitt, B. R. E. Wright, and P. A. Silva. 1999. "Low Socioeconomic Status and Mental Disorders: A Longitudinal Study of Selection and Causation during Young Adulthood." *American Journal of Sociology* 104: 1096–1131.

Mignolo, Walter. 2010. "De-Coloniality: Decolonial Thinking and Doing in the Andes: A Conversation by Walter Mignolo with Catherine Walsh." *Reartikulacija* 10–13. http://www.reartikulacija. org/?p=1468 (accessed July 18, 2012).

Milkman, Ruth. 1987. *Gender at Work: The Dynamics of Job Segregation by Sex during World War II*. Urbana: University of Illinois Press.

Miller, Alan S., and Rodney Stark. 2002. "Gender and Religiousness: Can Socialization Explanations Be Saved?" *American Journal of Sociology* 107: 1399–1423.

Miller, Francesca. 1999. "Feminism and Transnationalism." In *Feminisms and Internationalism*, edited by Mrinalini Sinha, Donna Guy, and Angela Woollacott. Oxford, UK: Blackwell Publishers.

Millet, Kris. 2008. "The Naxalite Movement: Exposing Scrapped Segments of India's Democracy." *Culture Magazine*. January 5. http://culturemagazine.ca/politics/the_naxalite_movement_exposing_ scrapped_segments_of_indias_democracy.html (accessed July 18, 2012).

Mills, C. Wright. 1948. *The New Men of Power*. New York: Harcourt, Brace.

———. 1956. *The Power Elite*. New York: Oxford University Press.

———. 1959. *The Sociological Imagination*. New York: Oxford University Press.

Mills, Charles W. 1997. *The Racial Contract*. Ithaca, NY: Cornell University Press.

Minh-ha, Trinh T. 2009. *Woman, Native, Other: Writing Postcoloniality and Feminism*. 1st ed. Bloomington: Indiana University Press.

Mink, Gwendolyn. 1986. *Old Labor and New Immigrants in American Political Development: Union, Party, and the State, 1875–1920*. Ithaca, NY: Cornell University Press.

Minkov, Anton. 2009. *Counterinsurgency and Ethnic/Sectarian Rivalry in Comparative Perspective: Soviet Afghanistan and Iraq*. Ottawa, Canada: Centre for Operational Research and Analysis, Defense Research and Development Canada.

Minow, Martha. 1998. *Between Vengeance and Forgiveness: Facing History after Genocide and Mass Violence*. Boston: Beacon Press.

———. 2002. *Breaking the Cycles of Hatred: Memory, Law, and Repair*. Introduced and with commentaries by N. L. Rosenblum. Princeton, NJ: Princeton University Press.

Mirowsky, J., C. E. Ross, and J. R. Reynolds. 2000. "Links between Social Status and Health Status." In *Handbook of Medical Sociology*, edited by Chloe Bird, Peter Conrad, and Alan M. Fremont, 47–67. 5th ed. Upper Saddle River, NJ: Prentice Hall.

Mishel, Lawrence, and Matthew Walters. 2003. "How Unions Help All Workers." Economic Policy Institute Briefing Paper 143. Economic Policy Institute. August. http://www.epi.org/publications/ entry/briefingpapers_bp143.

Mishra, Ramesh. 1984. *Welfare State in Crisis*. New York: St. Martin's Press.

Mitchell, Neil, and James McCormick. 1988. "Economic and Political Explanations of Human Rights Violations." *World Politics* 40: 476–498.

Modic, Dolores. 2008. "Stigma of Race." *Raziskave and Razprave/Research and Discussion* 1: 153–185.

Moghadam, Valentine M. 2005. *Globalizing Women: Transnational Feminist Networks*. Baltimore: Johns Hopkins University Press.

Mohanty, Chandra Talpade. 2006. *Feminism without Borders: Decolonizing Theory, Practicing Solidarity*. Durham, NC: Duke University Press.

Mohanty, Chandra Talpade, Ann Russo, and Lourdes Torres, eds. 1991. *Third World Women and the Politics of Feminism*. Bloomington: Indiana University Press.

Mojab, Shahrzad. 2009. "'Post-War Reconstruction,' Imperialism and Kurdish Women's NGOs." In *Women and War in the Middle East*, edited by Nadje Al-Ali and Nicola Pratt, 99–128. London: Zed Books.

Moncada, Alberto, and Judith Blau. 2006. "Human Rights and the Role of Social Scientists." *Societies without Borders* 1: 113–122.

BIBLIOGRAPHY 185

Moody, Kim. 1997. *Workers in a Lean World: Unions in the International Economy*. New York: Verso.

Moore, D. 2003. "A Signaling Theory of Human Rights Compliance." *Northwestern University Law Review* 97: 879–910.

Moore, Jason. 2000. "Sugar and the Expansion of the Early Modern World-Economy." *Review: A Journal of the Fernand Braudel Center* 23, no. 33: 409–433.

Moore, Kelly. 2008. *Disrupting Science: Social Movements, American Scientists, and the Politics of the Military, 1945–1975*. Princeton, NJ: Princeton University Press.

Moore, S. F. 1978. "Law and Social Change: The Semi-Autonomous Social Field as an Appropriate Field of Study." In *Law as Process: An Anthropological Approach*, edited by S. F. Moore, 54–81. London: Routledge.

Moore, Wendy Leo. 2008. *Reproducing Racism: White Space, Elite Law Schools, and Racial Inequality*. Lanham, MD: Rowman & Littlefield.

Morales, Maria Cristina. 2009. "Ethnic-Controlled Economy or Segregation? Exploring Inequality in Latina/o Co-Ethnic Jobsites." *Sociological Forum* 24: 589–610.

Morales, Maria Cristina, and Cynthia Bejarano. 2009. "Transnational Sexual and Gendered Violence: An Application of Border Sexual Conquest at a Mexico-U.S. Border." *Global Networks* 9: 420–439.

Morin, Alain, and James Everett. 1990. "Inner Speech as a Mediator of Self-Awareness, Self-Consciousness, and Self-Knowledge: An Hypothesis." *New Ideas in Psychology* 8: 337–356.

Morrell, Ernest. 2008. *Critical Literacy and Urban Youth: Pedagogies of Access, Dissent, and Liberation*. New York: Routledge.

Morris, Lydia. 2010. *Asylum, Welfare and the Cosmopolitan Ideal*. London: Routledge.

Morse, Janice M., and Linda Niehaus. 2009. *Mixed-Method Design: Principles and Procedures*. Walnut Creek, CA: Left Coast Press.

Morsink, Johannes. 1999. *The Universal Declaration of Human Rights: Origins, Drafting and Intent*. Philadelphia: University of Pennsylvania Press.

Moser, Annalise. 2007. *Gender and Indicators: Overview Report*. Brighton, UK: Institute of Development Studies.

Mossakowski, K. N. 2008. "Dissecting the Influence of Race, Ethnicity, and Socioeconomic Status on Mental Health in Young Adulthood." *Research on Aging* 30: 649–671.

Motley, Susan. 1987. "Burning the South: U.S. Tobacco Companies in the Third World." *Multinational Monitor* 8, no. 7–8: 7–10.

Moulier Boutang, Yann. 1998. *De l'esclavage au salariat: economie histoire du salariat bride*. Paris: Partner University Fund.

Mousin, Craig B. 2003. "Standing with the Persecuted: Adjudicating Religious Asylum Claims after the Enactment of the International Religious Freedom Act of 1998." *Brigham Young University Law Review* 2003: 541–592.

Moyn, Samuel. 2010. *The Last Utopia: Human Rights in History*. Cambridge, MA: Belknap Press.

Mueller, John. 1989. *Retreat from Doomsday: The Obsolescence of Major War*. New York: Basic Books.

Muller, Mike. 1983. "Preventing Tomorrow's Epidemic: The Control of Smoking and Tobacco Production in Developing Countries." *New York State Journal of Medicine* 83, no. 13: 1304–1309.

Mullins, Christopher W., David Kauzlarich, and Dawn L. Rothe. 2004. "The International Criminal Court and the Control of State Crime: Prospects and Problems." *Critical Criminology* 12: 285–308.

Muraven, Mark, Dianne M. Tice, and Roy F. Baumeister. 1998. "Self-Control as Limited Resource: Regulatory Depletion Patterns." *Journal of Personality and Social Psychology* 74: 774–789.

Myers, Kristen, and Laura Raymond. 2010. "Elementary School Girls and Heteronormativity: The Girl Project." *Gender & Society* 24: 167–188.

Nadarajah, Saralees. 2002. "A Conversation with Samuel Kotz." *Statistical Science* 17: 220–233.

Nagarjuna. 2007 [1300]. *In Praise of Dharmadhꓹtu*. With commentary by the Third Karmapa. Translated by Karl Brunnhölzl. Ithaca, NY: Snow Lion Publications.

Nagel, Joane. 2003. *Race, Ethnicity, and Sexuality: Intimate Intersections, Forbidden Frontiers*. New York: Oxford University Press.

Naples, Nancy A. 1991, "Socialist Feminist Analysis of the Family Support Act of 1988."*AFFILIA: Journal of Women and Social Work* 6: 23–38.

———. 1998. *Community Activism and Feminist Politics: Organizing across Race, Gender and Class*. New York: Routledge.

———. 2009. "Teaching Intersectionality Intersectionally." *International Feminist Journal of Politics* 11: 566–577.

———. 2011. "Women's Leadership, Social Capital and Social Change." In *Activist Scholar: Selected Works of Marilyn Gittell*, edited by Kathe Newman and Ross Gittell, 263–278. Thousand Oaks, CA: Sage Publications.

186 BIBLIOGRAPHY

Naples, Nancy A., and Manisha Desai. 2002. *Women's Activism and Globalization: Linking Local Struggles and Transnational Politics*. New York: Routledge.

Narayan, Uma. 1997. *Dislocating Cultures: Identities, Traditions, and Third World Feminism*. New York: Routledge.

———. 1998. "Essence of Culture and a Sense of History: A Feminist Critique of Cultural Essentialism." *Hypatia* 13: 86–106.

Nash, J. C. 2008. "Re-thinking Intersectionality." *Feminist Review* 89: 1–15.

National Center on Addiction and Substance Abuse (CASA) at Columbia University. 2001. "Malignant Neglect: Substance Abuse and America's Schools." CASA. http://www.casacolumbia.org/templates/Publications.aspx?articleid=320&zoneid=52.

National Drug Strategy Network. 1997. "18-Year-Old Texan, Herding Goats, Killed by U.S. Marine Corps Anti-Drug Patrol; Criminal Investigation of Shooting Underway." National Drug Strategy Network News Briefs. July. http://www.ndsn.org/july97/goats.html (accessed March 23, 2011).

Navarro, Vicente. 2004. "The Politics of Health Inequalities Research in the United States." *International Journal of Health Services* 34, no. 1: 87–99.

Neckerman, Kathryn. 2010. *Schools Betrayed: Roots of Failure in Inner-City Education*. Chicago: University of Chicago Press.

Nee, Victor. 2005. "The New Institutionalisms in Economics and Sociology." In *The Handbook of Economic Sociology*, edited by N. J. Smelser and R. Swedberg, 49–74. Princeton, NJ: Princeton University Press and Russell Sage Foundation

Neilson, Brett, and Mohammed Bamyeh. 2009. "Drugs in Motion: Toward a Materialist Tracking of Global Mobilities." *Cultural Critique* 71: 1–12.

Nettle, Daniel, and Thomas V. Pollet. 2008. "Natural Selection on Male Wealth in Humans." *American Naturalist* 172: 658–666.

Nevins, Joseph. 2003. "Thinking Out of Bounds: A Critical Analysis of Academic and Human Rights: Writings on Migrant Deaths in the U.S.-Mexico Border Region." *Migraciones Internacionales* 2: 171–190.

New York City Human Rights Initiative. 2011. http://www.nychri.org (accessed May 25, 2011).

Newman, Katherine S. 2008. *Chutes and Ladders: Navigating the Low-Wage Labor Market*. Cambridge, MA: Harvard University Press.

Ngai, Mae M. 2004. *Impossible Subjects: Illegal Aliens and the Making of Modern America*. Princeton, NJ: Princeton University Press.

Niazi, Tarique. 2002. "The Ecology of Genocide in Rwanda." *International Journal of Contemporary Sociology* 39, no. 2: 219–247.

———. 2005. "Democracy, Development, and Terrorism: The Case of Baluchistan (Pakistan)." *International Journal of Contemporary Sociology* 42, no. 2: 303–337.

———. 2008. "Toxic Waste." In *International Encyclopedia of the Social Sciences*, edited by William A. Darity, 407–409. 2nd ed. Farmington Hills, MI: Gale.

Nibert, David. 2002. *Animal Rights/Human Rights*. Lanham, MD: Rowman & Littlefield.

———. 2006. "The Political Economy of Beef: Oppression of Cows and Other Devalued Groups in Latin America." Paper presented at the annual meeting of the American Sociological Association, Montreal, Quebec, August 11, 2006.

Nichter, Mark, and Elizabeth Cartwright. 1991. "Saving the Children for the Tobacco Industry." *Medical Anthropology Quarterly*, New Series 5, no. 3: 236–256.

Nickel, James. 2010. "Human Rights." Stanford Encyclopedia of Philosophy. http://plato.stanford.edu/entries/rights-human (accessed July 18, 2012).

Nielsen, Francois. 2004. "The Ecological-Evolutionary Typology of Human Societies and the Evolution of Social Inequality." *Sociological Theory* 22: 292–314.

———. 2006. "Achievement and Ascription in Educational Attainment: Genetic and Environmental Influences on Adolescent Schooling." *Social Forces* 85: 193–216.

Nobis, Nathan. 2004. "Carl Cohen's 'Kind' Arguments for Animal Rights and against Human Rights." *Journal of Applied Philosophy* 21: 43–49.

Noguchi, Y. 2008. "Clinical Sociology in Japan." In *International Clinical Sociology*, edited by J. M. Fritz, 72–81. New York: Springer.

Nolan, James. 2001. *Reinventing Justice: The American Drug Court Movement*. Princeton, NJ: Princeton University Press.

Nolan, P., and G. Lenski. 2011. *Human Societies: An Introduction to Macrosociology*. Boulder, CO: Paradigm Publishers.

Nordberg, Camilla. 2006. "Claiming Citizenship: Marginalised Voices on Identity and Belonging." *Citizenship Studies* 10: 523–539.

Nöth, Winfried. 1995. *Handbook of Semiotics*. Bloomington: Indiana University Press.

BIBLIOGRAPHY 187

Nouwen, S., and W. Werner. 2010. "Doing Justice to the Political: The International Criminal Court in Uganda and Sudan." *European Journal of International Law* 21: 941–965.

Núñez, Guillermina, and Josiah McC. Heyman. 2007. "Entrapment Processes and Immigrant Communities in a Time of Heightened Border Vigilance." *Human Organization* 66: 354–365.

Nyland, Chris, and Mark Rix. 2000. "Mary van Kleeck, Lillian Gilbreth and the Women's Bureau Study of Gendered Labor Law." *Journal of Management History* 6: 306–322.

Nystrom, P. C. 1981. "Designing Jobs and Assigning Employees." In *Handbook of Organizational Design*. Vol. 2: *Remodelling Organizations and Their Environments*, edited by P. C. Nystrom and William Starbuck, 272–301. New York: Oxford University Press.

O'Connor, Alice. 2002. *Poverty Knowledge: Social Science, Social Policy and the Poor in Twentieth-Century U.S. History*. Princeton, NJ: Princeton University Press.

O'Connor, Alice, Chris Tilly, and Lawrence D. Bobo. 2001. *Urban Inequality: Evidence from Four Cities*. New York: Russell Sage Foundation.

Offe, Claus. 1984. *Contradictions of the Welfare State*. Cambridge, MA: MIT Press.

———. 1985. *Disorganized Capitalism*. Cambridge, MA: MIT Press.

Office of the High Commissioner for Human Rights (OHCHR). 1998. *Basic Human Rights Instruments*. 3rd ed. Geneva: Office of the High Commissioner for Human Rights.

———. 2010. *2009 OHCHR Report on Activities and Results*. New York: United Nations.

———. 2011. "Human Rights at the Centre of Climate Change Policy." OHCHR. www.ohchr.org/EN/NewsEvents/pages/climate change policy (accessed January 1, 2011).

Ogien, A. 1994. "L'usage de drogues peut-il etre un object de recherché?" In *La Demande sociale de drogues*, edited by A. Ogien and P. Mignon, 7–12. Paris: La Documentation Française.

Okin, Susan Moller. 1989. *Justice, Gender, and the Family*. New York: Basic Books.

Okonta, I., and O. Douglas. 2001. *Where Vultures Feast: Shell, Human Rights, and Oil in the Niger Delta*. San Francisco: Sierra Club Books.

Oliver, Kelly. 2009. *Animal Lessons: How They Teach Us to Be Human*. New York: Columbia University Press.

Olshansky, S. Jay, and A. Brian Ault. 1986. "The Fourth Stage of the Epidemiologic Transition: The Age of Delayed Degenerative Disease." *Milbank Memorial Fund Quarterly* 64: 355–391.

Olson, Mancur. 1982. *The Rise and Decline of Nations: Economic Growth, Stagflation, and Social Rigidities*. New Haven, CT: Yale University Press.

Omi, M., and H. Winant. 1986. *Racial Formation in the United States: From the 1960s to the 1980s*. New York: Routledge.

———. 1994. *Racial Formation in the United States: From the 1960s to the 1980s*. 2nd ed. New York: Routledge.

Omran, Abdel R. 1971. "The Epidemiological Transition." *Milbank Memorial Fund Quarterly* 49: 509–538.

Oneal, John, and Bruce Russett. 2011. *Triangulating Peace: Democracy, Interdependence, and International Organizations*. New York: Norton.

Onken, S. J., and E. Slaten. 2000. "Disability Identity Formation and Affirmation: The Experiences of Persons with Severe Mental Illness." *Sociological Practice: A Journal of Clinical and Applied Sociology* 2: 99–111.

Ontario Human Rights Commission (OHRC). 2001. *An Intersectional Approach to Discrimination, Addressing Multiple Grounds in Human Rights Claims*. OHRC. http://www.ohrc.on.ca/sites/default/files/attachments/An_intersectional_approach_to_discrimination%3A_Addressing_multiple_grounds_in_human_ rights_claims.pdf (accessed July 18, 2012).

Oppenheimer, Gerald. 1991. "To Build a Bridge: The Use of Foreign Models by Domestic Critics of US Drug Policy." *Milbank Quarterly* 69, no. 3: 495–526.

Oppenheimer, Martin, Martin Murray, and Rhonda Levine. 1991. *Radical Sociologists and the Movement: Experiences, Legacies, and Lessons*. Philadelphia: Temple University Press.

Orellana, Marjorie Faulstich. 1999. "Space and Place in an Urban Landscape: Learning from Children's Views of Their Social Worlds." *Visual Sociology* 14: 73–89.

Orentlicher, Diane F. 1990. "Bearing Witness: The Art and Science of Human Rights Fact-Finding." *Harvard Law School Human Rights Journal* 3: 83–136.

Orr, David W. 1979. "Catastrophe and Social Order." *Human Ecology* 7: 41–52.

Ortiz, Victor M. 2001. "The Unbearable Ambiguity of the Border." *Social Justice* 28: 96–112.

Osiel, Mark J. 1997. *Mass Atrocities, Collective Memory, and the Law*. New Brunswick, NJ: Transaction Publishers.

Ostrom, Elinor. 1990. *Governing the Commons: The Evolution of Institutions for Collective Action*. Cambridge, UK: Cambridge University Press.

188 BIBLIOGRAPHY

Ouellette-Kuntz, H., P. Burge, H. K. Brown, and E. Arsenault. 2010. "Public Attitudes towards Individuals with Intellectual Disabilities as Measured by the Concept of Social Distance." *Journal of Applied Research in Intellectual Disabilities* 23: 132–142.

Oxtoby, Willard G., and Allan F. Segal, eds. *A Concise Introduction to World Religions*. New York: Oxford University Press.

Page, Charles Hunt. 1982. *Fifty Years in the Sociological Enterprise: A Lucky Journey*. Amherst: University of Massachusetts Press.

Park, Robert E. 1914. "Racial Assimilation in Secondary Groups with Particular Reference to the Negro." *American Journal of Sociology* 19: 606–623.

———. 1928a. "Human Migration and the Marginal Man." *American Journal of Sociology* 33: 881–893.

———. 1928b. "The Bases of Race Prejudice." *Annals of the American Academy of Political and Social Science* 140: 11–20.

Parker, Karen. 2008. *Unequal Crime Decline: Theorizing Race, Urban Inequality, and Criminal Violence*. New York: New York University Press.

Parreñas, Rhacel Salazar. 1998. "The Global Servants: (Im)Migrant Filipina Domestic Workers in Rome and Los Angeles." Unpublished PhD diss., Department of Ethnic Studies, University of California, Berkeley.

Parsons, Talcott. 1951. *The Social System*. New York: The Free Press.

———. 1959. "The School as a Social System." *Harvard Educational Review* 29: 297–318.

Pascal, Celine-Marie. 2007. *Making Sense of Race, Class and Gender: Commonsense, Power and Privilege in the United States*. New York: Routledge.

Pascoe, C. J. 2007. *Dude, You're a Fag: Masculinity and Sexuality in High School*. Berkeley: University of California Press.

Pastor, Eugenia Relaño. 2005. "The Flawed Implementation of the International Religious Freedom Act of 1998: A European Perspective." *Brigham Young University Law Review* 2005: 711–746.

Patai, Raphael. 2002. *The Arab Mind*. New York: Hatherleigh Press.

Patterson, Charles. 2002. *Eternal Treblinka: Our Treatment of Animals and the Holocaust*. New York: Lantern Books.

Pattillo, Mary. 2007. *Black on the Block: The Politics of Race and Class in the City*. Chicago: University of Chicago Press.

Paust, Jordan J. 2004. "Post 9/11 Overreaction and Fallacies Regarding War and Defense, Guantanamo, the Status of Persons, Treatment, Judicial Review of Detention, and Due Process in Military Commissions." *Notre Dame Law Review* 79: 1335–1364.

Payne, Leigh. 2009. "Consequences of Transitional Justice." Paper presented at the Department of Political Science, University of Minnesota, Minneapolis.

PDHRE (People's Movement for Human Rights Learning). 2011. http://www.pdhre.org (accessed May 24, 2011).

Pearlin, L., and C. Schooler. 1978. "The Structure of Coping." *Journal of Health and Social Behavior* 19: 2–21.

Pécoud, Antoine, and Paul de Guchteneire. 2006. "International Migration, Border Controls and Human Rights: Assessing the Relevance of a Right to Mobility." *Journal of Borderlands Studies* 21: 69–86.

Peffley, Mark, and John Hurwitz. 2007. "Persuasion and Resistance: Race and the Death Penalty in America." *American Journal of Political Science* 51: 996–1012.

Pellow, D. N. 2007. *Resisting Global Toxics: Transnational Movements for Environmental Justice*. Cambridge, MA: MIT Press.

Penn, Michael, and Aditi Malik. 2010. "The Protection and Development of the Human Spirit: An Expanded Focus for Human Rights Discourse." *Human Rights Quarterly* 32, no. 3: 665–688.

Penna, David R., and Patricia J. Campbell. 1998. "Human Rights and Culture: Beyond Universality and Relativism." *Third World Quarterly* 19: 7–27.

Pennebaker, James W. 1997. "Writing about Emotional Experiences as a Therapeutic Process." *Psychological Science* 8: 162–166.

Perelman, Michael. 1978. "Karl Marx's Theory of Science." *Journal of Economic Issues* 12, no. 4: 859–870.

Peretti-Watel, Patrick. 2003. "How Does One Become a Cannabis Smoker? A Quantitative Approach." *Revue Française de Sociologie* 44: 3–27.

Peritz, Rudolph J. R. 1996. *Competition Policy in America, 1888–1992: History, Rhetoric, Law*. New York: Oxford University Press.

Perlman, Selig. 1922. *History of Trade Unionism in the United States*. New York: Macmillan.

———. 1928. *A Theory of the Labor Movement*. New York: Macmillan.

Perrin, Andrew J., and Lee Hedwig. 2007. "The Undertheorized Environment: Sociological Theory and the Ontology of Behavioral Genetics." *Sociological Perspectives* 50: 303–322.

Perrow, Charles. 1967. *Complex Organizations: A Critical Essay*. New York: Random House.
———. 1999. *Normal Accidents: Living with High-Risk Technologies*. Princeton, NJ: Princeton University Press.
———. 2002. *Organizing America, Wealth, Power, and the Origins of Corporate Capitalism*. Princeton, NJ, and Oxford, UK: Princeton University Press.
———. 2008. "Complexity, Catastrophe, and Modularity." *Sociological Inquiry* 78: 162–173.
Perrucci, Robert, and Carolyn C. Perrucci. 2009. *America at Risk: The Crisis of Hope, Trust, and Caring*. Lanham, MD: Rowman & Littlefield.
Perry, Michael J. 1997. "Are Human Rights Universal? The Relativist Challenge and Related Matters." *Human Rights Quarterly* 19, no. 3: 461–509.
Pescosolido, Bernice A., Brea L. Perry, J. Scott Long, Jack K. Martin, John I. Nurnberger Jr., and Victor Hesselbrock. 2008. "Under the Influence of Genetics: How Transdisciplinarity Leads Us to Rethink Social Pathways to Illness." *American Journal of Sociology* 114: S171–S201.
Peters, Julie, and Andrea Wolper. 1995. *Women's Rights, Human Rights: International Feminist Perspectives*. New York: Routledge.
Petersen, W. 1978. "International Migration." *Annual Review of Sociology* 4: 533–575.
Peterson, Ruth D., and Lauren J. Krivo. 2010. *Neighborhood Crime and the Racial-Spatial Divide*. New York: Russell Sage Foundation.
Pettigrew, T. F., and L. R. Tropp. 2006. "A Meta-Analytic Test of Intergroup Contact Theory." *Journal of Personality and Social Psychology* 90: 751–783.
PEW Forum on Religion in Public Life. 2009. "Global Restrictions on Religion." PEW Forum on Religion and Public Life, Washington, DC. http://www.pewforum.org/uploadedFiles/Topics/Issues/Government/ restrictions-fullreport.pdf (accessed July 18, 2012).
PEW Research Center for the People and the Press. 2010. "Favorability Ratings of Labor Unions Fall Sharply." PEW Research Center for the People and the Press. http://pewresearch.org/pubs/1505/labor-unions -support-falls-public-now-evenly-split-on-purpose-power (accessed February 23, 2010).
Pfeiffer, D. 1993. "Overview of the Disability Movement: History, Legislative Record, and Political Implications." *Policy Studies Journal* 21: 724–734.
———. 2001. "The Conceptualization of Disability." In *Exploring Theories and Expanding Methodologies: Where We Are and Where We Need to Go*, edited by S. N. Barnartt and B. M. Altman, 2:29–52. Oxford: Elsevier Science.
Phemister, A. A., and N. M. Crewe. 2004. "Objective Self- Awareness and Stigma: Implications for Persons with Visible Disabilities." *Journal of Rehabilitation* 70: 33–37.
Picou, J. S., D. A. Gill, and M. J. Cohen, eds. 1997. *The Exxon-Valdez Disaster: Readings on a Modern Social Problem*. Dubuque, IA: Kendall-Hunt Publishers.
Picq, Ardant du. 2006. *Battle Studies*. Charleston, SC: BiblioBazaar.
Pierce, Jennifer L. 1995. *Gender Trials: Emotional Lives in Contemporary Law Firms*. Berkeley and Los Angeles: University of California Press.
Pilgrim, D., and A. A. Rogers. 1999. *A Sociology of Mental Health and Illness*. 2nd ed. Buckingham, UK: Open University Press.
Piven, Frances Fox, and Richard P. Cloward. 1977. *Poor People's Movements: Why They Succeed, How They Fail*. New York: Vintage Books.
Playle, J., and P. Keeley. 1998. "Non-Compliance and Professional Power." *Journal of Advanced Nursing* 27: 304–311.
Poe, Steven C., C. Neal Tate, and Linda Camp Keith. 1999. "Repression of the Human Right to Personal Integrity Revisited: A Global Cross-National Study Covering the Years 1976–1993." *International Studies Quarterly* 43: 291–313.
Polanyi, Karl. 1944. *The Great Transformation*. New York: Farrar and Rinehart.
Polletta, Francesca, and James M. Jasper. 2001. "Collective Identity and Social Movements." *Annual Review of Sociology* 27: 283–305.
Pollis, Adamantia. 2004. "Human Rights and Globalization." *Journal of Human Rights* 3, no. 3: 343–358.
Pollner, Melvin. 1987. *Mundane Reason: Reality in Everyday and Sociological Discourse*. Cambridge, UK: Cambridge University Press.
Ponse, Barbara. 1978. *Identities in the Lesbian World: The Social Construction of Self*. Westport, CT: Greenwood Press.
Poole, Michael. 1975. *Workers' Participation in Industry*. London: Routledge & K. Paul.
Popkin, Eric. 1999. "Guatemalan Mayan Migration to Los Angeles: Constructing Transnational Linkages in the Context of the Settlement Process." *Ethnic and Racial Studies* 22: 267–289.
Popper, Karl R. 1963. *Conjectures and Refutations: The Growth of Scientific Knowledge*. New York: Basic Books.

190 BIBLIOGRAPHY

Population Research Bureau (PRB). 2007. "Is Low Birth Weight a Cause of Problems, or a Symptom of Them?" PBR. http://www.prb.org/Journalists/Webcasts/2007/LowBirthWeight.aspx (accessed January 25, 2012).

Porio, E. 2010. Personal communication with J. M. Fritz. December 12.

Portes, Alejandro, and Rubén Rumbaut. 2001. *Legacies: The Story of the Immigrant Second Generation*. Berkeley: University of California Press.

Poussaint, Alvin F. 1967. "A Negro Psychiatrist Explains the Negro Psyche." *New York Times Magazine*. August 20, 52.

Powell, Walter W., and Paul J. DiMaggio, eds. 1991. *The New Institutionalism in Organizational Analysis*. Chicago: University of Chicago Press.

Power, Samantha. 2002. *A Problem from Hell*. New York: Basic Books.

Prechel, Harland. 2000. *Big Business and the State: Historical Transitions and Corporate Transformation, 1880s–1990s*. Albany: State University of New York Press.

Preeves, Sharon E. 2003. *Intersex and Identity: The Contested Self*. New Brunswick, NJ: Rutgers University Press.

Preis, Ann-Belinda S. 1996. "Human Rights as Cultural Practice: An Anthropological Critique." *Human Rights Quarterly* 18, no. 2: 286–315.

Preston, Julia. 2011. "Risks Seen for Children of Illegal Immigrants." *New York Times*. September 20.

Prew, Paul. 2003. "The 21st Century World-Ecosystem: Dissipation, Chaos, or Transition?" In *Emerging Issues in the 21st Century World-System*. Vol. 2: *New Theoretical Directions for the 21st Century World System*, edited by Wilma A. Dunaway, 203–219. Westport, CT: Praeger Publishers.

Prior, L. 1996. *The Social Organization of Mental Illness*. London: Sage Publications.

Prunier, Gérard. 1997. *The Rwanda Crisis: History of a Genocide*. New York: Columbia University Press.

———. 2005. *Darfur: The Ambiguous Genocide*. Ithaca: Cornell University Press.

Pubantz, Jerry. 2005. "Constructing Reason: Human Rights and the Democratization of the United Nations." *Social Forces* 84: 1291–1302.

Pugh, Allison J. 2009. *Longing and Belonging: Parents, Children, and Consumer Culture*. Berkeley: University of California Press.

Purdy, Laura. 1989. "Surrogate Mothering: Exploitation or Empowerment?" *Bioethics* 3: 18–34.

Putnam, Robert D. 2000. *Bowling Alone: The Collapse and Revival of American Community*. New York: Simon and Schuster.

Quadagno, Jill. 1988. *The Transformation of Old Age Security*. Chicago: University of Chicago Press.

———. 2005. *One Nation, Uninsured: Why the U.S. Has No National Health Insurance*. New York: Oxford University Press.

Quadagno, Jill, and Debra Street, eds. 1995. *Aging for the Twenty-First Century*. New York: St. Martin's Press.

Quataert, Jean H. 2009. *Advocating Dignity: Human Rights Mobilizations in Global Politics*. Philadelphia: University of Pennsylvania Press.

———. 2010. "Women, Development, and Injustice: The Circuitous Origins of the New Gender Perspectives in Human Rights Visions and Practices in the 1970s." Paper presented at a conference titled "A New Global Morality? Human Rights and Humanitarianism in the 1970s," Freiburg Institute for Advanced Studies, Freiburg, Germany, June 10–12.

Queen, Stuart. 1981. "Seventy-Five Years of American Sociology in Relation to Social Work." *American Sociologist* 16: 34–37.

Quesnel-Vallee, Amelie. 2004. "Is It Really Worse to Have Public Health Insurance Than to Have No Insurance at All?" *Journal of Health and Social Behavior* 45, no. 4: 376–392.

Quigley, John. 2009. "The US Withdrawal from the ICJ Jurisdiction in Consular Cases." *Duke Journal of Comparative and International Law* 19, no. 2: 263–305.

Quinney, Richard. 1970. *The Social Reality of Crime*. Boston: Little, Brown and Co.

Rabben, Linda. 2002. *Fierce Legion of Friends: A History of Human Rights Campaigns and Campaigners*. Hyattsville, MD: Quixote Center.

Rainwater, Lee, and Timothy M. Smeeding. 2005. *Poor Kids in a Rich Country*. New York: Russell Sage Foundation.

Raskoff, Sally. 2011. "Welcome Back: Adjusting to Life after Military Service." Everday Sociology Blog. www.everydaysociologyblog.com/2011/12/welcome-back-adjusting-to-civilian-life-after-military-service.html (accessed December 17, 2011).

Ratner, S. R., J. S. Abrams, and J. L. Bischoff. 2009. *Accountability for Human Rights Atrocities in International Law: Beyond the Nuremberg Legacy*. 3rd ed. Oxford: Oxford University Press.

Rawls, A. 2000. "Harold Garfinkel." In *The Blackwell Companion to Major Social Theorists*, edited by George Ritzer, 545–576. Oxford: Blackwell.

———. 2003. "Conflict as a Foundation for Consensus: Contradictions of Industrial Capitalism in Book III of Durkheim's Division of Labor." *Critical Sociology* 29: 195–335.

———. 2006. "Respecifying the Study of Social Order: Garfinkel's Transition from Theoretical Conceptualization to Practices in Details." In *Seeing Sociologically: The Routine Grounds of Social Action* by Harold Garfinkel, 1–97. Boulder, CO: Paradigm.

Rawls, John. 1971. *A Theory of Justice.* Cambridge, MA: Belknap Press.

———. 1995. "Reply to Habermas." *Journal of Philosophy* 92: 132–180. Reprinted in *Political Liberalism,* edited by John Rawls, 372–434. New York: Columbia University Press.

———. 1996. *Political Liberalism.* New York: Columbia University Press.

Ray, Raka, and A. C. Korteweg. 1999. "Women's Movements in the Third World: Identity, Mobilization, and Autonomy." *Annual Review of Sociology* 25: 47–71.

Razack, Sherene. 1998. *Looking White People in the Eye: Gender, Race, and Culture in Courtrooms and Classrooms.* Toronto: University of Toronto Press.

Read, Jen'nan Ghazal. 2007. "Introduction: The Politics of Veiling in Comparative Perspective." *Sociology of Religion* 68: 231–236.

Reading, R., S. Bissell, J. Goldhagen, J. Harwin, J. Masson, S. Moynihan, N. Parton, M. S. Pais, J. Thoburn, and E. Webb. 2009. "Promotion of Children's Rights and Prevention of Child Maltreatment." *The Lancet* 373: 322–343.

Readings, Bill. 1996. *The University in Ruins.* Cambridge, MA: Harvard University Press.

Reardon, Betty. 1985. *Sexism and the War System.* New York: Teachers College Press.

Redwood, Loren K. 2008. "Strong-Arming Exploitable Labor: The State and Immigrant Workers in the Post-Katrina Gulf Coast." *Social Justice* 35: 33–50.

Reed, Michael. 1985. *Redirections in Organizational Analysis.* London: Tavistock. Regan, Tom. 2004. *The Case for Animal Rights.* Berkeley: University of California Press.

Regnerus, Mark D. 2007. *Forbidden Fruit: Sex and Religion in the Lives of American Teenagers.* New York: Oxford University Press.

Reilly, Niamh. 2007. "Cosmopolitan Feminism and Human Rights." *Hypatia* 22: 180–198.

———. 2009. *Women's Human Rights: Seeking Gender Justice in a Globalizing Age.* Cambridge, MA: Polity Press.

Reimann, Kim. 2006. "A View from the Top: International Politics, Norms and the Worldwide Growth of NGOs." *International Studies Quarterly* 50: 45–67.

Reinarman, Craig, and Harry Levine. 1997. *Crack in America: Demon Drugs and Social Justice.* Berkeley: University of California Press.

Reisch, Michael. 2009. "Social Workers, Unions, and Low Wage Workers: A Historical Perspective." *Journal of Community Practice* 17: 50–72.

Renteln, Alison Dundes. 1985. "The Unanswered Challenge of Relativism and the Consequences for Human Rights." *Human Rights Quarterly* 7, no. 4: 514–540.

———. 1988. "The Concept of Human Rights." *Anthropos* 83: 343–364.

Rheaume, J. 2008. "Clinical Sociology in Quebec: When Europe Meets America." In *International Clinical Sociology,* edited by J. M. Fritz, 36–53. New York: Springer.

———. 2010. Personal communication with J. M. Fritz. December 16.

Rhoades, Lawrence. 1981. "A History of the American Sociological Association, 1905–1980." American Sociological Association. www.asanet.org/about/Rhoades_Chapter3.cfm (accessed December 10, 2011).

Rice, James. 2009. "The Transnational Organization of Production and Uneven Environmental Degradation and Change in the World Economy." *International Journal of Comparative Sociology* 50, no. 3/4: 215–236.

Rich, Adrienne. 1980. "Compulsory Heterosexuality." In *Powers of Desire: The Politics of Sexuality,* edited by Ann Snitow, Christine Stansell, and Sharon Thompson, 177–205. New York: Monthly Review Press.

Rich, Michael, and Richard Chalfen. 1999. "Showing and Telling Asthma: Children Teaching Physicians with Visual Narratives." *Visual Sociology* 14: 51–71.

Richards, Patricia. 2005. "The Politics of Gender, Human Rights, and Being Indigenous in Chile." *Gender and Society* 19: 199–220.

Richardson, L., and T. Brown. 2011. "Intersectionality of Race, Gender and Age in Hypertension Trajectories across the Life Course." Presented at the eighty-first annual meeting of the Eastern Sociological Society, Philadelphia, Pennsylvania, February.

Ridge, D., C. Emslie, and A. White. 2011. "Understanding How Men Experience, Express and Cope with Mental Distress: Where Next?" *Sociology of Health and Illness* 33: 145–159.

Rieker, Patricia P., Chloe E. Bird, and Martha E. Lang. 2010. "Understanding Gender and Health." In *Handbook of Medical Sociology,* edited by Chloe Bird, Peter Conrad, Allen Fremont, and Stephan Timmermans, 52–74. 6th ed. Nashville, TN: Vanderbilt University Press.

192 BIBLIOGRAPHY

Right to the City Alliance. 2011. http://www.righttothecity.org (accessed May 28, 2011).

Riley, J. 2004. "Some Reflections on Gender Mainstreaming and Intersectionality." *Development Bulletin* 64: 82–86.

Riley, M. W., M. E. Johnson, and A. Foner. 1972. *Aging and Society*. Vol. 3: *A Sociology of Age Stratification*. New York: Russell Sage Foundation.

Riley, M. W., R. L. Kahn, and A. Foner. 1994. *Age and Structural Lag: Society's Failure to Provide Meaningful Opportunities in Work, Family, and Leisure*. New York: Wiley.

Riley, M. W., and J. W. Riley Jr. 1994. "Age Integration and the Lives of Older People." *Gerontologist* 3–4, no. 1: 110–115.

Ringelheim, Julie. 2011. "Ethnic Categories and European Human Rights Law." *Ethnic and Racial Studies* 34: 1682–1696.

Rios, Victor M. 2010. "Navigating the Thin Line between Education and Incarceration: An Action Research Case Study on Gang-Associated Latino Youth." *Journal of Education for Students Placed At-Risk* 15, no. 1–2: 200–212.

Risse, Thomas. 2000. "The Power of Norms versus the Norms of Power: Transnational Civil Society and Human Rights." In *The Third Force: The Rise of Transnational Civil Society*, edited by A. Florini, N. Kokusai, K. Senta, and Carnegie Endowment for International Peace. Tokyo: Japan Center for International Exchange, Washington Carnegie Endowment for International Peace, and Brookings Institution Press (distributor).

Risse, Thomas, S. C. Ropp, and K. Sikkink, eds. 1999. *The Power of Human Rights: International Norms and Domestic Change*. Cambridge, UK: Cambridge University Press.

Rist, Ray. 1970. "Student Social Class and Teacher Expectations: The Self-Fulfilling Prophecy in Ghetto Education." *Harvard Educational Review* 40: 411–451.

———. 1973. *The Urban School: Factory for Failure*. Cambridge, MA: MIT Press.

———. 1977. "On Understanding the Processes of Schooling: The Contributions of Labeling Theory." In *Power and Ideology in Education*, edited by Jerome Karabel and A. H. Halsey, 292–305. New York: Oxford University Press.

Rivera Vargas, Maria Isabel. 2010. "Government Influence and Foreign Direct Investment: Organizational Learning in an Electronics Cluster." *Critical Sociology* 36, no. 4: 537–553.

Robert, Stephanie A., and James S. House. 2000. "Socioeconomic Inequalities in Health: An Enduring Sociological Problem." In *Handbook of Medical Sociology*, edited by C. E. Bird, P. Conrad, and A. M. Fremont, 79–97. 5th ed. Upper Saddle River, NJ: Prentice Hall.

Roberts, Christopher N. J. Forthcoming. Untitled Work. Cambridge, UK: Cambridge University Press.

Roberts, Dorothy. 2010. "The Social Immorality of Health in the Gene Age: Race, Disability, and Inequality." In *Against Health: How Health Became the New Morality*, edited by Jonathan M. Metzl and Anna Kirkland, 61–71. New York: New York University Press.

Robertson, Roland. 1992. *Globalization: Social Theory and Global Culture*. London: Sage.

Robinson, Dawn T., Christabel L. Rogalin, and Lynn Smith-Lovin. 2004. "Physiological Measures of Theoretical Concepts: Some Ideas for Linking Deflection and Emotion to Physical Responses during Interaction." *Advances in Group Processes* 21: 77–115.

Rodan, Garry. 2006. "Singapore in 2005: 'Vibrant and Cosmopolitan' without Political Pluralism." *Asian Survey* 46: 180–186.

Rodríguez, Havidán, Rogelio Sáenz, and Cecilia Menjívar, eds. 2008. *Latina/os in the United States: Changing the Face of América*. New York: Springer.

Rodríguez, Nestor. 2008. "Theoretical and Methodological Issues of Latina/o Research." In *Latina/os in the United States: Changing the Face of América*, edited by H. Rodríguez, R. Sáenz, and C. Menjívar, 3–15. New York: Springer.

Roediger, D. R. 1991. *Wages of Whiteness: Race and the Making of the American Working Class*. London: Verso.

Roethlisberger, F. J., and W. J. Dickson. 1947. *Management and the Worker*. Cambridge, MA: Harvard University Press.

Rogers, Leslie. 1998. *Mind of Their Own: Thinking and Awareness in Animals*. Boulder, CO: Westview Press.

Rogoff, Barbara. 2003. *The Cultural Name of Human Development*. Oxford: Oxford University Press.

Rojas, Fabio. 2007. *From Black Power to Black Studies: How a Radical Social Movement Became an Academic Discipline*. Baltimore: Johns Hopkins University Press.

Rokeach, Milton. 1973. *The Nature of Human Values*. New York: The Free Press.

Romero, Mary. 1988. "Sisterhood and Domestic Service: Race, Class and Gender in the Mistress-Maid Relationship." *Humanity and Society* 12: 318–346.

———. 2006. "Racial Profiling and Immigration Law Enforcement: Rounding Up of Usual Suspects in the Latino Community." *Critical Sociology* 32: 449–475.

————. 2011. "Are Your Papers in Order? Racial Profiling, Vigilantes and 'America's Toughest Sheriff.'" *Harvard Latino Law Review* 14: 337–357.

Romero-Ortuno, Roman. 2004. "Access to Health Care for Illegal Immigrants in the EU: Should We Be Concerned?" *European Journal of Health Law* 11: 245–272.

Roschelle, Anne R., Jennifer Turpin, and Robert Elias. 2000. "Who Learns from Service Learning." *American Behavioral Scientist* 43: 839–847.

Rosenfield, S. 1999. "Gender and Mental Health: Do Women Have More Psychopathology, Men More, or Both the Same (and Why)?" In *Handbook for the Study of Mental Health*, edited by A. Horwitz and T. Scheid, 348–361. Cambridge, UK: Cambridge University Press.

Rosenhan, D. L. 1991. "On Being Sane in Insane Places." In *Down to Earth Sociology*, edited by J. M. Henslin, 294–307. New York: The Free Press.

Ross, J. S. Robert. 1991. "At the Center and the Edge: Notes on a Life in and out of Sociology and the New Left." In *Radical Sociologists and the Movement: Experiences, Lessons, and Legacies*, edited by Martin Oppenheimer, Martin J. Murray, and Rhonda F. Levine, 197–215. Philadelphia: Temple University Press.

Ross, Lauren. 2009. "Contradictions of Power, Sexuality, and Consent: An Institutional Ethnography of the Practice of Male Neonatal Circumcision." PhD diss., University of Connecticut, Storrs.

Rossi, Alice S. 1970. "Status of Women in Graduate Departments of Sociology, 1968–1969." *American Sociologist* (February): 1–12.

————. 1983. "Beyond the Gender Gap: Women's Bid for Political Power." *Social Science Quarterly* 64: 718–733.

————. 1984. "Gender and Parenthood." *American Sociological Review* 49, no. 1: 1–19.

Rossi, Federico M. 2009. "Youth Political Participation: Is This the End of Generational Cleavage?" *International Sociology* 24, no. 4: 467–497.

Roth, Brad. 2004. "Retrieving Marx for the Human Rights Project." *Leiden Journal of International Law* 17: 31–66. Roth, Wendy D., and Gerhard Sonnert. 2011. "The Costs and Benefits of 'Red-Tape': Anti-Bureaucratic Structure and Gender Inequity in a Science Research Organization." *Social Studies of Science*. January 17. http://sss.sagepub.com/content/early/2011/01/15/0306312710391494 (accessed July 19, 2012).

Rothschild, Joyce. 1979. "The Collectivist Organization: An Alternative to Rational-Bureaucratic Models." *American Sociological Review* 44: 509–527.

Rowe, John, Lisa Berkman, Robert Binstock, Axel Boersch-Supan, John Cacioppo, Laura Carstensen, Linda Fried, Dana Goldman, James Jackson, Matin Kohli, Jay Olshansky, and John Rother. 2010. "Policies and Politics for an Aging America." *Contexts* 9, no. 1: 22–27.

Rowland, Robyn. 1995. "Symposium: Human Rights and the Sociological Project (Human Rights Discourse and Women: Challenging the Rhetoric with Reality)." *Australian and New Zealand Journal of Sociology* 31: 8–25.

Roy, William G. 1997. *Socializing Capital: The Rise of the Large Industrial Corporation in America*. Princeton, NJ: Princeton University Press.

Rubin, Gayle. 1984. "Thinking Sex: Notes for a Radical Theory of the Politics of Sexuality." In *Pleasure and Danger: Exploring Female Sexuality*, edited by Carol Vance, 267–319. London: Pandora Press.

Rumbaut, Rubén. 1994. "Origins and Destinies: Immigration to the United States since World War II." *Sociological Forum* 9: 583–621.

Rumbaut, Rubén, and Walter A. Ewing. 2007. "The Myth of Immigrant Criminality." Border Battles. May 23. http://borderbattles.ssrc.org/Rumbault_Ewing/index.html (accessed November 9, 2010).

Rumbaut, Rubén, and Alejandro Portes. 2001. *Ethnicities: Children of Immigrants in America*. Berkeley: University of California Press.

Rummel, R. J. 1994. *Death by Government*. New Brunswick, NJ: Transaction.

Rupp, Leila J. 1997. *Worlds of Women: The Making of an International Women's Movement*. Princeton, NJ: Princeton University Press.

————. 2009. *Sapphistries: A Global History of Love between Women*. New York: New York University Press.

Ruppel, Oliver C. 2009. "Third Generation Human Rights and the Protection of the Environment in Namibia." Konrad-Adenauer-Stiftung. http://www.kas.de/namibia/en/publications/16045 (accessed December 2, 2010).

Russon, John. 1997. *The Self and Its Body in Hegel's Phenomenology of Spirit*. Toronto: University of Toronto Press.

Rutherford, Markella B. 2011. *Adult Supervision Required*. Piscataway, NJ: Rutgers University Press.

Rytina, Nancy, Michael Hoefer, and Bryan Baker. 2010. "Estimates of the Unauthorized Immigrant Population Residing in the United States: January 2009." Department of Homeland Security. January. http://www.dhs.gov/xlibrary/assets/statistics/publications/ois_ill_pe_2009.pdf (accessed October 12, 2010).

194 BIBLIOGRAPHY

Sabel, Charles, and Jonathan Zeitlin. 1997. *World of Possibilities: Flexibility and Mass Production in Western Industrialization.* Cambridge, UK: Cambridge University Press.

Sachs, A. 1996. "Upholding Human Rights and Environmental Justice." In *State of the World,* edited by Lester Brown, 133–151. New York: W. W. Norton.

Sacks, Harvey. 1972a. "An Initial Investigation of the Usability of Conversational Data for Doing Sociology." In *Studies in Social Interaction,* edited by David Sudnow, 31–74. New York: The Free Press.

———. 1972b. "On the Analyzability of Stories by Children." In *Directions in Sociolinguistics: The Ethnography of Communication,* edited by John J. Gumperz and Dell Hymes, 325–345. New York: Holt, Rinehart and Winston.

———. 1984. "Notes on Methodology." In *Structures of Social Action: Studies in Conversation Analysis,* edited by J. Maxwell Atkinson and John Heritage, 21–27. Cambridge, UK: Cambridge University Press; Paris: Les Éditions de la Maison des Sciences de l'Homme.

———. 1992. *Lectures on Conversation,* edited by Gail Jefferson with introductions by Emanuel A. Schegloff. 2 vols. Oxford: Basil Blackwell.

Sacks, Harvey, Emanuel A. Schegloff, and Gail Jefferson. 1974. "A Simplest Systematics for the Organization of Turn Taking for Conversation." *Language* 50, no. 4: 696–735.

Sadovnik, A. R., ed. 2007. *Sociology of Education: A Critical Reader.* New York: Routledge.

Sáenz, Rogelio. 2010a. "Latinos in the United States 2010." Population Reference Bureau. http://www.prb .org/pdf10/latinos-update2010.pdf (accessed July 19, 2012).

———. 2010b. "Latinos, Whites, and the Shifting Demography of Arizona." Population Reference Bureau. http://www.prb.org/Articles/2010/usarizonalatinos.aspx (accessed March 24, 2011).

Sáenz, Rogelio, Cynthia M. Cready, and Maria Cristina Morales. 2007. "Adios Aztlan: Mexican American Outmigration from the Southwest." In *The Sociology of Spatial Inequality,* edited by L. Lobao, G. Hooks, and A. Tickamyer, 189–214. Albany: State University of New York Press.

Sáenz, Rogelio, Cecilia Menjívar, and San Juanita Edilia Garcia. 2011. "Arizona's SB 1070: Setting Conditions for Violations of Human Rights Here and Beyond." In *Sociology and Human Rights: A Bill of Rights for the Twenty-First Century,* edited by J. Blau and M. Frezzo. Newbury Park, CA: Pine Forge Press.

Sáenz, Rogelio, Maria Cristina Morales, and Maria Isabel Ayala. 2004. "United States: Immigration to the Melting Pot of the Americas." In *Migration and Immigration: A Global View,* edited by M. I. Toro-Morn and M. Alicea, 211–232. Westport, CT: Greenwood Press.

Sáenz, Rogelio, and Lorena Murga. 2011. *Latino Issues: A Reference Handbook.* Santa Barbara, CA: ABC-CLIO.

Safran, S. P. 2001. "Movie Images of Disability and War: Framing History and Political Ideology." *Remedial and Special Education* 22: 223–232.

Said, Edward W. 1979. *Orientalism.* 1st ed. Vintage.

Saito, Leland T. 1998. *Race and Politics: Asian Americans, Latinos, and Whites in a Los Angeles Suburb.* Chicago: University of Illinois Press.

———. 2009. *The Politics of Exclusion: The Failure of Race-Neutral Policies in Urban America.* Palo Alto, CA: Stanford University Press.

Salvo, J. J., M. G. Powers, and R. S. Cooney. 1992. "Contraceptive Use and Sterilization among Puerto Rican Women." *Family Planning Perspectives* 24, no. 5: 219–223.

Salzinger, Leslie. 2005. *Genders in Production: Making Workers in Mexico's Global Factories.* Berkeley: University of California Press.

Sampson, Robert J., and Stephen W. Raudenbush. 1999. "Systematic Social Observation of Public Spaces: A New Look at Disorder in Urban Neighborhoods." *American Journal of Sociology* 105: 603–651.

Sampson, Robert J., Patrick Sharkey, and Stephen W. Raudenbush. 2008. "Durable Effects of Concentrated Disadvantage on Verbal Ability among African-American Children." *Proceedings of the National Academy of Sciences of the United States of America* 105, no. 3: 845–852.

Sampson, Robert J., and William J. Wilson. 1995. "Toward a Theory of Race, Crime, and Urban Inequality." In *Crime and Inequality,* edited by John Hagan and Ruth D. Peterson, 37–54. Stanford, CA: Stanford University Press.

San Miguel, Guadalupe. 2005. *Brown, Not White: School Integration and the Chicano Movement in Houston.* College Station: Texas A&M University Press.

Sanbonmatsu, John, ed. 2011. *Critical Theory and Animal Liberation.* Lanham, MD: Rowman & Littlefield.

Sanchez-Jankowski, Martin. 2008. *Cracks in the Pavement: Social Change and Resilience in Poor Neighborhoods.* Berkeley: University of California Press.

Sanders, Joseph. 1990. "The Interplay of Micro and Macro Processes in the Longitudinal Study of Courts: Beyond the Durkheimian Tradition." *Law and Society Review* 24, no. 2: 241–256.

BIBLIOGRAPHY 195

Sanderson, Matthew R., and Jeffrey D. Kentor. 2008. "Foreign Direct Investment and International Migration: A Cross-National Analysis of Less-Developed Countries, 1985–2000." *International Sociology* 23, no. 4: 514–539.

Sanderson, Stephen K. 2001. *The Evolution of Human Sociality*. Lanham, MD: Rowman & Littlefield.

———. 2007. "Marvin Harris, Meet Charles Darwin: A Critical Evaluation and Theoretical Extension of Cultural Materialism." In *Studying Societies and Cultures: Marvin Harris's Cultural Materialism and Its Legacy*, edited by Lawrence A. Kuznar and Stephen K. Sanderson, 194–228. Boulder, CO: Paradigm Publishers.

———. 2008. "Adaptation, Evolution, and Religion." *Religion* 38: 141–156.

Sanford, Victoria. 2003. *Buried Secrets: Truth and Human Rights in Guatemala*. New York: Palgrave Macmillan.

Santos, B. S. 2009. "A Non-Occidentalist West? Learned Ignorance and Ecology of Knowledge." *Theory, Culture and Society* 26, no. 7–8: 103–125.

Sarbin, T. R., and E. Keen. 1998. "Classifying Mental Disorders: Nontraditional Approaches." In *Encyclopedia of Mental Health*, edited by H. S. Friedman, 2:461–473. San Diego: Academic Press.

Sarver, Joshua H., Susan W. Hinze, Rita K. Cydulka, and David W. Baker. 2003. "Racial/Ethnic Disparities in Emergency Department Analgesic Prescription." *American Journal of Public Health* 93, no. 12: 2067–2073.

Sassen, Saskia, ed. 1989. "America's 'Immigration Problem.'" *World Policy* 6: 811–832.

———. 1999. *Globalization and Its Discontents: Essays on the New Mobility of People and Money*. New York: The New Press.

———. 2001. *The Global City: New York, London, Tokyo*. Updated ed. Princeton, NJ: Princeton University Press.

———. 2006a. *Cities in a World Economy*. 3rd ed. Boulder, CO: Pine Forge Press.

———. 2006b. *Territory, Authority, Rights: From Medieval to Global Assemblages*. Princeton, NJ: Princeton University Press.

———, ed. 2007. *Deciphering the Global: Its Spaces, Scales and Subjects*. New York: Routledge.

Satterthwaite, Margaret L. 2005. "Crossing Borders, Claiming Rights: Using Human Rights Law to Empower Women Migrant Workers." *Yale Human Rights and Development Law Journal* 8: 1–66.

Savage, Joanne, and Bryan J. Vila. 2003. "Human Ecology, Crime, and Crime Control: Linking Individual Behavior and Aggregate Crime." *Social Biology* 50: 77–101.

Savelsberg, Joachim J. 2010. *Crime and Human Rights: Criminology of Genocide and Atrocities*. London: Sage.

Savelsberg, Joachim J., and Ryan D. King. 2007. "Law and Collective Memory." *Annual Review of Law and Social Science* 3: 189–211.

———. 2011. *American Memories: Atrocities and the Law*. New York: Russell Sage.

Scambler, Graham. 2004. *Medical Sociology, Major Themes in Health and Social Welfare*. New York: Taylor and Francis.

Scarritt, James R. 1985. "Socialist States and Human Rights Measurement in Africa." *Africa Today* 32, no. 1/2: 25–36.

Scheff, Thomas J. 1988. "Shame and Conformity: The Deference-Emotion System." *American Sociological Review* 53: 395–406.

———. 1990a. *Microsociology: Discourse, Emotion, and Social Structure*. Chicago: University of Chicago Press.

———. 1990b. "Socialization of Emotions: Pride and Shame as Causal Agents." In *Research Agendas in the Sociology of Emotions*, edited by T. D. Kemper, 281–304. Albany: State University of New York Press.

———. 1994. *Bloody Revenge: Emotions, Nationalism, and War*. Boulder, CO: Westview.

———. 1999. *Being Mentally Ill: A Sociological Theory*. 3rd ed. New York: Aldine De Gruyter.

———. 2000. "Shame and the Social Bond: A Sociological Theory." *Sociological Theory* 18, no. 1: 84–99.

Scheff, Thomas J., and Suzanne M. Retzinger. 1991. *Emotions and Violence: Shame and Rage in Destructive Conflicts*. Lexington, MA: Lexington Books.

Schegloff, Emanuel A. 2007a. "A Tutorial on Membership Categorization." *Journal of Pragmatics* 39: 462–482.

———. 2007b. "Categories in Action: Person-Reference and Membership Categorization." *Discourse Studies* 9: 433–461.

———. 2007c. *Sequence Organization in Interaction: A Primer in Sequential Analysis*. Vol. 1. Cambridge, UK: Cambridge University Press.

Schegloff, Emanuel A., Gail Jefferson, and Harvey Sacks. 1977. "The Preference for Self-Correction in the Organization of Repair in Conversation." *Language* 53, no. 2: 361–382.

196 BIBLIOGRAPHY

Scheid, T. L. 2005. "Stigma as a Barrier to Employment: Mental Disability and the Americans with Disabilities Act." *International Journal of Law and Psychiatry* 28: 670–690.

Schenkein, Jim. 1978. "Sketch of an Analytic Mentality for the Study of Conversational Interaction." In *Studies in the Organization of Conversational Interaction*, edited by Jim Schenkein, 1–6. New York: Academic.

Schnittker, Jason. 2008. "Happiness and Success: Genes, Families, and the Psychological Effects of Socioeconomic Position and Social Support." *American Journal of Sociology* 114: S233–S259.

Schofer, Evan, and John W. Meyer. 2005. "The Worldwide Expansion of Higher Education in the Twentieth Century." *American Sociological Review* 70: 898–920.

Schrag, Peter. 2002. "A Quagmire for Our Time: The War on Drugs." *Journal of Public Health Policy* 23, no. 3: 286–298.

Schrecker, Ellen. 1986. *No Ivory Tower: McCarthyism and the Universities*. Oxford: Oxford University Press.

Schulz, William F. 2009. *Power of Justice: Applying International Human Rights Standards to American Domestic Practices*. Washington, DC: Center for American Progress.

Schulze, B., and M. C. Angermeyer. 2003. "Subjective Experiences of Stigma: Schizophrenic Patients, Their Relatives and Mental Health Professionals." *Social Science and Medicine* 56: 299–312.

Schwalbe, Michael L., and Douglas Mason-Schrock. 1996. "Identity Work as Group Process." In *Advances in Group Processes*, edited by Barry Markovsky, Michael J. Lovaglia, and Robin Simon, 13:113–147. Greenwich, CT: JAI Press.

Schwartz, Pepper, and Virginia Rutter. 1998. *The Gender of Sexuality*. Lanham, MD: AltaMira Press.

Schwartz, Shalom H. 1992. "Universals in the Content and Structure of Values: Theoretical Advances and Empirical Tests in 20 Countries." In *Advances in Experimental Social Psychology*, edited by Mark P. Zanna, 24: 1–65. San Diego: Academic Press.

———. 2006. "Basic Human Values: Theory, Measurement, and Applications." *Revue Française de Sociologie* 47: 249–288.

Schwartz, Shalom H., and Galit Sagie. 2000. "Value Consensus and Importance: A Cross-National Study." *Journal of Cross-Cultural Psychology* 31, no. 4: 465–497.

Schwed, Uri, and Peter Bearman. 2010. "The Temporal Structure of Scientific Consensus Formation." *American Sociological Review* 75: 817–840.

Schwerner, Cassie. 2005. "Building the Movement for Education Equity." In *Rhyming Hope and History: Activists, Academics, and Social Movement Scholarship*, edited by David Croteau, William Hoynes, and Charlotte Ryan, 157–175. Minneapolis: University of Minnesota Press.

Scimecca, Joseph A. 1976. "Paying Homage to the Father: C. Wright Mills and Radical Sociology." *Sociological Quarterly* 17: 180–196.

Scott, J. 2000. "Rational Choice Theory." In *Understanding Contemporary Society: Theories of the Present*, edited by G. Browning, A. Halcli, and F. Webster, 126–138. London: Sage.

Scott, W. Richard. 1998. *Organizations: Rational, Natural and Open Systems*. 4th ed. New Brunswick, NJ: Prentice Hall.

———. 2001. *Institutions and Organizations*. 2nd ed. Thousand Oaks, CA: Sage.

Scott, Tony. 2004. "Teaching the Ideology of Assessment." *Radical Teacher* 71: 30–37.

Scruton, Roger. 2000. *Animal Rights and Wrongs*. London: Claridge Press.

Scull, A. T. 1984. *Decarceration: Community Treatment and the Deviant—a Radical View*. Cambridge, UK: Polity Press.

Segura, Denise. 1989. "Chicana and Mexican Immigrant Women at Work: The Impact of Class, Race, and Gender on Occupational Mobility." *Gender and Society* 3: 37–52.

Seiwert, Hubert. 1999. "The German Enquete Commission on Sects: Political Conflicts and Compromises." *Social Justice Research* 12: 323–340.

———. 2003. "Freedom and Control in the Unified Germany: Governmental Approaches to Alternative Religions since 1989." *Sociology of Religion* 64: 367–375.

Sekulic, D., G. Massey, and R. Hodson. 2006. "Ethnic Intolerance and Ethnic Conflict in the Dissolution of Yugoslavia." *Ethnic and Racial Studies* 29: 797–827.

Selmi, Patrick, and Richard Hunter. 2001. "Beyond the Rank and File Movement: Mary Van Kleeck and Social Work Radicalism in the Great Depression, 1931–1942." *Journal of Sociology and Social Welfare* 28: 75–100.

Seltzer, William, and Margo Anderson. 2002. "Using Population Data Systems to Target Vulnerable Population Subgroups and Individuals: Issues and Incidents." In *Statistical Methods for Human Rights*, edited by Jana Asher, David Banks, and Fritz J. Scheuren, 273ff. New York: Springer.

Selznick, Philip. 1947. *TVA and the Grass Roots*. Berkeley and Los Angeles: University of California Press.

———. 1957. *Leadership in Administration: A Sociological Interpretation*. New York: Harper and Row.

———. 1959. "The Sociology of the Law." In *Sociology Today: Problems and Prospects*, edited by Robert K. Merton, Leonard Broom, and Leonard Cottrell Jr., 115–127. New York: Basic Books.

Sen, Amartya. 1981. *Poverty and Famines: An Essay on Entitlement and Deprivation*. New York: Oxford University Press.

———. 1992. *Inequality Reexamined*. New York: Russell Sage Foundation.

———. 1999a. "Democracy as a Universal Value." *Journal of Democracy* 10: 3–17.

———. 1999b. *Development as Freedom*. New York: Random House.

———. 2006. *Identity and Violence: The Illusion of Destiny*. New York: W. W. Norton and Co.

Sengupta, Amit. 2003. "Health in the Age of Globalization." *Social Scientist* 31, no. 11–12: 66–85.

Serrano, P. A., and L. Magnusson, eds. 2007. *Reshaping Welfare States and Activation Regimes in Europe*. Brussels and New York: PIE–Peter Lang.

Serrano, Susan K., and Dale Minami. 2003. *"Korematsu vs. United States*: A 'Constant Caution' in a Time of Crisis." *Asian Law Journal* 10: 37–50.

Settersten, R. A., Jr. 2005. "Linking the Two Ends of Life: What Gerontology Can Learn from Childhood Studies." *Journals of Gerontology, Series B: Psychological Sciences* 60B, no. 4: 173–180.

Settersten, R. A., Jr., and J. L. Angel, eds. 2011. *Handbook of Sociology of Aging*. New York: Springer.

Settersten, R. A., Jr., and G. Hagestad. 1996a. "What's the Latest? Cultural Age Deadlines for Family Transitions." *Gerontologist* 36, no. 2: 178–188.

———. 1996b. "What's the Latest II: Cultural Age Deadlines for Educational and Work Transitions." *Gerontologist* 36, no. 5: 602–613.

Settersten, Richard, and Barbara E. Ray. 2010. *Not Quite Adults: Why 20-Somethings Are Choosing a Slower Path to Adulthood, and Why It's Good for Everyone*. New York: Bantam.

Sevigny, R. 2010. Personal communication with J. M. Fritz. December 14.

Shah, Natubhai. 1998. *Jainism: The World of Conquerors*. Sussex, UK: Sussex Academic Press.

Shakespeare, T., and N. Watson. 2001. "The Social Model of Disability: An Outdated Ideology?" In *Exploring Theories and Expanding Methodologies: Where We Are and Where We Need to Go*, edited by S. N. Barnartt and B. M. Altman, 2:9–28. Oxford, UK: Elsevier Science.

Shakespeare, Tom. 2006. *Disability Rights and Wrongs*. New York: Routledge.

Shanahan, Michael J., Shawn Bauldry, and Jason Freeman. 2010. "Beyond Mendel's Ghost." *Contexts* 9: 34–39.

Shanahan, Michael J., Stephen Vaisey, Lance D. Erickson, and Andrew Smolen. 2008. "Environmental Contingencies and Genetic Propensities: Social Capital, Educational Continuation, and Dopamine Receptor Gene DRD2." *American Journal of Sociology* 114: S260–S286.

Shanks, Cheryl, Harold K. Jacobson, and Jeffrey H. Kaplan. 1996. "Inertia and Change in the Constellation of International Governmental Organizations, 1981–1992." *International Organization* 50: 593–627.

Sharrock, W. W. 1980. "The Possibility of Social Change." In *The Ignorance of Social Intervention*, edited by D. C. Anderson, 117–133. London: Croom Helm.

———. 2001. "Fundamentals of Ethnomethodology." In *Handbook of Social Theory*, edited by George Ritzer and Barry Smart, 250–259. London: Sage.

Sharrock, W. W., and D. R. Watson. 1988. "Autonomy among Social Theories: The Incarnation of Social Structures." In *Actions and Structure: Research Methods and Social Theory*, edited by Nigel Fielding, 56–77. London: Sage.

Sharrock, Wes, and Bob Anderson. 1991. "Epistemology: Professional Skepticism." In *Ethnomethodology and the Human Sciences*, edited by Graham Button, 51–76. Cambridge, UK: Cambridge University Press.

Sharrock, Wes, and Graham Button. 1991. "The Social Actor: Social Action in Real Time." In *Ethnomethodology and the Human Sciences*, edited by Graham Button, 137–175. Cambridge, UK: Cambridge University Press.

Shaw, Martin. 2000. *The Theory of the Global State: Globality as Unfinished Revolution*. Oxford: Cambridge University Press.

Shell-Duncan, B. 2008. "From Health to Human Rights: Female Genital Cutting and the Politics of Intervention." *American Anthropologist* 110: 225–236.

Shergill, S. S., D. Barker, and M. Greenberg. 1998. "Communication of Psychiatric Diagnosis." *Social Psychiatry and Psychiatric Epidemiology* 33: 32–38.

Shevelow, Kathryn. 2008. *For the Love of Animals: The Rise of the Animal Protection Movement*. New York: Henry Holt and Co.

Shields, Joseph, Kirk M. Broome, Peter J. Delany, Bennett W. Fletcher, and Patrick M. Flynn. 2007. "Religion and Substance Abuse Treatment: Individual and Program Effects." *Journal for the Scientific Study of Religion* 46, no. 3: 355–371.

Shils, Edward. 1968. "Deference." In *Social Stratification*, edited by John A. Jackson, 104–132. Cambridge, UK: Cambridge University Press.

198 BIBLIOGRAPHY

———. 1975. *Center and Periphery: Essays in Macrosociology*. Chicago: University of Chicago Press.

Shin, Y., and S. Raudenbush. 2011. "The Causal Effect of Class Size on Academic Achievement: Multivariate Instrumental Variable Estimators with Data Missing at Random." *Journal of Educational and Behavioral Statistics* 34, no. 2: 154–185.

Shirazi, Farid, Ojelanki Ngwenyama, and Olga Morawczynski. 2010. "ICT Expansion and the Digital Divide in Democratic Freedoms: An Analysis of the Impact of ICT Expansion, Education and ICT Filtering on Democracy." *Telematics and Informatics* 27: 21–31.

Shiva, Vandana. 1997. *Biopiracy: The Plunder of Nature and Knowledge*. Cambridge, MA: South End Press.

Shor, Eran. 2008. "Conflict, Terrorism, and the Socialization of Human Rights Norms: The Spiral Model Revisited." *Social Problems* 55, no. 1: 117–138.

Shor, Ira. 1992. *Empowering Education: Critical Teaching for Social Change*. Portsmouth, NH: Heinemann.

Shorter, Edward. 1977. *The Making of the Modern Family*. New York: Basic Books.

Shostak, Sara, and Jeremy Freese. 2010. "Gene-Environment Interaction and Medical Sociology." In *Handbook of Medical Sociology*, edited by Chloe Bird, Peter Conrad, Allen Fremont, and Stephan Timmermans, 418–434. 6th ed. Nashville, TN: Vanderbilt University Press.

Shukin, Sharon. 2009. *Animal Capital: Rendering Life in Biopolitical Times*. Minneapolis: University of Minnesota Press.

Shupe, Anson D. 1998. *Wolves within the Fold: Religious Leadership and Abuses of Power*. New Brunswick, NJ: Rutgers University Press.

———. 2007. *Spoils of the Kingdom: Clergy Misconduct and Religious Community*. Urbana: University of Illinois Press.

Shura, Robin, Rebecca A. Siders, and Dale Dannefer. 2010. "Culture Change in Long-Term Care: Participatory Action Research and the Role of the Resident." *Gerontologist* 51, no. 2: 212–225.

Shuval, Judith T. 2001. "Migration, Health and Stress." In *The Blackwell Companion to Medical Sociology*, edited by W. Cockerham, 126–143. Oxford, UK: Blackwell.

Shwed, U., and Peter Bearman. 2010. "The Temporal Structure of Scientific Consensus Formation." *American Sociological Review* 75, no. 6: 817–840.

Sibley, David. 1995a. "Gender, Science, Politics and Geographies of the City." *Gender, Place and Culture: A Journal of Feminist Geography* 2: 37–50.

———. 1995b. "Women's Research on Chicago in the Early 20th Century." *Women and Environments* 14, no. 2: 6–8.

SIECUS. 1917. *Der Krieg und die Geistigen Entscheidungen*. Munich: Duncker and Humblot.

———. 1950. *The Sociology of Georg Simmel*. Translated by Kurt H. Wolff. New York: The Free Press.

———. 1955. *Conflict and the Web of Group Affiliations*. Glencoe, IL: The Free Press.

———. 2010. "Fact Sheet: State by State Decisions: The Personal Responsibility Education Program and Title V Abstinence-Only Program." http://www.siecus.org/index.cfm?fuseaction=Page.View Page&PageID=1272 (accessed September 5, 2012).

Sienkiewicz, Dorota. 2010. "Access to Health Services in Europe." *European Social Watch Report* 2010: 17–20.

Sigmon, Robert. 1990. "Service Learning: Three Principles." In *Combining Service and Learning: A Resource Book for Community and Public Service*, edited by Jane Kendall and Associates, 1: 56–64. Raleigh, NC: National Society for Internships and Experiential Education.

Sikkink, Kathryn. 2011. *Justice Cascade*. New York: Knopf.

Sikkink, Kathryn, and Hunjoon Kim. 2009. "Explaining the Deterrence Effect of Human Rights Prosecutions in Transitional Countries." *International Studies Quarterly*.

Silbey, Susan. 2005. "Everyday Life and the Constitution of Legality." In *The Blackwell Companion to the Sociology of Culture*, edited by Mark D. Jacobs and Nancy Weiss Hanrahan, 332–345. Malden, MA: Blackwell.

Silvers, A. 1998a. "Formal Justice." In *Disability, Difference, Discrimination: Perspectives on Justice in Bioethics and Public Policy*, edited by A. Silvers, D. Wasserman, and M. B. Mahowald, 13–145. Lanham, MD: Rowman & Littlefield.

———. 1998b. "Introduction." In *Disability, Difference, Discrimination: Perspectives on Justice in Bioethics and Public Policy*, edited by A. Silvers, D. Wasserman, and M. B. Mahowald, 1–12. Lanham, MD: Rowman & Littlefield.

Simmel, Georg. 1968. "The Conflict in Modern Culture." In *The Conflict in Modern Culture and Other Essays*, edited and translated by K. Peter Etzkorn. New York: Teachers College Press.

———. 1990. *The Philosophy of Money*. London: Routledge.

Simon, H. 1957. *Models of Man, Social and Rational: Mathematical Essays on Rational Human Behavior in a Social Setting*. New York: Wiley.

BIBLIOGRAPHY 199

Simon, Herbert Alexander. 1947. *Administrative Behavior: A Study of Decision-Making Processes in Administrative Organization*. New York: Macmillan.
Simon, Karla W. 2010. "International Non-Governmental Organizations and Non-Profit Organizations." *International Lawyer* 44: 399–414.
Sims, Beth. 1992. *Workers of the World Undermined: American Labor's Role in U.S. Foreign Policy*. Boston: South End Press.
Singer, Peter. 1993. *Practical Ethics*. 2nd ed. Cambridge, UK: Cambridge University Press.
———. 2005. *Animal Liberation*. New York: Harper Perennial.
———. 2009. *The Life You Can Save*. New York: Random House.
Sinha, Mrinalini, Donna Guy, and Angela Woollacott, eds. 1999. *Feminisms and Internationalism*. Oxford, UK: Blackwell Publishers.
Sjoberg, Gideon. 1999. "Some Observations on Bureaucratic Capitalism: Knowledge about What and Why?" In *Sociology for the Twenty-First Century: Continuities and Cutting Edges*, edited by Janet Abu-Lughod, 43–64. Chicago: University of Chicago Press.
Sjoberg, Gideon., E. A. Gill, B. Littrell, and N. Williams. 1997. "The Reemergence of John Dewey and American Pragmatism." *Studies in Symbolic Interaction* 23: 73–92.
Sjoberg, Gideon., E. A. Gill, and J. E. Tan. 2003. "Social Organization." In *Handbook of Symbolic Interactionism*, edited by Larry T. Reynolds and Nancy J. Herman-Kinney, 411–432. New York: AltaMira Press.
Sjoberg, Gideon., E. A. Gill, N. Williams, and K. E. Kuhn. 1995. "Ethics, Human Rights and Sociological Inquiry: Genocide, Politicide and Other Issues of Organizational Power." *American Sociologist* 26: 8–19.
Sjoberg, Gideon., and T. R. Vaughan. 1993. "The Ethical Foundations of Sociology and the Necessity for a Human Rights Alternative." In *A Critique of Contemporary American Sociology*, edited by T. R. Vaughan, G. Sjoberg, and L. T. Reynolds, 114–159. Dix Hills, NY: General Hall.
Sjoberg, Gideon, Elizabeth A. Gill, and Leonard Cain. 2003. "Counter System Analysis and the Construction of Alternative Futures." *Sociological Theory* 21, no. 3: 214–235.
Sjoberg, Gideon, Elizabeth A. Gill, and Norma Williams. 2001. "A Sociology of Human Rights." *Social Problems* 48, no. 1: 11–47.
Sklar, Martin J. 1988. *The Corporate Reconstruction of American Capitalism, 1890–1916: The Market, the Law, and Politics*. New York: Cambridge University Press.
Skocpol, Theda. 1979. *States and Social Revolutions: A Comparative Analysis of France, Russia, and China*. Cambridge, UK: Cambridge University Press.
———. 1984. "Sociology's Historical Imagination." In *Vision and Method in Historical Sociology*, edited by Theda Skocpol. New York and Cambridge, UK: Cambridge University Press.
———. 1992. *Protecting Soldiers and Mothers: The Political Origins of Social Policy in the United States*. Cambridge, MA: Belknap Press.
Skrentny, John D. 2002. *The Minority Rights Revolution*. Cambridge, MA: Harvard University Press.
Slovic, Paul. 2000. *The Perception of Risk*. London: Routledge.
Smaje, Chris. 2000. *Natural Hierarchies: The Historical Sociology of Race and Caste*. Malden, MA: Blackwell.
Small, Mario Luis. 2009. *Unanticipated Gains: Origins of Network Inequality in Everyday Life*. New York: Oxford University Press.
Smith, Adam. 2002 [1759]. *The Theory of Moral Sentiments*, edited by Knud Haakonssen. New York: Cambridge University Press.
Smith, Christian. 2010. *What Is a Person?* Chicago: University of Chicago Press.
Smith, Dorothy E. 1987. *The Everyday World as Problematic: A Feminist Sociology*. Toronto: University of Toronto Press.
———. 1990. *Texts, Facts, and Femininity: Exploring the Relations of Ruling*. New York: Routledge.
———. 1999. *Writing the Social: Critique, Theory, and Investigations*. Toronto: University of Toronto Press.
Smith, Jackie. 1999. "Human Rights and the Global Economy: A Response to Meyer." *Human Rights Quarterly* 21, no. 1: 80–92.
———. 2004. "Exploring Connections between Global Integration and Political Mobilization." *Journal of World-Systems Research* 10, no. 1: 255–285.
———. 2005. "Response to Wallerstein: The Struggle for Global Society in a World System." *Social Forces* 83, no. 3: 1279–1285.
———. 2008. *Social Movements and Global Democracy*. Baltimore: Johns Hopkins University Press.
Smith, Jackie, Melissa Bolyard, and Anna Ippolito. 1999. "Human Rights and the Global Economy: A Response to Meyer." *Human Rights Quarterly* 21, no. 1: 207–219.
Smith, Jackie, and Hank Johnston, eds. 2002. *Globalization and Resistance: Transnational Dimensions of Social Movements*. Lanham, MD: Rowman & Littlefield.

Smith, Jackie, Marina Karides, Marc Becker, Christopher Chase Dunn, Dorval Brunelle, Donnatella Della Porta, Rosalba Icaza, Jeffrey Juris, Lorenzo Mosca, Ellen Reese, Jay Smith, and Rolando Vasquez. 2008. *The World Social Forums and the Challenges for Global Democracy*. Boulder, CO: Paradigm Publishers.

Smith, Jackie, Ron Pagnucco, and George A. López. 1998. "Globalizing Human Rights: The Work of Transnational Human Rights NGOs in the 1990s." *Human Rights Quarterly* 20, no. 2: 379–412.

Smith, Jackie, and Dawn Wiest. 2005. "The Uneven Geography of Global Civil Society: National and Global Influences on Transnational Association." *Social Forces* 84, no. 2: 621–652.

Smith, Linda Tuhiwai. 1999. *Decolonizing Methodologies: Research and Indigenous Peoples*. New York: Zed Books.

———. 2005. "On Tricky Ground: Researching the Native in an Age of Uncertainty." In *Handbook of Qualitative Research*, edited by Norman Denzin and Yvonna Lincoln, 18–108. Beverly Hills, CA: Sage Publications.

Smith, Philip. 2008. *Punishment and Culture*. Chicago: University of Chicago Press.

Smith, Robert. 2005. *Mexican New York: Transnational Lives of New Immigrants*. Berkeley: University of California Press.

Smith, Sylvia. 2005. "The $100 Laptop—Is It a Wind-Up?" CNN.com. http://edition.cnn.com/2005/WORLD/africa/12/01/laptop (accessed January 23, 2010).

Smith, Thomas Spence. 2004. "Where Sociability Comes From: Neurosociological Foundations of Social Interaction." In *The Dialogical Turn: New Roles for Sociology in the Postdisciplinary Age*, edited by Charles Camic and Hans Joas, 199–220. Lanham, MD: Rowman & Littlefield.

Smith, Tom W. 2009. "National Pride in Comparative Perspective." In *The International Social Survey Programme, 1984–2009: Charting the Globe*, edited by Max Haller, Roger Jowell, and Tim W. Smith, 197–221. New York: Routledge.

Smith-Doerr, Laurel. 2004. *Women's Work: Gender Equality vs. Hierarchy in the Life Sciences*. Boulder, CO: Lynne Rienner Publishers.

Snipp, C. Matthew. 2003. "Racial Measurement in the American Census: Past Practices and Implications for the Future." *Annual Review of Sociology* 29: 563–588.

Snow, David A. 2004. "Framing Processes, Ideology, and Discursive Fields." In *The Blackwell Companion to Social Movements*, edited by David A. Snow, Sarah A. Soule, and Hanspeter Kreisi, 380–412. Oxford: Blackwell.

Snow, David A., and Leon Anderson. 1987. "Identity Work among the Homeless: The Verbal Construction and Avowal of Personal Identities." *American Journal of Sociology* 92: 1336–1371.

Snow, David, E. Burke Rochford Jr., Steven K. Worden, and Robert D. Benford. 1986. "Frame Alignment Processes, Micro-Mobilization and Movement Participation." *American Sociological Review* 51: 464–481.

Snyder, Howard. 2011. "Arrest in the United States: 1980–2009." Bureau of Justice Statistics. http://bjs.ojp .usdoj.gov/content/pub/pdf/aus8009.pdf (accessed October 2011).

Snyder, Jack, and Leslie Vinjamuri. 2003/2004. "Trials and Errors: Principle and Pragmatism in Strategies of International Justice." *International Security* 28: 5–44.

Sobell, L. C., M. B. Sobell, D. M. Riley, F. Klajner, G. I. Leo, G. Pavan, and A. Cancill. 1986. "Effect of Television Programming and Advertising on Alcohol Consumption in Normal Drinkers." *Journal Studies of Alcohol and Drugs* 47: 333–340.

Sok, Chivy, and Kenneth Neubeck. Forthcoming. "Building U.S. Human Rights Culture from the Ground Up: International Human Rights Implementation at the Local Level." In *In Our Own Backyard: Human Rights, Injustice, and Resistance in the United States*, edited by Bill Armaline, Bandana Purkayastha, and Davita Silfen Glasberg, 231–243. Philadelphia: University of Pennsylvania Press.

Soley, Lawrence. 1999. *Leasing the Ivory Tower: The Corporate Takeover of Academia*. Boston: South End Press.

Sombart, Werner. 1913. *Krieg und Kapitalismus*. Munich: Duncker and Humblot.

Somers, Margaret R. 2008. *Genealogies of Citizenship: Markets, Statelessness, and the Right to Have Rights*. New York: Cambridge University Press.

Somers, Margaret R., and Christopher Roberts. 2008. "Towards a New Sociology of Rights: A Genealogy of 'Buried Bodies' of Citizenship and Human Rights." *Annual Review of Law and Social Science* 4: 385–425.

Soohoo, Cynthia, Catherine Albisa, and Martha F. Davis, eds. 2008. *Bringing Human Rights Home: Portraits of the Movement*. Vol. 3. Westport, CT: Praeger.

Sorenson, John. 2011. "Constructing Extremists, Rejecting Compassion: Ideological Attacks on Animal Advocacy from Right and Left." In *Critical Theory and Animal Liberation*, edited by John Sanbonmatsu, 219–238. Lanham, MD: Rowman & Littlefield.

BIBLIOGRAPHY 201

Sørensen, Aage B. 1979. "A Model and a Metric for the Analysis of the Intragenerational Status Attainment Process." *American Journal of Sociology* 85: 361–84.

South African Human Rights Commission (SAHRC). 1998. *My Rights, Your Rights: Respect, Responsibilities and the SAHRC*. English ed. Pretoria: Government of South Africa.

Soysal, Yasemin. 1994. *Limits of Citizenship: Migrants and Postnational Membership in Europe*. Chicago: University of Chicago Press.

Speier, Matthew. 1973. *How to Observe Face-to-Face Communication: A Sociological Introduction*. Pacific Palisades, CA: Goodyear.

Spencer, Herbert. 1967. *Evolution of Society*. Chicago: University of Chicago Press.

Spirer, Herbert F. 1990. "Violations of Human Rights: How Many? The Statistical Problems of Measuring Such Infractions Are Tough, but Statistical Science Is Equal to It." *American Journal of Economics and Sociology* 49: 199–210.

Spring, Joel. 2000. *The Universal Right to Education*. Mahwah, NJ: Lawrence Erlbaum Associates.

———. 2007. *A New Paradigm for Global School Systems*. New York: Routledge.

Squires, Gregory, and Charis B. Kubrin. 2006. *Privileged Places: Race, Residence, and the Structure of Opportunity*. Boulder, CO: Lynne Rienner Publishers.

St. Jean, Peter K. B. 2007. *Pockets of Crime: Broken Windows, Collective Efficacy, and the Criminal Point of View*. Chicago: University of Chicago Press.

Stacey, Judith. 1988. "Can There Be a Feminist Ethnography?" *Women's Studies International Forum* 11: 21–27.

———. 1991. "Can There Be a Feminist Ethnography?" In *Women's Words*, edited by Sherna B. Gluck and Daphne Patai, 111–119. New York: Routledge.

Stack, Carol. 1974. *All Our Kin: Strategies for Survival in a Black Community*. New York: Harper and Row.

Stacy, Helen. 2009. *Human Rights in the 21st Century*. Stanford, CA: Stanford University Press.

Staggenborg, Suzanne. 1988. "The Consequences of Professionalization and Formalization in the Pro-Choice Movement." *American Sociological Review* 53, no. 4: 585–605.

Stammers, Neil. 1999. "Social Movements and the Social Construction of Human Rights." *Human Rights Quarterly* 21: 980–1008.

———. 2009. *Human Rights and Social Movements*. New York: Pluto Press.

Stamp Dawkins, Marian. 2006. "The Scientific Basis for Assessing Suffering of Animals." In *In Defense of Animals: The Second Wave*, edited by Peter Singer. Cambridge, MA: Blackwell Publishers.

Stanton, Timothy, Dwight Giles, and Nadine Cruz. 1999. *Service Learning: A Movement's Pioneers Reflect on Its Origins, Practice, and Future*. San Francisco, CA: Jossey-Bass.

Stark, Barbara. 1992–1993. "Economic Rights in the United States and International Law: Towards an Entirely New Strategy." *Hastings Law Journal* 44: 79–130.

Staudt, Kathleen. 1990. *Women, International Development, and Politics: The Bureaucratic Mire*. Philadelphia: Temple University Press.

———. 1997. "Gender Politics in Bureaucracy: Theoretical Issues in Comparative Perspective." In *Women, International Development, and Politics*, edited by Kathleen Staudt, 3–36. Philadelphia: Temple University Press.

Stearns, Peter N. 1994. *American Cool: Constructing a Twentieth-Century Emotional Style*. New York: New York University Press.

Stein, Dorothy. 1988. "Burning Widows, Burning Brides: The Perils of Daughterhood in India." *Pacific Affairs* 61: 465–485.

Steiner, Gary. 2010. *Anthropocentrism and Its Discontents: The Moral Status of Animals in the History of Western Philosophy*. Pittsburgh, PA: University of Pittsburgh Press.

Steiner, Henry J., Phillip Alston, and Ryan Goodman. 2008. *International Human Rights in Context: Law, Politics, Morals*. Oxford: Oxford University Press.

Steinmetz, George. 2007. *The Devil's Handwriting: Precoloniality and the German Colonial State in Qingdao, Samoa, and Southwest Africa*. Chicago: University of Chicago Press.

Steinmo, Sven, Kathleen Thelen, and Frank Longstreth, eds. 1992. *Structuring Politics: Historical Institutionalism in Comparative Analysis*. New York: Cambridge University Press.

Stephan, W. G., C. W. Stephan, and W. B. Gudykunst. 1999. "Anxiety in Intercultural Relations: A Comparison of Anxiety/Uncertainty Management Theory and Integrated Threat Theory." *International Journal of Intercultural Relations* 23: 613–628.

Stephens, Lowndes. 1979. "The Goebbels Touch." *Journal of Communication* 29: 2205–2206.

Stets, Jan E., and Emily K. Asencio. 2008. "Consistency and Enhancement Processes in Understanding Emotions." *Social Forces* 86: 1055–1078.

Stets, Jan E., and Jonathan H. Turner, eds. 2007. *Handbook of the Sociology of Emotions*. New York: Springer.

202 BIBLIOGRAPHY

Stevens, Fred. 2001. "The Convergence and Divergence of Modern Health Care Systems." In *The Blackwell Companion to Medical Sociology*, edited by William Cockerham, 159–176. Malden, MA: Blackwell Publishing.

Stevenson, Betsey, and Justin Wolfers. 2007. "Marriage and Divorce: Changes and Their Driving Forces." *Journal of Economic Perspectives* 21, no. 2: 27–52.

Stinchcombe, Arthur L. 1997. "On the Virtues of the Old Institutionalism." *Annual Review of Sociology* 23: 1–18.

Stolleis, Michael. 2007. "Law and Lawyers Preparing the Holocaust." *Annual Review of Law and Social Science* 3: 213–232.

Stover, Eric. 2005. *The Witnesses: War Crimes and the Promise of Justice in The Hague*. Philadelphia: University of Pennsylvania Press.

Straus, Scott, and Robert Lyons. 2006. *Intimate Enemy: Images and Voices of the Rwandan Genocide*. Cambridge, MA: MIT Press.

Strauss, Anselm L. 1978. *Negotiations*. New York: Wiley.

———. 1993. *Continual Permutations of Action*. New York: Aldine De Gruyter.

Streeck, Wolfgang. 1992. *Social Institutions and Economic Performance: Studies of Industrial Relations in Advanced Capitalist Economies*. London: Sage Publications.

Streeter, Sonya, Jhamirah Howard, Rachel Licata, and Rachel Garfield. 2011. "The Uninsured, a Primer: Facts about Americans without Health Insurance." Kaiser Family Foundation. http://www.kff.org/uninsured/upload/7451.pdf (accessed July 19, 2012).

Strickland, D. E. 1983. "Advertising Exposure, Alcohol Consumption and Misuse of Alcohol." In *Economics and Alcohol: Consumption and Controls*, edited by M. Grant, M. Plant, and A. Williams, 201–222. New York: Gardner.

Strom, Elizabeth A., and John H. Mollenkopf, eds. 2006. *The Urban Politics Reader*. New York: Routledge.

Stryker, Sheldon. 1980. *Symbolic Interactionism: A Social Structural Version*. Menlo Park, CA: Benjamin Cummings.

Stryker, Sheldon, and Kevin D. Vryan. 2003. "The Symbolic Interactionist Frame." In *Handbook of Social Psychology*, edited by John DeLamater, 3–28. New York: Kluwer.

Stuart, Alan, and J. Keith Ord. 1987. *Kendall's Advanced Theory of Statistics*. Vol. 1: *Distribution Theory*. 5th ed. Originally by Sir Maurice Kendall. New York: Oxford University Press.

Stuart, Tristram. 2006. *The Bloodless Revolution: A Cultural History of Vegetarianism from 1600 to Modern Times*. New York: W. W. Norton and Co.

Stuhr, John J. 2010. *100 Years of Pragmatism: William James's Revolutionary Philosophy*. Bloomington: Indiana University Press.

Substance Abuse and Mental Health Services Administration (SAMHSA). 2010. *Results from the 2009 National Survey on Drug Use and Health*. SAMHSA. http://oas.samhsa.gov/NSDUH/2k9NSDUH/2k9Results.htm#7.3.1 (accessed January 1, 2011).

Sunder, Madhavi. 2003. "Piercing the Veil." *Yale Law Journal* 112: 1401–1472.

Sutter, Molly Hazel. 2006. "Mixed-Status Families and Broken Homes: The Clash between the U.S. Hardship Standard in Cancellation of Removal Proceedings and International Law." *Transnational Law and Contemporary Problems* 783: 1–28.

Swedberg, Richard. 2010. "The Structure of Confidence and the Collapse of Lehman Brothers." In *Markets on Trial: The Economic Sociology of the U.S. Financial Crisis*, edited by Michael Lounsbury and Paul M. Hirsch, 71–114. Research in the Sociology of Organizations 30A. London: Emerald Group Publishing.

Swidler, Anne. 1986. "Culture in Action: Symbols and Strategies." *American Sociological Review* 51: 273–286.

Switzer, J. V. 2003. *Disabled Rights: American Disability Policy and the Fight for Equality*. Washington, DC: Georgetown University Press.

Symington, Alison. 2004. "Intersectionality: A Tool for Gender and Economic Justice." Association for Women's Rights in Development. http://www.awid.org/content/download/48805/537521/file/intersectionality_en.pdf (accessed September 17, 2012).

Szell, G. 1994. "Technology, Production, Consumption and the Environment." *International Social Science Journal* 140: 213–225.

Tabak, Mehmet. 2003. "Marxian Considerations on Morality, Justice, and Rights." *Rethinking Marxism* 15, no. 4: 523–540.

Tajfel, H. 1970. "Experiments in Intergroup Discrimination." *Scientific American* 223: 96–102.

Takacs-Santa, A. 2004. "The Major Transitions in the History of Human Transformation of the Biosphere." *Human Ecology Review* 11, no. 1: 51–66.

Takagi, Dana. 1994. "Maiden Voyage: Excursion into Sexuality and Identity Politics in Asian America." *Amerasia Journal* 20, no. 1: 1–17.

BIBLIOGRAPHY 203

Takeuchi, David T., Emily Walton, and ManChui Leung. 2010. "Race, Social Contexts and Health: Examining Geographic Spaces and Places." In *Handbook of Medical Sociology*, edited by Chloe Bird, Peter Conrad, Allen Fremont, and Stephan Timmermans, 92–105. 6th ed. Nashville, TN: Vanderbilt University Press.

Takeuti, N. 2010. Personal communication with J. M. Fritz. December 14.

Tarnas, Richard. 1991. *The Passion of the Western Mind: Understanding the Ideas that Have Shaped Our World View*. New York: Ballantine Books.

Tarrow, Sidney G. 1998. *Power in Movement: Social Movements and Contentious Politics*. New York and Cambridge, UK: Cambridge University Press.

———. 2005. *The New Transnational Activism*. New York: Cambridge University Press.

Tatum, Beverly Daniel. 2003. *"Why Are All the Black Kids Sitting Together in the Cafeteria?" and Other Conversations about Race*. New York: Basic Books.

Taylor, Frederick W. 1910. *The Principles of Scientific Management*. New York: Harper and Brothers.

Taylor, Greg. 2003. "Scientology in the German Courts." *Journal of Law and Religion* 19: 153–198.

Taylor, J. 1999. "The New Economics of Labour Migration and the Role of Remittances in the Migration Process." *International Migration* 37, no. 1: 63–68.

Tazreiter, Claudia. 2010. "Local to Global Activism: The Movement to Protect the Rights of Refugees and Asylum Seekers." *Social Movement Studies* 9, no. 2: 201–214.

Teitel, Ruti. 1997. "Human Rights Genealogy (Symposium: Human Rights on the Eve of the Next Century)." *Fordham Law Review* 66: 301–317.

———. 2000. *Transitional Justice*. Oxford: Oxford University Press.

TenHouten, Warren D. 2005. "Primary Emotions and Social Relations: A First Report." *Free Inquiry in Creative Sociology* 33, no. 2: 79–92.

Terl, Allan H. 2000. "An Essay on the History of Lesbian and Gay Rights in Florida." *Nova Law Review* 24 (spring): 793–853.

Thayer, Carlyle A. 2004. "Laos in 2003: Counterrevolution Fails to Ignite." *Asian Survey* 44, no. 1: 110–114.

Thayer-Bacon, Barbara. 2004. "An Exploration of Myles Horton's Democratic Praxis: Highlander Folk School." *Educational Foundation* 18, no. 2, 5–23.

Theil, Henri. 1967. *Economics and Information Theory*. Amsterdam: North-Holland.

Therborn, G. 1980. *The Ideology of Power and the Power of Ideology*. London: Verso.

Thomas, George. 2004. "Constructing World Civil Society through Contentions over Religious Rights." *Journal of Human Rights* 3: 239–251.

Thomas, George M. 1987. *Institutional Structure: Constituting State, Society, and the Individual*. Newbury Park, CA: Sage Publications.

———. 2001. "Religions in Global Civil Society." *Sociology of Religion* 62: 515–533.

Thomas, James. 2010. "The Racial Formation of Medieval Jews: A Challenge to the Field." *Ethnic and Racial Studies* 33: 1737–1755.

Thomas, James, and David Brunsma. 2008. "Bringing Down the House: Reparations, Universal Morality, and Social Justice." In *Globalization and America: Race, Human Rights, and Inequality*, edited by Angela Hattery, David G. Embrick, and Earl Smith, 65–81. Lanham, MD: Rowman & Littlefield.

Thomas, John, John W. Meyer, Francisco O. Ramirez, and John Boli. 1987. *Institutional Structure: Constituting State, Society, and the Individual*. Newbury Park, CA: Sage.

Thomas, Nigel, Brian K. Gran, and Karl Hansen. 2011. "An Independent Voice for Children's Rights in Europe? The Role of Independent Children's Rights Institutions in the EU." *International Journal of Children's Rights* 19, no. 3: 429–449.

Thomas, Robert J. 1994. *What Machines Can't Do: Politics and Technology in the Industrial Enterprise*. Berkeley: University of California Press.

Thomas, W. H. 2004. *What Are Old People For? How Elders Will Save the World*. Acton, MA: VanderWky and Burnham.

Thompson, E. P. 1963. *The Making of the English Working Class*. London: V. Gollancz.

———. 1978. *The Poverty of Theory*. London: Merlin Press.

Thompson, Silvanus P. 1946 [1910]. *Calculus Made Easy*. 3rd ed. New York: St. Martin's Press.

Thorne, B. 1993. *Gender Play: Boys and Girls in School*. Piscataway, NJ: Rutgers University Press.

Thorne, S., B. Paterson, S. Acorn, C. Canam, G. Joachim, and C. Jillings. 2002. "Chronic Illness Experience: Insights from a Metastudy." *Qualitative Health Research* 12, no. 4: 437–452.

Tiefer, Lenore. 2004. *Sex Is Not a Natural Act and Other Essays*. Boulder, CO: Westview Press.

Tilly, Charles. 1978. *From Mobilization to Revolution*. New York: McGraw-Hill Companies.

———. 1992. *Coercion, Capital and European States*. Oxford: Blackwell.

Timasheff, N. S. 1941. "Fundamental Problems of the Sociology of Law." *American Catholic Sociological Review* 2, no. 4: 233–248.

204   BIBLIOGRAPHY

Timmermans, S. 2001. "Social Death as Self-Fulfilling Prophecy." In *Sociology of Health and Illness: Critical Perspectives*, edited by P. Conrad, 305–321. New York: Worth.

Tinkler, Penny. 1995. *Constructing Girlhood*. Oxfordshire, UK: Taylor and Francis.

Tisdall, E. K. M. 2008. "Is the Honeymoon Over? Children and Young People's Participation in Public Decision-Making." *International Journal of Children's Rights* 16, no. 3: 343–354.

Tocqueville, Alexis de. 1960 [1835]. *Democracy in America*. New York: Alfred A. Knopf.

Tolman, Deborah L. 1994. "Doing Desire: Adolescent Girls' Struggles for/with Sexuality." *Gender and Society* 8, no. 3: 324–342.

Tomasevski, Katerina. 1995. *Women and Human Rights*. London: Zed Books.

Toney, Jeffery H., H. Kaplowitz, R. Pu, F. Qi, and G. Chang. 2010. "Science and Human Rights: A Bridge towards Benefiting Humanity." *Human Rights Quarterly* 32, no. 4: 1008–1017.

Tonry, Michael H. 1995. *Malign Neglect—Race, Crime, and Punishment in America*. New York: Oxford University Press.

Torres, Bob. 2007. *Making a Killing: The Political Economy of Animal Rights*. Oakland, CA: AK Press.

Toulmin, Stephen. 1953. *The Philosophy of Science: An Introduction*. London: Hutchinson.

———. 1978. "Science, Philosophy of." In *The New Encyclopaedia Britannica, Macropaedia* 16: 375–393. 15th ed. Chicago: Britannica.

Touraine, Alain. 1981. *The Voice and the Eye*. Cambridge, UK: Cambridge University Press.

———. 1983. *Solidarity: The Analysis of a Social Movement, Poland 1980–1981*. Cambridge, UK: Cambridge University Press.

Townsend, Peter. 2006. "Policies for the Aged in the 21st Century: More 'Structured Dependency' or the Realisation of Human Rights?" *Aging and Society* 26: 161–179.

Traer, Robert. 1991. *Faith in Human Rights: Support in Religious Traditions for a Global Struggle*. Washington, DC: Georgetown University Press.

Trevino, Javier A. 1996. *The Sociology of Law: Classical and Contemporary Perspectives*. New York: St. Martin's Press.

———. 1998. "The Influence of C. Wright Mills on Students for a Democratic Society: An Interview with Bob Ross." *Humanity and Society* 22: 260–277.

Tripp, Aili, and Myra Marx Ferree, eds. 2006. *Global Feminism: Transnational Women's Activism, Organizing, and Human Rights*. New York: New York University Press.

Trucios-Haynes, Inid. 2001. "Why 'Race Matters': LatCrit Theory and Latina/o Racial Identity." *La Raza Law Journal* 12, no. 1: 1–42.

Tsutsui, Kiyoteru. 2004. "Global Civil Society and Ethnic Social Movements in the Contemporary World." *Sociological Forum* 19, no. 1: 63–87.

Tuan, Mia. 1999. *Forever Foreigners or Honorary Whites? The Asian Ethnic Experience Today*. New Brunswick, NJ: Rutgers University Press.

Tuchman, Gaye. 2011. *Wannabe U: Inside the Corporate University*. Chicago: University of Chicago Press.

Turk, Austin. 1969. *Criminality and Legal Order*. Chicago: Rand McNally.

———. 1982. *Political Criminology*. Thousand Oaks: Sage.

Turmel, André. 2008. *A Historical Sociology of Childhood*. New York: Cambridge University Press.

Turner, Bryan S. 1993. "Outline of the Theory of Human Rights." In *Citizenship and Social Theory*, edited by Bryan S. Turner, 162–190. London: Sage.

———. 1995. "Symposium: Human Rights and the Sociological Project (Introduction)." *Australian and New Zealand Journal of Sociology* 31: 1–8.

———. 1996. *Vulnerability and Human Rights: Essays on Human Rights*. University Park: Penn State University Press.

———. 2002. "The Problem of Cultural Relativism for the Sociology of Human Rights: Weber, Schmitt and Strauss." *Journal of Human Rights* 1, no. 4: 587–605.

———. 2006. "Global Sociology and the Nature of Rights." *Societies without Borders* 1: 41–52.

———. 2010. "The Problem of Cultural Relativism for the Sociology of Human Rights: Weber, Schmitt and Straus." *Journal of Human Rights* 1, no. 4: 587–605.

Turner, Jonathan H. 2007. *Human Emotions: A Sociological Theory*. New York: Routledge.

Turner, Jonathan H., and Alexandra Maryanski. 2005. *Incest: The Origin of the Taboo*. Boulder, CO: Paradigm Publishers.

———. 2008. *On the Origins of Societies by Natural Selection*. Boulder, CO: Paradigm Publishers.

Turner, Jonathan H., and Jan E. Stets. 2005. *The Sociology of Emotions*. Cambridge, UK: Cambridge University Press.

———. 2006. "Sociological Theories of Human Emotions." *Annual Review of Sociology* 32: 25–52.

Turner, R. J., B. Wheaton, and D. A. Lloyd. 1995. "The Epidemiology of Social Stress." *American Sociological Review* 60: 104–125.

Turner, Ralph. 1976. "The Real Self: From Institution to Impulse." *American Journal of Sociology* 81: 989–1016.

Turner, Ralph H., and Steven Gordon. 1981. "The Boundaries of the Self: The Relationship of Authenticity in the Self-Conception." In *Self-Concept: Advances in Theory and Research*, edited by Mervin D. Lynch, Ardyth A. Norem-Hebeisen, and Kenneth J. Gergen, 39–57. Cambridge, MA: Ballinger.

Turner, Stephanie S. 1999. "Intersex Identities: Locating New Intersections of Sex and Gender." *Gender and Society* 13, no. 4: 457–479.

Turner, Stephen. 1977. "Blau's Theory of Differentiation: Is It Explanatory?" *Sociological Quarterly* 18: 17–32.

———. 2007. "A Life in the First Half-Century of Sociology: Charles Ellwood and the Division of Sociology." In *Sociology in America: A History*, edited by Craig Calhoun, 115–154. Chicago: University of Chicago Press.

Udehn, L. 2001. *Methodological Individualism. Background, History, and Meaning*. London: Routledge.

Udry, J. Richard. 2000. "Biological Limits of Gender Construction." *American Sociological Review* 65, no. 3: 443–457.

Uhlenberg, Peter. 2009a. "Children in an Aging Society." *Journals of Gerontology, Series B: Psychological Sciences* 64B: 489–496.

———, ed. 2009b. *International Handbook of Population Aging*. Dordrecht, The Netherlands: Springer.

Uhlenberg, Peter, and Michelle Cheuk. 2010. "The Significance of Grandparents to Grandchildren: An International Perspective." In *Sage Handbook of Social Gerontology*, edited by D. Dannefer and C. Phillipson, 447–458. London: Sage.

Uhlenberg, Peter, and Jenny de Jong Gierveld. 2004. "Age-Segregation in Later Life: An Examination of Personal Networks." *Ageing and Society* 24: 5–28.

Underhill, Kristen, Paul Montgomery, and Don Operario. 2007. "Systematic Review of Abstinence-Only Programmes Aiming to Prevent HIV Infection in High-Income Countries." *British Medical Journal* 335: 248.

United Nations. 1948. "The Universal Declaration of Human Rights." United Nations. www.un.org/en/documents/udhr/index.shtml (accessed December 10, 2010).

———. 1991. "The Protection of Persons with Mental Illness and the Improvement of Mental Health Care." United Nations. http://www.un.org/documents/ga/res/46/a46r119.htm (accessed November 10, 2010).

———. 1992. *Rio Declaration on Environment and Development*. 31 ILM874. United Nations. www.un-documents .net/rio-dec.htm (accessed January 20, 2012).

———. 1993. "Vienna Declaration and Programme of Action." Office of the United Nations High Commissioner for Human Rights. http://www.unhchr.ch/huridocda/huridoca.nsf/(symbol)/a.conf.157.23 .en (accessed July 20, 2012).

———. 1995. *UN Report of the Fourth World Conference on Women*. New York: United Nations.

———. 2000. "Gender and Racial Discrimination Report of the Expert Group Meeting." United Nations. http://www.un.org/womenwatch/daw/csw/genrac/report.htm (accessed January 11, 2012).

———. 2001. "Background Briefing on Intersectionality, Working Group on Women and Human Rights, 45th Session of the UN CSW." Center for Women's Global Leadership. http://www.cwgl.rutgers.edu/csw01/ background.htm (accessed March 31, 2011).

———. 2002. "Johannesburg Declaration on Sustainable Development." United Nations. http://www.un.org/ esa/sustdev/documents/WSSD_POI_PD/English/POI_PD.htm (accessed July 20, 2012).

———. 2007. "United Nations Declaration on the Rights of Indigenous Peoples." New York: Official Records of the General Assembly, Sixty-First Session, Supplement No. 53 (A/61/53), Pt. One, Ch. 2, Sect. A, and 107th Plenary Meeting, September 13.

———. 2008. "International Migrant Stock: The 2008 Revision." United Nations. http://esa.un.org/migration/ index.asp?panel=1 (accessed October 12, 2010).

———. 2009. *15 Years of the United Nations Special Rapporteur on Violence against Women, Its Causes and Consequences*. Office of the High Commissioner for Human Rights. http://www2.ohchr.org/english/issues/women/ rapporteur/docs/15YearReviewofVAWMandate.pdf (accessed January 11, 2012).

———. 2010. "Gender Dimensions of Agricultural and Rural Employment: Differentiated Pathways out of Poverty." UN Food and Agriculture Organization. http://www.fao.org/docrep/013/i1638e/i1638e00 .htm (accessed January 21, 2011).

United Nations Development Program (UNDP). 1987. *Brundtland Report*. New York: UNDP.

United Nations Educational Scientific and Cultural Organization (UNESCO). 1990. "Meeting Basic Learning Needs: A Vision for the 1990s." UNESCO. http://www.unesco.org/en/efa/the-efa-movement/jomtien-1990.

206 Bibliography

United Nations Food and Agriculture Organization (UNFAO). 2006. "Livestock's Long Shadow: Environmental Issues and Options." UNFAO. http://www.fao.org/docrep/010/a0701e/a0701e00.htm (accessed July 20, 2012).
———. 2010. *Gender Dimensions of Agricultural and Rural Employment: Differential Pathways out of Poverty*. Rome: UNFAO, International Fund for Agricultural Development, and International Labour Office.
United Nations High Commissioner for Refugees (UNHCR). 1966. "International Covenant on Economic, Social, and Cultural Rights." UNHCR. http://www2.ohchr.org/english/law/cescr.htm (accessed January 11, 2012).
———. 2010. "UNHCR Refugee Figures." UNHCR. http://www.unhcr.org/pages/49c3646c1d.html (accessed on January 11, 2012).
United Nations Human Development Reports. 2010. "The Real Wealth of Nations: Pathways to Human Development." UN Human Development Reports. http://hdr.undp.org/en/reports/global/hdr2010 (accessed July 20, 2012).
United Nations Human Rights Council. 2008. "Human Rights and Climate Change." UN Human Rights Council Resolution 7/23, March 28.
United Nations Office on Drugs and Crime (UNODC). 2010. *Drug Control, Crime and Prevention: A Human Rights Perspective*. International Centre on Human Rights and Drug Policy. http://www.humanrightsanddrugs.org/wp-content/uploads/2010/03/UNODC-Human-Rights-Conference-Paper. pdf (accessed January 1, 2011).
United States 111th Congress. 2009. *Afghan's Narco War: Breaking the Link between Drug Traffickers and Insurgents*. Government Printing Office. http://www.gpoaccess.gov/congress/index.html (accessed January 1, 2011).
United States Census Bureau. 2008. "U.S. Population Projections." US Census Bureau. http://www.census.gov/population/www/projections/summarytables.html (accessed January 29, 2012).
United States Department of Defense. 2003. *An Abrupt Climate Change Scenario and Its Implications for United States National Security*. Washington, DC: US Department of Defense.
United States Department of Health and Human Services. 2010. "Fact Sheet: Sex Trafficking." Administration for Children and Families. http://www.acf.hhs.gov/trafficking/about/fact_sex.html (accessed December 21, 2010).
United States Department of State. 2009. "2009 Human Rights Report: Singapore." US Department of State. http://www.state.gov/g/drl/rls/hrrpt/2009/eap/136008.htm (accessed October 1, 2011).
———. 2010a. "2010 Human Rights Report: Saudi Arabia." US Department of State. http://www.state.gov/documents/organization/160475.pdf (accessed October 1, 2012).
———. 2010b. "2010 Human Rights Report: China (Includes Tibet, Hong Kong, and Macau)." US Department of State. http://www.state.gov/g/drl/rls/hrrpt/2010/eap/154382.htm (accessed October 20, 2011).
United States Government Accountability Office (GAO). 2005. "Drug Offenders: Various Factors May Limit the Impacts of Federal Laws that Provide for Denial of Selected Benefits." GAO-05-238. GAO. http://www.gao.gov/new.items/d05238.pdf (accessed September 2011).
United States Human Rights Fund. 2010. *Perfecting Our Union: Human Rights Success Stories from across the United States*. New York: US Human Rights Fund.
United States Human Rights Network. 2011. http://www.ushrnetwork.org (accessed May 26, 2011).
United States National Institute of Standards and Technology (NIST). 2003. *Engineering Statistics Handbook*. NIST. http://www.itl.nist.gov/div898/handbook (accessed January 20, 2012).
University of Warwick, Sociology Department. n.d. "The Module in 10 Points." University of Warwick. http://www2.warwick.ac.uk/fac/soc/sociology/staff/emeritus/robertfine/home/teachingmaterial/humanrights/tenpoints (accessed January 1, 2011).
Unno, Mark T. 1999. "Review: Questions in the Making: A Review Essay on Zen Buddhist Ethics in the Context of Buddhist and Comparative Ethics." *Journal of Religious Ethics* 27, no. 3: 507–536.
Updegraff, K., A. Booth, and Shawna Thayer. 2006. "The Role of Family Relationship Quality and Testosterone Levels in Adolescents' Peer Experience: A Biosocial Analysis." *Family Psychology* 20: 21–29.
US Constitution Online. "U.S. Constitution—Amendment 1." 1791. US Constitution Online. http://www.usconstitution.net/xconst_Am1.html (accessed July 20, 2012).
Vaillancourt, Jean-Guy. 2010. "From Environmental Sociology to Global Ecosociology: The Dunlap-Buttel Debates." In *The International Handbook of Environmental Sociology*, edited by Michael R. Redclift and Graham Woodgate, 48–62. Northampton, MA: Edward Elgar Publishing.
Valentine, David. 2007. *Imagining Transgender: An Ethnography of a Category*. Durham, NC: Duke University Press.

BIBLIOGRAPHY 207

Valenzuela, Angela. 1999. *Subtractive Schooling*. Albany: State University of New York.

Valliant, George E. 1983. *The Natural History of Alcoholism*. Cambridge, MA: Harvard University Press.

Van Aelst, Peter, and Stefaan Walgrave. 2002. "New Media, New Movements? The Role of the Internet in Shaping the 'Anti-Globalization' Movement." *Information, Communication, & Society* 5, no. 4: 465–493.

Van Bockstaele, J., M. Van Bockstaele, J. Malbos, M. Godard-Plasman, and N. Van Bockstaele. 2008. "Socioanalysis and Clinical Intervention." In *International Clinical Sociology*, edited by J. M. Fritz, 170–187. New York: Springer.

Van den Berghe, Pierre L. 1979. *Human Family Systems*. New York: Elsevier.

———. 1981. *The Ethnic Phenomenon*. New York: Elsevier.

Van der Kroef, Justus M. 1976. "Indonesia's Political Prisoners." *Pacific Affairs* 49, no. 4: 625–647.

Van Krieken, Robert. 1999. "The 'Stolen Generations': On the Removal of Australian Indigenous Children from Their Families and Its Implications for the Sociology of Childhood." *Childhood* 6, no. 3: 297–311.

Van Sertima, Ivan. 1976. *They Came Before Columbus: The African Presence in Ancient America*. New York, NY: Random House.

Vanwesenbeeck, I. 1997. "The Context of Women's Power(lessness) in Heterosexual Interactions." In *New Sexual Agendas*, edited by L. Segal. New York: New York University Press.

Vaughan, Diane. 1999. "The Dark Side of Organizations: Mistake, Misconduct, and Disaster." *Annual Review of Sociology* 25: 271–305.

———. 2002. "Criminology and the Sociology of Organizations." *Crime, Law, and Social Change* 37: 117–136.

Vaughan, T. R., and G. Sjoberg. 1984. "The Individual and Bureaucracy: An Alternative Meadian Interpretation." *Journal of Applied Behavioral Science* 20: 57–69.

Vaughn, Michael G, Matt Delisi, Kevin M. Beaver, and John Paul Wright. 2009. "DAT1 and 5HTT Are Associated with Pathological Criminal Behavior in a Nationally Representative Sample of Youth." *Criminal Justice and Behavior* 36, no. 11: 1103–1114.

Vaughn, Ted R., Gideon Sjoberg, and Larry Reynolds, eds. 1993. *A Critique of Contemporary American Sociology*. Dix Hills, NY: General Hall.

Veblen, Thorstein. 1991. *The Theory of the Leisure Class*. Fairfield, CT: A. M. Kelley.

———. 1998. *The Nature of Peace*. New Brunswick, NJ: Transaction Publishers.

Vegans of Color. 2011. "Liberation Veganism." Vegans of Color. http://vegansofcolor.wordpress.com/tag/animal-rights (accessed March 28, 2011).

Velez, Veronica, Lindsay Perez Huber, Corina Benavides López, Ariana de la Luz, and Daniel G. Solorzano. 2008. "Battling for Human Rights and Social Justice: A Latina/o Critical Race Media Analysis of Latina/o Student Youth Activism in the Wake of 2006 Anti-Immigrant Sentiment." *Social Justice* 35, no. 1: 7–27.

Veltmeyer, Henry, and Mark Rushton. 2011. *The Cuban Revolution as Socialist Human Development*. Leiden, the Netherlands: Brill.

Venetis, Penny M. 2012. "Making Human Rights Treaty Law Actionable in the United States." *Alabama Law Review* 63, no. 1: 97–160.

Venkatesh, Sudhir Alladi. 2009. *Off the Books: The Underground Economy of the Urban Poor*. Cambridge, MA: Harvard University Press.

Verkutyten, Maykel, Jochem Thijs, and Hidde Bekhuis. 2010. "Intergroup Contact and Ingroup Reappraisal: Examining the Deprovincialization Thesis." *Social Psychology Quarterly* 73, no. 4: 358–379.

Vermeersch, Peter. 2003. "Ethnic Minority Identity and Movement Politics: The Case of the Roma in the Czech Republic and Slovakia." *Ethnic and Racial Studies* 26: 879–901.

Verrijn, Stuart, H. 2008. "The ICC in Trouble." *Journal of International Criminal Justice* 6: 409–417.

Vialles, Noelie. 1994. *Animal to Edible*. Translated by J. A. Underwood. Cambridge, UK: Cambridge University Press.

Vinck, Patrick, Phuong N. Pham, Laurel E. Fletcher, and Eric Stover. 2009. "Inequalities and Prospects: Ethnicity and Legal Status in the Construction Labor Force after Hurricane Katrina." *Organization and Environment* 22, no. 4: 470–478.

Virchow, R. 1848. *Die Medizinische Reform*. Berlin: Druck und Verlag von G. Reimer.

Viscusi, Kip W. 1998. "Constructive Cigarette Regulation." *Duke Law Journal* 47, no. 6: 1095–1131.

Volti, R. 1995. *Society and Technological Change*. New York: St. Martin's Press.

Voss, Kim. 1992. "Disposition Is Not Action: The Rise and Demise of the Knights of Labor." *Studies in American Political Development* 6: 272–321.

Wagner, David, and Joseph Berger. 1985. "Do Sociological Theories Grow?" *American Journal of Sociology* 90: 697–728.

208 BIBLIOGRAPHY

Wagner, Jon. 1999a. "Beyond the Body in a Box: Visualizing Contexts of Children's Action." *Visual Sociology* 14: 143–160.

———. 1999b. "Visual Sociology and Seeing Kids' Worlds." *Visual Sociology* 14.

Waites, Matthew. 2009. "Critique of 'Sexual Orientation' and 'Gender Identity' in Human Rights Discourse: Global Queer Politics beyond the Yogyakarta Principles." *Contemporary Politics* 15, no. 1: 137–156.

Waitzkin, H. 1981. "The Social Origins of Illness: A Neglected History." *International Journal of Health Services* 11: 77–103.

Wakefield, Sara E. L., and J. Baxter. 2010. "Linking Health Inequality and Environmental Justice: Articulating a Precautionary Framework for Research and Action." *Environmental Justice* 3, no. 3: 95–102.

Walby, Sylvia. 2007. "Introduction: Theorizing the Gendering of the Knowledge Economy: Comparative Approaches." In *Gendering the Knowledge Economy: Comparative Perspectives*, edited by Heidi Gottfried, Karin Gottschall, Mari Osawa, and Sylvia Walby, 3–50. Houndsmill, UK: Palgrave.

———. 2009. *Globalization and Inequalities: Complexity and Contested Modernities*. Los Angeles and London: Sage.

Wales, Steven. 2002. "Remembering the Persecuted: An Analysis of the International Religious Freedom Act." *Houston Journal of International Law* 24: 579–648.

Wallace, John, Ryoko Yamaguchi, Jerald G. Bachman, Patrick M. O'Malley, John E. Schulenberg, and Lloyd D. Johnston. 2007. "Religiosity and Adolescent Substance Use: The Role of Individual and Contextual Influences." *Social Problems* 54, no. 2: 308–327.

Wallace, Michael, Beth A. Rubin, and Brian T. Smith. 1988. "American Labor Law: Its Impact on Working-Class Militancy, 1901–1980." *Social Science History* 12: 1–29.

Wallerstein, Immanuel. 1974. *The Modern World System I: Capitalist Agriculture and the Origins of the European World-Economy in the Sixteenth Century*. New York: Academic Press.

———. 1979. *The Capitalist World System*. Cambridge, UK: Cambridge University Press.

———. 1980. *The Modern World System II: Mercantilism and the Consolidation of the European World Economy, 1600–1750*. New York: Academic Press.

———. 1983. *Historical Capitalism*. London: Verso.

———. 1984. *The Politics of the World-Economy: The States, the Movements, and the Civilizations*. Cambridge, UK: Cambridge University Press.

———. 2002. "The Itinerary of World Systems Analysis: or, How to Resist Becoming a Theory." In *New Directions in Contemporary Sociological Theory*, edited by Joseph Berger and Morris Zelditch, 358–376. Lanham, MD: Rowman & Littlefield.

———. 2005a. "After Development and Globalization, What?" *Social Forces* 83, no. 3: 1263–1278.

———. 2005b. "Render unto Caesar? The Dilemmas of a Multicultural World." *Sociology of Religion* 66: 121–133.

Walsh, Catherine. 2010. "De-Coloniality, Decolonial Thinking and Doing in the Andes: A Conversation by Walther Mignolo with Catherine Walsh." *Reartikulacija* 10–13. http://www.reartikulacija.org/?p=1468 (accessed February 25, 2011).

Walters, Kerry S., and Lisa Portness, eds. 1999. *Ethical Vegetarianism: From Pythagoras to Peter Singer*. Albany: State University of New York Press.

Walters, Suzanna Danuta. 2001. "Take My Domestic Partner, Please: Gays and Marriage in the Era of the Visible." In *Queer Families, Queer Politics: Challenging Culture and the State*, edited by Mary Bernstein and Renate Reimann, 338–357. New York: Columbia University Press.

Waltz, Kenneth N. 1979. *Theory of International Politics*. New York: Random House.

Wang, Guang-zhen, and Vijayan K. Pillai. 2001. "Women's Reproductive Health: A Gender-Sensitive Human Rights Approach." *Acta Sociologica* 44, no. 3: 231–242.

Wardell, Mark L., and Stephen P. Turner, eds. 1986. *Sociological Theory in Transition*. Boston: Allen and Unwin.

Waring, Marilyn. 2003. "Counting for Something! Recognising Women's Contributions to the Global Economy through Alternative Accounting Systems." *Gender and Development* 11, no. 1: 35–43.

Warner, R. 1994. *Recovery from Schizophrenia*. Routledge: London.

Warner, Michael. 2000. *The Trouble with Normal: Sex, Politics and the Ethics of Queer Life*. Cambridge, MA: Harvard University Press.

Warner-Smith, Penny, Lois Bryson, and Julie Ellen Byles. 2004. "The Big Picture: The Health and Well-Being of Women in Three Generations in Rural and Remote Areas of Australia." *Health Sociology Review* 13, no. 1: 15–26.

Warren, John T. 2001. "Doing Whiteness: On the Performative Dimensions of Race in the Classroom." *Communication Education* 50, no. 2: 91–108.

Washington, DC, City Council. 2008. "Washington D.C. Human Rights City Resolution." American Friends Service Committee. December 10. http://afsc.org/resource/washington-dc-human-rights-city-resolution (accessed May 24, 2011).

Washington, Silvia H. 2010. "Birth of a Sustainable Nation: The Environmental Justice and Environmental Health Movements in the United States." *Environmental Justice* 3, no. 2: 55–60.

Waters, Malcolm. 1995. "Globalisation and the Social Construction of Human Rights." Symposium: "Human Rights and the Sociological Project." *Australian and New Zealand Journal of Sociology* 31: 29–36.

———. 1996. "Human Rights and the Universalization of Interests: Towards a Social Constructionist Approach." *Sociology* 30, no. 3: 593–600.

Watkins-Hayes, Celeste. 2009. "Two-Faced Racism: Whites in the Backstage and Frontstage (review)." *Social Forces* 87: 2183–2185.

Watson, D. R. 1981. "Conversational and Organisational Uses of Proper Names: An Aspect of Counselor-Client Interaction." In *Medical Work: Realities and Routines*, edited by Paul Atkinson and Christian Heath, 91–106. Farnborough, UK: Gower.

———. 1983. "The Presentation of Victim and Motive in Discourse: The Case of Police Interrogations and Interviews." *Victimology* 8: 31–52.

———. 1984. "Racial and Ethnic Relations." In *Applied Sociological Perspectives*, edited by R. J. Anderson and W. W. Sharrock, 43–65. London: George Allen and Unwin.

———. 1997. "Some General Reflections on 'Categorization' and 'Sequence' in the Analysis of Conversation." In *Culture in Action: Studies in Membership Categorization Analysis*, edited by Stephen Hester and Peter Eglin, 49–75. Washington, DC: International Institute for Ethnomethodology and Conversation Analysis and University Press of America.

Weber, Bruce. 2011. "Harold Garfinkel, a Common-Sense Sociologist, Dies at 93." *New York Times*. May 3.

Weber, Max. 1946. "Religious Rejections of the World and Their Direction." In *From Max Weber*, edited by H. H. Gerth and C. Wright Mills, 24–26. New York: Oxford University Press.

———. 1948a. "Class, Status, Party." In *Max Weber: Essays in Sociology*, edited by H. H. Gerth and C. Wright Mills, 180–195. Oxford: Oxford University Press.

———. 1948b. "Politics as a Vocation." In *Max Weber: Essays in Sociology*, edited by H. H. Gerth and C. Wright Mills, 77–128. New York: Oxford: Oxford University Press.

———. 1949. *The Methodology of the Social Sciences*. New York: The Free Press.

———. 1968 [1920]. *Economy and Society*. Translated by Guenther Roth and Claus Wittich. 3 vols. Berkeley: University of California Press.

———. 1978. *Economy and Society*, edited by Guenther Roth and Claus Wittich. Berkeley: University of California Press.

———. 2002. *The Protestant Ethic and the Spirit of Capitalism*. London: Penguin Books.

———. 2007 [1914]. "Basic Sociological Terms." In *Classical Sociological Theory*, edited by Craig Calhoun et al., 211–227. New York: Blackwell.

———. 2011. *The Protestant Ethic and the Spirit of Capitalism*. Rev. 1920 ed. USA: Intercultural Publishing.

Weeramantry, C. G., ed. 1993. *The Impact of Technology on Human Rights: Global Case Studies*. Tokyo: United Nations University Press.

Weglyn, Michi Nishiura. 1976. *Years of Infamy: The Untold Story of America's Concentration Camps*. Seattle: University of Washington Press.

Weibel-Orlando, Joan C. 1989. "Pass the Bottle, Bro!: A Comparison of Urban and Rural Indian Drinking Patterns." In *Alcohol Use among U.S. Ethnic Minorities*, edited by D. Spiegler, D. Tate, S. Aitken, and C. Christian, 269–289. Rockville, MD: National Institute on Alcohol Abuse and Alcoholism.

Weinstein, J. 2010. *Social Change*. 3rd ed. Lanham, MD: Rowman & Littlefield.

Weir, Margaret. 1992. *Politics and Jobs: The Boundaries of Employment Policy in the United States*. Princeton, NJ: Princeton University Press.

Weis, L., ed. 2008. *The Way Class Works: Readings on School, Family, and the Economy*. New York: Routledge.

Weissbrodt, David S., and Clay Collins. 2006. "The Human Rights of Stateless Persons." *Human Rights Quarterly* 28, no. 1: 245–276.

Weitz, Eric D. 2003. *A Century of Genocide: Utopias of Race and Nation*. Princeton, NJ: Princeton University Press.

———. 2008. "From the Vienna to the Paris System: International Politics and the Entangled Histories of Human Rights, Forced Deportations, and Civilizing Missions." *American Historical Review* 113, no. 5: 1313–1343.

210 BIBLIOGRAPHY

Weitzer, Ronald, ed. 2000. *Sex for Sale: Prostitution, Pornography, and the Sex Industry*. New York: Routledge.

Wejnert, Barbara. 2005. "Diffusion, Development, and Democracy, 1800–1999." *American Sociological Review* 70: 53–81.

Wendt, Alexander. 1999. *Social Theory of International Politics*. Cambridge, UK: Cambridge University Press.

West, Nathaniel. 1841. "A Coppie of the Liberties of the Massachusetts Colonie in New England." In *American History Leaflets 25*, edited by Albert Bushnell Hart and Edward Channing. New York: A. Lovell and Co., 1896. http://www.lonang.com/exlibris/organic/1641-mbl.htm (accessed September 4, 2012).

Westra, Laura. 2011. *Globalization, Violence and World Governance*. Leiden, the Netherlands: Brill.

Whitbeck, Les B. 2009. *Mental Health and Emerging Adulthood among Homeless Young People*. New York: Psychology Press.

White, Geoffry D., ed. 2000. *Campus, Inc.: Corporate Power in the Ivory Tower*. New York: Prometheus Books.

White, Orion. 1974. "The Dialectical Organization: An Alternative to Bureaucracy." *Public Administration Review* 29, no. 1: 32–42.

Whitmeyer, Joseph M. 1997. "Endogamy as a Basis for Ethnic Behavior." *Sociological Theory* 15, no. 2: 162–178.

Whyte, William Foote. 1943. *Street Corner Society*. Chicago: University of Chicago Press.

Wieder, D. Lawrence. 1974. *Language and Social Reality: The Case of Telling the Convict Code*. The Hague: Mouton.

Wieviorka, Michael. 2005. "From Marx to Braudel and Wallerstein." *Contemporary Sociology* 34, no. 1: 1–7.

WILD for Human Rights. 2006. *Making Rights Real: A Workbook on the Local Implementation of Human Rights*. San Francisco: Women's Institute for Leadership Development for Human Rights.

Wilentz, Sean. 1984. "Against Exceptionalism: Class Consciousness and the American Labor Movement, 1790–1920." *International Labor and Working-Class History* 26: 1–24.

Wiley, Norbert. 1994. *The Semiotic Self*. Chicago: University of Chicago Press.

Wilkinson, Lindsey, and Jennifer Pearson. 2009. "School Culture and the Well-Being of Same-Sex-Attracted Youth." *Gender and Society* 23, no. 4: 542–568.

Wilkinson, Richard. 1992. "National Mortality Rates: The Impact of Inequality?" *American Journal of Public Health* 82: 1082–1084.

———. 1996. *Unhealthy Societies: The Afflictions of Inequality*. New York: Routledge.

Wilkinson, Richard, and Michael Marmot, eds. 2003. *Social Determinants of Health: The Solid Facts*. Geneva: World Health Organization.

William, Archbishop of Tyre. 1943. *A History of Deeds Done beyond the Sea*. Translated and annotated by Emily Atwater Babcock and A. C. Krey. New York: Columbia University Press.

Williams, B. 1994. "Patient Satisfaction—a Valid Concept?" *Social Science and Medicine* 38, no. 4: 509–516.

Williams, D. R., Y. Yu, J. S. Jackson, and N. B. Anderson. 1997. "Racial Differences in Physical and Mental Health: Socio-Economic Status, Stress and Discrimination." *Journal of Health Psychology* 2, no. 3: 335–351.

Williams, David R., and Michelle Sternthal. 2010. "Understanding Racial-Ethnic Disparities in Health: Sociological Contributions." *Journal of Health and Social Behavior* 51, no. 1: S15–S27.

Williams, William Appleman. 1962. *The Tragedy of American Diplomacy*. New York: Dell.

Williamson, Oliver E. 1985. *The Economic Institutions of Capitalism, Firms, Markets, Relational Contracting*. New York: The Free Press.

Willmott, Hugh, Todd Bridgman, and Mats Alvesson, eds. 2009. *The Oxford Handbook of Critical Management Studies*. New York: Oxford University Press.

Wilsnack, R. W., and R. Cheloha. 1987. "Women's Roles and Problem Drinking across the Lifespan." *Social Problems* 34: 231–248.

Wilson, Edward O. 1978. *On Human Nature*. Cambridge, MA: Harvard University Press.

Wilson, R. A. 1997. *Human Rights, Culture and Context: Anthropological Perspectives*. London: Pluto Press.

Wilson, William Julius. 1987. *The Truly Disadvantaged: The Inner City, the Underclass and Public Policy*. Chicago: University of Chicago Press.

———. 2009. *More Than Just Race: Being Black and Poor in the Inner City*. New York: W. W. Norton.

Winant, Howard. 2006. "Race and Racism: Towards a Global Future." *Ethnic and Racial Studies* 29, no. 5: 986–1003.

Winch, Peter. 2008. *The Idea of a Social Science and Its Relation to Philosophy*. 3rd ed. London: Routledge Classics.

Wines, Michael. 2011. "Deadly Violence Strikes Chinese City Racked by Ethnic Tensions." *New York Times*. July 31. http://www.nytimes.com/2011/08/01/world/asia/01china.html (accessed September 4, 2012).

Winter, Bronwyn. 2006. "Religion, Culture, and Women's Human Rights: Some General and Theoretical Considerations." *Women's Studies International Forum* 29, no. 4: 381–394.

Wirth, L. 1931a. "Clinical Sociology." *American Journal of Sociology* 37: 49–66.

———. 1931b. *Sociology: Vocations for Those Interested in It*. Vocational Guidance Series 1. Chicago: University of Chicago, Department of Special Collections. Louis Wirth Collection. Box LVI, Folder 6.

Wise, Steven. 2005. *Rattling the Cage: Toward Legal Rights for Animals*. New York: Perseus Press.

Wisner, Ben, Piers Blaikie, Terry Cannon, and Ian Davis. 2004. *At Risk: Natural Hazards, People's Vulnerability and Disasters*. New York: Routledge.

Witz, Ann. 2000. "Whose Body Matters? Feminist Sociology and the Corporeal Turn in Sociology and Feminism." *Body and Society* 6, no. 2: 1–24.

Wodak, Alex. 1998. "Health, HIV Infection, Human Rights, and Injecting Drug Use." *Health and Human Rights* 2, no. 4: 24–41.

Woddiwiss, A. 1998. *Globalisation, Human Rights, and Labour Law in Pacific Asia*. Cambridge, UK: Cambridge University Press.

———. 2003. *Making Human Rights Work Globally*. London: The Glass House Press.

———. 2005. *Human Rights*. London: Routledge.

Woehrle, Lynne M., Patrick G. Coy, and Gregory M. Maney. 2008. *Contesting Patriotism: Culture, Power and Strategy in the Peace Movement*. Lanham, MD: Rowman & Littlefield.

Wolf, Diane L., ed. 1996. *Feminist Dilemmas in Fieldwork*. Boulder, CO: Westview.

Wolf, Kurt. 1950. "Introduction." In *The Sociology of Georg Simmel*, edited and translated by Kurt H. Wolff, xvii–xiv. New York: The Free Press.

Women's Refugee Commission. 2011. *The Living Ain't Easy: Urban Refugees in Kampala*. New York: Women's Refugee Commission.

Wood, Charles. 1999. "Losing Control of America's Future: The Census, Birthright Citizenship, and Illegal Aliens." *Harvard Journal of Law and Public Policy* 22, no. 2: 465–522.

Woolford, Andrew. 2006. "Making Genocide Unthinkable: Three Guidelines for a Critical Criminology of Genocide." *Critical Criminology* 14: 87–106.

World Conference against Racism. 2001. "World Conference against Racism, Racial Discrimination, Xenophobia and Related Intolerance: Declaration." United Nations. http://www.un.org/durbanreview2009/pdf/DDPA_full_text.pdf (accessed July 20, 2012).

World Health Organization (WHO). 1948. *Constitution of the World Health Organization*. Geneva: WHO.

———. 2000. *Maternal Mortality in 2000: Estimates Developed by WHO, UNICEF, and UNFPA*. Relief Web. http://www.reliefweb.int/library/documents/2003/who-saf-22oct.pdf (accessed January 20, 2012).

———. 2001. *The World Health Report 2001: Mental Health: New Understanding, New Hope*. WHO. http://www.who.int/whr/2001/en (accessed July 20, 2012).

———. 2007. "Community Mental Health Services Will Lessen Social Exclusion, Says WHO." WHO. http://www.who.int/mediacentre/news/notes/2007/np25/en/index.html (accessed January 20, 2012).

———. 2010. *Global Strategies for Women's and Children's Health*. New York: Partnership for Maternal, Newborn, and Child Health.

World People's Conference on Climate Change and the Rights of Mother Earth. 2010. "Draft Universal Declaration of the Rights of Mother Earth." Global Alliance for the Rights of Nature. http://therightsofnature.org/wp-content/uploads/pdfs/FINAL-UNIVERSAL-DECLARATION-OF-THE-RIGHTS-OF-MOTHER-EARTH-APRIL-22-2010.pdf (accessed March 20 2011).

World Resources Institute's Earth Trends. 2008. World Resources Institute. http://earthtrends.wri.org/pdf_library/data_tables/food_water_2008.pdf (accessed January 22, 2011).

Wotipka, Christine Min, and Kiyoteru Tsutsui. 2008. "Global Human Rights and State Sovereignty: State Ratification of International Human Rights Treaties 1965–2001." *Sociological Forum* 23, no. 4: 724–754.

Wrench, John. 2011. "Data on Discrimination in EU Countries: Statistics, Research and the Drive for Comparability." *Ethnic and Racial Studies* 34: 1715–1730.

Wright, Eric R., and Brea L. Perry. 2010. "Medical Sociology and Health Services Research: Past Accomplishments and Future Policy Challenges." *Journal of Health and Social Behavior* 51: S107–S119.

Wright, James D. 2009. *Address Unknown: The Homeless in America*. Piscataway, NJ: Transaction Publishers.

Wright, Quincy. 1948. "Relationship between Different Categories of Human Rights." In *Human Rights: Comments and Interpretations*, edited by United Nations Educational Scientific and Cultural Organization (UNESCO). Paris: UNESCO.

212 BIBLIOGRAPHY

Wronka, J. 1998. *Human Rights and Social Policy in the 21st Century*. Lanham, MD: University Press of America.

Yang, Alan S. 1998. *From Wrongs to Rights: Public Opinion on Gay and Lesbian American's Moves toward Equality*. Washington, DC: National Gay and Lesbian Task Force Policy Institute.

Yates, Michael D. 2009. *Why Unions Matter*. New York: Monthly Review Press.

Yeung, W. J., and D. Conley. 2008. "Black-White Achievement Gap and Family Wealth." *Child Development* 79: 303–324.

Yosso, T., M. Ceja, W. Smith, and D. Solorzano. 2009. "Critical Race Theory, Racial Microaggressions, and Campus Racial Climate for Latina/o Undergraduates." *Harvard Educational Review* 79: 659–690.

Young, Iris. 1990. *Justice and Politics of Difference*. Princeton, NJ: Princeton University Press.

Youngers, Coletta. 2005. "The Collateral Damage of the U.S. War on Drugs: Conclusions and Recommendations." In *Drugs and Democracy in Latin America*, edited by Eileen Rosin and Coletta Youngers. Boulder, CO: Lynne Rienner Publishers.

Youngers, Coletta, and Eileen Rosin. 2005. *Drugs and Democracy in Latin America: The Impact of U.S. Policy*. Boulder, CO: Lynne Rienner Publishers.

Yuker, H. E. 1994. "Variables that Influence Attitudes toward People with Disabilities: Conclusions from the Data." *Journal of Social Behavior and Personality* 9, no. 5: 3–22.

Yuval-Davis, N. 2006a. "Intersectionality and Feminist Politics." *European Journal of Women's Studies* 13, no. 3: 193–209.

———. 2006b. "Women, Citizenship and Difference." *Feminist Review* 57: 4–27.

Zajdow, Grazyna. 2005. "What Are We Scared Of? The Absence of Sociology in Current Debates about Drug Treatments and Policies." *Journal of Sociology* 41, no. 2: 185–199.

Zajdow, Grazyna, and Jo M. Lindsay. 2010. "Editorial: Sociology, Recreational Drugs and Alcohol." *Health Sociology Review* 19, no. 2: 146–150.

Zakaria, Fareed, and Kuan Yew Lee. 1994. "Culture Is Destiny: A Conversation with Lee Kuan Yew." *Foreign Affairs* 73, no. 2: 109–126.

Zald, Mayer N. 1992. "Looking Backward to Look Forward: Reflections on the Past and Future of the Resource Mobilization Research Program." In *Frontiers in Social Movement Theory*, edited by Aldon D. Morris and Carol McClurg Mueller, 326–348. New Haven, CT: Yale University Press.

Zeitlin, Irving M. 2000. *Ideology and the Development of Sociological Theory*. 7th ed. Englewood Cliffs, NJ: Prentice Hall.

———. 2009. "Education for Democracy in Peirce, James, Dewey and Mead: The North Central Sociological Association's Ruth and John Unseem Plenary Address." *Sociological Focus* 43, no. 4: 317–329.

Zellner, Robert, et al. 2008. "Brandeis in the Sixties." A panel presented at the annual meeting of the Association for Humanist Sociology, Boston, Massachusetts.

Zheng, Tiantian. 2010. *Sex Trafficking, Human Rights, and Social Justice*. New York: Routledge.

Zimmerman, Don H. 1970. "The Practicalities of Rule Use." In *Understanding Everyday Life: Toward the Reconstruction of Sociological Knowledge*, edited by Jack D. Douglas, 221–238. Chicago: Aldine.

Zinn, Maxine Baca, Lynn Weber Cannon, Elizabeth Higginbotham, and Bonnie Thornton Dill. 1986. "The Costs of Exclusionary Practices in Women's Studies." *Signs: Journal of Women in Culture and Society* 11: 290–303.

Zitzelsberger, Hilde. 2005. "(In)visibility: Accounts of Embodiment of Women in Physical Disabilities and Differences." *Disability and Society* 20, no. 4: 389–403.

Žižek, Slavoj. 2005. "Against Human Rights." *New Left Review* 34 (May–June): 115–131.

Zolberg, Aristide. 1986. "How Many Exceptionalisms?" In *Working-Class Formation: Nineteenth-Century Patterns in Western Europe and the United States*, edited by I. Katznelson and A. Zolberg, 397–455. Princeton, NJ: Princeton University Press.

Zou, M., and Zwart, T. 2011. "Rethinking Human Rights in China: Towards a Receptor Approach.' In *Human Rights in the Asia-Pacific Region: Towards Institution Building*, edited by H. Nasu and B. Saul, 249–263. London: Routledge.

Zuberi, Tukufu, and Eduardo Bonilla-Silva. 2008. *White Logic, White Methods: Racism and Methodology*. Lanham, MD: Rowman & Littlefield.

Zukin, Sharon. 2011. *Naked City: The Death and Life of Authentic Urban Places*. New York: Oxford University Press.

Zuo, J., and Robert D. Benford. 1995. "Mobilization Processes and the 1989 Chinese Democracy Movement." *Sociological Quarterly* 36: 131–156.

Zweigenhaft, R., and G. Domhoff. 2006. *Diversity in the Power Elite*. Lanham, MD: Rowman & Littlefield.

About the Editors

David L. Brunsma is Professor of Sociology at Virginia Tech. His areas of research include sociologies of human rights and human rights sociologies, racial identity and racism, cognitive sociology and epistemologies, and multi-raciality and whiteness. He is currently working on a major textbook about the social construction of difference. He is currently coeditor of *Societies without Borders: Human Rights and the Social Sciences* and section editor of the Race and Ethnicity Section of *Sociology Compass*. He lives and loves with his family in Blacksburg, Virginia.

Keri E. Iyall Smith's research explores the intersections between human rights doctrine, the state, and indigenous peoples in the context of a global-izing society. She has published articles on hybridity and world society, human rights, indigenous peoples, and teaching sociology. She is author of *States and Indigenous Movements* (2006), editor of *Sociology of Globalization* (2012), and coeditor of *Public Sociologies Reader* (with Judith R. Blau, 2006) and *Hybrid Identities: Theoretical and Empirical Examinations* (with Patricia Leavy, 2008). She is Associate Professor of Sociology at Suffolk University in Boston, Massachusetts, where she teaches courses on globalization, sociological theory, Native Americans, and introductory sociology. She is a former vice president of Sociologists Without Borders.

Brian K. Gran is a former lawyer whose sociological research focuses on human rights and institutions that support and hinder their enforcement, with a par-ticular interest in whether law can intervene in private spheres. A cofounder of the ASA Human Rights Section, Gran is directing a project funded by the National Science Foundation (NSF) to develop an international Children's Rights Index. He serves on the Council of the Science and Human Rights Project of the American Association for the Advancement of Science. Gran was recently elected president of the ISA Thematic Group on Human Rights and Global Justice (TG03). For his research on independent children's rights institutions, he was a Visiting Fellow of the Fulbright grant to research and teach at the School of Law at Reykjavik University in Iceland.